Milton to Pope, 1650–17

D0077271

WITHDRAWN

transitions

General Editor: Julian Wolfreys

---

transitions Series
Series Standing Order ISBN 0–333–73684–6
(*outside North America only*)

You can receive future titles in this series as they are published by placing a standing order. Please contact your bookseller or, in case of difficulty, write to us at the address below with your name and address, the title of the series and the ISBN quoted above.

Customer Services Department, Macmillan Distribution Ltd
Houndmills, Basingstoke, Hampshire RG21 6XS, England

---

transitions

Milton to Pope, 1650–1720

Kay Gilliland Stevenson

palgrave

First published 2001 by
PALGRAVE
Houndmills, Basingstoke, Hampshire RG21 6XS and
175 Fifth Avenue, New York, N.Y. 10010
Companies and representatives throughout the world

PALGRAVE is the new global academic imprint of
St. Martin's Press LLC Scholarly and Reference Division and
Palgrave Publishers Ltd (formerly Macmillan Press Ltd).

ISBN 0–333–69612–3 hardback
ISBN 0–333–69613–1 paperback

This book is printed on paper suitable for recycling and
made from fully managed and sustained forest sources.

A catalogue record for this book is available
from the British Library.

Library of Congress Cataloging-in-Publication Data
Stevenson, Kay Gilliland.
    Milton to Pope, 1650–1720 / Kay Gilliland Stevenson.
        p. cm. – (Transitions)
    Includes bibliographical references and index.
    ISBN 0–333–69612–3 — ISBN 0–333–69613–1 (pbk.)
        1. English Literature—Early modern, 1500–1700—History and
criticism. 2. English literature—18th century—History and
criticism. 3. Milton, John, 1608–1674—Criticism and
interpretation. 4. Pope, Alexander, 1688–1744—Criticism and
interpretation. 5. Authors and readers—Great Britain—History—
17th century. 6. Authors and readers—Great Britain—History—
18th century. 7. Literature and society—Great Britain—History—
17th century. 8. Literature and society—Great Britain—History—
18th century. I. Title. II. Transitions (St Martin's Press)
PR431 .S74 2000
820.9'004—dc21   00–040439

10 9 8 7 6 5 4 3 2 1
10 09 08 07 06 05 04 03 02 01

Printed in China

Contents

General Editor's Preface

Transitions: *transition–*, n. of action. 1. A passing or passage from one condition, action or (rarely) place, to another. 2. Passage in thought, speech, or writing, from one subject to another. 3. **a**. The passing from one note to another **b**. The passing from one key to another, modulation. 4. The passage from an earlier to a later stage of development or formation … change from an earlier style to a later; a style of intermediate or mixed character … the historical passage of language from one well-defined stage to another.

The aim of *Transitions* is to explore passages and movements in language, literature and culture from Chaucer to the present day. The series also seeks to examine the ways in which the very idea of transition affects the reader's sense of period so as to address anew questions of literary history and periodisation. The writers in this series unfold the cultural and historical mediations of literature during what are commonly recognised as crucial moments in the development of English literature, addressing, as the OED puts it, the 'historical passage of language from one well-defined stage to another'.

Recognising the need to contextualise literary study, the authors offer close readings of canonical and now marginalised or overlooked literary texts from all genres, bringing to this study the rigour of historical knowledge and the sophistication of theoretically informed evaluations of writers and movements from the last 700 years. At the same time as each writer, whether Chaucer or Shakespeare, Milton or Pope, Byron, Dickens, George Eliot, Virginia Woolf or Salman Rushdie, is shown to produce his or her texts within a discernible historical, cultural, ideological and philosophical milieu, the text is read from the vantage point of recent theoretical interests and concerns. The purpose in bringing theoretical knowledge to the reading of a wide range of works is to demonstrate how the literature is always open to transition, whether in the instance of its production or in succeeding moments of its critical reception.

The series desires to enable the reader to transform her/his own reading and writing transactions by comprehending past developments. Each book in the second tranche of the series offers a pedagogical guide to the poetics and politics of particular eras, as well as to the subsequent critical comprehension of periods and periodisation. As well as transforming the cultural and literary past by interpreting its transition form the perspective of the critical and theoretical present, each study enacts transitional readings of a number of literary texts, all of which are themselves conceivable as having effected transition at the moments of their first appearance. The readings offered in these books seek, through close critical reading, historical contextualisation and theoretical engagement, to demonstrate certain possibilities in reading to the student reader.

It is hoped that the student will find this series liberating because the series seeks to move beyond rigid definitions of period. What is important is the sense of passage, of motion. Rather than providing a definitive model of literature's past, *Transitions* aims to place you in an active dialogue with the writing and culture of other eras, so at to comprehend not only how the present reads the past, but how the past can read the present.

Julian Wolfreys

Acknowledgements

A page from Comenius' *Orbis sensualium pictus*, trans. Charles Hoole (E2116.1) and an advertisement for *The Tempest, Or, the Distressed Lovers* at Bartholemew-Fair (Harl. 5932, 271) are reproduced by permission of the British Library.

The titlepage of *Biblia polyglotta* (Young 7) and the titlepage of Elizabeth Cellier's *Malice Defeated* (Sel.1.116^{35}) are reproduced by permission of the Syndics of the Cambridge University Library.

The courtesy of librarians added to the pleasures of hours of reading. Special thanks go to Stella Clarke and her staff in the Rare Books Room of Cambridge University Library, and to librarians at the British Library, the Albert Sloman Library of the University of Essex, Dr Williams Library, and the Pitts Theology Library of Emory University. For assistance in visiting libraries I am grateful to the Research Endowment Fund of the Department of Literature, University of Essex. The Arts and Humanities Research Board and the Research Fund of the University of Essex provided additional study leave time during the final months of completing the book.

Julian Wolfreys was generous in his comments, from his initial invitation to contribute to the series through the difficult final task of pruning the length of discussions.

Abbreviations

Lives: Samuel Johnson. *Lives of the English Poets* (1779–81). Ed. George Birkbeck Hill. 3 vols. Oxford: Clarendon Press, 1905.

London Stage: The London Stage 1660–1800: A Calendar of Plays, Entertainments & Afterpieces Together with Casts, Box-Receipts and Contemporary Comment, compiled from the Playbills, Newspapers and Theatrical Diaries of the Period. Part I: 1660–1700. Ed. William Van Lennep, with intro. by Emmet L. Avery and Arthur H. Scouten. *Part II: 1700–1729.* Ed. and intro. Emmet L. Avery. Carbondale: Southern Illinois University Press, 1965, 1960.

POAS: Poems on Affairs of State: Augustan Satirical Verse, 1660–1714. Ed. George deForest Lord, *et al.* 7 vols. New Haven: Yale University Press, 1963–75.

1 Contexts

'In the twentieth century, they thought ...' What cogent generalisations about beliefs and attitudes could be offered in three centuries' time, based on the evidence of the written word? Is there anything that could not be convincingly contradicted by some other piece of evidence? As historians together with literary scholars are fond of saying, there is no such thing as an unproblematical factual background against which the complexities of a literary text can be teased out. Rather than beginning with assertions about cultural concepts, this introductory chapter presents a sampler of particular texts from which pathways for exploration of relations between writing and performance or politics, language and interpretation, myth and history, might be opened. Following brief description of eight texts – a dancing manual, an extremist's pamphlets, a schoolbook, an edition of the Bible in multiple languages, a royal proclamation, an accused traitor's account of her trial and vindication, and a masque – are a few practical comments. These focus on publication, reading and the physical characteristics of older printed books.

The arbitrariness of the dates 1650–1720 originally seemed to me one of the interesting things about the Macmillan series of 'period' *Transitions* volumes. Established bibliographical practices cut the century in ways that give a particular slant to literary history, obscuring some continuities and emphasising others. The *Cambridge Bibliography of English Literature* places in one volume literature of 'the Renaissance to the Restoration (1500–1660)', and in another 1660–1800, a span often called 'the long eighteenth century'. Beginning with different dates seemed a useful way of finding new patterns. The chosen dates cut in two the careers of both authors mentioned in the title, whose names serve primarily as a reminder of who was active at the time. Neither a study concentrating on 'major' figures nor an attempt to 'cover' everything, which would reduce the chapters to hectic thumbnail entries, this volume explores the multiplicity of writing in what one ballad calls 'this scribbling age',[1] and some pleasures or problems related to the always ongoing process of learning about it. Pattern will declare itself, no matter what dates are adopted as a starting point. In 1650 Playford entered *The English Dancing Master* in the Stationers' Register; in 1720 another important publisher, Jacob Tonson, retired. What the successful booksellers of the period found marketable, and how publishing practices affect assessment of writers, will be a minor, recurrent theme.

John Playford, *The English Dancing Master* (1651)

The date of publication of John Playford's *The English Dancing Master: or Plaine and easie Rules for the Dancing of Country Dances, with the Tune to each Dance* (1651) is a useful caveat against assumptions about Puritan suppression of amusements. In a preface 'To the Ingenious Reader', Playford claims that he reluctantly agreed to bring out the volume, based on an excellent text he happened to have by him, only because 'there was a false and surreptitious Copy at the Printing Presse, which if it had been published, would have been a disparagement to the quality and the Professors thereof, and a hinderance to the Learner'; he thus neatly sets out a convention which readers of various early texts quickly learn to recognise. There were, certainly, some pirated texts published, but the claim of being forced into print is a hardy one. As an increasing number of women writers appear, noting how they call on such firmly established conventions strengthens analysis of their prefaces and prevents over-ingenuous literal readings of their self-presentation. Playford's handbook serves as a useful introductory text, too, in posing questions about the process of passive or active understanding of a printed page. Like the script of a play, the words, music and diagrams of *The English Dancing Master* are, even more obviously, incomplete without performance.

The English Dancing Master was kept in print through expanded edition after edition, the twelfth in 1703. Today Playford's name remains familiar to country dancers and to ballad collectors, grateful that he preserved old tunes. From *The English Dancing Master* through Purcell's *Orpheus Britannicus* (1698) and D'Urfey's collections of songs in the multi-volume *Wit and Mirth* (1699), John

Playford and then his son Henry were the outstanding music publishers of their time, rivalled only as the century neared its end by John Walsh. Through their books, the interplay between music and words, on the street, at the court, in the theatres, in homes and in churches is kept easily available for study. At the Playford shop in the porch of the Temple Church (1647–90), Samuel Pepys stopped to read, to buy, to trade (13 February 1660 and seven other references in the *Diary*). Access to current songs and new compositions, revealing changes in musical tastes, is provided in such publications as the Playford *Choice Ayres, Songs, and Dialogues*, repeatedly issued and expanded. Many of Walsh's beautifully engraved books, too, preserve recently written poetry in the context of its first settings. He emphasises the timeliness of his offerings in a long-running periodical called *The Monthly Mask of Vocal Music, or the Newest Songs Made for the Theatres & Other Occasions* (1702–11, 1717–24).

Arise Evans, *The Voice of King Charls* and *The Voice of the Iron Rod* (1655)

While Playford's publications and their popularity unsettle any simple killjoy image of the Commonwealth and Protectorate periods, the works of another royalist active in the 1650s produce a second surprise. It is easy to assume that the royalists were the party of dashing cavaliers. Arise Evans, however, in a series of impassioned little books calling for the restoration of monarchy, defines the cause of many of England's ills as failures in Sabbath observance. In two complementary pamphlets published in 1655, Arise Evans addresses Charles Stuart and Oliver Cromwell, setting the tone in a long titlepage:

THE
VOICE
OF
King CHARLS the Father, to CHARLS the Son;
And, the Bride say, *Come*.
Being, An Invitation of King
Charls to come in peaceably, and
be reconciled to his Kingdoms, according
to his Father's minde; and shewing

the integrity of his Highness
OLIVER CROMWEL.
Also, That the Author's Prophesie is fulfilled in part and shall
    perfectly be verified in 1655.
The Sabbath straightly to be sanctified & kept.
The Vindication of Infant-baptism, and re-baptising proved by
    Scriptures and Fathers to be a Truth.
With an exhortation to the Royalists. And many other discoveries of
    Truth.
Noble Royalists, this is your way of advancement.
By ARISE EVANS.
Heb. 4.7. *Today if ye will, hear his voice,* &c.
Printed at London for the Author, 1655.

Trained as a tailor, Evans had a grander sense of vocation. His entry in
the *Dictionary of National Biography* is cross-referenced from his own
preferred and prophetic name Arise to the more common Welsh
name Rhys, and identified with the dry occupational label 'fanatic'.
He was scandalised by the exceptions made by members of the long
Parliament against Sabbath-observance, reporting with indignation
that they went abroad in coaches and boats (thus causing the
boatmen and coachmen to work): 'when no Boat on the Thames durst
stir on the Sabbath, the Lord Bradshaw's Boat may; and when other
men must go afoot on the Sabbath, a Parliament-man sends his ticket
for a Coach, and will have it; then God brings them down also' (*Charls*
1655, 32–33). He waxes nostalgic about the piety observed in the days
of Charles I, and emphasises the religious divisions of the time, when

> the Master goeth one way, the Mistress another, the Children and
> Servants another; every one goeth several wayes; and when they
> come home, Mum is best, for they can neither pray together nor
> speak any thing of God; if they do, there is a hot house presently with
> their damning and confounding another; God is not the Author of
> such confusion, but of peace and concord, 1 Chron. 14.33. and how
> can there be religious Government, or a keeping of the Sabbath in
> Families, when the Church is without Government? (34–5)

Highly reactionary, and with as much zeal as logic, Evans reduces the
complex religious and political history of the nation to a single issue:

> The granting Liberty of Conscience was the overthrow of the late

King; for had he been severe to make all men keep holy the Sabbath, he had not fallen, and his tolerating men to use, on that day, their own Conscience and wills as they listed, was his failing, so that he and his lost all by it: and now there is no way left to pacifie God's wrath, but by fasting and prayer to seek the Lord in publick and private, and specially to keep holy the Sabbath-day. (35)

Evans' writing is a curious mixture of wild-eyed prophecy (including misdated forecasts of a rising against Cromwell to restore the Stuarts), and practical proposals, such as a match between Charles II and one of Cromwell's daughters, both of whom did in the event marry English noblemen. There is some shrewdness in his analysis of barriers to such a match, including a hypothetical objection 'That if the King should match with his Highness's Daughter, he would be in scorn among all the Princes in Christendom.' Evans' response is telling: 'Alas! he is more in scorn among them now as he is: for what do the Princes do, for to restore him? If they send him a little maintenance for a time, they are soon weary of him and account of him but as a poor man that craveth Alms' (12–13).

In *The Voice of the Iron Rod, To His Highness The Lord Protector: Being A seasonable Admonition presented to him and to all Judicious men*, also printed at his own expense, Evans continues to argue for unity between Cromwell and Charles, setting himself apart from Plotters 'foolishly thinking, that God is well pleased with blood, and that it is impossible for the King and his Highness to agree' (A2^r; for folio referencing see note 27). Aligning himself with Jeremiah giving good advice to King Zedekiah, he calls on Cromwell to bring in Charles as king and to establish firm church government, claiming that 'I had a Vision which shewed that the King was come in to you upon an agreement, and that all the haters of the Lord were to be destroyed' (1, 6–7). Exhortation is mixed with warning. By 1655, expectation that Cromwell would assume the title of Emperor or King was common talk, and the court of 'His Highness' was a site of ceremonial pomp, its regal splendour probably reassuring to foreign ambassadors although dismaying to many who had fought with Cromwell in the 1640s (Sherwood 1977, 1997). Evans notes public unease about the legal status of the government and the cost of the military forces that sustain it, but he takes comfort from Cromwell's title of 'Protector' which he interprets as marking a temporary custodianship of power (*Charls*, 6–7).

In 1659, during the awkward uncertainties which followed the death of Cromwell, Evans published *A Rule from Heaven*, proposing that a king be chosen by lot from among the poor. He might have done better to reprint his 1652 pamphlet *A Voice from Heaven to the Common-wealth of English*, which proclaims the return of Charles II as the fulfilment of scripture: 'there is a day nigh at hand, in which, God will judge the World, by a man which he hath appointed to the word of Jesus Christ in righteousness. And this man, is not Jesus; but a man ordained, appointed, and sent, by the Father and his Son Jesus' (3). Voluble but harmless, Evans was a lone prophet, failing to attract a following. He distanced himself from the proliferating separatist groups, even explicitly warning Cromwell 'not to seek the welfare of these Sectaries, whose spirits are fired to do evil, and to bring evil upon themselves and you' (*Iron Rod*, 1). Evans' privately printed pamphlets, and his appearances at Whitehall with a Bible under his arm were, in fact, a mild version of witness based on religious conviction.[2]

Much more threatening were visionaries like the Diggers or Levellers, who put into practice their sense that all land should be held in common. Direct action, the occupying of wasteland, accompanied their attempts at persuasion by words. In *An Humble Request to the Ministers of Both Universities and to All Lawyers in Every Inns-a-Court* (1650) Gerrard Winstanley set out to prove that

> The whole Earth: By the Law of Creation, is the Common treasury of free Livelyhood, to whole Mankind. And those Lords of Mannors, and others, that deny any part of mankind, this creation-freedome in the earth, are sinners in the highest degree, and are upholders of the fall & curse of Mankind. (*Works* 1941, 423)

Despite his distinction, in the final sentence of the tract, between the carnal weapons of the sons of bondage – fire, club and sword – and the spiritual weapons of the sons of freedom – love, patience and righteousness – any owner of property might well be uneasy. More violent sects reinforced conservative prejudices. Notoriously, the Fifth-Monarchists were ready to resort to fire and the sword to establish the reign of King Jesus. Their armed revolt in London, in January 1661, accomplished nothing for their cause, but inflamed a reaction against all who interpreted Scripture as a call to social and political reform.

Quakers, the fastest-growing of the radical sects in the second half of the seventeenth century, were not at first notable for grey sobriety. Walking toward Lichfield on a winter day in 1651, George Fox, who had recently emerged from over a year's imprisonment for 'the avowed uttering and broaching of divers blasphemous opinions', felt a sudden command from the Lord to take off his shoes. Following further commands, according to his report, he entrusted his shoes to some shepherds, entered the town, and went up and down the streets crying 'Woe to the bloody city of Lichfield' (*Journal* 1694; 1952, 52, 71). The most flamboyant of the Quaker testimonies was that of James Nayler, from whom Fox soon distanced himself. In October 1655, Nayler's riding into Bristol accompanied by women singing 'Holy, holy, holy, Lord God of Israel' brought a violent reaction, just short of crucifixion, from conservatives unwilling or unable to read the event symbolically. Although one member of Parliament argued against pressure to 'hang every man that says Christ is in you, the hope of glory', Nayler was pilloried, whipped, branded, and he had his tongue bored with a hot iron (Watts 1978, 210–11).

Prophetic voices more successful than Evans' raised enormous fear. 'Enthusiasm' becomes the standard word for extravagance, treated with distrust.[3] Reactions against enthusiasm, easily associated with rabble-rousing or anarchy, contribute to a conscious stress on reason, which, taken at face value, used to give the period the label Age of Reason.

Comenius, *Orbis sensualium pictus*, trans. Charles Hoole (1658)

A page from Charles Hoole's translation of Comenius's *Orbis sensualium pictus*, 'A World of Things Obvious to the Senses drawn in Pictures', looks so familiar, so much like children's 'First Dictionaries' published in large numbers in the eighteenth century and on into modern times, that it takes a small effort to recognise or remember that this is indeed a 'first', the earliest illustrated textbook (Figure 1.1). First published on the continent, it was 'Englished' (halfway) to improve educational practice. Pages showing a printshop or farmyard, with objects in the pictures keyed to words on a facing page, form a simple and practical teaching manual. Presenting a classroom of young boys with a page of physical deformities, and providing them with terms for insulting opponents – giant, dwarf, great-nosed,

(172)

LXXXIV.

Carriages.   *Vehicula.*

We are carried
on a Sled 1.
over Snow,
and Ice.
   A Carriage with one
Wheel, is called
a Wheel-barrow ; 2.
with two Wheels
a Cart; 3.
with four Wheels

Trahâ 1.
vehimur
super nivibus
& Glacie.
   Vehiculum unirotum,
dicitur
Pabo ; 2.
birotum,
Carrus ; 3.
quadrirotum
                    a Wa-

Figure 1.1 A page from Comenius, *Orbis sensualium pictus,* trans. Hoole (1658). Reproduced by permission of the British Library.

goggle-eyed or worse – seems rash, but might be necessary prepara-tion for reading and writing satire. An engraving of Adam and Eve appears within the run of homelier topics, apparently no more remote from everyday experience than the preceding pages of sea-fish and shell-fish or the seven ages of man that follow. The simple pages of this textbook could lead in practical, historical and theoretical direc-tions: it opens up questions about education in general, about communication between England and continental Europe, about assumptions as to the relationship between words and things, or even speculation about the language of Eden.[4]

Without wanting to impose too heavy a load on a practising school-master's day-to-day teaching of Latin vocabulary, one notes that the *Orbis sensualium pictus* literally illustrates a view of language which was championed not long afterward by the Royal Society. Here is something like Thomas Sprat's ambition 'to return back to the primi-tive purity and shortness, when men deliver'd so many *things*, almost in an equal number of *words*' (Sprat 1667; 1959, 113). As Sprat's own words 'return back to the primitive purity' indicate, even the Royal Society for the Advancement of Learning could consider transitions as a recovery of a hypothetical, past ideal as well as a way forward. Another glance backward is, paradoxically, contained in the society's title, for in echoing the title of Francis Bacon's *The Advancement of Learning* (1605), it links past and future so that 'advancement' consists as fulfilment of an earlier plan. On the frontispiece designed by John Evelyn for Sprat's *History of the Royal Society* (1667), a bust of Charles II is flanked by the society's president and by Bacon, with 'Artium Instaurator' engraved on the tiles at his feet. At the outset of its formal history, the Royal Society visually provides a tribute to continuity of vision.[5]

Bacon's own sense of language, summed up in his image of idols of the marketplace, is part of his analysis of how easily false notions, or erroneous ways of looking at nature, distort human knowledge. The idols of the marketplace are words which introduce false ways of looking at the world. Some words do not correspond to anything that really exists, although the name of the (non-existent) thing makes people assume it does. Other words are based on inaccurate generali-sation and imperfect analogy (*Novum organum* I. 39). In paragraphs which John Locke added in 1700 to the fourth edition of *An Essay Concerning Human Understanding* (1690), he painstakingly explains his terms, and echoes Bacon's conviction that verbal confusion is a major obstacle to knowledge, 'The greatest part of the Questions and Controversies that perplex Mankind depending on the doubtful and uncertain use of Words, or (which is the same) *indetermined* Ideas, which they are made to stand for' (Locke 1770; 1975, 13).

The project of the Royal Society to match words and things runs counter to more sophisticated ideas about language, found as far back as St Augustine's *De doctrina Christiana*. Augustine distinguishes crisply between natural signs, such as smoke for fire, and arbitrary signs, based on social convention. This second, and larger, category is emphasised by Hobbes: 'That is a true sign, which by the consent of men becomes a sign' (*Philosophical Rudiments*, XV. 17; *Works* II. 221). Words 'have their signification by agreement, and constitution of men' (*Leviathan*, XXXI; *Works* III. 355). Augustine recognises, too, the fact that differences among languages have an important effect on what can be said (or as modern linguists such as Shafer and Whorf have argued, what can be thought). Moreover, Augustine is by no means the first to make the point; in the prologue to Ecclesiasticus, its second-century translator into Greek observes that 'what was originally expressed in Hebrew does not have exactly the same sense when translated into another language'.[6]

Scholarly projects on the history of the English language were perhaps part of the general surge of antiquarianism in the period. Although historical linguistics seems a curious site for enlarged educational opportunities, among the distinguished pioneers of Old English studies are not only fellows of colleges, such as George Hickes (1642–1715), but also those who were working against disadvantages of birth. Humfrey Wanley (1672–1726), a draper's clerk before he became an assistant at the Bodleian Library, laid the foundations for later work by his catalogue of Anglo-Saxon manuscripts (1705). Elizabeth Elstob (1683–1756), once released from the guardianship of an uncle who thought one language was quite enough for any woman,[7] was supported and encouraged by her scholarly brother William (1673–1715). She published a translation of Aelfric, prefaced by an essay defending women's education, and *The rudiments of grammar for the English-Saxon tongue, first given in English; with an apology for the study of northern antiquities* (1715); after her brother's death, however, she had fewer opportunities for research, while supporting herself as a schoolteacher and then as governess in the household of the Duchess of Portland. Academic work at Oxford and Cambridge on the history of the language, on which subsequent grammatical and lexical studies rest, was a good bit more informed and less sentimental than the Royal Society's nostalgia for primitive purity. Sprat and his fellows parallel the religious sects who long to return to a former time when words, doctrines and behaviour were as yet uncorrupted. In an autobiography focused on his search for 'the Knowledge of the Truth', John Crook recalls earnest, prolonged discussions within an Independent congregation about 'whether we were in the right Order of the Gospel, according to the Primitive Patterns' (Crook 1706; 1998, 159, 166).

In *An Essay on Criticism*, Pope worries about how rapidly English changes.

> Our Sons their Fathers' failing Language see,
> And such as Chaucer is, shall Dryden be. (ll. 482–3)

Earlier, in 'Of English Verse', Edmund Waller compares writing in Latin or Greek with carving in marble. To him English seemed as unstable as sand, its rapid shifting mimicked metrically by enjambement and, after one regular iambic line, the unexpected rhythms of the next.

> But who can hope his Lines should long
> Last in a daily-changing Tongue? (ll. 5–6)

Classical languages had further advantages; studying them was rewarded by the ability to communicate with any other educated man in Europe. Even within England, learned controversies were conducted in Latin. A sidelight on linguistic practice, and a link to the next example in this sampler of texts, is the indignation expressed by Bishop Walton when criticism of his polyglot Bible was published in English. Why, he asks, if the attacker 'had no sinister ends', did he write in English rather than 'in that Language wherein Learned men debate such things, as are not fit for popular judgements?' (1659, 21).

On the other hand, while nourished by classical writing, Dryden was not alone in his concern that 'the greater part of our Youth is spent in learning the words of dead Languages' ('Life of Plurarch', 1693, 20). For boys, the language of instruction in all advanced subjects, at school and university, was Latin.[8] The education of girls, a topic which prompts considerable discussion, was more variable.[9] In *The Gentlewomans Companion*, attributed to Hannah Woolley, a brief gesture toward approval of Latin as an aid to understanding English is made, but the book grows much more authoritative when it turns to recipes for food or medicines.[10] As the anonymous lady who wrote *An Essay in Defence of the Female Sex* points out, commonly girls 'are taught only our Mother Tongue, or perhaps French, which is now very fashionable'; having asked 'whether the disadvantage be so great as it is commonly imagined', she turns to attack men who restrict 'learned' to classical languages, having 'given that to the knowledge of words, which belongs more properly to Things' (1696, 36–8, 46–8). When Bathsua Makin published an energetic treatise on female education and set up her own school for girls in London, she advertised that half the students' time would be spent on the usual decorative and useful activities – Dancing, Music, Singing, Writing, Keeping accounts – but 'The other half to be employed in gaining the Latin and French tongues; and those that please may learn Greek and Hebrew, the Italian and Spanish: in all which this Gentlewoman hath a competent knowledge' (1673, 42).

The intersection of language with social, political and academic practice can be seen in a book partly by George Fox, *A Battle-Door for Teachers & Professors to Learn Singular & Plural* (1660), which on historical and grammatical grounds defends the democratic linguistic practices of the Quakers. Their use of the familiar 'thou' rather than the deferential plural 'you' caused as much trouble as their refusal to take off their hats as a sign of respect. In a modern situation, the cheekiness of using 'tu' to address a respectable, and hardly known, Frenchwoman is a bare approximation of the affront caused daily by Quaker speakers; they were often beaten for their insolence (Whiting 1715). Fox vigorously attacks the inconsistency of teaching 'Thou to one, and You to many' in school, but then punishing those who carry over this grammatically correct pattern into everyday life, where 'thou' to social superiors is called 'clownish and unmannerly' (A2^r). The final note, signed with Fox's initials, marks a curious leap from the two hundred pages of sober comparative linguistics to wild suspicion of the Roman Catholic Church as the root of all ills: 'The Pope set up *you* to one in his pride, and it is the pride which cannot bear *thou* and *thee* to one but must have, and would have *you* from the Author their Father in their pride, which must not but have the word *thou*, which was before their Father the Pope was, which was Gods language, and will stand when the Pope is ended.'

Bishop Walton ed., *Biblia polyglotta* (1656)

The six massive folio volumes of Bishop Brian Walton's *Biblia poly-glotta* remain a monument of scholarship (*Cambridge History of the Bible* 1963, 64, 93). They form a culmination of the humanist desire to establish accurate texts of religious as well as secular writing. The precedents include Erasmus's edition of the Greek New Testament, and, in the early centuries of Christian scholarship, Origen's comparative edition of six texts called the *Hexapla*. For a general student of early modern literature, a minor interest of this impressive, multilingual Bible is its illumination of publishing practice, including reasons why 'preliminaries' such as prefaces are not paginated in the same way as the main text of a book. Whereas the small books and pamphlets described so far were modest in price, the *Biblia polyglotta* was so expensive a project that it was financed in advance by subscription. A small extra sheet, 'An Advertisement to the Subscribers and others, unto whom any Copies of the first Volume of the BIBLE shall be delivered', dated 4 September 1654, survives with some copies[11] as a clear reminder that what the subscriber received was not yet ready for display; the letter advises delay in having the books bound as they come from the press, since the preface and 'some other things which belong to the first Volume cannot be Printed till the whole Work be done'. The bookseller advises buyers that 'to prevent the danger of losing any sheets if they be loose, they may have them sewed together with Pasteboard covers at a little charge'.[12]

Hasty or careless buyers evidently disregarded this warning, for the magnificent titlepage engraved by Wenceslaus Hollar (Figure 1.2) is missing from some copies of the *Biblia polyglotta*, or bound in the final volume. The reading of visual images, like the reading of words, is an acquired skill – but one expected of the educated person of the day.[13] The architectural framework of this titlepage shows Old Testament and New Testament as parts of a unified building, the New Testament smaller but superior. Peter with a key and Paul with a sword frame the central depiction of the day of Pentecost, when the disciples gathered in Jerusalem were 'all filled with the Holy Ghost, and began to speak with other tongues, as the Spirit gave them utterance' (Acts 2: 4). Gospel accounts of Jesus' life are condensed into five small scenes: Nativity, Last Supper, Crucifixion, Resurrection and Ascension; the four evangelists Matthew, Mark, Luke and John appear

Figure 1.2 Title-page of Walton, *Biblia polyglotta* (1659). Reproduced by permission of the Syndics of Cambridge University Library.

in their standard iconographical form as angel, lion, ox and eagle. On the porch supporting the Christian superstructure are Moses, with his tablets of the law, and Aaron the priest. Below Moses is the sad origin of need for law; Adam and Eve stand before the forbidden tree, a moment away from eating the fruit. On the right, more promisingly, is Noah's ark, a symbol for salvation through the church.

The most significant link between general study of early modern literature and this splendid edition of the Bible is a pair of questions keenly contested in the seventeenth century: who is able to interpret, and how? The learned boldly claimed exclusive rights. In John Bunyan's account of his exchanges with a Bedford lawyer, William Foster, the tinker presents a strong counter-argument.

> *Foster.* He said, that I was ignorant, and did not undertand Scriptures; for how (said he) can you understand them, when you know not the original Greek? &c.
> *Bunyan.*   To whom I said, that if that was his opinion, that none could understand the Scriptures, but those that had the original Greek, &c. then but a very few of the poorest sort should be saved, (this is harsh) yet the Scripture saith, *That God hides his things from the wise and prudent,* (that is from the learned of the world) *and reveals them to babes and sucklings.* (*A Relation of the Imprisonment of Mr. John Bunyan* 1765; 1998, 103)

George Fox goes further, denying authority to those with learning alone. Not only does the Spirit of God continue to speak directly 'now as in the days of the apostles', it is impossible to interpret the Bible aright without entering 'into the same power and Spirit that the prophets and apostles were in' (*Journal* 1952, 23, 33). Another Quaker, Samuel Fisher, attacks academic study of the scripture as rabbinical focus on the letter rather than the spirit. With vigorous alliterative scorn, he dismisses 'the misty ministers of the meer letter' who value 'the bare External Text of Scriptures (which they themselves confess to be corrupted, vitiated, altered and adulterated in all Translations' above 'inward Light and Spirit' (Wright 1932, 51–52).

Women claiming direct authority for Biblical interpretation further extend the competition between the instructed and the inspired. Both the Old Testament and New Testament provided support. The standard proof texts are Joel 2: 28, 'I will pour out my spirit upon all flesh: and your sons and your daughters shall prophesy' (quoted by Peter in

Acts 2: 17–18), and Galatians 3: 28, 'There is neither Jew nor Greek, there is neither bond nor free, there is neither male nor female: for ye are all one in Christ Jesus.' This statement of radical equality among Christians is especially important as an antidote to Paul's words in the first epistle to Timothy: 'Let the woman learn in silence with all subjection. But I suffer not a woman to teach, nor to usurp authority over the man, but to be in silence' (1 Timothy 2: 11–12). When Margaret Fell set out in *Womens Speaking Justified, Proved and Allowed of by the Scriptures* (1667) to combat this often-quoted prohibition on women's preaching, she moves beyond the usual proof texts to develop interpretations of passages in Revelation and Genesis. Her logical dexterity in commenting on the aftermath of the fall, the punishments of Adam, Eve and the serpent, is particularly striking, for she manages to align with Satan anyone who is opposed to women. In Genesis 3: 15, the Lord says to the serpent, 'I will put enmity between thee and the woman.' Margaret Fell provides a strong reading: 'Let this Word of the Lord, which was from the beginning, stop the mouths of all that oppose Womens speaking in the Power of the Lord', for 'it is manifest, that those that speak against the Woman and her Seeds Speaking, speak out of the enmity of the old Serpent's Seed' (4).[14]

How the Bible was, or should be, read intersects with general questions about interpetation of texts. Typology, or the recognition of parallels between earlier and later stories – often with one a shadowy foreshadowing and the other the fulfilment of a significant pattern – is a habit of mind more familiar to students who define their field as mediaeval and Renaissance texts than to those who think of themselves as modernists, whether 'early modern' or later. Seeing Jonah and his three-day sojourn in the whale as a 'type' of Christ's death and resurrection, for example, or reading Hercules' descent into Hades to rescue Alcestis as an approximation of the Harrowing of Hell is common among writers and their readers from Dante to Milton.[15]

In the flood of autobiographical writing in the seventeenth century, the matching of story to story takes on a particularly intense and personal quality. Repeatedly, almost routinely, those describing their own experiences find in them parallels with lives of Old Testament and New Testament figures. The word 'identify', often casually used in talking about modern novels ('I could really identify with the heroine') has larger resonance in these spiritual autobiographies. Identity-formation is clearly evident in the search for, or recognition and citing of, Biblical characters whose history and words give pattern and meaning to personal awareness in seventeenth century Britain. In Bunyan's *Grace Abounding to the Chief of Sinners*, the title announces his link to Paul, who resoundingly declared 'This is a faithful saying, and worthy of all acceptation, that Christ Jesus came into the world to save sinners; of whom I am chief' (1 Timothy 1: 15).

The community of interpreters includes men now better known in other fields of learning. Robert Boyle and John Locke would have been surprised by the fissures that opened in the nineteenth century between science and religion. Like Voltaire they were confident that knowing nature and knowing the author of nature are complementary.[16] Boyle's *Some Considerations Touching the Style of the H. Scriptures* (1661) reached a fourth edition in 1675. Locke's Biblical commentary in *An Essay for the Understanding of St. Paul's Epistles, By Consulting St. Paul himself* (1707) is especially interesting because he gives conscious attention to the effect that the physical layout of a page has on perception. The practice of printing the Scriptures 'crumbled into Verses', with each verse set out as a separate paragraph, was in his time a convention of relatively recent standing, first found in the Geneva Bible (1560). Locke complains of the eye's being 'constantly disturb'd with loose Sentences, that by their standing and separation, appear as so many distinct Fragments.' St Paul's words are

> so chop'd and minc'd, and as they are now Printed, stand so broken and divided, that not only the Common People take the Verses usually for distinct Aphorisms, but even Men of more advanc'd Knowledge in reading them, lose very much of the strength and force of the Coherence, and the Light that depends on it. (1707, ix, vii)

Charles II, *Declaration of Breda*, $\frac{4}{14}$ April 1660[17]

> And because the Passion and Uncharitableness of the Times have produced several Opinions in Religion by which men are engaged in Parties and Animosities against each other, which, when they shall hereafter unite in a Freedom of conversation, will be composed, or better understood; we do declare a liberty to tender Consciences; and that no man shall be disquieted or called in question, for Differences of Opinion in Matters of Religion which do not disturb the Peace of the Kingdom; and that we shall be ready to consent to such an Act of

> Parliament, as, upon mature Deliberation, shall be offered to us, for
> the full granting that Indulgence.

The stirring, unequivocal promise 'we do declare a liberty to tender Consciences' is compromised by the end of the sentence. Clear as the declaration looks at first glance, it leaves room for plenty of interpretative work. Optimism that those engaged in animosities can and will unite in freedom of conversation, and that the differences will be composed, is tempered by a phrase which in the ongoing rhythm of reading might be taken as simply rhetorical doubling, a strengthening restatement of 'composed'. Do the three words 'or better understood' contribute primarily to a view of controversialists coming to understand one another in charitable sympathy, as 'unite' has suggested, or does the phrase open up possibilities that sharpening definitions of differences might harden the lines? There is, furthermore, the question of discriminating between opinions in religion which do and do not disturb the peace. Finally, before the sentence reaches a full stop, Charles' confident 'we do declare' is qualified by the movement from active proclamation to passive assent; his hopeful assertion of liberty to tender consciences is dependent on what the Parliament, after mature deliberation, will offer for his consent.

In the event, the promises of Breda were unfulfilled. The Act of Uniformity (1662) required all clergymen, university fellows and teachers to declare 'unfeigned assent and consent' to a newly revised Book of Common Prayer, *before* this prayerbook was available for thorough study.[18] The act drove out of the established church a large number of its most scrupulous leaders. Men such as Richard Baxter (1615–91), briefly a royal chaplain and more than once offered a bishopric, were now classed among the rebellious and were criminalised for preaching. Despite penalties of fines and imprisonment, many of these nonconformists continued to preach and, in or out of prison, to extend their pastoral reach through writing. There are 2523 names in the 1713 version of Edmund Calamy's *Account of the Ministers, Lecturers, Masters and Fellows of Colleges and Schoolmasters, who were Ejected or Silenced after the Restoration in 1660, by or before the Act for Uniformity*; biographical entries in the modern *Calamy Revised* (Matthews 1934) often end with the dry word 'Publications'.

In the more radical Protestant sects, extreme antinomians escaped from problems of conscience. Chopping out of its context Paul's injunction that 'Unto the pure all things are pure' (Titus 1: 15), they scandalised their neighbours by sexual licence; Laurence Clarkson's autobiography *The Lost Sheep Found* (1660) sketches such episodes. That religious doctrine could actually encourage immorality was more generally suspected of papists. When 'liberty to tender Consciences' was withheld from even moderate dissenters, Roman Catholics had an extremely slim chance of toleration. In *Of True Religion, Hæresie, Schism, Toleration* (1673), Milton catalogues abuses grown more prominent in recent years – 'Pride, Luxury, Drunkenness, Whoredom, Cursing, Swearing, bold and open Atheism every where abounding' – and finds a direct correlation with the spread of papist doctrine, which lulled a sinner's conscience through 'easy Confession' and superstitious dependence on masses, pardons, relics rather than on true repentence (*Prose Works* 1982, VIII. 438–9). Widespread uneasiness about Roman Catholics mounted towards hysterical accusations that there was a Popish Plot to assassinate the king and so hurry on the succession to the throne of his more openly Catholic brother James. Modern readers are sometimes much in the position of readers of the late 1670s, bewildered by the mass of pamphlets, poems, transcripts of trials, and politically charged plays, struggling to sort out exactly what did and did not happen. Fear of Communists during the McCarthy era in America provides an analogy for the obsessive distrust of papists in the late seventeenth century. 'Papism' was represented as an ideology to which almost any particular form of suspicion might cogently be attached. The consequences are by turns farcical, heroic or fatally arbitrary.

Elizabeth Cellier, *Malice Defeated* (London 1680)

Given the mixtures of real and imaginary plotting, incredulity and hysteria, individual courage and incidental humour, a range of rogues, sturdy commonsensical witnesses and heroic stalwarts, assaying the facts behind 'the Popish Plot' was not easy in the 1670s and early 1680s – nor is it easy now.[19] That transcripts of trials sold well is indicated by the advertisement of 'Books lately Printed' at the end of *The Tryal and Conviction of John Tasborough and Ann Price* (1680). Among many others 'sold by Robert Pawlet, at the Bible in Chancery-Lane, near Fleet-Street' is listed one of the secondary prosecutions: 'The Tryal and Conviction of *Thomas Knox*, and *John Lane*, for a Conspiracy to defame and Scandalise *Dr. Oates*, and *Mr. Bedloe*;

thereby to discredit their Evidence about the *Horrid* Popish-Plot.' The mass of printed works associated with such public events, political and religious, contains a great deal of material interesting to a student of rhetoric, although literary interest was not the primary intent of the writers. Fashions in literary scholarship shift rapidly; there is little here that a student of English literature in, say, the 1950s would have considered central.

Caught up in the aftermath of the Popish Plot, a Catholic midwife named Elizabeth Cellier herself prepared for the press a volume called, in brief, *Malice Defeated*. Conveniently made available in facsimile by the Augustan Reprint Society, it provides a self-portrait of a figure implicated in the ludicrous but potentially disastrous forgery of papers hidden in her meal-tub. Its full titlepage deserves close reading (Figure 1.3). The top half sets out a description of the book's contents. Next comes an emblematic design, presenting an anchor attached to a cross on which a dove is perched, with an olive twig in its beak. The motto claiming 'I never change' (=*semper eadem*, said of the eternal law) is here also associated with Mrs Cellier as steadfast, harmless dove. The framing Latin motto is an inaccurately printed quotation from Juvenal, Satire II. 63, spoken by a woman who is complaining of the injustice of the law, made by men and unfair to women. In its correct form it reads *dat veniam corvis, vexat censura columbas* (Our censor absolves the ravens and passes judgment on the doves).[20] Elizabeth Cellier's defence continues in two passages quoted from the Psalms. Here, as throughout the pamphlet, she combines or juxtaposes defence of her innocence with an attack on the malicious accuser, Thomas Dangerfield. Finally, the titlepage records that the book was printed for Elizabeth Cellier, and sold at her house. This is not quite vanity publishing, in the modern fashion, but it indicates – as similar information on Arise Evans' pamphlets does – the use of the press for private ends of self-presentation.

From Mrs Cellier's pamphlet, a curious reader could move to the less highly charged, semi-official account of her trial, or to the second trial which followed in which her publication of *Malice Defeated* is the central issue: libel against the king and his ministers, for which she was fined £1000 and sentenced to stand in the pillory three times. Street-ballads mocking the Papist Midwife join the cluster of publications directly related to the events of 1680.[21] The voice of this confidently assertive woman can be heard in a second composition of her own. 'A Scheme for the Foundation of a Royal Hospital and ... for the

Malice Defeated :

Or a Brief Relation of the Accusation and Deliverance of

Elizabeth Cellier,

Wherein her Proceedings both before and during her Confinement, are particularly Related, and the Myftery of the *Meal-Tub* fully
difcovered.
Together with an Abftract of her Arraignment
and Tryal, written by her felf, for the fa-
tisfaction of all Lovers of undifguifed Truth.

Pfal. 35. 11. 12. *Falfe witneffes did rife up againft me, they laid to my charge things
that I knew not.
They rewarded me Evil for Good, to the fpoiling of my Soul.*
Pfal. 7. 14, 16. *Behold he Travelleth with Iniquity, and conceived Mifchief, and
brought forth Falfehood.
His Mifchief fhall return upon his own Head, and his violent Dealing fhall come down
upon his own Pate.*

LONDON, Printed for *Elizabeth Cellier,* and are to be fold at
her Houfe in *Arundel-ftreet* near St. *Clements* Church, 1680.

Figure 1.3   Title-page of Cellier, *Malice Defeated* (1680). Reproduced
by permission of the Syndics of Cambridge University Library.

Maintenance of a Corporation of skilful Midwives, of such Found-lings, or Exposed Children, as shall be admitted therein' (1687), presented to James II during his brief reign, remained in manuscript until the mid-eighteenth century. Her carefully thought-through proposals join, or for a student can open the way towards, other prac-tical educational, medical and social treatises of the time. As is almost always the case, reading a single publication leads in many directions. Trials as a form of dramatic entertainment will recur in a later chapter of this book. Mrs Cellier's accuser reappears as the hero and narrator of *Don Tamazo* (1680), a jaunty fictionised celebration of Dangerfield as a resilient rogue.[22] It belongs in the stream of criminal narratives which runs from Elizabethan coney-catching pamphlets to Defoe's *Moll Flanders* and beyond.

John Dryden, *Secular Masque* (1700)

In the year of his death, Dryden's *Secular Masque* provides, compressed into ninety-seven lines of verse, a panoramic review of the century. 'Secular' in the title, from Latin *saeculum*, means age or generation; here as in many works of the period continuities and change, often very conscious awareness of change, are intermingled. For this last of his dramatic scripts Dryden chose an old-fashioned form, one associated more with the early Stuart court than with the post-Restoration public theatres.[23] During the reign of James I, Ben Jonson and Inigo Jones had collaborated in yearly displays of poetry and stage design mingled with political flattery and instruction. In Dryden's script, there is less didacticism than nostalgia and disillu-sionment, however gracefully or jauntily expressed: ''Tis better to Laugh than to Cry' (l. 20). Although the *Secular Masque* ends with anticipation of a new age, the context of performance at Drury Lane has a large measure of attachment to the past, at least as much conti-nuity as innovation. Dryden's work was produced as an afterpiece for one of the dozens of pre-1642 plays revived and revised after the reopening of the theatres in 1660, a play by Jonson's even more popular contemporary John Fletcher, *The Pilgrim* (first performed 1621), in a version 'corrected' by Dryden's friend, the younger play-wright John Vanbrugh.

Janus, the two-faced god who looks backward and forward, has the opening lines. All the characters with speaking parts are Roman deities, a choice of imagery so commonplace that a moment's pause is needed to contemplate the ease with which English writers, and their readers, move between seventeenth-century Britain and classical Italy or Greece, or on other occasions (as in Dryden's *Absalom and Achitophel*, 1681) between seventeenth-century Britain and ancient Palestine. Without quite being considered contemporary, Augustus and (at an extra literal millenium's distance) David offer an enlarged but familiar world, a vocabulary of images with which to consider modern affairs. While, for poets, the implicit evaluative qualities of classical and Hebrew allusions are usefully economical, in other contexts such as Sprat's *History of the Royal Society*, calling on what everyone knows (certainly the king, to whom the *History* is dedicated) can be explicitly argumentative. Two of Sprat's three paragraphs in the dedicatory epistle set out a case for technical innovation as more glorious than warfare. In pagan antiquity, 'the Gods they Worshipped with Temples and Altars, were those who instructed the World to Plow, to Sow, to Plant, to Spin, to build Houses, and to find out New Countries.' Parallel arguments rest on Genesis:

> In the whole History of the first Monarchs of the World, from Adam to Noah, there is no mention of their Wars, or their Victories: All that is Recorded is this, They lived so many years, and taught their Posterity to keep Sheep, to till the Ground, to plant Vineyards, to dwell in Tents, to build Cities, to play on the Harp and Organs, and to work in Brass and Iron.

Dryden neatly deploys as his cast two trios of Roman divinities, along with attendant musicians and dancers. Janus is an obvious choice for the first of the trio of presenters, in which weary Chronos, god of time, too tired to fly towards the new century, is balanced by laughing Momus, god of discord or ridicule. Music and dance must be imagined as a significant part of the masque. To the sound of hunting-horns Diana appears, representing the age of James I and Charles I:

> *Janus.*   Then our Age was in its Prime,
> *Chronos.*   Free from Rage,
> *Diana.*   And free from Crime,
> *Momus.*   A very Merry, Dancing, Drinking,
>   Laughing, Quaffing, and unthinking Time. (ll. 37–40)

Accompanied by drums and trumpets, Mars (so conveniently ignored by Sprat) brings to an end the dance of Diana's attendants. His evocation of the Civil Wars and Interregnum leads to Momus' comment on that period's futility: 'neither side a winner, / For things are as they were.' Third, to unspecified music, comes Venus as patroness of the days of Restoration, when 'Joy ruled the Day, and Love the Night' but as the chorus implies, that era was gone long before Charles was followed by James and James by William and Mary. Despite lilting rhythms, the conclusion of the masque is far from merry.

> All, all, of a piece throughout;
> Thy Chase had a Beast in view;
> Thy Wars brought nothing about;
> Thy Lovers were all untrue.
> 'Tis well an Old Age is out,
> And time to begin a New. (ll. 86–91)

Stage directions call for Momus to point in turn to Diana, Mars and Venus during the second to fourth of these verses; Janus and Chronos chime in at the end. Possibly the final dance of huntsmen, nymphs, warriors, and lovers established a more festive conclusion to the evening.[24]

What was published and how it looked

Learning about contexts is progressive rather than preliminary. Once past the most neatly packaged anthology, selected and annotated, each new text sets up questions about what one would like to know. In the phrase 'literature 1650–1720', both the noun and the dates are interestingly problematical. If literature includes everything 'lettered', written or printed, then – for one thing – who could read it all? Among mediaeval scholars, there was a small recurrent joke that anyone who claimed to have read all of Augustine's work was a liar. Among scholars alive today, few other than Neil Keeble can have read all the published work of Richard Baxter. The work of enumerative bibliographers, even though always at least a little incomplete, is both stimulating and daunting. Even within carefully defined limits, temporal or topical, there is a wealth of material. When the London bookseller George Thomason set out, during the Civil Wars and Interregnum, to acquire practically everything published, he built up a collection of 23 926 texts. When enormous stocks of printed materials were destroyed in the Great Fire of London (1666), Thomason's collection was fortunately at Oxford; it is now in the care of the British Library.[25] The merest glance at the two-volume printed catalogue of the Thomason Tracts – and any student of the mid-seventeenth century should do more than glance at it – is enough to support one of the recurrent themes of this discussion: the jostling together of disparate views, the multiplicity of voices. Evocative long titles give a much fuller sense of subject and tone than the crisp spine-titles common now. The very low proportion of literature in obviously belle-lettrist categories prompts attention to questions about what was actually bought and read – and read, one must assume, with both pleasure and profit.

John Whiting's early bibliography, *A Catalogue of Friends Books; Written by many of the People, called Quakers, from the Beginning or First Appearance of the said People* (1708) again demonstrates both the mass of published texts and the early, self-conscious valuing and preserving of recent records. How prolific the early Quakers were can be seen and counted in the 232 quarto pages of Whiting's catalogue. It is a quirk of the alphabet that the major listing (216 pages, followed by a list of Quaker books in continental languages) runs from Margaret Abbot's pamphlet *A Testimony against the false Teachers of this Generation* to Judith Zins-Penninck's *Some worthy Proverbs ... to be Read in the Congregation of the Saints*. It is a happy quirk given that this frame emphasises the relative prominence of women within the Quaker community.[26] Margaret Fell's twenty-one titles include a number of genres: there are warnings and exhortations, pastoral epistles, an account of *The Examination and Tryal of Margaret Fell & George Fox at the several Assizes held at Lancaster* (1664), two public letters addressed to the king, and the treatise that is now the best-known of her publications, *Womens Speaking Justified, proved & allowed of by the Scriptures* (1666, with additions 1667), an argument briefly discussed earlier in this chapter in relation to controversy over who was entitled to interpret the Bible. On his titlepage Whiting quotes Isaiah 30: 8: 'Go, write it before them in a Table and note it in a Book, that it may be for the time to Come.'

An active student of literature 1650–1720 quickly begins to be a scholar. A great deal of the writing of the period has been published in modernised editions; a great deal has not. Reading an original text, or a facsimile, involves growing familiar with conventions of earlier printing. Whiting, in his 1708 bibliography, does not note, as modern book reviews often do, how long each text is by giving the number of pages, but instead specifies the number of sheets of paper and supplies information about format: folio, quarto, octavo, duodecimo.[27] Recognising the choices made by publishers in presenting the book is a key to understanding what book-buyers might expect. A folio, like a modern 'coffee-table book' could be seen as pretentious or as dignified. The smaller volumes were easily portable. More was not always seen as better. Richard Brome's 'Upon *Aglaura* in Folio', included in the anthology *Musarum deliciae* (1655), is a sour comment on an expensive printing of Suckling's play *Aglaura* (1638), with wide margins and a slender rivulet of text occupying only fifty pages. Brome's poem on 'This great Voluminous Pamphlet' ends

> Give me the sociable pocket books,
> These empty Folio's onely please the looks.

When the poem was reprinted in Brome's *Five New Playes* (1659), a variant final line, 'These empty Folio's only please the Cooks' strengthens the satiric attack; unsold printed paper was thriftily reused, supporting pies which were the seventeenth-century's fast food.

At first glance, early editions look typographically odd. The interchangeability of i and j, or of u and v, is less apt to present difficulties than the double use of y to represent not only the letter Y but also the Old Enlish *thorn*, for a phoneme now usually represented by *th*. Thus *ye* often means, and should be pronounced as, *the*, and in texts making use of contractions, y^t can stand for either *that* or *yet*; context is the only guide. 'Long S' is a special problem. In handwriting as well as in print, a different form of the letter s was used at the end of a word and in initial or medial place, and since the 'long s' resembles an f, it is easy to start lisping – in reading 'mifs' (miss) for example. Mistakes are easily made, even in the seventeenth century, contributing to the many textual variants found in early printed texts. In the 1650 anthology *Academy of Complements*, Ben Jonson's 'Slow, slow fresh fount, keep time to my salt tears' appears as 'Flow, flow, fresh fount' (205). It is possible that a copyist intended to improve Jonson's line, emphasising fluidity rather than pace, but it is also possible that a hasty typesetter introduced the variant.

Old dating and old money call for brief explanation. The simpler of two possible confusions about dating is whether a new year is assumed to begin, on 1 January or on 25 March, the feast of the Annunciation. (Students of mediaeval literature will remember how resonant 25 March is for Dante, for whom the creation of the world and the incarnation of Christ coincide.) Some caution is needed with dates of publication and premières of plays. The occasional appearance of an odd-looking date such as February $16\frac{79}{80}$ (found, for example, on the titlepage of *The Tryal and Conviction of John Tasborough and Ann Price*) reflects the fact that from January to almost the end of March the year could be written either 1679 or 1680. In modern scholarly books, a careful double date may be used to avoid any ambiguity about how many months separate the premières of Sedley's *Antony and Cleopatra* (February 1676/7) and Dryden's *All for Love* (December 1677), since a contemporary reference to February 1676 could misleadingly suggest a longer gap between the rival plays. Although the modern British economic year is still linked with 25 March, that link is obscured by the difference between Julian and Gregorian calendars.[28] This is a second potential although less common cause for confusion. From the time of Julius Caesar, an error of one day every 128 years accumulated in the Julian calendar, corrected by Pope Gregory XIII in 1582. Most continental countries adopted the Gregorian calendar, but partly because of Protestant aversion to anything 'papist', it was not accepted in England until 1752. When comparing English documents with those of other parts of Europe, it is often important to know whether old style (o.s.) or new style (n.s.) dating is used. The official publication of Charles II's Declaration of Breda shows the date in both forms. Later in the century, William of Orange could be seen to leave Holland on 12 November 1688 (n.s.) but arrive in England, three days later, on the fifth of November (o.s.).[29] Old money and its abbreviations present fewer difficulties. A pound (£) contained twenty shillings (s.) and each shilling contained twelve pence (d.). The guinea, a gold coin first issued from 1663, was worth slightly more than a pound because the gold of Guinea was thought especially fine.

Whether in this book to present quotations with scholarly faithfulness to original spelling, punctuation, even abbreviations, was not an easy decision.[30] Apparently reader-friendly, modernisation in the process of making a text look easy, up-to-date, hides pitfalls. There are changes of meanings in common words, such as awful (awe-inspiring), or comfortable (comforting, in Alice Thornton's catalogue of letters sent to her after her husband's death). Two other common words which are traps for the unwary are prevent (come before or anticipate, rather than obstruct) and pretend (claim rather than feign). The general question of how useful it is to keep in sight, or not, the differences between one era and another, including assumptions that standardised spelling is the mark of education, is also important. Some spellings which are now non-standard are useful because the small pause in interpretation may cause a pun to become more prominent. Careful poets often use an apostrophe in past participles to indicate that the -ed was not to be pronounced as a separate syllable, so *call'd* and *called* have different metrical effects. On the other hand, the use of apostrophes in possessives, and their absence from plurals, had not yet been standardised. Only occasionally can spelling, capitalisation or punctuation safely be assigned to the author; such matters are frequently accidents of the copyist, typesetter or editor. When working directly from the early texts, I have occasionally adopted an uneasy compromise, lightly modernising spelling which seems apt to confuse ('bade' rather than 'bad' as the past tense of 'bid', Jonson and Rowe for the playwrights' surnames rather than Johnson and Roe).[31] Typographically, the unpredictable capitalisation and extravagant italics of the time may produce a mildly alienating effect. Titles are a special case, as in *The New Academy of Complements* (for *Compliments*) or *The Voice of King Charls*; here original spelling is preserved as an aid to finding works in library catalogues.

Dashes in quotation are another special problem, and an interesting one for a modern reader. How does the presence of a 'blanking' dash, or full spelling out of a name or indecorous term, affect reading? When, in 'An Allusion to Horace', Rochester attacks Dryden for unimaginative foul-mouthedness, the couplet

> But when he would be sharp, he still was blunt,
> To frisk his frolic fancy, he'd cry, 'C___' (ll. 74–5)[32]

is stronger with the blank than without it; the typographical convention hardly conceals the word that is meant, but calls attention to it. Similarly when dashes are used for proper names, the blank is hardly a secret; if so, the force of either attack or praise would be lost. On a titlepage, initials may proclaim fame rather than disguising authorship. The 1689 *Poems on Affairs of State* which attributed many of them to A___ M___ is better evidence of Marvell's reputation as a satirist than spelling out his name in full would have been. Editors who silently fill in the blanks usually need (and provide) annotation for proper names in any case, but they obscure some of the effect of early printings. A dash emphasises knowledge shared between poet and audience, establishing an in-group of understanding and, potentially, of judgment. Occasionally, there is an extra sting, as in Dryden's *MacFlecknoe*. Although the metrical pattern of the poem, as well as common literary knowledge, establishes that Sh___ means Shadwell, on the page sh___ suggests to the eye an alternative monosyllabic reading.

Reading on

The chronological chart and bibliogaphies at the end of this volume succinctly point towards a great deal more writing of and about the time than can be discussed within these pages. Any single good book leads to dozens more. In the early decades of the twenty-first century, coming to terms with texts produced three hundred years ago may produce clashes of keenly felt recognition and a sense of alterity. Occasionally, something particularly 'modern' also seems particularly odd. Air pollution in London, the topic of John Evelyn's *Fumifugium* (1661), is so severe that it drives John Locke to the countryside; Sir William Temple, in an essay 'Of Health and Long Life', gravely considers the medicinal advantages claimed for 'friction' (massage) and for what is now called aromatherapy. The gap in time increases the danger of imposing alien expectations, or of assuming with self-satisfied arrogance that one can uncover others' unconscious motivations without revealing one's own. Reading, now, is further complicated by the mass of critical commentary written since 1720, or even since 1970. It is also complicated in practical ways, by publishing practices and by the proximity or remoteness of major libraries. Publishers now as in the past have an unsystematic but powerful influence on what is available. Books rapidly go out of print; the Penguin edition of Dorothy Osborne's letters, for example, is now a happy find in a second-hand bookshop. Electronic databases, on the Net or on CD-ROM, are not an immediate cure for all deficiencies. Availability of material is spotty and editing is uneven. Commercially produced materials for computers may for independent scholars seem as remote as a distant Rare Book Room; the Chadwyck-Healy 'Early English Prose Fiction' (1997) provides a great many narratives (although not their prefatory matter) from the years 1500–1700, but the CD-ROM version was originally announced at a price of £5500, and subscribing to the Internet version is also out of the budgetary range of individuals, and often even of university libraries.

Underexamined assumptions about earlier times linger in some apparently authoritative modern publications. Margaret J.M. Ezell, in the bracing arguments of *Writing Women's Literary History* (1993) includes an incisive critical review of the anthologies of women's writing published in the 1970s and 1980s. She notes that despite the contribution made by these anthologies to making available (and academically respectable) texts which had not been easily obtainable, texts written before the nineteenth century are underrepresented. In *The Norton Anthology of Literature by Women: The Tradition in English* (1985), for example, pre-Romantic writing occupies only 172 pages out of 2390; such a proportion reinforces the view 'that women writing before the eighteenth century were rare and eccentric creatures' (41–2). As significant evidence to the contrary, Ezell cites Patricia Crawford's checklist of published writing by women between 1600 and 1700, which identifies some three hundred authors.[33] In addition, as recent studies on the significance of manuscript circulation have demonstrated, publication and literary productivity, even literary recognition, are not to be equated (Love 1993). *Caveat lector*, here and elsewhere; although rapid changes in women's studies are particularly obvious in recent decades,[34] almost any generalisation about a 'period' as long and diverse as 1650–1720 invites sceptical scrutiny.

Selection, Serendipity and System: Given the thousands of items in the Thomason Tract collection alone, which covers only two decades, exhaustive investigation is the task of an exhausting – or for a scholar of the right temperament, exhilarating – lifetime. What should and could one read first? There are many possible models for learning about the literature of this or any other period. Alliteratively, a group of approaches could be characterised as canon, coterie or cornflake packet. For canon, syllabus might be a more useful idea; invoking the word canon often serves as tactical preparation for challenging it. Either term is loaded with implications of authority, of order, and of limits. These days, many readers meet literature of 1650–1720 in a university course, where someone has drawn up a list supportive of doctrine (literally, 'teaching') and sufficient for salvation in the form of a pass mark. If at the end of such a course the student has not accumulated a substantial additional list, for rereading or new reading, something has gone wrong. At the other extreme from canon is the cornflake packet, or attention to whatever comes to hand, whatever the local library has on its shelves. There is something to be said for this approach. Like the classroom, it is a success only if it leads on to further exploration. Outside an academic structure, or within the limited freedom of a class project, interest in a coterie provides a structure for reading. A letter by Dorothy Osborne leads to the work of William Temple, and to the early activities of his young kinsman Jonathan Swift. Or the other way around. One natural metaphor for the coterie approach is throwing a stone in a pond and seeing its widening circles. A web, the Web, is now the obvious alternative image.

At the risk of asking the reader of this book to throw it away, but aware that time is short and art is long, I strongly urge anyone confronting a choice between reading anything from the years 1650 and 1720 and reading *about* it, to choose the primary text.

Notes

1. The stanza of 'Upon the Popish Plot' in which this phrase appears is printed in Greer's introduction to the anthology *Kissing the Rod* (1988, 22).
2. See Hill (1991, 48–71) on Evans; Mack (1992) on prophetic women; Capp (1972) on Fifth Monarchy Men; Watts (1978) on a range of dissenting behaviour.
3. Locke's vigorous attack on enthusiasm as distinguished from both reason and revelation is in *An Essay Concerning Human Understanding* (1690), Book 4, Chapter 19.
4. As epigraph to the volume, Comenius uses Genesis 2: 19–20, 'The Lord God brought unto Adam every Beast of the Field, and every Fowl of the air, to see what he would call them. And Adam gave names to all Cattle, and to the Fowl of the air, and to every beast of the Field.' In the continental editions (Noribergae, 1664 for example), the Latin text of these verses emphasises the significant words about sight and speech typographically, either by using full capitals or by a distinction between italic and Roman type, so that VIDERET, VACARET, *Appellavitque*, and *Nominibus* stand out.

5. This is not an isolated example of conscious emphasis on links between past and future, particularly notable in a series called *Transitions*. In 1650–1720 looking back is as prominent an image as looking forward. Major projects for change, in government, religion, language or scientific enquiry, are more often presented as restoration or continuity than as innovation. For a stimulating study of intersections of science, religion, and linguistics, with trenchant reviews of earlier work, see Markley (1993). On language and the Royal Society, see also Reed 1989.

6. The Apocryphal books, among which Ecclesiasticus (not to be confused with Ecclesiastes) belongs, were separated from the fully canonical books in the Authorised Version of 1611, but they remained familiar to seventeenth-century readers. Having searched the Scriptures to find a half-remembered verse, Bunyan finally locates it in Ecclesiasticus (*Grace Abounding* ¶ 65).

7. Elizabeth Elstob reported her uncle's attitude in a letter to George Ballard, whose compilation of *Memoirs of Several Ladies of Great Britain who have been Celebrated for their Writings or Skill in the Learned Languages, Arts and Sciences* she encouraged (Ballard 1752).

8. There were a few exceptions. A progressive academy set up by Charles Morton at Newington Green, where Samuel Wesley and Daniel Defoe were educated, had a wide curriculum and a well-equipped laboratory for what was then called natural philosophy and is now called science. Michael R. Watts comments, 'That Morton was able to achieve so much is no doubt largely explained by the fact that, unusually for a late-seventeenth-century tutor, whether Dissenting or Anglican, he gave all his instruction in English' (Watts 1978, 368).

9. Ezell (1987) gives a succinct account of female education, warning against oversimplification of the evidence.

10. The name Hannah Woolley appears on the titlepage, but, as Elaine Hobby points out, she was indignant about the false attribution, along with plagiarism and distortion of her earlier writing; significantly, a bookseller saw her works as 'a saleable commodity' (Hobby in MacLean 1995, 181, 189–90).

11. In the Cambridge University Library, there are several copies, of which Young 7 includes the 'advertisement' to subscribers. In Bury 4.1.6 the engraved titlepage is bound in the sixth volume; a plainer titlepage only, dated 1657, is found in Bury 4.1.1.

12. Amusingly, there is also an edgy sentence about 'unworthy dealing' which implies that some who had promised to support the work 'have performed nothing'.

13. See for example, the volume published by John Ogilby, master of the

revels, with illustrations and descriptions of the four triumphal arches erected for Charles II's progress through London to his coronation (Ogilby 1662, facsimile 1988). A generous array of Hollar's engravings, contributing to a sense of seventeenth-century landscape and architecture as well as book design, is provided in Parry (1980).

14. On women's prophecy and interpretation of scripture, see Hobby (1988, 26–53) and Thickstun (1991l).

15. See Korshin (1982) on the survival of typological approaches, to secular as well as religious texts, well into the eighteenth century.

16. Note the titles of three of Richard Baxter's many books, *The Unreasonableness of Infidelity* (1655), *Reasons for the Christian Religion* (1667), and *More Reasons for the Christian Religion* (1672), which anticipate John Locke's *The Reasonableness of Christianity as delivered in the Scriptures* (1695). The compatibility of interest in nature – or as we might now say, in science – and in religion is everywhere to be found. John Tillotson (later Archbishop of Canterbury) was elected to the Royal Society and appointed Dean of Canterbury in the same year, 1672.

17. For double dating, see explanation below, under 'What was published and how it looked'.

18. The Act of Uniformity was one of the cluster of measures often referred to as the Clarendon Code, which heavily penalised unauthorised meetings for worship, treating those who led such gatherings as fomenters of sedition. Corporation Act 1661, Act of Conformity 1662, Conventicle Act 1664, Five Mile Act 1665.

19. For guidance see Kenyon (1972); in McHenry (1986) are facsimiles of twenty-five documents related to the plot, presented as background to Dryden's *Absalom and Achitophel*.

20. Contrary to the notes at the head of the Augustan Reprint Society's edition, the whole of *Malice Defeated* was set in type at least twice. The incorrect endings on CORVUS and COLUMBUS were marked by a presumably puzzled reader on the copy which the Society used for its reproduction. They stand wholly uncorrected (and largely meaningless) in the alternative setting of the titlepage in a copy held by the Cambridge University Library (Syn.4.68.8[5]).

21. 'On Mrs. Cellier in the Pillory' can be found in *POAS* II. 364–6.

22. That his name was already a byword for rhetorical effrontery can be seen in Thomas Rymer's essay on *The Tragedies of the Last Age* (1678). Offhandedly, he writes of a comic character: 'all his words are brags; no Dangerfield nor Captain Thundergun could sit near him' (Spingarn II. 198). For *Don Tamazo*, see Peterson (1961), Salzman (1991).

23. With a still later work in this genre, *The Judgment of Paris: A Masque*

(1701), Congreve may be deliberately inviting comparison with Dryden, who in 'To my dear Friend Mr. Congreve on his Comedy, call'd The Double-Dealer' (1694) names him as the proper recipient of his laurels.

24. The surviving music for the masque is briefly described in Fiske (1986), 14, 210–11.

25. While Thomason's serious collecting runs from the Long Parliament in November 1640 to the coronation of Charles II in April 1661, there is a lull in 1658 when he considered discontinuing the project, and throughout the period he was less assiduous in collecting broadside ballads and Quaker tracts than other materials (Fortescue 1908, I. xxii; McAleer 1961, 172).

26. A recent, substantial anthology of Quaker women's writing 1650-1700, ed. Garman *et al.* (1996), provides convenient samples of this material.

27. Briefly, a folio is made from folding each sheet of printed paper once, and since printing paper was a cheaper replacement for parchment, whose size was dependent on the width and breadth of a sheepskin, this produces an impressively large book. A quarto was made up of paper folded twice, thus providing four leaves. Progressively smaller, an octavo from paper folded four times has eight leaves to a gathering, and a duodecimo has twelve. See diagrams in Gaskell (1971, 88–105).

'Folio' can also mean a single leaf in a book of any size. For books or parts of books without page numbers, references are given by identifying whether the front (recto, abbreviated r, usually in superscript) or back (verso, abbreviated v) of the leaf (fol. or f.) is meant. Thus f. 4^v for what in a modern book would be p. 8. Printers usually 'signed', with alphabetical letters or other symbols, the large sheets used for printing and then folded to make up gatherings for binding; assuming the printer began with A, the front of the third leaf of the second gathering (folded sheet) of a quarto would be f. $B3^r$ (=page 13).

28. When the Gregorian calendar was finally adopted in Britain, in the mid-eighteenth century, the time lag between the calendars caused the beginning of the tax year to become 6 April rather than 25 March.

29. Quaker dating presents additional difficulties; John Nichall's edition of *The Journal of George Fox* provides a lucid explanation and handy table (1952, xiii–xiv). For full information on calendars, see Cappelli (6th edn 1988).

30. A clear comparative example of editorial practices is available in Patrick Colborn Cullen's 1994 edition of Anna Weamys' *A Continuation of Sir Philip Sidney's 'Arcadia'* (1657), in the Oxford University Press series Women Writers in English 1350–1850. After a modernised annotated text, Cullen also provides an old-spelling

reprint (dispensing with long S, but retaining other typographical details such as italics for proper names). See McKenzie (1986) for a forceful argument, illustrated with four lines from Congreve's prologue to *The Way of the World* which were used as an epigraph to Wimsatt and Beardsley's influencial essay on 'The Intentional Fallacy', on the distortions of meaning resulting from editorial modernising.

31. What is important to note is that editorial practice is problematical and controversial. In the most recent edition of Rochester's *Complete Works*, Frank H. Ellis sets out the argument for modernisation as 'elucidation' (1995, xv). Elucidation is, one notes, an unobtrusive but strong nudge towards a particular reading. In contrast, Barbara Everett roundly criticises the 'toneless text', with loss or shifts of meaning, which results from so common a form of modernisation as eliminating capitals (Everett 1982, 15–16).

32. The couplet is missing from Rochester's poem as printed in *The Oxford Book of Seventeenth Century Verse*, ed. H.J.C. Grierson and G. Bullough (1934), with no indication of ellipsis. Is this bowdlerisation, or an innocent choice of copy-text? Most modern editions follow the 1680 *Poems*; Grierson and Bullough the 1685 edition. For a brief description of how the publisher Andrew Thorncome in 1685 omits materials he 'may have considered blasphemous or obscene', see Vieth (1963, 10).

33. Crawford, in Prior (1985), 211–82. The biographical directory of English women writers 1580–1720 compiled by Maureen Bell *et al.* (1990) includes some four hundred women who were published, along with about one hundred and fifty whose writing survived in manuscript.

34. In an autobiographical essay on 'Memory and Women's Studies' in *Gender, Art, and Death* (1993) Janet Todd sketches a history of feminist writing from the 1970s into the 1990s, tracing shifts in the academic vocabulary used for thinking about women writing. See also Donna Landry, 'Commodity Feminism' in Damrosch (1992, 154–74).

2 Poems and Occasions

Milton

Had Milton been executed in 1660, as could well have happened, his name might be less familiar to students of poetry than that of Edmund Waller. Both in 1645 published their first collections of poetry. Waller's was an immediate success, while, despite its inclusion of 'Lycidas' and 'A Mask Presented at Ludlow Castle', Milton's volume did not sell well enough to prompt a second edition until after the appearance of *Paradise Lost* (1667), and of *Paradise Regained* and *Samson Agonistes* (1671). Well into his fifties, his general reputation was based on his prose tracts, notorious for advocating divorce and defending regicide. When John Evelyn engaged a tutor for his son, he noted that this young man, Edward Phillips, 'was Nephew to Milton who writ against Salmasius's *Defensio*' and then added reassuringly 'but not at all infected with his principles, & though brought up by him, yet in no way tainted' (*Diary*, 24 October 1663).

At the Restoration, Milton was perilously close to death. A royal proclamation dated 13 August 1660 directed against Milton and John Goodwin notes that they 'are both fled, or obscure themselves, that no endeavours used for their apprehension can take effect, whereby they might be brought to Legal Tryal, and deservedly receive condigne punishment for their Treasons and Offences'. Milton's *Pro Populo Anglicano Defensio* (1651) is condemned as containing 'sundry Treasonable Passages against Us and Our Government, and most Impious endeavors to justify the horrid and unmatchable Murther of Our late Dear Father, of Glorious Memory'. The proclamation commands that all copies be called in and publicly burned, 'to the end that Our good Subjects may not be corrupted in their Judgments'.

His survival, after brief imprisonment later in 1660, changed the map of English literature. When Dryden rewrote the epic as an opera, *The State of Innocence,* he was only the first of a long series of writers stimulated to new creative efforts by Milton's work (Griffin 1986; Stevenson and Seares 1998). Acclaim was not, of course, immediate, universal or unqualified. Nonetheless, as Falstaff was not only witty himself but the cause of wit in others, so Milton tends to encourage in critics some of the qualities for which he was praised by the first Earl of Shaftesbury: 'solid Thought, strong Reasoning, noble Passion' (1710, 118). In 1688, half a dozen years after Milton's death, the book-seller Jacob Tonson, with a combination of literary and commercial acumen, produced *Paradise Lost* in a handsome folio volume, financed by advance payment from some five hundred aristocratic and well-to-do buyers. For the first time the method of subscription publication is used for an English poet; it had been established for major scholarly works such as the *Biblia polyglotta* (discussed in Chapter 1). Tonson was proud of the book; when the series of Kit-Kat Club portraits, now in the National Portrait Gallery, was painted, Tonson chose to be shown holding a copy of *Paradise Lost*. In 1712, Addison's famous set of eighteen *Spectator* papers argue that the English epic is worthy to be set beside its great classical predecessors, and imply that any moderately urbane person – to whom the *Spectator* is addressed – will be ready to take an interest in it.

Is the seventeenth century 'an age too late' for epic? Milton himself raises the question (IX. 44), and boldly reinterprets heroic traditions. Unlike many of the epic topics he jotted down in his younger days, and unlike the epics written by Spenser and Davenant, *Paradise Lost* does not take knightly adventure as its focus. Explicitly at the begin-ning of Book IX, and implicitly in Books VI–VII, the narrator dismisses war as central to heroism. In this respect it differs markedly from the contemporary heroic drama of Dryden and Davenant.[1] Oddly insensi-tive to its tone and implications, Dryden thought *Paradise Lost* too tragic for an epic.[2] The opposite could be argued; it is almost too comic. Or, like the scope of the acting troupe that visits Elsinore, it is admirably and eclectically tragical-comical-historical-pastoral.

The great classical epics are dominated by heroic individuals: Aeneas in Virgil, Odysseus and (more ironically) Achilles in Homer. The perennial question, 'Who is the hero of *Paradise Lost*?' is in some ways a non-starter – although it started early. John Dennis names Satan as the hero on the grounds that he wins the conflict with mankind (1704; 1939 I. 334). Milton sets up multiple heroes, certainly including Satan, but heroic positions are repeatedly undermined. Simple allegiance to the idea of Satan as hero is often a mark of someone who has not read attentively past the opening book. At the bridge between Books V and VI, which in the first, ten-book edition was the centre of the poem, Milton invents an episode in which the seraph Abdiel repents (literally, 'turns back') from following Satan to the north of heaven. Milton gives Abdiel a magnificent speech and a valiant march, then half deflates the dramatic moment of return when he finds 'Already known what he for news had thought / To have reported' (VI. 20–1). God does not need his information. Yet he is praised in words which, in the New Testament, Jesus uses in his parable of the talents. Moreover, the seraph foreshadows solitary, faithful figures of Hebrew history who are shown to Adam in Book XI. Brilliant at exploiting a single scene for multiple effects, Milton also designs Abdiel's reception as parallel and opposite to Satan's surprise when he returns from earth to hell. At no point in the story is Satan more pleased with himself, but while he might well expect a chorus of 'hail the conquering hero comes' Milton invents a rude burlesque instead; suddenly transformed into serpents, Satan's followers involuntarily greet him with hisses (X. 384–547). Among other characters who have more or less strong claims to heroic status, Adam in Book IX resembles the romantic, self-sacrificing lovers of drama. Eve, however, is the stronger of the two human figures, more rational than Adam in Book IX before taking the apple, quicker to seek reconciliation, and willing to assume all the punishment. Her final word, the final word spoken by a character, is 'restore' (XII. 623). Throughout the epic, dramatic and thematic contrasts between Satan and God the Son, whom he fervently envies, invite evaluation. Among many parallel passages, the most obvious are scenes in Books II and III when Satan and the Son both volunteer to go to earth, the glorious light-centred week of creation by the Son in Book VII in contrast to Satan's dark seven days hiding in the shadow of the earth (IX. 58–67), and on a smaller scale Satan's parodies of gospel promises to mankind (IV. 377–85).

Reading a long poem is, as C.S. Lewis wrote some decades ago in his brief, stimulating *Preface to Paradise Lost*, different from reading a lyric. More recently, general reader-response studies such as those by Wolfgang Iser on the dynamics of anticipation and retrospection emphasise the importance of memory and readjustment in literary interpretation. There are, to be sure, many individual passages with dense local patterning: doctrinal – 'was she thy God ... ?' where Adam's inverted priorities are condemned by mere word order (X.

145–55); lyrical – Eve's celebration of Eden and of love 'Sweet is the breath of morn . . .', which has often been set to music (IV. 641–56); dramatic – the revelation of Satan's character through dialogue, oration, and monologue (I. 84–91, I. 254–8, IV. 75–86). As Satan's cluster of significantly contradictory speeches indicates, large-scale commentary on *Paradise Lost* demands attending to its rhythms of repetition, parody, refinement and redefinition, developed and sustained throughout the work. Eve's early celebratory speech, twice reviewing the sweetness of Eden and finding nothing sweet without Adam, seems self-contained, but it takes on added resonance when balanced in Book XI by her lament, 'Must I leave thee, Paradise?' (XI. 268–85).

In 1695, Patrick Hume published the first scholarly annotations on *Paradise Lost*, giving to the modern Milton the kind of attention until then reserved for classical texts. Before the mid-eighteenth century, Milton's epic gathered a formidable reputation. For those easily daunted by length, learning or verse, selected 'ELEGANCIES Taken out of Milton's *Paradise Lost*' (1725) were published, and A Gentleman of Oxford produced a version in which the text is 'rendered into prose' (1745). At the same time, this adapter wrote so intemperately about 'what you must know' before reading the poem that few could ever venture to do so. The length of *Paradise Lost* and the demands that it makes should not, however, be exaggerated. It can be read aloud in a day, and reading it fast *but whole* creates understanding much more significant than the meaning of individual words or allusions. Informative as magisterial footnotes may be, the help offered can also be a distraction. There are advantages to owning a plain text, as well as an annotated edition, to facilitate concentration on the flow of the narrative, uninterrupted. In recent years, the Milton discussion group on the Internet has reported a dozen or more all-day or all-night group readings, with comments on their exhilarating effects: an enhanced sense of drama, of different voices, of changes in pace. Most important is awareness of echoes or an intensified sense of relationships among parts.

Its long-breathed character is signalled at the start in the announce-ment of theme. While in the third word of the *Aeneid* Virgil tells us that he sings of arms and the man – *Arma virumque cano* – Milton, clearly intending that the reader should note the contrast, delays for five lines his introduction of the word 'Sing' – now not an indicative in reference to himself, but an imperative addressed to heaven:

> Of man's first disobedience, and the fruit
> Of that forbidden tree, whose mortal taste
> Brought death into the world, and all our woe,
> With loss of Eden, till one greater man
> Restore us, and regain the blissful seat,
> Sing, heavenly Muse ...

Note the patterns of repetition and contrast. The noun 'man' (no longer Virgil's male *vir*, but the Vulgate's *homo*, a human being) is significantly doubled. In the first line, it can mean Adam, or both Adam and Eve.[3] At line 4, 'one greater man' is clearly Christ. Not until 'loss' has been balanced by 'restore' (reinforced by 'regain') does the sentence arrive at its main verb. Within these opening lines the involvement of the reader is twice invoked, in the negative and in the positive movements of the plot ('all *our* woe' and 'restore *us*'). The double movement announced here helps explain why, throughout the epic, allusions to the New Testament intertwine with Old Testament episodes. Justifying the ways of God to man is, for the poet, not a matter of theological debate (parodied in the fallen angels' pastimes, II. 557–61), but of a narrative in which God the Son pronounces a judgment (Book X) which he has already agreed to take upon himself (Book III). When the narrator speaks of his 'great argument' (I. 24), a reader may better attend to the story told than try to translate it into abstract assertions about divinity; the short 'arguments' added before each book in its second edition are a reminder that argument can mean summary rather than contention.

Words which echo through the poem acquire changed and enriched meaning. The first fruit of the forbidden tree is death (with a pun on 'mortal taste'). Near the beginning of Book XI (combined in the first edition of *Paradise Lost* with what is now Book XII as a single final unit), prayers of the repentant Adam and Eve are described to God the Father as 'Fruits of more pleasing savour, from thy seed / Sown' than all the trees of Paradise could have produced (XI. 26–9), and there is a cluster of words which, like 'restore' and 'regain' at the opening of the epic, reaffirm the return to happiness. The Son redefines death, seen no longer as punishment but as a respite from prolonged woe on earth and as a gate to heaven for mankind

refined
By faith and faithful works, to second life,

> Waked in the *renovation* of the just,
> *Resigns* him up with heaven and earth *renewed*. (XI. 63–6, italics added)

When in the 1640s Milton jotted down four plans for a play on the early chapters of Genesis, he intended to begin after the Fall. Both continuities and major shifts in plan can be seen by comparing these early drafts (easily consulted in the introduction to Fowler's edition of *Paradise Lost*) and the epic. Very little of what is now Books I–IX is indicated in the preliminary plans. Milton's interest is not simply in the drama of disobedience, but in working out the consequences of that act and the possibility of redemption. The final three books of *Paradise Lost* had long been contemplated.

Two of the early stage adaptations, by Dryden in the seventeenth century and by Benjamin Stillingfleet in the eighteenth, simplify and accelerate the movement towards an essentially comic, that is to say happy, outcome. Dryden closes *The State of Innocence* with a vision which elaborates the lines quoted above from Book XI. Stillingfleet, emphasising the means by which this blessedness is to be achieved, quotes Michael's forecast of the Nativity (XII. 360–7). Milton's own ending is more subtle, a muted consolation. Although 'far happier days' (XII. 465) are to come, facile celebration like that of the still immature Adam is rebuked by the archangel. Addison wished the epic two lines shorter than it is; he suggested that the last picture of Adam and Eve might well have been

> The world was all before them, where to choose
> Their place of rest, and providence their guide (XII. 646–7)

rather than

> They hand in hand with wandering steps and slow,
> Through Eden took their solitary way. (XII. 648–9)

Milton's shorter epic, *Paradise Regained*, despite its positive title, is also bracing rather than consoling. Choosing as his plot the temptations in the desert, a setting antithetical to Eden, Milton makes the debates between Jesus and his tempter Satan a struggle to define, precisely, the terms of redemptive power. The ending is far from a triumphal conclusion; rather it is the beginning of the Son of

God's earthly ministry, but, wittily, Milton makes the final word 'returned'.

Samuel Johnson's famous pronouncement on *Paradise Lost*, 'None ever wished it longer than it is', is balanced elsewhere in his 'Life of Milton' by comments that the design is so 'interwoven ... that every part appears to be necessary' and that 'There is perhaps no poem of the same length from which so little can be taken without apparent mutilation' (*Lives*, I. 183, 171, 175).

How long is a poem?

> How shall we please this Age? If in a Song
> We put above six Lines, they count it long;
> If we contract it to an Epigram,
> As deep the dwarfish Poetry they damn;
>
> (Sedley, in the *Gentleman's Journal*, November 1692)

To ask 'how long is a poem?' may seem to be like asking 'how long is a piece of string?' At different periods, however, those pressed to give a simple answer will be likely to respond rather differently. In 'Of Poetry' (1690), Sir William Temple scorns verse which merely develops a witty idea or explores a metaphor. Focusing attention on large narratives, he dismisses smaller genres as the choice of those 'wanting either Genius or Application for Nobler or more Laborious Productions, as Painters that cannot Succeed in great Pieces turn to Miniature' (Spingarn 1908, III. 99–100). Epics are grand by definition, and grandeur includes sheer size as well as large conceptions. *Paradise Lost* is somewhat more than ten thousand lines long, roughly two and a half times the length of *Hamlet*. The four-book short epic *Paradise Regained* has 2070 lines. While Milton's works are the only seventeenth-century English epics easily available to modern readers, he was hardly alone in his time in choosing the most spacious of genres. Extensive works by ambitious writers attempting to make a name through what was called 'heroic poetry' frame Milton's achievement. Davenant's mediaeval Italian epic adventures, *Gondibert* (1651) in rhyming quatrains, was warmly commended by Hobbes (Spingarn 1908, II. 54–67) before it was complete; in the event, it was never completed, but its three (of a planned five) books total something over six thousand lines. Cowley, too, follows Spenser's precedent in describing more than he finishes. In a preface defending the use of Scriptural material in poetry, Cowley announces that his *Davideis* (1656) would eventually include a Virgilian dozen books, concluding with David's lament over Saul and Jonathan. In Samuel Johnson's words, however, 'he had leisure or perseverance only to write the third part' (*Lives*, I. 49). For sheer perseverance Sir Richard Blackmore, physician to William III, deserves notice. He wrote four epics on English monarchs, beginning with a Spenserian hero in *Prince Arthur* (1695). Pope drily calls him 'Everlasting Blackmore' in a footnote to the episode in the *Dunciad* where Blackmore, 'Who sings so loudly, and who sings so long', wins a contest on the grounds of volume and voluminousness.

At the other extreme from epic is the epigram, sometimes no longer than two lines of verse. Like the heroic poem it can claim classical descent. Although for Temple it was merely one of the 'Scraps or Splinters into which Poetry was broken' (Spingarn 1908, III. 100), Alastair Fowler, in his preface to *The New Oxford Book of Seventeenth Century Verse*, makes strong claims for the significance of the revival of epigrams. He suggests that the compression of 'metaphysical' imagery and the pointedness of closed couplets both owe much to the epigram, which 'brought a lasting change of scale: even now we take for granted that every word in a poem must count' (1991, xxxix). Etymologically the epigram is an inscription, and stone is a medium which invites concision rather than amplification. Tossed off (or privately polished) in their hundreds, these lapidary turns of thought and language seldom bulk large in anthologies or classroom discussions. A colleague of mine once managed, for fifty minutes, to focus the thinking of a seminar on Pope's late epigram (1737) composed for a pet's collar:

> I am His Highness' Dog at Kew;
> Pray tell me Sir, whose Dog are you?

A taste for the closed couplet may be nourished by concentrating on an example such as this, before moving on to larger works of the period in which the couplet plays an egregious part. Tight patterning of words and thoughts invites the opposite of speed-reading. In these two octosyllabic lines, a foot shorter than the iambic pentameter which is the most common line in English verse, there are multiple parallelisms and oppositions: courtliness in the first four words of each line, followed by deflation; geographical and social placing, the shifting significance of *dog* as literal or metaphorical; the framing words *I* and *you*. As a dramatic situation, the couplet implies the posture of an imagined reader, who must be bending over, almost bowing, to read an inscription on a collar. Information that Pope had his couplet engraved on a collar for the puppy he presented to Frederick, Prince of Wales, is not essential to understanding the lines. Because epigrams are often topical, however, they can pose for editors, classrooms or common readers a difficulty which all occasional poetry involves: how much space, time or patience is needed to elucidate that original occasion? As Samuel Johnson says, 'occasional poetry must often content itself with occasional praise' (*Lives*, II. 67).

Between two and several thousand lines, many poems written between 1650 and 1720 are of a generous intermediate length which has grown rather less common in recent decades and which – perhaps for that reason – presents problems for modern editors. For anthologies, many of the most notable poems of the period seem to be too long. Butler's *Hudibras* (2578 lines in its first part, published in 1662), Dryden's *Absalom and Achitophel* (1031 lines), Marvell's *The Last Instructions to a Painter* (990 lines), Mary, Lady Chudleigh's *The Ladies Defence* (845 lines) are not often included in full. Even Denham's famous and influential *Cooper's Hill*, only 358 lines long in its most expansive version, is often represented only by extracts. Marvell's *Upon Appleton House* (776 lines), despite forming a magnificent climax to the country-house tradition, is seldom given a place.[4]

The intersection of literary judgments and of commercial publishing has interesting, and sometimes disquieting, effects. *Paradise Lost* is not only easily available in both inexpensive and sumptuous editions, it can take a lion's share in anthologies intended for teaching purposes. In DeMaria's 1211-page Blackwell volume *British Literature 1640–1789* (1996), it occupies slightly over a sixth of the pages. Is institutional convenience dominant here, so that a single textbook can be bought for a course? How much is the shunning of moderately long poems due to publishers' sense of marketing? The blurb on the back of DeMaria's anthology emphasises the range of the book: 'a great many authors' and 'wide variety of genres, forms, opinions, viewpoints, and styles'. But while three lines in the headnote to Dryden's poetry identify *Absalom and Achitophel*, as 'perhaps the most famous of his political poems', it is completely squeezed out of the selections. As John Wain notes, 'Obviously one gets more diversity, and crowds one's table of contents more impressively with names, by printing ten poems of twenty lines than one of two hundred' (1990, xxii). Elimination of longish poems from the anthologies may also indicate uneasy trust in modern readers' attention spans.

What does the limitation of space do to a sense of poetry? 'Substantial extracts' as promised by many editors are rarely a satisfactory compromise. Selections 'from *Absalom and Achitophel*' (as in many academic anthologies, and even in the Oxford Poetry Library volume devoted entirely to Dryden, 1994) tend to highlight the portraits but give no idea of the satire's structural symmetries, with two contrasting versions of a Golden Age framing the whole (Erskine-Hill 1983, 227). When in the Blackwell 1640–1789 anthology, only the final 160 lines of Chudleigh's *The Ladies Defence* are printed, any sense of the shape of the poem, as a dramatic debate in which the three male speakers condemn themselves, is completely lost. An even shorter extract (fifty-two lines) in *The Norton Anthology of Literature by Women* reduces Chudleigh's play of voices to a simple manifesto.

Questions about the length of poems, and of what a student is apt to encounter in textbooks, are important both for the individual poems and for a general sense of poetry in any given age. Despite the many important long poems of the romantic period and later – Wordsworth's *Prelude*, Browning's *The Ring and the Book*, Eliot's *The Waste Land*, Pound's *Cantos* – the modern reader's quick answer to 'How long is a poem?' is likely to indicate something shorter than what a reader in the late seventeenth century would propose. As John Wain comments, 'It is a modern fad to think of poetry as primarily a vehicle for short utterances' (1990, xxiii). To reduce poetry as a category to a brief outpouring of emotion would mean ignoring a very large proportion of the verse produced in the decades 1650–1720.

Poetic kinds

The grand genres and the poets laureate

> As Philosophers have divided the Universe, their subject, into three Regions, *Celestial, Aerial,* and *Terrestrial,* so the Poets (whose work it is, by imitating human life in delightful and measured lines, to avert men from vice and incline them to virtuous and honourable actions) have lodged themselves in the three Regions of mankind, *Court, City,*

and *Country* ... From hence have proceeded three sorts of Poesy, *Heroic*, *Scommatic*, and *Pastoral*. Every one of these is distinguished again in the manner of Representation, which sometimes is Narrative, wherein the Poet himself relateth, and sometimes Dramatic, as when the persons are every one adorned and brought upon the Theatre to speak and act their own parts. There is therefore neither more or less than six sorts of Poesy.

> (Thomas Hobbes, 'The Answer to Sir William D'Avenant's Preface before Gondibert' 1650, in Hobbes, *English Works* IV. 443–4)

When I speak of Poetry, I mean not an Ode or an Elegy, a Song or a Satyr, nor by a Poet the Composer of any of these, but of a just Poem.

> (Sir William Temple, 'Of Poetry' 1690, in Spingarn III. 82)

The most perfect work of poetry, says our master Aristotle, is tragedy. His reason, is, because it is the most united ... But after all these advantages, an heroic poem is certainly the greatest work of human nature ... But considering satire as a species of poetry, here the war begins amongst the critics.

> (Dryden, 'A Discourse Concerning Satire' 1693, in *Essays* 1962, 2. 95–7)

Despite its theoretical clarity and diagrammatic neatness (scommatic = scoffing), Hobbes' systematic sorting of poetry into 'neither more or less than six sorts' is less informative about the genres jostling for the attention of a verse-reading public than Temple's off-hand and dismissive catalogue, or than Dryden's terse statements focused on tensions in critical opinion. For Temple 'true poetry' means epic, and at his most extreme, Homer and Virgil: 'these two immortal Poets must be allowed to have so much excelled in their kinds as to have exceeded all Comparison, to have even extinguished Emulation, and in a Manner confined true Poetry not only to their two Languages, but to their very Persons' (1690, Spingarn 1908, III. 83). Dryden, in the preface to his translation of the *Aeneid*, is apologetic, or edgily defensive, about never having attempted an original epic. He goes out of his way in his critical prefaces to elevate the genres which he did practise by attempting to align them with epic. Pope, at the end of his life, was planning an epic in blank verse on Brutus, the legendary founder of Britain. Aside from the heroic poem, what are the dominant kinds of poetry actually practised rather than simply praised?

In Dryden's liveliest critical essay, after four friends begin by talking of good and bad poetry in general, they agree that they must limit their topic, but the category they choose seems neither obvious nor narrow by modern standards; indeed it looks generically askew. A conversation sparked by dismay at the flood of panegyrics which an English naval victory would produce turns into *An Essay of Dramatick Poesie*. Verse drama established the reputations of the series of poets recognised as 'Laureate' in the seventeenth century. Before the Civil War, Ben Jonson and Sir William Davenant claimed the title. It was officially conferred upon Dryden (1668–89) who, because of his loyalty to James II, lost it to Thomas Shadwell (1689–92), the 'MacFlecknoe' of Dryden's attack on dullness. Then the metaphorical bay wreath was given to Nahum Tate (1692–1715), Nicholas Rowe (1715–18), and Laurence Eusden (1718–30). All except the obscure Eusden produced major work for the stage, along with varying amounts of other verse. Shadwell, whose comedies are more attractive than Dryden was willing to admit (at least after their estrangement in 1682), also turned his hand to satire, and was one of many to translate the tenth satire of Juvenal. In theatrical circles, Tate's name survives because of his version of *King Lear* and his libretto for Purcell's *Dido and Aeneas*; outside the theatre, he collaborated with Nicholas Brady on metrical versions of the psalms. In *Tamerlane* (1701), written long before he was named laureate, Rowe took up the tacit duties of the post, propagating a positive view of the government and its policies. Those who know Tamberlaine through Marlowe's play are apt to be astonished by the metamorphosis of the hero into a complimentary version of William III, and of his major rival Bajazet into a caricature of Louis XIV. Rowe also wrote a series of successful tragedies with pathetic heroines; he produced a notable translation of Lucan; and in editing Shakespeare's plays for the publisher Tonson he established useful precedents for the division of acts and scenes. In an age when almost everyone could turn out a set of complimentary or elegiac verses as occasions for celebration or grief occurred, Eusden demonstrated the minimal requirements of an official laureate. He evidently attracted brief approval at court for a poem on the marriage of the Lord Chamberlain, the duke of Newcastle. Pope gives him two lines in *The Dunciad*. Whether recognition of poetic talent, rather than of political correctness, had much to do with appointments of the others is hard to say. In the event, most are respectable choices, but now they are apt to be categorised as 'playwrights' rather than as 'poets'.

Panegyric and satire

Dryden makes a valiant attempt to align both panegyric and satire with the dignity of epic. Poems of praise define public virtues, pronouncing 'Worthy things of worthy men' ('To Sir Robert Howard', l. 99). Similarly, Waller writes, in 'Upon the Earl of Roscommon's Translation of Horace':

> Well-sounding verses are the charm we use,
> Heroic thoughts and virtue to infuse. (ll. 23–4)

In 'A Discourse Concerning Satire' (1693), Dryden writes that 'beautiful turns of words and thought' are 'as requisite in this, as in heroic poetry itself, of which the satire is undoubtedly a species' (*Essays* 1962, II. 149). As he tucks into a dependent clause this claim that satire is a sub-category of epic, and rests his assertion only on the word 'undoubtedly' (sign of a weak argument in published work, as in student essays), he leaves open questions about how clearly or consistently its qualities are related to epic. Mock-epic is (undoubtedly, one might say?) a particular species of satire.

Much that is now presented as prose journalism appeared in 1650-1720 as verse. George deF. Lord notes the sheer volume of this material:

> In quantity and popularity satire stood first among the various kinds of non-dramatic verse written between 1660 and 1714. More than 3,000 satirical pieces from this period survive in print. Of these approximately 1,200 were published in various collections between 1689 and 1716, the best known of which were entitled *Poems on Affairs of State*. POAS (also commonly called *State Poems*) was a leading poetical miscellany for thirty years. About thirty such volumes were printed. In addition some 2,500 poems on state affairs survive only in manuscript. (*POAS* 1963, I. xxv–xxvi)

For a general survey of public events, and climates of opinion, the modern, seven-volume edition of selected *Poems on Affairs of State 1660–1714* provides at least as useful a source as a standard history textbook.[5] A shift in expectations about poetry and its subject-matter can be registered within the next century. In the life of Matthew Prior, Johnson notes the mass of occasional verse produced in the late seventeenth and early eighteenth centuries, contrasting the observation that 'Through the reigns of William and Anne no prosperous event passed undignified by poetry' with more recent history when 'the fame of our counsellors and heroes was intrusted to the Gazetteer' (*Lives*, II. 186–7). In particular, he amusingly writes, 'The death of queen Mary (in 1695) produced a subject for all the writers: perhaps no funeral was so poetically attended. Dryden, indeed, as a man discountenanced and deprived, was silent; but scarcely any other maker of verses omitted to bring his tribute of tuneful sorrow' (*Lives*, II. 183). Those interested in the intersections of words and images should consult the catalogue of political prints in the British Library (Stephens 1870) as a supplement to the *Poems on Affairs of State*.

At best, perhaps, elaborate poems of praise form part of a Renaissance tradition; poets give advice to princes in diplomatically oblique ways. At their most blatant, the political panegyrics are what now is called propaganda (a word which originally had a more positive meaning: spreading the true faith). From a distance of three centuries, the panegyrics seem overblown and the satiric poems obscure. Writers closer in time were well aware of the dangers. Granville, in a verse 'Essay upon Unnatural Flights in Poetry' (1701) wryly describes the excesses of Restoration poems:

> Our King return'd, and banisht Peace restor'd,
> The Muse ran Mad to see her exil'd Lord. (In Spingarn III. 294)

The judiciousness of Samuel Johnson, describing Prior's praise of King William in the *Carmen seculare* (1700), where the poet 'exhausts all his powers of celebration', mingles as much charity as is consistent with dry good sense: 'I mean not to accuse him of flattery; he probably thought all that he writ, and retained as much veracity as can be properly exacted from a poet professedly encomiastick' (*Lives*, II. 185).

Another danger is the predictability of panegyrics. In a satiric poem attacking Dryden, the political expediency of those who celebrate every change of government is the major target, but repetitiousness is also at stake:

> We Cromwell call the best of Kings,
> And of dead Charles say the same things;
> And when his successor shall die,
> Like strains shall eternize his memory.
>
> ('Dryden's Ghost' ll. 47–50; *POAS* IV. 148)

Milton and Marvell present exceptions to the run-of-the-mill political poems. Milton's sonnet addressed to 'Cromwell, our chief of men' (1652) is stern. Marvell's odes on Charles and Cromwell are fascinating partly because of their poised ambiguities. His panegyric on a Scottish naval captain and his *Last Instructions to a Painter* will be discussed below, in relation to Cleveland and to Waller.

The obscurity of some of the poems on public events, a problem at the other extreme from predictability, is a barrier to modern readers. Addison notes that satire is 'more difficult to be understood by those that are not of the same Age with it, than any other kind of Poetry' because of 'the remoteness of the Customs, Persons and Things' to which the satirist alludes (1721, I. 525). As in Arden editions of Shakespeare, the poetical text in the modern *Poems on Affairs of State* volumes sometimes all but disappears, squeezed up to a few lines at the top of a page by the bulk of notes below.

Odes

> 'tis pleasant to observe what a notable Trade hath been driven of late in Pindaric Odes.
>
> (Edward Phillips, *Theatrum poetarum*, 1675)

> The Character of these late Pindariques, is a Bundle of rambling, incoherent Thoughts, expressed in a like parcel of irregular Stanzas, which also consist of such another Complication of disproportioned, uncertain, and perplexed Verses and Rhymes.
>
> (Congreve, 'A Discourse on the Pindarique Ode', 1706)

The popularity of the ode in the later seventeenth century seems at first glance odd; it sits curiously in an era when the decasyllabic couplet is the more prominent vehicle for serious poetry. Emotional or associative rather than logical in its transitions, the ode fits more easily with assumptions about the Romantics than about a period sometimes called the Age of Reason.

The irregular shape of its stanzas makes an ode easy enough to recognise. Definition is harder. Cowley, the poet who established the vogue for the genre, claimed to be following Pindar, though thorough classicists are apt to comment on how vague the understanding of Pindar's metrical patterns was. As in Cowley's 'Ode on Wit', description of odes in the later seventeenth century is largely a matter of negatives: stanzas of no definite length, lines of no set number of feet, rhyme-schemes without predictable pattern. It is tempting to suspect a temperamental difference between poets particularly fond of the ode and those who are more apt to choose the heroic couplet. Riffle through a collected edition of Cowley or Norris, and at a glance it is obvious that while the couplet is not foreign to them, they prefer irregular, stanzaic forms.

Adaptable to ruminative or ecstatic tones, the ode waxed and waned in importance during these decades. Except for Cowley, 'major' poets after Jonson choose the ode only for particular subjects. Dryden and Pope find it especially suitable for poems on music for Saint Cecilia's Day. Dryden uses it for some panegyrics, including his elegy for Anne Killigrew, who herself wrote odes. When Mary, Lady Chudleigh explains her choice of form for an ambitious 2065-line ode, 'The Song of the Three Children Paraphras'd' (from Daniel 3: 23–34), she claims that it is particularly fit for 'exalted' celebration. Her suggestion that the ode is easier than other poetic forms is not to be taken altogether seriously. She claims with mocking self-deprcciation that 'The Reason why I chuse this sort of Verse, is, because it allows me that Liberty of running into large Digressions, gives a great Scope to the Fancy, and frees me from the trouble of tying my self up to the stricter Rules of other Poetry' (1703; 1993, 169). So many women admired and imitated Cowley's odes that a *Spectator* paper patronisingly and offhandedly refers to irregular verse 'as loose and unequal as those in which the *British* ladies sport their *Pindariques*' (no. 366, 30 April 1712). When Dryden contrasted Cowley's performances with those of his imitators (1695), or Congreve complained about the incoherence of odes (1706, quoted above), or Gay advised the publisher Lintot to omit them from his new anthology ('On a Miscellany of Poems, To Bernard Lintot', 1712) their reaction against the form is partly a sign of how successful it had become. Not until the Romantics rediscovered its suitability for creating an immediate sense of powerful emotion, spontaneously overflowing, did it return to full favour.

The liberty Lady Chudleigh notes is strikingly obvious in work by one of the most enthusiastic of minor practitioners, John Norris, better known as a Platonic philosopher than as a poet. In a 467-page collection of his miscellaneous works in verse and prose, he gives pride of place to 'The Passion of Our Blessed Saviour represented in a Pindarique Ode', followed by 'Annotations' in which he asserts that 'This Ode is after the Pindaric way; which is the highest and most magnificent kind of writing in Verse, and consequently fit only for great and noble Subjects; such as are boundless as its *own Numbers'* (1687, 8). Both the grand subject and the 'boundless Numbers' – a phrase which also appears in the fourth line of his poem – are significant. Although the English odes use rhyme, they are otherwise very far from the numerical, that is metrical, regularity of the heroic couplet. Norris emphasises the variability of tone and pace when, in terms that echo the second stanza of Cowley's 'Praise of Pindar', he enlarges on the 'numbers' of the ode: 'The nature of which is to be loose and free, and not to keep one settled pace, but sometimes like a gentle stream to glide peaceably within its own Channel, and sometimes, like an impetuous Torrent, to *roll* on extravagantly, and carry all before it' (1687, 8). Although extravagance is not the word which first springs to mind in describing poetic taste of the period, it is evident in the first of Norris's seven stanzas:

> Say bold Licentious Muse,
>   What Noble Subject wilt thou choose,
> Of what great Hero, of what mighty thing,
>   Wilt thou in boundless numbers sing?
>   Sing the unfathom'd Depths of Love,
> (For who the Wonders done by Love can tell,
> By Love, which is itself all Miracle?)
> Here in vast endless Circles mayst thou rove,
> And like the travelling Planet of the day
>   In an Orb unbounded stray.
> Sing the great Miracle of Love Divine,
> Great by thy Genius, sparkling every Line,
>   Love's greatest Mystery rehearse,
>   Greater than that
> Which on the teeming Chaos brooding sat,
> And hatched, with kindly heat, the Universe
> How God in Mercy chose to bleed, and die
>   To rescue Man from Misery,
> Man, not his Creature only, but his Enemy.

From the imperative verb with which it begins, the ode sweeps on in words which may seem to be over-egging a rich pudding: bold, licentious, noble, great, mighty, boundless, unfathomed, wonders, miracle, vast, endless, rove, unbounded, stray. All those within the first ten lines.

Translation and imitation

> If a man should undertake to translate *Pindar* word for word, it would
> be thought that *one Mad-man* had translated *another*.
>
> (Cowley, Preface to 'Pindaric Odes, Written in Imitation of the Stile
> and Maner of the Odes of Pindar', 1656)

The decades 1650–1720 are rich in translation, and in critical discussion of translation, theoretical and practical.[6] By 'the obliging
Humour' of translators, writes the author of *An Essay in Defence of the
Female Sex* (1696), 'scarce any thing either Ancient or Modern that
might be of general use either for Pleasure, or Instruction is left
untouch'd' and ''tis possible for an ingenious Person to make a
considerable progress in most parts of Learning, by the help of
English only' (41–2). The market for translations, however, was not
only, or even primarily, those who because of limited educational
opportunities could not read the originals. As subscription lists for
Dryden's and Pope's epic translations indicate, the audience of
subscribers willing to pay in advance for these works was full of those
who had been trained to read classical languages and were therefore
equipped to relish a particular new version. (Similarly in the 1990s the
first wave of buyers for Robert Fagles' *Odyssey* was made up of those
who already had at least one other translation and perhaps the Greek
text on their bookshelves.) Translation is a phenomenon particularly
interesting when considering self-consciousness about periods, or
transitions. It involves a sense of distance (from another age, civiliza-
tion, language, metrical structure or personality); yet the translator
also claims intimacy and understanding. Both feelings are explored in
Cowley's preface. The words *difference, changes, distance, strangers*
stand out in his statement of difficulties:

> We must consider in *Pindar* the great difference of time betwixt his
> age and ours, which changes, as in *Pictures*, at least the *Colours* of
> *Poetry*; the no less difference betwixt the *Religions* and *Customs* of our
> Countreys, and a thousand particularities of places, persons, and
> manners, which do but confusedly appear to our eyes at so great a
> distance. And lastly (which were enough alone for my purpose) we
> must consider that our Ears are strangers to the Music of his
> *Numbers*.

With all this, Cowley yet claims an affinity of spirit, confidently promising that he will illuminate not so much 'precisely what he spoke, as what was his *way* and *manner* of speaking'. Dryden builds on Cowley's foundation when he distinguishes among three kinds of translation: metaphrase, paraphrase, and imitation. He recommends the middle path, between word-for-word literalness and free variations on a theme, and he stresses catching the individual 'character of an author, what distinguishes him from all others' so that Virgil and Ovid are not flattened into sameness (Preface to *Sylvae*, 1685).

With a few exceptions – such as Ted Hughes with *Tales from Ovid* – the translator in modern times is seen as less praiseworthy than an 'original' poet. The skills of the translator were more often prized in the seventeenth and early eighteenth centuries. Addison's first published poem, 'To Mr. Dryden' (1693), celebrates him primarily as a translator, of Virgil, Horace, Persius, Juvenal, and especially of 'thy Ovid':

> Thy charming Verse, and fair Translations, show
> How thy own Laurel first began to grow. (ll. 23–4)

An ode 'To Mr. Dryden, on his excellent Translation of Virgil' (1697) by Mary, Lady Chudleigh opens with extravagant apostrophe:

> Thou matchless Poet, whose capacious Mind
> Contains the whole that Knowledge can impart,
>   Where we each charming Science find,
>   And ev'ry pleasing Art:

The history of English poetry, as she traces it from Chaucer through Spenser, then Waller, Milton and Cowley, reaches its full triumph in Dryden and culminates in his work of translation, which transforms the Roman poet into a 'Native of our Isle' (l. 56).

The range of names involved in translation is very wide, and the number of texts large. Hobbes, though better known for other publications, thought it worthwhile to turn his hand to translations from Greek (along with original compositions in Latin verse: an autobiography and a poem in praise of the Peak District). His translation of the historian Thucydides survives as a standard text. With the sharp eye and tongue of a competitor, Dryden sneers at Hobbes' 'bald' translation of *The Iliad* and mocks him for 'studying poetry as he did mathematics, when it was too late' (Preface to *Fables Ancient and Modern* 1700). By far the most prolific translator of the period, Dryden turned some 40 000 lines of classical poetry into English: Virgil complete, large chunks of Ovid, Juvenal, Horace, selections from five books of Lucretius's *De rerum natura*, and Book I of *The Iliad*. Dryden's version of the *Aeneid* and Pope's of *The Iliad* in readily found Penguin editions have, during the last decade of the twentieth century, been welcome reprints. Clusters of familiar names are noticeable in several versions of Ovid's work. Along with Dryden, Aphra Behn, Butler, Otway and Rymer contributed to the 1680 edition of Ovid's imaginary letters from classical heroines, the *Heroides*. A group of Charles II's courtiers cooperated in translating Corneille's *Pompey*, shortly after Katherine Philips had produced her much-admired version, with original poems added between the acts. Lucy Hutchinson, when allowed to study Latin as well as the usual feminine skills, records that she was 'so apt that I outstripped my brothers who were at school, although my father's chaplain, that was my tutor was a pitiful dull fellow'. When she presented the manuscript of her full, six-book translation of *De rerum natura* to the Earl of Anglesey, her allusion to the partial translation by John Evelyn is tinged with asperity; 'a masculine Witt hath thought it worth printing his head in a laurel crown for the version of one of these books' (1996, 23). Elizabeth Elstob was a pioneer in Anglo-Saxon translation (Aelfric, 1709).

Intertextual alertness was intensified both because among the readers were a substantial number of gentlemen who had spent their schooldays immersed in classical languages and because rival translations of major authors were appearing thick and fast. Women aware of the gap between their own education and that of men of their class might well, as Mary, Lady Chudleigh does, celebrate the appearance of Greek and Latin works in English dress. The translators, however, were drawn to their task not so much to fill a pedagogical gap as to meet a poetic challenge. Hardly twenty-one years old when his version of 'The Episode of Sarpedon' from Books 12 and 16 of the *Iliad* was published (1709), the young Pope calls attention to an earlier version. Sarpedon's 'admirable Speech' urging his companion into perilous battle, he comments in a headnote, 'has been rendered in English by Sir John Denham; after whom the Translator had not the Vanity to attempt it for any other reason, than that the Episode must have been very imperfect without so Noble a part of it'. However modest Pope's wording, the invitation to comparison is plain. In response to this invitation, a very short sample, corresponding to *The Iliad* XII. 322–8, is printed below. Hobbes' translation is also given, as a foil for the other two.

Denham:

Could the declining of this Fate (oh friend)
Our Date to Immortality extend?
Or if Death sought not them, who seek not Death,
Would I advance? Or should my vainer breath
With such a Glorious Folly thee inspire?
But since with Fortune Nature doth conspire,
Since Age, Disease, or some less noble End,
Though not less certain, doth our days attend;
Since 'tis decreed, and to this period lead
A thousand ways, the noblest path we'll tread;
And bravely on, till they, or we, or all,
A common Sacrifice to Honour fall.

Pope:

Could all our Care elude the greedy Grave,
Which claims no less the Fearful than the Brave,
For Lust of Fame I should not vainly dare
In fighting Fields, nor urge thy Soul to War.
But since, alas, ignoble Age must come,
Disease, and Death's inexorable Doom;
The Life which others pay, let Us bestow,
And give to Fame what we to Nature owe;
Brave, though we fall; and honour'd, if we live;
Or let us Glory gain, or Glory give!

Hobbes (1677):

Glaucus, if we could death eschew and age
    By running from the battle cowardly,
D'ye think I foremost would myself engage,
    Or ever counsel you to follow me?
You know the ways to death are infinite.
    Though we ne'er fight we cannot always live.
Therefore come on, and let us bravely fight,
    And either honour gain, or honour give.

Even so short a sample demonstrates how much Pope learned from
Denham about the use of balance, antithesis and compression.
Parsimonious with adjectives and generous with verbs, as his model
was, the younger poet intensifies Denham's 'if Death sought not
them, who seek not Death' by bracketing 'the greedy Grave' with
'elude' and 'claims'. And while in general Pope scorned Hobbes'
translation (described as 'too low for criticism' in the preface to the
Iliad), he was willing to borrow a neatly balanced line when he saw it.

Occasionally poets deliberately double a challenging task. The title
of Addison's 'Milton's Stile imitated, in a Translation of a Story out of
the Third Aeneid' (1704) asks readers to admire skilful handling of
relationships with two poetic masters. The imitation of Milton is not,
to my ear, a success. Obvious choices of vocabulary and heavily
enjambed blank verse are not enough to sound Miltonic. The extent
to which the translation seems Virgilian, or accords with any preconceptions about neoclassical tastes in the early eighteenth century, is
also open to question. When the unhappy Achaemenides, left on
Polyphemus' island by Odysseus, recounts his story, Addison magni-
fies Gothic gore in the description of the cyclop's cave:

> A dungeon wide and horrible, the walls
> On all sides furr'd with mouldy damps, and hung
> With clots of ropy gore, and human limbs,
> His dire repast ... (ll. 67–70)

Having grasped a Greek in each hand, Polyphemus

> dasht and broke 'em on the grundsil edge;
> The pavement swam in blood, the walls around
> Were spattered o'er with brains. He lapt the blood,
> And chew'd the tender flesh still warm with life,
> That swell'd and heav'd itself amidst his teeth
> As sensible of pain. (77–82)

Addison makes the blinding of Polyphemus equally revolting:

> We gather'd round, and to his single eye,
> The single eye that in his forehead glar'd
> Like a full moon, or a broad burnish'd shield,
> A forky staff we dex'trously apply'd,

> Which, in the spacious socket turning round,
> Scoopt out the big round gelly from its orb. (89–94)

Comparison either directly with Virgil's *Aeneid* (III. 588–681 for the full passage translated by Addison; III. 620–39 in particular) or with Dryden's version of the same passage is instructive. Here, in contrast to the Denham–Pope translations of Homer, the interest lies in the extraordinarily different ways in which Dryden and Addison render Virgil's passage. In Dryden's translation the parallel lines are:

> The cave, tho' large, was dark; the dismal floor
> Was pav'd with mangled limbs and putrid gore.
>
>   ...
>
> Stretch'd on his back, he dash'd against the stones
> Their broken bodies, and their crackling bones:
> With spouting blood the purple pavement swims,
> While the dire glutton grinds the trembling limbs.
>
>   ...
>
> We pray; we cast the lots, and then surround
> The monstrous body, stretch'd along the ground:
> Each, as he could approach him, lends a hand
> To bore his eyeball with a flaming brand.
> Beneath his frowning forehead lay his eye;
> For only one did the vast frame supply –
> But that a globe so large, his front it fill'd,
> Like the sun's disk or like a Grecian shield.
> The stroke succeeds; and down the pupil bends:
> This vengeance follow'd for our slaughtered friends.

In any version it is not a pretty scene. The 'trembling limbs' ground by Polyphemus in Dryden's version are very slightly less gruesome than their warm quivering (*tepidi tremerent*) originals; Addison extends the disturbing description from two words to two lines. Virgil and Dryden after him frame the blinding of Polyphemus by lines which emphasise ceremony and comradeship,[7] reduced by Addison to 'we gathered round'.

What looks like 'straight' translation may have an additional contemporary edge. Most of Dryden's translations were produced in the final dozen years of his life, after he lost the laureateship. A number of literary historians have in recent decades teased out the political overtones of these texts, and those by other seventeenth-century translators (Fujimura 1983; Lynch 1998). More openly, a particular type of 'imitation' established by John Wilmot, Earl of Rochester, in 'An Allusion to Horace. The 10th Satire of the 1st Book' (about 1675), reworks the allusions of a classical poem. Samuel Johnson whose 'Vanity of Human Wishes', based on Juvenal's tenth satire, is part of the tradition, praises Rochester's achievement: 'In the reign of Charles the Second began that adaptation, which has since been very frequent, of ancient poetry to present times; and perhaps few will be found where the parallelism is better preserved than this' (*Lives*, I. 224). Rochester's poem can be read on its own, but placing it beside a parallel passage from Horace's satire (quoted here from the Loeb edition) doubles the pleasure by showing how deftly Rochester adopts or adapts the structure and subject of the earlier poem. The opening lines of the two poems are particularly close in both tone and organisation. Rochester is following Horace in a three-part movement: an offhand admission that he has criticised a fellow-poet, a rhetorical question about this poet's admirers, and a reminder that the earlier criticism had been accompanied by due credit to achievements.

> Well sir, 'tis granted I said Dryden's rhymes
> Were stol'n, unequal, nay dull many times.
> What foolish patron is there found of his
> So blindly partial to deny me this?
> But that his plays, embroidered up and down
> With wit and learning, justly pleased the town
> In the same paper I as freely own.

> Nempe incomposito dixi pede currere versus
> Lucili. quis tam Lucili fautor inepte est,
> ut non hoc fateatur? at idem, quod sale multo
> urbem defricuit, charta laudatur eadem.
> (To be sure I did say that the verses of Lucilius run on with halting foot. Who is a partisan of Lucilius so in-and-out of season as not to confess this? And yet on the self-same page the self-same poet is praised because he rubbed the city down with much salt.)

Until the sixth line, where 'justly' takes the sting from what might otherwise be praise attributed only to others, Rochester is harsher than Horace, multiplying the single word on technical ineptitude by three critical adjectives, and doubling the partiality of fans (both blind and foolish, not simply consistently loyal).

Translation is a two-way street. In tribute to the qualities of Milton's *Paradise Lost*, and perhaps to make it more accessible to continental readers, four translations into Latin (only one, to be sure, complete) appeared before 1700 (Hale 1984). Translation as a lighter amusement can be seen in the thirty-five English songs with facing Latin translations by Henry Bold, identified on his title-page as 'formerly of New College in Oxford', which appeared in 1685. While authors of the originals are not named, some are easily recognisable. The fourth song is Rochester's 'My dearest Mistress hath an heart ...'. The longest (no. 21), completed 'by order of the Bishop of London', should be easy enough to identify by anyone who, like the bishop, is a lover of traditional ballads.[8]

> Vivat Rex noster nobilis,
>   Omnis in tuto sit,
> Venatus, olim flebilis,
>   Chevino Luco fit.
>
> Cane, feras ut abigat,
>   Percaeus abiit,
> Vel embruo elugeat,
>   Quod hodie accidit.[8]

A bawdy ballad about the baker of Mansfield who castrated the devil (no. 19) is improved by Bold. At any rate, he finds Latin rhymes more telling than those of the original: 'A pretty Jest I will you tell / O' th' gelding of the Devil of Hell' is neatly transformed to 'Hoc erit vobis Joculo, / De castrante Diabolo'. A different sort of comic transposition, also primarily for educated readers, was travesty of classical texts. When Charles Cotton rewrote Virgil's account of Dido and Aeneas as the farcical *Scarronides* (1664), its appeal was certainly to those who already know the *Aeneid*. Pepys enjoyed looking over this 'pretty Burlesque poem' at a bookstall in Saint Paul's churchyard, and found it 'extraordinary good' (*Diary*, 2 March 1664).

The idea of translation can be stretched further. Along with transfers from foreign languages to English (or the other way around), English works could be brought up to date. In 1687, 'A Person of quality' published *Spencer redivivus, containing the first book of the Fairy queen, his essential design preserv'd, but his obsolete language and manner of verse totally laid aside. Deliver'd in heroick numbers.* Others had complained about Spenser's obsolete language; this writer refurbishes his epic 'in more fashionable English and Verse' (A7^v), replacing Spenser's 'tedious Stanza' with heroic couplets 'much more suitable to an Epic poem' (A4^r). Canto one, thus improved, opens:

> A worthy Knight was Riding on the Plain,
> In Armour Clad, which richly did Contain
> The Gallant Marks of many Battels fought,
> Tho' he before no Martial Habit sought.

Regularised versions of poems by Chaucer and by Donne are among the youthful exercises written by Pope.

Songs

> The town may da-da-damn me for a poet ... but they si-si-sing my songs for all that. (Thomas Brown, 'Laconicks' 1715, IV. 117, purportedly a comment by Thomas D'Urfey)

The mass of late seventeenth-century and early eighteenth-century songs attracted about as much serious critical analysis as do the words of our pop ballads (which is to say that fans are plentiful but that most often the printed words are prompts for or reminders of performance). Many lyric poems – in the literal sense of poetry intended to be sung – were written and published, but, as poetry, they were low in the pecking order. On the negative side, there are the pungent remarks from John Norris, the philosopher and writer of religious odes:

> It may appear strange indeed that in such a Refining Age as this, wherein all things seem ready to receive their *last turn* and *finishing stroke*, Poetry should be the only thing that remains unimproved.

Worse than unimproved, both music and poetry seem to him to be trivialised,

> now for the most part dwindled down to light, frothy stuff, consisting either of mad extravagant Rants, or slight Witticisms, and little amorous Conceits, fit only for a Tavern entertainment ... Poetry is grown almost out of Repute, and men come strongly prejudiced to any thing of this kind, as expecting nothing but Froth and Emptiness,

and to be a Poet goes for little more than a Country Fiddler. (Norris of
Bemerton, 'To the Reader', *Miscellanies*, a4^{r-v})

On the positive side, there is the fact that the joy in country fiddlers,
and their more urbane cousins of the court and theatre, is clearly
attested. The superb bibliography by Day and Murrie, *English Song-
Books 1651–1702*, includes a first-line index of 4150 lyrics. The index,
along with descriptions of more than two hundred and fifty songbooks, provides tempting paths for statistical exploration. Whose
songs, old or new, were most popular? Fifteen poems by Herrick,
mainly with Henry Lawes' settings, are printed, some repeatedly.
Seven songs from Shakespearean plays are present; there are sixty-
two from Dryden's plays, and fifteen from Aphra Behn. On a different line of enquiry, how can songs be weighed against poems on
affairs of state in assertions about what were the dominant forms of
poetry? The editors of *Poems on Affairs of State 1660–1714* estimate
some 3000 poems in print and 2500 in manuscript. That total
exceeds the number of Day and Murrie's lyrics, but given that they
include only songs in print, and moreover in books (as contrasted
with single broadsheets used for ballads), the 4150 songs listed are
only a sample of those circulating at the time. Moreover, Day and
Murrie deal only with secular songbooks, omitting religious songs
and hymnals. Attempts at comparison are further complicated by
questions of dating and definition. Some songs are topical, some
continue in the popular repertoire long after composition. Furthermore, are lines to be counted along with numbers of individual texts?
Songs are by definition, or by the limitations of a singer's stamina,
fairly short.

   Day and Murrie's choice of dates, 1651–1702, centred on the careers
of John and Henry Playford, indicates the importance of publishers in
making available, or positively promoting, poetry of particular kinds.
Authorship of the poems, however, was not the Playfords' concern. In
the series of songbooks they published, notably *Select Ayres and
Dialogues* (1652–63) followed by *Choyce Ayres, Songs, and Dialogues ...
being Most of the Newest Ayres and Songs, Sung at Court and at the
Public Theatres* (5 vols, 1673–84), and *The New Treasury of Music*
(1695) the name of the composer is generally given, but not the name
of the poet, and only occasionally the titles of plays for which many
songs – by Dryden, Behn, Lee, Otway and others – were designed.
John Playford's preface to *Choyce Ayres* emphasises the point that the

combination of words and music, rather than either in isolation, is important; alone, either is incomplete:

> These *Songs* and *Ayres* are such as were lately Composed, and are very suitable and acceptable to the *Genius* of these *Times*. Many of the Words have been already Published, which gave but little content to divers Ingenious Persons, who thought them as dead, unless they had the *Airy Tunes* to quicken them. (1676, A2^r; Spink 1989)

The Playford volumes of *Select Ayres* helped keep alive the poetry of Herrick and the music of Lawes; the *Choyce Ayres*, as its long title indicates, allowed the most contemporary work for performance which was being produced by Purcell, Dryden and their contemporaries to spread from court and theatre into private musical gatherings.

A number of hymns written between 1650 and 1720 remain familiar. Try testing Playford's comments on the interplay of words and music by reading the words of Addison's 'The Spacious Firmament on High' (1712) or Isaac Watts' 'Our God, our Help in Ages Past' (from *The Psalms of David Imitated*, 1719) without humming.

Broadside ballads

> More solid things do not shew the Complexion of the times so well as Ballads and Libels. (Selden, *Table-Talk* 1689, 31*)*

Generically, the broadside ballad falls between songbooks and *Poems on Affairs of State*. Alternatively, one might think of the broadside ballads as being something like a modern newsagent's miscellaneous stock, or halfway between pop songs and the more sensational tabloids or cheap magazines. Given a predilection for self-congratulation on living in a refined and polished age, contempt for popular ballads might be expected. Nonetheless, for their preservation, the seventeenth century is an important time. For Thomas Percy's *Reliques of Ancient English Poetry* (1765) the most important source was the manuscript, in a mid-seventeenth-century hand, in which someone recorded 195 old songs, historical poems and metrical romances. Another was the collection of almost two thousand black-letter ballads, amassed by the antiquarian John Selden (1584–1654) and after him by Samuel Pepys, and arranged by Pepys into five large folios.

A glance at facsimile volumes of Pepys' ballads gives some sense of the characteristic appearance of poetry performed and vended in great quantity. The large sheets, printed on one side only, combining illustrative woodcuts and text, were also used as simple wall-decoration, as posters are today. In *The Compleat Angler* (1653) Walton makes them characteristic of an inviting alehouse, 'where we shall find a cleanly room, lavender in the window and twenty ballads stuck about the wall'. Addison, a bit over half a century later, attests the continuity of the custom in country houses, and the pleasure it gives him: 'I can't, for my Heart, leave a Room, before I have thoroughly studied the Walls of it, and examined the several printed Papers which are usually pasted upon them' (*Spectator* no. 85, 7 June 1711).

Selden suggested the sociological value of ballads; Addison, in two *Spectator* papers focusing on 'The Two Children in the Wood' and on 'Chevy Chase', argues for the ballads' aesthetic significance, a victory of nature over artefice, and of appreciation of the 'genuine and unaffected'. A combative tone in Addison's defence of the ballad indicates that the taste for which he makes a case is not universal; 'the little conceited Wits of the Age, who can only show their Judgment by finding Fault ... cannot be supposed to admire these Productions which have nothing to recommend them but the Beauties of Nature'. He calls on the prestige of Dorset and Dryden and 'several of the most refined Writers of our present Age, who are of the same Humour'. Long before Wordsworth and Coleridge's *Lyrical Ballads*, there was interest in these songs.

Music and dating provide the appeal of a treasure hunt, and the ballads offer a rewarding training-ground for literary historians. Almost always the broadsheets specify, but do not print, a tune. Occasionally this is as familiar as 'Greensleaves', but more often needs a search. Simpson's *The British Broadside Ballad and its Music* (1966) supplies over four hundred melodies, with notes on their history. As performances rather than simply as texts, the ballads invite comparison with Playford's *The Dancing Master* (with which they often share tunes) and with the stage. Dating, when not established by topical events, leads to familiarity with the careers of seventeenth and early eighteenth-century printers. John Hollander's introduction to the Euing Collection of English broadside ballads in the University of Glasgow describes resources for tracking down the rapidly changing partnerships among printers of the time. Woodcuts reused for new ballads also provide clues, for as time goes on the blocks accumulate more wormholes and wider cracks.

The Pack of Autolycus, Rollins' sampler of forty ballads printed between 1624 and 1693, emphasises in its title a line of sensational stories binding late seventeenth-century examples to Shakespeare's roguish peddler in *The Winter's Tale*. Marvels abound; the selection ranges from ghost stories and visitations by the devil, through Siamese twins, to an account of the eruption of Mount Etna in 1669. With just over four hundred ballads, almost all from the seventeenth century, the Euing Collection provides further variety. For those with access to the clearly printed modern volume (1971), the Euing Collection has some advantages over the Pepys ballads. Despite its immense size, the Pepys collection has awkward gaps at its centre, between the broadsides acquired from Selden and those Pepys bought during the last quarter of the century; his most vigorous collecting begins about 1680 and ends by 1700, when as he noted, the visual style of the broadside printers was changing, with Roman type superseding Gothic typeface.

Given the immense number of these penny publications which survive, it is rash to generalise about their literary qualities. A Euing ballad (no. 170) about the Great Fire of London, 'The Londoners Lamentation', links factual reporting with free imagery, a fluid verb with the subject of fire:

> It over-flow'd New *Fish-street-hill*,
>   and then gave fire to *Canon-street*,
> Then through the Lanes, about did wheel,
>   until it with the *Thames* did meet,
> *As if it would have dry'd the Flood,*
> *And left dust where the River stood.*

A patriotic ballad from the Pepys collection, 'The Protestants Prayer: Being Their hearty Wishes for the Prosperity of Their Majesties Fleet at Sea, and likewise Their Land-Forces, that our Foes may be put to Flight, and these Three Kingdoms flourish again in Peace' is jauntily amateur: 'King William and Mary, our Sovereigns they / I hope long may flourish the Sceptre to sway' (Pepys Ballads II. 70). Given that many of the ballad-singers selling copies of their songs on the streets were women, 'The Good Wives Fore-Cast, or, The Kind and Loving Mothers Counsel to her Daughter after Marriage' (Euing Ballads no. 132) has particular dramatic appeal. As a mirror of seventeenth-century views of marriage, it is a concise companion-piece to Lord Halifax's *The Ladies New-year Gift, or Advice to a Daughter* (1688).

Poetic topics and poetic diction

> The first beauty of the Epic poem consists in diction, that is, in the
> choice of words, and harmony of numbers. (Dryden, Preface to
> *Fables*, 1700)

Included in John Phillips' *The Mysteries of Love & Eloquence, Or, the
Arts of Wooing and Complementing* (1658) is a compendium of adjectives appropriate for various nouns. The entry for *tongue*, beginning
'seraphic, Nectarious, sweet, harmonious', also suggests 'oily,
venemous, glozing ... detracting, malicious ... smooth, flattering'.
Woman might be 'inconstant, crafty, deceitful, wanton, beauteous,
soft, tender ... '; *streams* 'silver, christal, purling, foaming, winding ...'.
Like the Latin lists of synonyms, epithets and exemplary sententious
observations (*loci communes*, literally commonplaces), which were
provided for schoolboys wrestling with composition exercises,[9] this
might be an aid for fluency, though hardly for originality. At a similarly low level of sophistication, what topics seemed particularly
poetic can be seen in Edward Bysshe's *Art of English Poetry* (1702),
which promises 'the most Natural, Agreeable, and Noble Thoughts'
on matters from Absence to Zeal (1452 quotations from 48 authors),
and in its imitation and rival, Charles Gildon's *Complete Art of Poetry*
(1718), 'A Collection of the most beautiful Descriptions, Similes,
Allusions, &c'. An eager market for such publications can be seen in
the present rarity of Phillips' volume (which may have been read to
pieces), and in the number of editions of Bysshe and Gildon.
Nonetheless, however natural, beautiful, agreeable (or in later
editions of Bysshe's selections, 'sublime') the listings in these publications are, they are as misleading about working poets' choices as a
paint-by-numbers kit would be for the visual arts.

Phillips' 'Alphabet of Epithets' is, in fact, offered primarily as an aid
to a fashionable word-game: 'the witty sport commonly named
Substantives and Adjectives'. The quotations chosen by Bysshe and
Gildon are wrenched from their contexts in plays and (often very
long) poems, creating a misleading focus on 'Thoughts' and
'Descriptions'. While *Poems on Several Occasions* is a common title for
collections, the occasions for poetry range from public affairs such as
the Great Fire of London to the most trivial events. Waller produces
neatly turned verses on the gift of a pen. Literary occasions regularly
brought forth additional literature: prologues and epilogues to plays,

compliments for friends' new books. Births, deaths, marriages are commemorated. In contemporary critical discussions of poetic diction, the touchstones are apt to be clarity and propriety; extremely dense descriptions or thoughts fall out of favour. Thomas Hobbes at mid-century voices antipathy to the extreme compression of imagery which later attracts the epithet 'metaphysical'. He attacks 'the ambitious obscurity of expressing more than is perfectly conceived; or perfect conception in fewer words than it requires. Which Expressions, though they have had the honour to be called strong lines, are indeed no better than Riddles ... dark and troublesome' (Answer to Davenant's Preface to *Gondibert* 1650, Spingarn II. 63). In a later critical essay, 'Concerning the Vertues of an Heroique Poem' (1675), Hobbes focuses on the choice of words for epic translations, and rejects technical terms, 'the names of Instruments and Tools of Artificers' as both unintelligible to a reader and inappropriate for a hero (Spingarn, II. 68–9). Since propriety means proper not in the limited sense of polite, but in the more interesting sense of specific, appropriate to the occasion, each poem or kind of poem sets up its own standards.[10]

When Charles II returned there was an outpouring of panegyrics and also a surge of printed work mocking Presbyterians and Parliamentarians. Samuel Butler's immensely popular *Hudibras* (1662, followed by second and third parts in 1664 and 1678) attacked the defeated Puritans. In 1662 there also appeared *Rump: or An Exact Collection of the Choycest Poems and Songs Relating to the Late Times. By the most Eminent Wits, from Anno 1639 to Anno 1661.*[11] The comedy of anatomical and excremental references proved irresistible to many Royalist contributors. A ballad called 'Bum-Fodder: or Waste-Paper, proper to wipe the Nations RUMP with, or your Own' is followed by a mock-panegyric: 'A Vindication of the RUMP: or The RUMP Re-advanced' (Part II, 54–60). By the end of the first stanza, anyone doubting a comic tone – conveyed in the bouncing metrical form, as well as in the specification of an appropriate tune ('To the Tune of *Up tails all*') – would be disabused, by the rhyme with 'Mars', of any tendency to take 'Vindication' seriously:

> Full many a Ballad hath been Penn'd
>   And scoffing Poem writ
> Against the RUMP; but I intend
>   To speak in Praise of it.

> Come *Jove* and *Apollo*, come *Venus* and *Mars*,
> And lend your assistance: to speak of the A___
>   Will require a prodigious wit.

As the poem proceeds, repeated references to buttocks or tail (both spelled out) link the parliament with farting and with (quite jolly) fornication. The final two stanzas grow coarser, suggesting that the Speaker of the House might as well have been called '*Anus* / Since he was the mouth of the *RUMP*' and the last stanza brings together the sexual and the excremental, an accusation of hypocrisy, and specific political references. Stinging word-play on 'purge' takes the history of the Rump Parliament from its creation (Pride's Purge, 1648) to General Monk's important role in bringing about the Restoration.

> Our zealous sticklers for Reformation
>   Will edifie on the Rump of a Sister,
> And it will never grow out of fashion
>   To Physick the Tayl with a Glister.
> But beware that *Monk* does not come with a bitter
> Purge to the Rump which will make her beshit her,
>   For she hath already bepist her.

Royalists did not bask long in high hopes. Bitter lines from Brome's 'The Cavalier' (1664) testify to disillusionment. At the Restoration Charles II had published a Proclamation of Oblivion and Indemnity, 'popularly said to be of Oblivion to his friends and Indemnity to his enemies' (Wedgwood 1960, 129). Alexander Brome speaks for Charles' disappointed supporters:

> We have laid all at stake
> For his Majesty's sake,
> We have fought, we have paid,
> We've been sold and betrayed,
> And tumbled from nation to nation;
> But now those are thrown down
> That usurped the Crown,
> Our hopes were that we
> All rewarded should be,
> But we're paid with a Proclamation. (ll. 8–16)

Until the four-syllable *Proclamation* which ends the stanza, the words are deliberately simple. Who else, asks Charles Cotton when praising Brome's verse:

> Writes in so pure, an unaffected strain,
> As shows wit's ornament, is to be plain.
>
> ('The Answer' ll. 19–20, in Brome 1982, 229)

Anglo-Saxon plainness was, however, a recurrent if minor matter of critical controversy. To some, including Dryden, it seemed obvious that a series of short words rarely sounds 'harmonious'; indeed that often 'a monosyllabic line turns verse to prose' (Preface to *Aeneid* 1697; 1962, II. 245). Waller's earliest editor agreed, and having attacked the 'harsh untunable' sound of verse before Waller wrote, asserts that as Waller brought in more polysyllables, he also brought in smoother measures (1690). For Addison, English seems inelegant because it lacks 'the multitude of Syllables, which makes the Words of other Languages more Tunable and Sonorous' (*Spectator* no. 135, 4 August 1711). Pope, in *An Essay on Criticism*, provides a parody of the issue: 'And ten low Words oft creep in one dull Line'. In vigorous opposition to received opinion, the Anglo-Saxon scholar Elizabeth Elstob argues that it is not short words, but poetic skill in handling them, that counts, and she illustrates her point by quotations first in Greek and Latin, then in major translations by Dryden and Pope, and finally in a brisk survey of English poetry from Chaucer to Lady Winchelsea (1715).

The vocabulary of praise, although sometimes playful, must be persuasive; it is often solemn and sonorous. The most indecorous rhymes, in contrast, have an emphatic place in satire. After the failure of Monmouth's rebellion, when the University of Cambridge not only took down the Lely portrait of its former chancellor but even had it publically burned, George Stepney ironically describes the occasion.

> Then his air was too proud, and his features amiss,
> As if being a traitor had altered his phiz!
> So the rabble of Rome, whose favor ne'er settles,
> Melt down their Sejanus to pots and brass kettles.
>
> ('On the University of Cambridge's Burning the Duke of
> Monmouth's Picture', *POAS* IV. 43)

These couplets hover between the seriousness of Juvenal's tenth satire, exposing how quickly the multitude desert a fallen statesman, and the comedy of throwaway rhyme-words, coming down heavily on the slang 'phiz' before bouncing jauntily on the feminine rhymes 'settles' and 'kettles'. Throughout Butler's *Hudibras*, comic two-syllable and three-syllable rhymes are prominent. The coy blanks which appear in satirical verse are sometimes silently filled by modern editors, although 'blanking' dashes not only draw attention to well-known individuals but also emphasise, rather than conceal, the deliberate coarseness of sexual or scatalogical vocabulary – as in a squib on Nell Gwyn and Charles II: 'She hath got a trick to handle his p___' (*POAS* I, 420), or in an attack on Blackmore: 'Go on brave Doctor, a third Volume write, / And find us Paper while you make us Sh___' (*POAS* VI, 188). (See also Chapter 1, pp. 28–9.)

Mere invective characterises the crudest satiric poets. Dryden's comments in his 'Essay on Satire' about hatchet-jobs or deft rapier strokes have added point given that he himself had been the butt of attack, especially after his change of religion. 'To Mr. Bays' relies on direct insult: 'Thou mercenary renegade, thou slave, / Thou ever changeling, still to be a knave' (*POAS* IV. 79). One need not dislike Dryden or doubt the sincerity of his religious conversion to enjoy another poem on the same topic, 'To Mr. Dryden, Upon his Declaring himself a Roman Catholic' (1686), which ends neatly: 'So, Jack of all faiths, and of none, adieu' (*POAS* IV, 78). Combining a pseudo-friendly nickname and variation on a familiar catchphrase, the line economically sums up, in its last word, the finality of dismissal and the hand-washing of 'God help you'.

The editors of *Poems on Affairs of State* assert that the enormous bulk of material in their collection tends to be underrepresented in modern anthologies. In contrast, poetry on love may be overrepresented. Love has a mildly surprising minor place as a poetic topic in popular 'drollery' collections and broadside publications. Some idealistic, tender verses can of course be found, but a more dominant tone is sceptical. The swaggering individuality of Donne's 'The Indifferent' becomes a public declaration of shared assumptions in lines from Henry Bold:

> I'll swear they Lie, who say they Love
>   One only Beauteous Face,
> He's Mad (or Honest) does not prove
>   A Score in three days space.

I'm *a la mode* Myself; pretend that I
Am here all-over Love and there could Die,
When Faith! there's no such matter seriously. (Song 5, 1664)

When Pepys, a methodical organiser, sorted his collection of broadside ballads, he provided a carefully lettered table in which love, pleasant and unpleasant, takes up two of his ten categories.

1 – Devotion & Morality
2 – History, True & Fabulous
3 – Tragedy viz. Murders, Executions, Judgments of God
4 – State & Times
5 – Love Pleasant
6 – Love Unfortunate
7 – Marriage, Cuckoldry &c.
8 – Sea – Love, Gallantry, & Actions
9 – Drinking & Good Fellowshipp
10 – Humour, Frollicks &c. mixt

The effect of this table is largely to emphasise how miscellaneous the subjects for popular poetry were. The range extends further, to poems on nothing – literally, in Rochester's 'On Nothing' and in an anonymous song of the same name which can be found along with its tune in D'Urfey's anthology *Wit and Mirth* (1719–20).

How does poetry appear?

Sedley indeed and *Rochester* might Write,
For their own Credit, and their Friends' Delight,
Showing how far they could the rest out-do,
As in their Fortunes, so their Writings too;
But should Drudge *Dryden* this Example take,
And *Absoloms* for empty Glory make,
He'd soon perceive his Income scarce enough,
To feed his Nostrils with Inspiring Snuff.
(Matthew Prior, 'Satyr on the Poets', ll. 143–52)

Here 'appearance' means, first, what the poem looks like on a page, and second how it was distributed. Typography alone sets up expectations about certain kinds of verse. Until about 1700, street ballads

were commonly printed in black-letter type. Soon afterwards, the
appearance of songbooks also changed when Walsh, who succeeded
the Playford family as the most active publisher of music, began to
use engraved plates. Furthermore, the shapes that poems present to
the eye give a quick indication of tastes of the times. Spenser's stanzas
are, to the taste of the later seventeenth century, outmoded. Almost
no one except Milton writes sonnets. Few poets attempt the metrical
variety and experimentation of the sixteenth and earlier seventeenth
centuries. There is no one as versatile as Sidney, who in the *Arcadia*
provides a sampler of poetic form, including attempts to write in
classic, quantitative meters (dependent on the length of syllables
rather than on stress). No lyricist is as inventive as Herbert, who uses
over a hundred different stanza patterns in the 169 poems of *The
Temple* (1633). Butler's short-lined 'hudibrastics' with doggerel
rhymes and rough rhythms might be seen as a revival of Skelton's
early sixteenth-century satiric lines, 'ragged, / Tattered and jagged'
(*Collyn Cloute*, 53–4), but Skelton practised aureate verse and formal
stanzas as well as 'skeltonics'. At the middle of the seventeenth
century, Davenant tried quatrains as a vehicle for epic. By the 1670s,
iambic pentameter couplets are so much the norm for narrative
poetry that in the second edition of *Paradise Lost* Milton adds a
defensive note on his choice of blank verse, attacking the 'jingling
sound of like endings' and asserting that in rhyme there is 'no true
musical delight, which consists only in apt numbers, fit quantity of
syllables, and the sense variously drawn out from one verse into
another'. He thus invites attention to subtle variations of syllable
length and the placing of pauses. Like other long serious poems of the
time, however, Milton's epic appears set out in unbroken blocks with
only mildly wavy right-hand margins. At the other extreme, the irregular Pindaric ode is visually as well as verbally extravagant.

Manuscript and print

Poetry appeared in public on single sheets and in grand folios; it was
passed from friend to friend, hawked in the streets, or displayed in
coffee-houses and booksellers' stalls and shops. Manuscript circulation was no more destroyed by the development of printing than
email has, yet, brought an end to letters through the post. Aristocratic
disdain, feminine modesty and censorship all encouraged quiet,
private publication within a sympathetic circle. Handwritten verse
passed from friend to friend was more intimate, more spontaneous or

more elegant, more 'polite' or less censored, than the public press (Love 1993). The greater prestige of manuscript over print extended even to newsletters. Those genuinely powerful and rich received regular reports from ambassadors and agents abroad; those willing to pay for the privilege could subscribe to handwritten accounts of international and national affairs, personalised at the start. When Margaret Cavendish, Duchess of Newcastle brought out her *Poems and Fancies* in 1653 as a printed volume, Dorothy Osborne considered the act as extravagant as the duchess's bizarre appearance. While her comments are sometimes quoted as a failure of feminine solidarity, they measure how idiosyncratic the duchess's display seemed. A rising young man could, and often did, venture into print in order to demonstrate his general talents and attract patronage. In the short term, he expected some financial reward for the standard flattery of a dedication; in the longer term he hoped the influential dedicatee would recognise abilities and help him towards a post.[12]

In 1661, in the preface to *Songs and Other Poems*, Alexander Brome amusingly reviews the standard apologies, and the combination of vanity and vulnerability, which accompanied voluntary public appearance:

> I might allege several reasons; namely, gratification of Friends, importunity, preventing of spurious impressions. But these are in print already in many grave Authors, with exact formulas to express the bashfulness of the Author ... There are another sort of reasons, not expressed but implied, as an ambition to be in print, to have a face cut in copper, with a laurel about my head; a motto and verses underneath made by my self in my own commendation; and to be accompted a wit, and called a Poet.
>
> All that is terrible in this case, is, that the Author may be laughed at, and Stationer beggered by the book's invendibility. It concerns him to look to the one, I am provided against the other. For it is unkind and unmanly to abuse me for being a bad poet, when as I could not help it; it being my desire to be as good as any that can jeer me. (A2^v–A4^r)[13]

Less breezily, the Earl of Shaftesbury devotes three pages in his prose *Advice to an Author* (1710) to 'Why a Writer for Self-Entertainment should not keep his Writings to himself, without appearing in Public, or before the World'. Self-defensively, he tries to dissociate himself from 'Merchant-Adventurers in the Letter-Trade'. At the risk of protesting too much, he argues first that his friends deserve better than to read his advice in his own handwriting, and then that although he could easily pay a copyist, he does not think 'that there can be any harm in a quick way of copying fair, and keeping Copies alike' (145–7).

Amateurs could be careless, or adopt a pose of carelessness, about verses written for pleasure rather than for fame or reward. When after the death of Henry Bold his brother tried to put together a collection of his Latin verses, he had difficulty in finding complete copies. He therefore appealed to 'all Gentlemen who have any of the Author's Latin Songs or Verses which are not found in this Impression, that they will be pleased to bring or send Copies of them to Mr. John Eglesfield Bookseller, at the Sign of the Marigold in Fleet-Street London' (A5^r). According to the brother's preface, the translations were produced at the request of the bishop of London, 'and some for other Honourable Persons, & some for his own humor, or his Familiar Friends, and these he distributed according as they were related in the first fair Corrected Copy, and left nothing in his own Custody but indigested, foul, torn, scattering Papers' (A4^v). For the disappearance as well as appearance of poetry, this little preface offers an account. The horrified brother 'very hardly rescued out of the hands of an illiterate welsh Cook wench' (A5^r) two poems in Latin; the English versions had already been used for lighting fires. Given the cost of paper, recycling was routine. Sheets saved from fire-lighting, like Bold's verses or the traditional ballads called the Percy manuscript, might be used as lining papers in book-binding. Satiric attacks on bad verse allude to less dignified fates, in the cookshop or privy.[14]

Printers and booksellers could and did make money from poetry, seldom the case today. For the poet, publication (apart from patronage) brought little direct financial profit except when publication by subscription was organised, a process which involved soliciting advance payment from enough buyers so that both author and printer were assured of immediate funds. This was how the translations of Virgil and Homer produced economic independence for Dryden and Pope. For original English poetry the method was established more slowly, but friends of Matthew Prior worked diligently to rescue him from poverty through such an edition of *Poems on Several Occasions* (1718). Until after the first Copyright Act (1710), writers had little leeway for negotiating contracts with members of the Stationers' Company, the guild of printers and booksellers.

How close are the extant texts to what a poet 'really' or at some point, or on final consideration, wrote? When pirated and unautho- rised texts were printed, these sometimes prompted living writers to issue corrected editions. The reliability of a posthumous poetic edition of Rochester or other court wit is apt to be very low, at the opposite end of the spectrum from the *Works* patiently supervised early in the century by Ben Jonson, or an *Iliad* corrected by Pope. Given the casual circulation of poems in manuscript, variant manuscript copies abound – occasionally in the handwriting of the author, more often in the personal anthologies or 'commonplace books' into which individ- uals copied out what they enjoyed. Since manuscript copies, like Chinese whispers, accumulate variants, defining a 'definitive' text may be a vain enterprise. The apparently arid inches of 'textual notes' in modern editions, however, preserve in small print the complicated sifting of different readings. It is not only authorial intention that is at stake here; variants encapsulate reception history, how a phrase might be understood, misunderstood, used to modify or strengthen implica- tions of a passage. Undergraduates as well as advanced scholars may well take an interest in small but significant differences made by a single word in Rochester's *Satire on Mankind*, line 45: 'at heart they hate' or 'at least they hate' or 'at last they hate'? Two readings rest on early transcriptions, one is a critical guess.[15] Not only individual words or lines, but whole poems are often in question. Even though Rochester reportedly left orders to burn all his profane writings, by the time of his death copies of his poems were in many hands, along with poems falsely attributed to him. In 'Timon. A Satyr' he himself sardon- ically describes a fool insisting that 'a libel of a sheet or two ... was so sharp it must be mine', despite his explicitly disowning it and disdain- fully criticising its insipidity. A number of printers eager to profit from Rochester's reputation brought out large editions purporting to be *Poems on Several Occasions by the Right Honourable, the E. of R__* (1680, 1685, 1691), providing scholarly puzzles in sorting what must be his from what is probably or certainly not. Only occasionally is this task as easy as spotting that two poems in the 1685 edition had been in print nine years before Rochester was born (Rochester, ed. Vieth 1963, 33). Modern editors have pruned the canon sharply. The most recent claim to represent *The Complete Works* prints ninety-five poems, less than two-thirds of those attributed to him in the seventeenth and early eighteenth centuries. Of these ninety-five, furthermore, only forty-two 'can be attributed to Rochester with certainty' (1994, xiv).

The printing of individual poems, on a single sheet ('a broadside') or small pamphlet, was far more common than it is at present. I have now forgotten why, in the rare books room of the Cambridge University Library, I first called up a volume which on its spine is identified simply as 'Tracts, Vol. 13' (Sel.2.126). Whatever the original motivation, it melted into fascination at the collection of 190 poems, mainly from the early 1680s, which had been bought separately and then bound together. (Pepys' *Diary* provides reminders, if they are needed, that visiting a bookseller and a bookbinder were separate enterprises. Some books were sold in loose sheets, others stitched; booksellers' catalogues make a note when simple bindings have already been supplied.) A list in the front flyleaf records the prices paid for 126 of the works – usually a penny, occasionally as much as a shilling for longer pamphlets. Having the collection bound was three times more expensive than the dearest text. The final item shows a payment of three shillings and fourpence 'For the binding'. There are a few familiar texts, including Rochester's *A Satire on Mankind* and the second part of Dryden's *Absalom and Achitophel*, but most of the poems are obscure. Of the first eight in the collection, five are political, two are jolly verses in praise of punch and of a drinking club, and one is a reprint of a reflective poem written some six decades earlier, 'The Pilgrimage' ('Give me my Scollop-Shell of Quiet ...') attributed to Sir Walter Raleigh. The bulk of singly-printed poems, when piled together, is striking. The collection is overwhelmingly political and satirical, although, in addition to the amusing poems in praise of punch and brandy, it contains a dialogue between Tea and Coffee, and a handful of elegies and panegyrics.

What is absent is also interesting. Landscape is even scarcer than love. Authors' names are given only when the bookseller or writer has something to gain. There may be some snob appeal in several songs attributed to 'A Person of Quality' (Rochester). Had the birth of a son to James II not precipitated his loss of the throne, a cluster of poems printed in 1688 might have been of advantage to loyal subjects. Commendatory verses include 'A Congratulatory Poem to Her Most Sacred Majesty, on the Universal Hopes of All Loyal Persons for a Prince of Wales' (1688) by Mrs A. Behn (its title soon to be disproved), D'Urfey's 'A Poem Congratulatory on the Birth of the Young Prince', and a short poem expressing 'The most Hearty and Unspeakable Rejoycings of the Kings-Bench Prisoners in Southwark, Upon the News of the Birth of the Prince of Wales'. A music-master turns his broadside into self-advertisement: 'To the King's Most Sacred Majesty, upon the Happy Birth of the Prince of Scotland and Wales, June the 10th, 1688; A Poem, by William Niven, late Master of the Musick School of Inverness, in Scotland, and now Practitioner of the Harpsicon, Flute, and Flagelot, at Deans-Court in Old-Bayly Street, in London'.

The volume as a whole is an example of an individually compiled anthology. Commercially assembled anthologies also proliferated.

Anthologies

Four major kinds of anthology appeared: songbooks with music, drolleries, miscellanies with a greater claim to art, and the collections of poems on affairs of state. There are also numerous volumes commemorating specific events. The two universities brought out loyal collections to celebrate the return of Charles and other royal occasions; the death of Dryden precipitated *The Nine Muses*, a group of elegies by women. As elsewhere in this volume, description is highly selective; as a short-title checklist in the *New Cambridge Bibliography of English Literature* shows, there was a flood of 'Miscellanies, Anthologies, and Collections of Poetry', never fewer than two in a year (1664 was one of the leaner years) and sometimes nearer two dozen.[16] In general, however, what might a reader expect?

In songbooks, such as John Playford's *Music's Recreation* (1652) and *Catch that Catch can, or, The Musical Companion* (1667, with many following, revised and expanded editions), the combination of music and words emphasises the social experience of performance. Other anthologies, with texts only, promote silent reading. The first of the drolleries was *Musarum deliciae: or, The Muses Recreation, Conteining severall select Pieces of sportive Wit* (1655). While 'drollery' is not a precise term, a prefatory note by the bookseller Henry Herringman, 'The Stationer to the Ingenious Reader', advertises the appeal of light and conversational verse:

> Plain Poetry is now disesteem'd, it must be *Drollery* or it will not please: I have therefore, to regale the curious Palates of these Times, made a Collection of Sir *John Mennis*, and Doctor *Smiths* Drollish Intercourses; which as they need no recommendation to your acceptance, the world being well acquainted with the ingenuity both of those persons, and their productions; so neither can you suspect them adulterate, since they are inimitable by any but themselves.

Read, Laugh, and enjoy.

                              H.H.

Mennis (now usually spelled Mennes) and Smith are no longer names
to conjure with, but they had a certain reputation at the time, and the
publisher had a shrewd sense of what would please 'the palates of
these times'; the volume was reprinted in 1656 and 1661. It is possible
that poems by the two named writers were carefully transcribed, but
'unadulterate' does not guarantee that all the contents are theirs.
Among the longest pieces is 'The Fart censured in the Parliament
House', a schoolboy joke, working names of parliamentarians into a
debate about an unfortunate windy comment or 'ill motion'. A sense
of popular taste, and its continuity, may be seen in the textual history
of this poem. Some half-century later it persists as an anthology selection in *Wit and Mirth* (1699 and 1707), there attributed to Sir John
Suckling (1609–42), although it seems to have been well-known by
1610.[17]

Promising only amusement, the collection nonetheless displays
links with writing now considered 'canonical'. It begins with a few
familiar epistles, in the line of Jonson and ultimately of Horace. The
opening poem 'To Parson Weeks. An Invitation to London' alludes to
the wine 'Young Herrick took to entertain / The Muses in a sprightly
vein'. In 'Upon Chesse-play. To Dr. Budden', there is a mock-heroic
celebration of the game of chess. The continuing popularity of
Sidney's *Arcadia* is seen in a 'Description of three Beauties' whose
names and descriptions are taken from the pastoral romance:
Philoclea and Pamela, who are both beautiful, and lure the poet to
love, and Mopsa, who provides an antidote:

> *Mopsa,* even *Mopsa,* pretty Mouse,
> Best piece of Wainscot in the House;
> Whose Saffron Teeth, and Lips of Leeks,
> Whose Corall Nose, and Parchment Cheeks;
> Whose Paste-board forehead, eyes of Ferret,
> Breast of brown Paper, Neck of Caret;
> And other parts, not evident,
> For which dame nature should be shent,
> Are Spells and Charms of great renown,
> Concupiscence to conjure downe.

This is mildly amusing on its own, more amusing as an imitation of Sidney's negative blazon 'What length of verse can serve ... ' which runs through Mopsa's bodily parts from rocky forehead and 'lips of sapphire blue' to 'those parts unknown, which hidden sure are best'. In their second drollery, *Wit Restor'd* (1658), Mennes and Smith playfully parody both classical story and pretentious scholarship in a deliberately rough poem about Penelope and Ulysses, accompanied by footnotes. Theatrical bits and pieces take a prominent place in popular post-Restoration collections such as *Covent Garden Drollery*. Compiled by 'A.B.' (probably Aphra Behn), it includes prologues, epilogues and songs from plays.

A culmination and combination of the songbook and drollery tradition, *Wit and Mirth: or, Pills to Purge Melancholy, in Six Volumes* appeared in 1719–20 (reprint 1959). Published by Henry Playford, who held the rights to some 70 settings by Purcell which are included, the compendium was edited by Thomas D'Urfey, who himself wrote 350 of the 1144 songs and unset poems. Wine and women go well with song, and as the running title indicates, these are 'Pleasant and Divertive' poems. Even when the theme is potentially mordant, as in 'The Power of Gold' (III. 348–9), which sets out to demonstrate that money is more powerful than love, cynicism dissolves into playfulness, as classical stories such as Jove's amours are rewritten to prove a point. Marking continuities rather than new directions, D'Urfey's massive compilation gives to a Georgian audience much that was written and sung in Charles II's time. There are songs by Wycherley, Dorset, Rochester, Sedley and Dryden; most, except for D'Urfey's, are anonymous. Throughout, the assumption that the aim is performance rather than silent reading is kept clear; tunes are supplied, or simply named if (evidently) familiar.

'Miscellany' today seems a singularly unappealing title, suggesting only a jumble of heterogeneous materials. In the seventeenth and eighteenth centuries, it retained some culinary overtones, from the stew which made up gladiators' diets or from mixed grain. Johnson's *Dictionary* (1755) illustrates *miscellane* by quoting from Bacon's *Natural History* the advice that 'if you sow a few beans with wheat, your wheat will be better'. While the catchy titles of songbooks and drolleries promise no more than an antidote to depression, miscellanies of the later seventeenth century are somewhat more nourishing. The enterprising publisher Jacob Tonson was not the first to issue a mixed collection of translations and original poems, serious and light, old and new. Nor was Tonson alone is seeing the advantage, for clear-ing stock and promoting authors whose work he owned, of joining earlier work with fresh compositions. Nonetheless, the six volumes of *Miscellany Poems* he published between 1684 and 1709 properly earn him a place in literary history. (The whole series is sometimes called *Dryden's Miscellanies*, although Dryden's editorial help is clear only for the first volume, 1684, and the second, *Sylvae*, 1685. Tonson includes substantial amounts of Dryden's translations and occasional poetry in what he called the 'Annual Miscellanies' of 1693 and 1694, and in the two volumes, and collected edition, published after Dryden's death.) Competitors rushed to imitate Tonson. Any computer search brings up dozens of books in the late seventeenth century with 'Miscellany Poems' in the titles. By the end of 1685, the bookseller J. Hindmarsh had, with assistance from Aphra Behn, assembled *Miscellany, Being A Collection of Poems by several Hands*, and Anthony Stephens brought out *Miscellany Poems and Translations. By Oxford Hands.* At first heavily weighed towards trans-lation, Tonson's volumes also include satire, theatrical epilogues and prologues, songs and other assorted verse. The final collected edition (1716) is not a reprint, but a selection from earlier volumes with addi-tional lyric poetry including some pre-Restoration work.[18] As a general overview of principles and practice, Gay's 'On a Miscellany of Poems, To Bernard Lintot' (1712) is entertaining. These instructions for concocting a miscellany, addressed to a rival of Tonson, invite being called a recipe, for Gay begins with a culinary metaphor:

> As when some skilful Cook, to please each Guest,
> Would in one Mixture comprehend a Feast,
> With due Proportion and judicious Care
> He fills his Dish with diff'rent sorts of Fare ...

He recommends a judicious combination of lyric, heroic and satiric verse, counsels that 'Translations should throughout the Work be sown' (l. 29), and then moves on to a catalogue of poets whose reputa-tions he thus confirms: Buckingham, Sheffield, Congreve, Prior, Waller, Addison, Garth, Pope. 'From these successful Bards collect thy Strains, / And Praise with Profit shall reward thy Pains' (ll. 87–8).

Grounds for reputation

In 1692, the popular bi-weekly *Athenian Mercury* printed the question, amusing to a modern eye, 'Whether Milton and Waller were not the best English Poets? and which the better of the two?' The answer is judiciously balanced:

> They were both excellent in their kind, and exceeded each other, and all besides. Milton was the fullest and loftiest, Waller the neatest and most correct Poet we ever had. But yet we think Milton wrote too little in Verse, and too much in Prose, to carry the Name of Best from all others. (Vol 5, no. 14, 16 January 1692)

Marvell, like Milton, seems to have written 'too much in Prose' for his poetic good. During his own lifetime, only ten of Marvell's poems were printed, and only five acknowledged by him. The posthumous *Miscellaneous Poems* (1681) attracted few buyers, and these were not prepared for the poems of pastoral dialogue and complaint, country house poems, or poems on love, the works that Graham Parry has called Marvell's 'tidying up and terminating the Caroline tradition, putting the finishing touches on various conventions, giving them one last perfect and unfollowable performance before the shadows of history close on them' (Parry 1985, 222). Satire was what contemporaries expected from Marvell. The 1681 volume sank almost without trace, not to surface to full enthusiastic approval until the twentieth century. Only Tonson seems to have had much sense of Marvell's lyric achievement; he printed nine of the lyrics in his 1716 *Miscellany*.

How can reputation be accurately gauged? Modern critics offer some contradictory views on which poets were most esteemed, and which were considered outmoded. Such matters are obviously interesting when considering transitions in tastes. Hugh Kenner asserts that by mid-century Herrick's work seemed old-fashioned, and notes that his 1648 collection *Hesperides* did not reach a second edition; he suggests that Herrick 'outlived ... the vogue of direct easy song' (1964, 284).[19] Statistics in Norman Ault's edition of *Seventeenth Century Lyrics from the Original Texts* could lead to a directly contrary judgment. Herrick's 'Gather ye rose-buds' (first printed in *Hesperides* 1648) is the most frequently reprinted lyric of any in Ault's anthology. Given, however, that 'Gather ye rose-buds' often appeared with William Lawes' setting, how much of its appeal was due to the poet and how much to the musician? How much is due to Playford, who kept Lawes' music before the public eye?

Theatrum poetarum, or A Compleat Collection of the Poets, Especially of The most Eminent of all Ages. The Ancients distinguish'd from the Moderns in their several Alphabets. With some Observations and Reflections upon many of them, particularly those of our own Nation. Together with a Prefatory Discourse of the Poets and Poetry in Generall (1675), by Milton's nephew Edward Phillips, is complete within limits. Phillips has not, he notes, gone 'so far as to condescend to the taking notice of every single-sheeted Pie-Corner Poet, who comes squirting out with an Elegy in mourning for every Great Person that dies'. In his estimation there is little to praise before the mid-century:

> As for the Antiquated & fallen into obscurity from their former credit & reputation, they are for the most part those that have written beyond the verge of the present Age, for let us look back as far as about 30 or 40 years, and we shall find a profound silence of the Poets beyond that time, except of some few Dramatists, of whose real worth the Interest of the now flourishing Stage, cannot but be Sensible ... nothing it seems relishes so well as what is written in the smooth style of our present Language taken to be of late so much refined. (**2)

He arranges his poets into ancients and moderns, separately paginated, with a special section at the end on 'Women among the Moderns Eminent for Poetry'. In Phillips' brief entries, Cowley and Waller are highly commended. Among earlier seventeenth-century poets, Quarles' emblems are contemptuously dismissed as 'the darling of our Plebeian Judgments', while Herbert's *Temple* is described as 'generally known and approved'. Of his uncle he hesitates to write effusively:

> *John Milton* ... how far he hath reviv'd the Majesty and true Decorum of Heroic Poesy and Tragedy: it will better become a person less related than myself, to deliver his judgement. (113–14)

More praise of Milton is, however, slipped into the entry on Edward Phillips' brother John, ' Nephew and Disciple of an Author of most deserved Fame late deceas't, being the exactest of Heroic Poets, (if the truth were well examin'd, and it is the opinion of many both Learned and Judicious persons) either of the Ancients or Moderns, either of our own or what ever Nation else' (114–15). In the pages on women poets, Phillips is generous to Aphra Behn, to Margaret (Cavendish), Duchess of Newcastle, and to Katherine Philips.

Poetic surveys of contemporaries, such as Rochester's 'An Allusion to Horace', can be suspect, since the stress of rivalries has to be taken into account. Commendatory verses which lard the preliminary pages of collected editions need several grains of salt, as do funeral elegies. When the young Addison produced 'An Account of the Greatest English Poets' (1694) his judgments may, however, be more or less a summary of received opinions. In 155 lines, he romps through a history of English poetry:

> Long had our dull Fore-fathers slept Supine,
> Nor felt the Raptures of the Tuneful Nine;
> 'Til *Chaucer* first, a merry Bard arose ...
> Old *Spenser* next, warmed with Poetic Rage,
> In Antique Tales amused a barb'rous Age ...

> Great *Cowley* then (a mighty Genius) wrote;
> O'er-run with Wit, and lavish of his Thought:
> His Turns too closely on the Reader press;
> He more had pleased us, had he pleased us less.
> One glitt'ring Thought no sooner strikes our Eyes
> With silent Wonder, but new Wonders rise ...

> But *Milton* next, with high and haughty Stalks,
> Unfettered in *Majestic Numbers* Walks;
> No vulgar *Heroe* can his Muse ingage
> Nor Earth's wide Scene confine his hallow'd Rage ...

> The courtly *Waller* next Commands thy Lays ...

More briefly, he reviews Roscommon (author of the poetic *Essay on Translated Verse*) and Denham, before pausing on 'artful *Dryden*' who is praised for his versatility, in comedy and tragedy, satire and heroic verse. Congreve and 'noble Montagu' round off the account.

Alternative sources of information about reputation may be found in early eighteenth-century dictionaries of quotations. In the last revised edition (1718) of Bysshe's *Art of English Poetry*, the top ten poets statistically (in ascending order, with number of extracts following the names) are: Lee 104, Rowe 116, Milton 117, Shakespeare 118,

Blackmore 125, Otway 127, Butler 140, Cowley 143, Pope 155 and Dryden 1201; almost five hundred of the Dryden quotations are from his translation of the *Aeneid*. Gildon's *Complete Art of Poetry* (1718) offers no challenges to Bysshe's estimates of poetic worth, except for adding passages from Spenser (Culler 1948, 868).

Individual reputations

Cleveland

Considered from a more distant perspective, who, in the second half of the seventeenth century, stands out as England's preeminent poet? Hugh Kenner once unequivocally claimed John Cleveland as 'the most popular poet of the mid-seventeenth century' (Kenner 1964, 284), although others would name Abraham Cowley. Assertions about contemporary repute stimulate inquiry in two directions. First, what evidence supports the claims? Secondly, given immediately striking differences between the qualities for which these poets were known and the styles of (now) better-known poets from near the end of the century, how much continuity or real change in taste can be perceived?

Kenner cites the large number of editions of Cleveland, twenty-five between 1647 and 1687. Further supportive evidence is provided in the early proliferation of reference books, defining or recording reputations. In *The History of the Worthies of England*, Thomas Fuller praises Cleveland as a master of 'Masculine Stile' and as

> A General Artist, Pure Latinist, Exquisite Orator, and (which was his Master-piece) Eminent Poet. His Epithets were pregnant with Metaphors, carrying in them a difficult plainness, difficult at the hearing, plain at the considering thereof. His lofty Fancy may seem to stride from the top of one Mountain to the top of another. (1662, 135–6)

In *Theatrum poetarum*, Edward Phillips gives Cleveland his due as a satirist on the king's behalf, describing him as foremost, both in time and in vigour, in attacking the Presbyterian party and the entire Scottish nation. An ironic note, however, is clear. Sounded when he identifies Cleveland as 'a Notable High soaring Witty Loyalist', it is amplified in the account of his reputation:

> In fine, so great a Man hath Cleaveland been in the Estimation of the generality, in regard his Conceits were out of the common road, and Wittily far fetch't, that Grave Men in outward appearance have not spar'd in my hearing to affirm him the best of English Poets, and let them think so still, who ever please, provided it be made no Article of Faith. (1675, 104–5)

On the one hand, this account verifies Cleveland's popularity. On the other, patronising indulgence towards 'the estimation of the generality' implies doubt that the measure of praise for figures of speech ('conceits' or elaborate imagery) should be their far-fetched originality. Reputation depends heavily, of course, on the degree to which a poet reflects and explores ideas and attitudes to which readers readily respond. Of the many editions of Cleveland published in the seventeenth century, most appeared in the 1650s and 1660s, when royalism and antagonism against the Scots were enough to attract buyers. All but five of the editions were published before 1670.

Today, one might well ask 'Who is Cleveland?' Or even, 'who is "Cleveland"?' His significance is partly an example of the question 'what is an author?': a person, a body of texts, a reputation, or a received notion about a particular manner or style; an image or a definition of a certain kind of writing. By 1677, a total of 147 poems had been printed as by Cleveland, and additional poems were attributed to him in manuscript commonplace books. Only in one edition, *Clievelandi vindiciae* (1677) prepared by two of Cleveland's former pupils at Cambridge, was there an attempt to weed the 'Genuine' works from 'the many False and Spurious Ones Which had usurped his Name'; the canon here shrinks to thirty-one poems. The standard modern edition is similarly slim: thirty poems, with thirteen more cautiously presented as 'probably' by Cleveland (1967, xxii–xli). Two-thirds of the material which first appeared under his name is thus discarded. A gap between possible understanding of 'Cleveland' in 1675 or thereabouts, and today, widens.

In the trimmed-down body of work, it is a challenge to find the far-fetched metaphors, what Dryden called 'common thoughts in abstruse words', for which he was known. Remarks on 'Clevelandisms' make him sound like a super-convoluted Donne, but the reputation and verses are not easily matched. Occasionally in the abrupt openings of a satire there is a family resemblance to Donne, but one which has more to do with a standard satiric dramatic situation – the exasperated outburst of a plain speaker who can stay contained no longer – than of direct imitation. In 'On the Powder Plot', a poem which may, or may not, be Cleveland's,[20] the approach is summed up:

> Satires run best when Clashing terms do meet,
> And Indignation makes them knock their feet.
> To be methodical in Verse, and rhyme
> In such invectives is the highest crime.
> Who Ever saw a fiery passion break
> But in abruptness? (ll. 5–10)

His reputation for rough satire meant that booksellers coupled his name with flat abuse. While in anthologies of the period poems are generally printed without attribution, an occasional name stands as a special recommendation, or as a signal for a kind of poem. Thus, in D'Urfey's *Wit and Mirth, or Pills to Purge Melancholy*, skeltonic verses beginning 'If you will be still, / Then tell you I will / Of a fusty old Gill, / That dwells under a Hill' appear as 'By Cleveland' (1719–20, III. 346–7). Poems describing ugly women go back a long time; they seem (on the basis of the number that occur in drolleries) to have been especially popular in the Restoration period, a conscious counter to flattery. The lines on Gill, however, are so straightforwardly repellent that they show the disadvantage of an acerbic reputation: 'Hair lousie with Nits, / She stinks i'th' Arm-pits'.

This reputation for abusiveness could, however, be used to good effect. A writer today much better known than Cleveland himself turns him into a fictional character in 'The Loyal Scot'. Marvell's poem depends on its contrast with the absolute scorn of Cleveland's 'The Rebel Scot', which contains what is probably Cleveland's best-known couplet, one which amused Samuel Johnson: 'Had Cain been Scot, God would have changed his doom / Not forced him wander, but confined him home'. In an elegy for Captain Douglas, who acted with fatal heroism in the Second Dutch War, Andrew Marvell imagines warlike ghosts gathering in the Elysian Fields to select

> Which of their poets should his welcome sing,
> And, as a favourable penance, chose
> Cleveland, on whom that task they would impose.
> He understood, but willingly addressed

His ready muse to court their noble guest.
Much had he cured the tumour of his vein,
He judged more clearly now, and saw more plain;
For those soft airs had tempered every thought,
And of wise Lethe he had took a draught. (4–10)

Converting Cleveland into a panegyrist gives the praise for this loyal
Scot an extra piquancy. Using Cleveland as a mouthpiece leaves room
for satiric bite in passages on church government, and Marvell echoes
Cleveland's hypothetical emendation of Cain's punishment when
contemplating what might have happened a bit later in the Old
Testament:

Instead of all the plagues, had bishops come,
Pharaoh at first would have sent Israel home. (119–20)

In the final lines, after Cleveland's explicit and generous apology to
Douglas for having written against the whole Scottish nation, the tone
shifts to genial, teasing friendship.

Here Douglas, smiling, said he did intend
After such frankness shown to be his friend,
Forewarned him therefore lest in time he were
Metempsychosed in some Scotch presbyter. (285–8)

This last line, completing the inversion of Cleveland's earlier views,
also neatly parodies his (reputed) fondness for long words.

Who, or what, then, was 'Cleveland', the most popular poet of the
1650s and 1660s? In summary one might use the name as a sign for
what was soon to become outmoded: a far-fetched, extravagant wit
giving way to a taste for what could be perceived as 'both natural and
new', and as a type of satire relying on blunt attack, to be superseded
by subtler, more sophisticated approaches.

Cowley

The reputation of Cowley has waned since Edward Phillips called him,
in 1675, 'the most applauded Poet of our Nation both of the present
and past Ages'. Given that applause came from Milton, Rochester and
Dryden, he should not be dismissed unread. Only Dryden, with a
patronising remark on Cowley as 'the darling of my Youth', implies

that he outgrew an immature infatuation. Institutionally, because of the organisation of university courses, he now tends to disappear in the crack between 'Metaphysical' poetry (where his imagery may ensure brief mention) and the eighteenth century. Major teaching anthologies seldom find space for more than his odes 'Of Wit' (the only Cowley poem in the Norton Anthology, 1993) and 'To Mr. Hobbes' (DeMaria includes both in his Blackwell volume, 1996).

'Bold', the term Cowley himself uses to describe Pindar, is a useful reminder that energy, not simply correctness, is a touchstone for admirable poetry in the second half of the seventeenth century and the beginning of the eighteenth. Pope's *Essay on Criticism* is at once the most precise and the most vigorous of statements rejecting mere precision as a poetic standard. The influence of Cowley, particularly through the fourteen odes he composed between 1651 and 1656, is alone reason to examine his work and consider its importance in the work of Killigrew, Dryden, Chudleigh, Pope and a host of other writers.

Reception of Cowley's unfinished epic *Davideis* (1656) marks a major shift in attitudes, within a single century, towards religious poetry. In Cowley's preface to his folio *Poems*, rhetorical questions juxtapose classical and Biblical stories: 'why will not the actions of *Sampson* afford as plentiful matter as the *Labours* of *Hercules*? Why is not *Jephtha's Daughter* as *good a woman* as *Iphigenia*?' Instead of the 'confused antiquated *Dreams* of senseless *Fables* and *Metamorphoses*', he proposes baptising poetry in Jordan (as Herbert had). Although he adds a caveat on unskilful artists, he is largely untroubled by the mingling of imagination and what Samuel Johnson in the next century will call 'awful' – that is awe-inspiring – truths (1656; Spingarn II. 88–90). The confidence and boldness with which Cowley, and after him Milton, can deal with religious materials marks one of the clear contrasts with the narrowing views of the eighteenth century, when Handel's oratorios were open to charges of impiety, and Johnson in his 'Life of Cowley' pronounced that in sacred history 'all amplification is frivolous and vain' (*Lives*, I. 49).[21]

At the outset, *Davideis* seems not so much frivolous as flat, despite the echo of Virgil:

> I sing the *Man* who *Judahs Sceptre* bore
> In that right hand which held the *Crook* before;
> Who from best *Poet*, best of *Kings* did grow;
> The two chief *Gifts* Heav'n could on *Man* bestow.

Reading habits nourished by new historicism, however, lead toward admiration for Cowley's tact in handling his announced double theme, political and poetical. Even if the epic had been complete, Cowley's plan was to end before David's accession to the throne, leaving implicit the providential inevitability of his reign. During the decade when Charles II had taken refuge in France, David's need to flee his country has extra force. Inset songs abound, and Cowley cleverly avoids assigning them all to the obvious musician, young David with his harp. The climax of Book I, introduced as if it were only a digression, is a psalm by Balaam, who, taught by his ass to acknowledge the error of his ways, returns to true allegiance.

Waller

Evidence for Waller's standing as 'one of the most fam'd Poets, and that not unworthily, of the present Age' (Phillips 1675, 36) is strong in the seventeenth and early eighteenth centuries. Statistics on numerous editions of his works and straightforward praise concur (Chernaik 1968, 5). Dryden speaks of Waller and Denham as 'these two Fathers of our English Poetry' ('Discourse concerning the Original and Progress of Satire', 1692). Pope in *An Essay on Criticism* sets up as an ideal 'the easy vigour of the line / Where Denham's strength and Waller's sweetness join'. The oxymoronic 'easy vigour' defines a combination of what is comfortable, poised, relaxed, with energy and power. Does Waller's sweetness need a combination with Denham's strength to achieve this ideal, or is Phillips' description of Waller's verse as 'smooth, yet strenuous' accurate?

In Rochester's survey of contemporary poets, 'An Allusion to Horace', Waller appears as preeminently a poet of praise. Some modulation occurs between Rochester's recognition of 'force and fire and fancy unconfined' to a triplet of verbs indicating the propagandist's artful presentation of things in the best possible light:

> Waller, by nature for the bays designed,
> With force and fire and fancy unconfined,
> In panegyrics does excel mankind.
> He best can turn, enforce, and soften things
> To praise great conquerors or to flatter kings. (ll. 54–8)

There is a sting in the line recalling that Waller wrote both for Cromwell and for Charles. In the service of Charles II, Waller introduced a new or modified genre into English verse. The price of this achievement, however, is that his poem became the background for a notable string of parodies. Setting out to celebrate the Duke of York's leadership at the Battle of Lowestoft (1665), one of the early naval engagements in the Second Dutch War, he gave a tweak to a strand of ekphrastic poetry that extends back to the shield of Achilles in the *Iliad* and to the painted temple walls of Carthage in the *Aeneid*. Following the lead of a recent Italian poem, Busenello's celebration of a Venetian naval victory (1656, translated Higgons 1658), Waller sets out, however, not to describe an artefact that purportedly already exists, but to give orders for creating it. His immediate gain is the energy of imperatives: 'First draw the sea' (l. 1) For the first quarter of the poem, a series of further imperatives drives description onwards, and solves problems of transition. Then, as in Homer, the idea of an artwork fades away as the poet seems to be caught up in a vision of figures moving, events unfolding in time. Much that the painter is earlier told to do could of course not be done in reality: 'Let thy bold pencil hope and courage spread, / Through the whole navy, by that hero led' (ll. 15–16). Willing suspension of literal-mindedness is required throughout. But the impossibility of capturing heroism in a static artefact is turned to advantage. When in the penultimate verse paragraph Waller dramatises a mock-apology to the painter who provides his major metaphor, he explores a distinction between what the verbal and visual arts can achieve which remains interesting long after smoke from the Battle of Lowestoft has settled. What can words and what can pictures do?

Within two years *Instructions to a Painter, for the Drawing of the Posture and Progress of His Majesty's Forces at Sea, under the Command of His Highness-Royal; together with the Battle and Victory obtained over the Dutch, June 3, 1665* attracted a flock of mocking imitations. The *Second Advice to a Painter* was followed by a Third, Fourth, Fifth and Sixth *Advice*, all anonymous. Marvell's *Last Instructions to a Painter*[22] was in fact far from the last. Dozens of other advice-to-a-painter poems appeared; it was a genre extensively practised until at least Blackmore's instructions to a tapestry-weaver in 1709.[23]

Satirists who took up Waller's poem and turned it to an attack on the government and the handling of the war had two major advantages. One is that – as in modern book-reviewing – ridicule is always easier than praise. Waller's classical allusions could be turned topsy-turvy. The satirists also had the advantage of facts. Lowestoft was not a great victory (although it might have been if the Duke of York had not been asleep at the crucial time for deciding whether to pursue the retreating Dutch fleet). When Waller compares the king's satisfaction after the battle to that of Octavius after Actium, the exaggeration of the compliment is all too obvious. The Duchess of York, who visited Harwich when the English ships retired there for supplies, might with a panegyrist's license be compared to Aphrodite, but the author of the *Second Advice* (probably Marvell, as Patterson 1978 persuasively argues) provides a stinging mock-compliment to the Duke and Duchess of York when he likens their parting at Harwich to that of Antony and Cleopatra. The *Last Instructions* ironically endow the Duchess (who was pregnant the the time of her marriage) with miraculous powers as she 'found how royal heirs might be matured / In fewer months than mothers once endured' (ll. 55–6).

The qualities for which Dryden especially praised Waller, a verse 'even, sweet, and flowing' (*An Essay of Dramatick Poesie*, 1668; 1962, I. 24) are not what those of us trained to enjoy Donne, or modern poets, find immediately exciting. What we have learned to hear as admirable and interesting is a tension between the speaking voice and a metrical pattern. It takes the careful suspension of impatience to savour the studied balance of Waller's couplets, which during his career tend increasingly towards pauses at midline, with closure at the end, combining native four-beat lines with the syllable counting of iambic pentameter (Allison 1962). Some retraining may be needed to appreciate what his first editor, Bishop Atterbury, attractively describes in the preface to *The Second Part of Mr. Waller's Poems* (1690):

> Before his time, men Rhym'd indeed, and that was all: as for the harmony of measure, and that dance of words, which good ears are so much pleased with, they knew nothing of it ... Besides, their Verses ran all into one another, and hung together, throughout a whole Copy, like the hooked Atoms, that compose a Body in Descartes. There was no distinction of parts, no regular stops, nothing for the ear to rest upon.

Despite a personal (or learned) taste for enjambment, I am lured by Atterbury's description towards understanding of what Waller did with the closed couplet.

> So that where-ever the natural stops of that were, he contriv'd the
> little breakings of his sense so as to fall in with 'em. And for that
> reason, since the stress of our Verse lies commonly upon the last
> Syllable, you'll hardly ever find him using a word of no force there ...
> he commonly closes with Verbs, in which we know the Life of
> Language consists.

Nonetheless, Waller in his maturity never wrote anything that to my
mind surpasses his early lyrics, especially 'Go lovely rose'. Born two
years earlier than Milton, whom he outlived by fourteen years, he
represents continuity between poetry of the early seventeenth
century and the eighteenth.

Rochester

In common with Cleveland, John Wilmot, second Earl of Rochester
(1647–80), had his name attached to a great many more poems than
he wrote. A drinking companion of the king, and the model for
Dorimant in Etherege's *The Man of Mode* (1676), the young aristocrat
can be cited as the supreme example of the Restoration court wit. He
may be best known now for uncensored exploration of sexual experience, such as his wry description of premature ejaculation in 'The
Imperfect Enjoyment'.[24] Those having no more than a slight acquaintance with Restoration poetry respond to his name with a nudge and a
wink, showing that they have picked up something of his reputation
for licentiousness. The reputation was established early, and
promoted by the publisher who gathered together cynical and sexually explicit poems under his name; one of his executors advertised in
The London Gazette for information about who was responsible for 'a
Libel of lewd scandalous Poems, lately Printed, under the name of the
Earl of Rochesters' (Vieth 1963, 60). In twentieth-century criticism as
in Victorian writing, one comes across offhand references to 'profane
wits like Rochester and Dorset' (Richetti 1977, 76), although in recent
decades much more discriminating and appreciative attention has
been given to the range of his achievements.

His name is not usually coupled with Marvell's. Different as the earl
and the MP for Hull were in behaviour and companions, their posthumous collections of poetry (1680 and 1681) combine lucidity and
simplicity of language with complexity of meaning. Variations on
well-known early seventeenth-century poems are prominent in some
of Rochester's shorter lyrics. 'Love and Life' ('All my past life is mine

no more') looks to be straight out of Donne's *Songs and Sonets*, an imitation of Donne's witty libertine defences of inconstancy, made explicitly 'metaphysical' as Rochester paraphrases Hobbes' views on time. 'A Song of a Young Lady to Her Ancient Lover', highly ambiguous in tone, expands Jonson's couplet on Charis – 'Of whose beauty it was sung / She shall make the old man young' – but Rochester's version is sung from the woman's point of view. In 'The Fall' ('How blest was the created state') Rochester, like Milton in *Paradise Lost*, builds on Saint Augustine's position that before the fall sexual experience was better, with no possibilities of the awkwardness and dismay explored in 'The Imperfect Enjoyment'. Instead of pursuing the history of ideas, a reader may be most struck by tone, reminded of writers from other periods and of poets who at first glance are very different. Similarities of temperament or of poetic tactics may be as striking as ideas or periods. 'The Fall' is poetry of statement, spare and painful. Some of Emily Dickinson's work creates an impression similar to that of its third quatrain:

> But we, poor slaves to hope and fear,
>   Are never of our joys secure;
> They lessen still as they draw near,
>   And none but dull delights endure.

Is Pope's criticism of poetic 'dull delight' in *An Essay on Criticism* a quotation, an allusion, or merely a sign of a common taste for oxymoron? Closer to home, Rochester's poem invites comparison with Marvell's 'The Definition of Love' with its terse tetrameters and paradoxical clarity, raw emotion and stark rationality in tandem.

Rochester's 'A Satyr against Mankind' neatly exposes the critical assumptions of a pompous questioner:

> What rage ferments in your degenerate mind
> To make you rail at reason and mankind? (ll. 58–9)

In some poems, Rochester plays with a stylised version of his own image as profligate and cynical, daring literal-minded interpreters to read them biographically. Only ironic distance between the breezy colloquial voice of 'To the Postboy' and the poet, however, makes possible its witty turn, when the question posed by 'a peerless peer' about the shortest way to hell is answered: 'by Rochester'. More obviously distanced and dramatised is the most elegantly shaped of his poems, 'Artemisa to Chloe. A Letter from a Lady in the Town to a Lady in the Country concerning the Loves of the Town'. Near its centre is a portrait of 'that wretched thing *Corinna*, who had run / Through all the sev'ral ways of being undone' (ll. 189–90). The elegant Ovidian name sits uneasily beside 'wretched thing'. A later summary phrase, 'Poor creature', hints at the prostitute's relation to her maker.

> Gay were the Hours, and wing'd with joy they flew,
> When first the Town her early Beauty knew:
> Courted, admired, and loved, with Presents fed;
> Youth in her Looks, and Pleasure in her Bed:
> Till Fate, or her ill Angel, thought it fit
> To make her dote upon a man of Wit:
> Who found 'twas dull to love above a day;
> Made his ill-natured jest, and went away.
> Now scorned of all, forsaken, and oppresed,
> She's a *Momento Mori* to the rest ... (ll. 193–202)

References to time, defining the brevity of Corinna's beauty, range from early gay hours through a day of love to the 'now' which stretches towards a skull's hollow durability when she is wretchedly reified as a reminder of death to the rest. Midway through the quoted passage, 'dote' and 'dull', placed at the same rhythmical point in their lines, point up the contrast between Corinna's attitude and that of her lover, a disparity soon to be made more obvious as he leaves jesting, and she is left scorned. In the phrase 'ill-natured jest', there is a flicker of connection between Rochester's satire and Pope's *Epistle to Dr. Arbuthnot*. As in Pope's portrait of Atticus, there is a hint of disappointment, even dismay, that cleverness is not naturally united with generosity.

Brilliant as the brief passage is, it is even more disquieting as part of a highly organised, highly concentrated three-part poem in three concentric, generically differentiated rings. Isolate the passage quoted above, and Corinna is a victim; she becomes a murderess. In a poem of only 264 lines, Rochester presents a tale within an episode within a letter. The first voice is that of Artemisa wrily sketching the risk a woman takes as a poet – 'Scorned if you fail and cursed if you succeed'. Aware that, for a woman, 'writing's a shame, / That whore is scarce a more reproachful name / Than poetess', she nonetheless continues and, for her friend's amusement, describes an unnamed 'fine lady' who has temporarily come up to town. This fine lady is also self-contradictory, voluble on fools but visibly foolish herself (making a fuss over a monkey after contemptuously dismissing her husband). In the midst of idle chatter, she relates Corinna's story as if its point were only women's ability to dominate. The unfolding of 'Artemisa to Chloe' involves readjusting and refining a view of all three of the major characters. When a feminist scholar asks 'Just what then, can be discerned in the poem about Rochester's attitudes toward women?' particularly careful analysis is required to avoid reductive generalisations, illustrating only what the critic starts by suspecting or assuming about gender and power relationships. How would one go about proving or disproving that Rochester's satires are 'less a means to contain aggression than a means to contain man's pain and vulnerability, and in addition, to gain power through wit and language in the articulation of that pain' (Nussbaum 1984, 74–5)? Similarly, it is easy enough to identify the period or climate of opinion which produces the assertion that 'Libertine wits like Rochester and Dorset tell us more about the inadequacy of their own promiscuity and dissipation than about their female targets. The fear of women and the self-hatred implicit in all misogynism are obtrusive in these lyrics' (Richetti 1977, 77). Unless the poems are to be used primarily to demonstrate the received ideas of an observer, it would be worth pausing to explore how alike Dorset and Rochester are, and to query 'all misogynism'.

Katherine Philips

> But if Apollo should design
>   A woman Laureat to make,
> Without dispute he would Orinda take,
>   Though Sappho and the famous Nine
>   Stood by, and did repine.
> (Abraham Cowley, 'On the Death of Mrs. Katherine Philips', ll. 37–41)

When, without her permission, a volume of *Poems* 'by the Incomparable, Mrs. K.P.' was printed early in 1664, Katherine Philips (1632–64) expressed in her letters extreme discomfort about having been exposed to public censure. In fact, 'the matchless Orinda' is rare in attracting little but praise. Commendatory verse epistles were addressed to her by the Earls of Orrery and of Roscommon, and by an unidentified 'Philo-Philippa'. Her early death by smallpox produced an outpouring of commendatory elegies, including tributes by Abraham Cowley and by Sir William Temple. When the highly principled John Evelyn refers to a performance before the king and queen of her translation of Corneille's *Horace*, he speaks of the tragedy as 'written by the virtuous Mrs. Philips' (*Diary*, 2 February 1668). Editions of her poems appeared in 1667, 1669, 1678 and 1710. An entry under 'Women among the Moderns Eminent for Poetry' in *Theatrum poetarum* presents her as

> the most applauded, at this time, Poetess of our Nation, either of the present or former Ages, and not without reason, since both her fame is of a fresh and lively date from the but late publisht Volume of her Poetical works, and those also of a style suitable to the humour and Genius of these times. (1675, 157)

How useful it would have been if this comment about style had been developed. What, in the 1670s, can be meant? Passionate celebration of female friendship is her major theme. That hardly seems to be the spirit of the age, although just possibly it might be compared to the intense male bonding Dryden presents on stage, from *The Indian Queen* to *All for Love*. Katherine Philips could turn her hand to witty occasional verses in heroic couplets ('On the numerous access of the English to wait upon the King in Holland') or panegyric ('On the death of the Queen of Bohemia'). I think it more interesting, however, that a number of her poems, like Rochester's, are closely related to well-known publications of the early seventeenth century. In both meter and delicacy, the touching epitaph for her infant son recalls Ben Jonson's laments for his own children.

> What on Earth deserves our trust?
> Youth and Beauty both are dust.
> Long we gathering are with pain,
> What one moment calls again.
> Seven years childless, marriage past,
> A Son, a son is born at last;
> So exactly lim'd and Fair,
> Full of good Spirits, Mien, and Air,
> As a long life promised,

Yet, in less than six weeks, dead.
Too promising, too great a mind
In so small room to be confin'd:
Therefore, fit in Heav'n to dwell,
He quickly broke the Prison shell.
So the subtle Alchemist,
Can't with Hermes seal resist
The powerful spirit's subtler flight,
But 'twill bid him long good night.
And so the Sun, if it arise
Half so glorious as his Eyes,
Like this Infant, takes a shroud,
Buried in a morning Cloud.[25]

Having avoided alliteration in the opening two couplets, she emphasises long anticipation, and after that rejoicing, by the stress on 'Seven
years' and the touching repetition of 'A Son, a son'. In the statement
of desolation, many lines stop on a word of bleak plainness: dust,
pain, dead. With the turn to muted consolation, which occupies
slightly more than half the poem, there is more freedom in imagery.
Release from the earth to heaven becomes a rebirth, and the progressive movement from shell to alchemist's laboratory to natural world
an imaginative enlargement. The cloud of the final line is precisely
poised between mourning and morning.

Donne's *Songs and Sonets* lie behind the lyric 'Friendship's
Mysteries, to my dearest Lucasia' which was set to music by Henry
Lawes. From the opening imperative and rush toward argument, she
imitates the style and tone of the earlier poet.

Come, my Lucasia, since we see
  That Miracles Men's faith do move
By wonder and by prodigy
  To the dull, angry world let's prove
  There's a Religion in our Love.

Within the six stanzas, she collects images and paradoxes from
Donne, transforming them into her own particular version of ecstasy.

Our hearts are doubled by the loss,
  Here Mixture is Addition grown;
We both diffuse, and both ingross:

And we whose minds are so much one,
Never, yet ever are alone. (stanza 3)

Although in routine complimentary verses 'To her royal highness the Duchess of York, on her command to send her some things I had wrote', she offers apologies as 'an artless Muse', such a modesty topos was suspect as early as in Chaucer's day.

Her importance is only partially a matter of her achievement. For women poets of the next half-century, the two major models were the virtuous Orinda and the more scandalous Astraea, Aphra Behn (Medoff 1992). Outside the theatre, Orinda was a safer model, her influence claimed by Ann Killigrew and by Ann Finch, Lady Winchilsea, among many others. Behn herself wished to be ranked with Katherine Philips. When she translated the sixth book of Cowley's 'Of Plants', she inserted an address to the laurel tree, asking to be numbered among poets:

I by a double right thy Bounties claim,
Both from my Sex, and in *Apollo's* Name:
Let me with *Sappho* and *Orinda* be
Oh ever sacred Nymph, adorn'd by thee;
And give my Verses Immortality. (1689, 143)

While both Cowley and Behn assume Philip's association with the laurel, in Swift's *The Battle of the Books* (1704) the single woman poet who appears is Behn. Here, however, given the the mock-heroic frame in which modern authors appear in assertive combat against the ancients, Swift's choice of the 'Aphra the Amazon' (paralleling Virgil's focus on one female warrior, Camilla) is apt.

More women wrote poetry than those who publicly acknowledged it, even within a limited circle. Seven poems in Lady Rochester's handwriting, four with deletions and modifications indicating that they are her own work in progress, came to light only in 1935 (Vieth 1963, 210–12). Lucy Hutchinson's authorship of *Order and Disorder; Or; The World Made and Undone. Being Meditations upon the Creation and Fall; as it is recorded in the beginning of Genesis*, published anonymously in 1679, has recently been persuasively argued (Norbrook 1999). Details such as the description of pregnancy and childbirth – 'pangs that prepare / The violent openings of life's narrow door' – are fascinating even in isolation. Alongside her translation of Lucretius, which stayed in manuscript until 1996, the lengthy meditations on Genesis quicken interest in further explorations of her work.

Pope

The career of Alexander Pope, like that of Milton, is cut in half by the dates of *Transitions 1650–1720*. There is, however, a curious symmetry in Pope's career, with a major mock-epic, verse essay, and Homeric translation before 1720, and also after. He was not yet out of his twenties when he put together a collected *Works* (1717), partly as he claims in the preface to distinguish poetry which is really his from inferior work attributed to him. One of the striking characteristics of his poetry is its homage to a host of earlier writers. Among the longer early works, the *Pastorals* follow in the footsteps of Virgil and of Spenser; *Windsor Forest* is in the line of Virgil's *Georgics* and of Denham's *Cooper's Hill*. Among his 'Imitations of English Poets' are tributes to the founding fathers Chaucer and Spenser, and more recent figures: Waller (seven imitations), Cowley (four) and the Earl of Dorset (two). The paradoxes of 'On Silence' are an imitation of the Earl of Rochester's 'On Nothing'. The 'Ode on Solitude' ('Happy the man, whose wish and care / A few paternal acres bound ...') sums up a long tradition of retirement poems; Pope claimed to have written it when he was only twelve.

The early decades of his poetic career include the romantic condensed narrative of 'Elegy to the Memory of an Unfortunate Lady' and the intense passion of *Eloisa to Abelard*. Adapting Ovid's form of an imaginary letter for retelling of a famous mediaeval story, Pope dramatises Eloisa's tension between erotic and religious fervour. In a couplet addressed to the statues of her convent's shrines, she sums up her failure to find serenity:

> Tho' cold like you, unmov'd, and silent grown,
> I have not yet forgot myself to stone. (ll. 23–4)

Commanding a wide variety of tones, Pope opens *An Essay on Criticism* with wry judiciousness, posing the question of which is worse, a bad critic or a bad poet. As he surveys the qualities needed by a good critic, and a good poet, Pope reviews controversies of neoclassical criticism, and wittily plays with some of its recurrent terms. When he damns a line which is 'Correctly cold and regularly low' (l.

240), the word *regularly* is a telling pun on rules and on monotony. In the early eighteenth century it was still possible for the word *wit* to indicate mental power in general, a meaning preserved now in the term 'half-wit'. Wit as mere cleverness with words, at the other extreme, had been recently attacked by Sir Richard Blackmore (reprieved from annihilation in Swift's *Battle of the Books* on the grounds that he was a good physician though a bad poet). Within this spectrum of meanings, Pope plays especially with the distinctions between wit and judgment made by Locke and Hobbes. In their writings, *wit* means capacity for bringing disparate things together, an ability central to poetic imagination and especially to metaphor, while *judgment* means ability to make distinctions. Only in the best of possible writing, poetic or critical, is there a happy marriage between them, 'For Wit and Judgment often are at strife, / Though meant each other's Aid, like Man and Wife' (11. 82–3).

In imitation of Horace's *Ars poetica*, Pope gives the organisation of *An Essay on Criticism* an air of conversational casualness. In contrast *The Rape of the Lock*, in its final five-canto form, attracts attention to its precise shapeliness, even as it simultaneously fulfils and inverts 'rules' for heroic poetry. There are many precedents, classical and modern, for mock-epic, including the game of chess in Smith and Mennes' first drollery. None, however, is as playful and as serious as this. Pope constructs multiple little jokes on form. The five cantos correspond to Davenant's dramatic model for *Gondibert*, while the time-scale, noon to evening, not only shrinks the span of years appropriate to epic, but exactly halves the day allowed to a neoclassical play. The great traditions of Western poetry, from Homer through Milton, resonate throughout the ridiculously inflated incidents of a voyage from London to Hampton Court, card-table and tea-table, and the snipping of a lock of hair. As in *Gulliver's Travels*, however, the miniature (precise or trivial) and the large (grand or gross) are not seen from a single perspective. Pope's subject and his method is disproportion. The poem is both an indictment and a celebration. All the world dwindles to Belinda's dressing table, but infinite riches in a little room can flash forth again, as 'all Arabia breathes from yonder box' (I. 134). The transformation of Belinda's hair to a comet, in the final canto, is a preposterous miracle, like this triumph of occasional poetry over its occasion.

Notes

1. For discussion of *Paradise Regained* and *Samson Agonistes* in relation to 'Milton's continuing engagement with the heroic drama', see Steven N. Zwicker, in MacLean (1995), 137–58.
2. 'As for Mr Milton, whom we all admire with so much justice, his subject is not that of an heroic poem, properly so called. His design is the losing of our happiness; his event is not prosperous, like that of all other epic works' ('A Discourse Concerning the Original and Progress of Satire', 1693; 1962, II. 84).
3. 'And God said, Let us make man in our image ... So God created man in his own image, in the image of God created he him; male and female created he them' (Genesis 1: 16–17).
4. *Upon Appleton House* is included neither in Wain's Oxford Anthology: *Spenser to Crabbe* (1990) nor in DeMaria's Blackwell textbook *British Literature 1640–1789* (1996); in both cases, the longest poem by Marvell is 'An Horatian Ode' (120 lines).
5. For a review of 'The Yale Poems on Affairs of State Thirty-Five Years Later', see DeLuna *et al.* (1998).
6. Steiner (1975) provides a useful anthology of contemporary comments on translation, including the Earl of Roscommon's verse *Essay on Translated Verse* (1684). Dryden's prefaces are a good place to begin; among others, the Preface to *Sylvae: or the Second Part of Poetic Miscellanies* (1685) engagingly analyses a translator's choices. The quantity of translations from Greek and Latin poetry is shown by Gillespie (1992).
7. Virgil, as literally translated in the Loeb Classics volume: 'we prayed to the great gods, then, with our parts allotted, pour round him ... And so at last we gladly avenged our comrades' shades'.
8. These are the first two of the sixty-four quatrains of 'Chevy-Chase':

    > God prosper long long our Noble King,
    >   our lives and safeties all
    > A woeful hunting once there did
    >   in Chevy-Chase befall.

    > To drive the Deer with Hound & Horn
    >   Earl Percy took his way;
    > The child may rue that is unborn
    >   the hunting of that day.

    Bold's version of 'Chevy Chase' also appeared in the second Dryden-Tonson *Miscellany* (1685).

9. *Gradus ad Parnassum* (1685) and *Synopsis communium locorum* (1700) are briefly described in Bradner (1940), 3.

10. Archaisms, neologisms and foreign words not yet fully absorbed into English were all attacked on the grounds of obscurity or indecorum. Dryden disapproved of Milton's vocabulary to the extent that it resembled Spenser's deliberate antiquarianism. James Wright in *Country Conversations* comments that 'mob' is 'a word but of Late Use, and not sufficiently Naturalised to appear in a serious Poem' (1694, 42).

11. The bibliographical relationship between this collection, *Ratts Rhimed to Death* (1660), and *Rump* (1660) is analysed by Brooks 1939.

12. For an overview of patronage, see Griffin (1996). The standard gift from patron to dedicatee was £10–£20, but sometimes much more (Griffin 1996, 39).

13. While care was less often taken, then than now, in the establishment of a reliable text, much attention was often paid to visual presentation. Engraved portraits of the author are common, commendatory verses still more so. These are a further incentive to consult early editions.

14. 'From dusty shops neglected authors come, / Martyrs of pies, and relics of the bum.' (Dryden, *MacFlecknoe*, ll. 100–1)

15. In their editions of Rochester, Veith (1968) and Ellis (1994) adopt 'least' and 'heart'; Barbara Everett proposes that 'the conclusive ring of "at last they hate" is both more Rochesterian and more generally Augustan' (1982, 28). Her emendation may have been influenced by the verbal sequence 'first ... then' five lines earlier in the poem.

16. Fuller bibliographical information is given in Case (1935) and in Day and Murrie (1940).

17. Suckling's editors, explaining why the poem cannot possibly be by him, note that Jonson alludes to it in *The Alchemist* (1610) and that it occurs in twenty-two early manuscripts in the British Library and the Bodleian Library, often dated 1609, the year of Suckling's birth (Suckling 1971, cv).

18. Raymond Havens' analysis of the shifting proportion of classical materials and lighter English poems in the Tonson miscellanies provides a fascinating and reliable basis for studies in taste and economics (1929). Barbara M. Benedict's study of early modern anthologies, while enticing in its general thesis that anthologies help to 'form and reform canons, confirm literary reputations, and establish taste and cultural literacy for generations of readers' (1996, 3), can be misleading on details.

19. In Edward Phillips' *Theatrum poetarum* (1675), the entry is dismissive, thus supporting Kenner's assessment: '*Robert Herric* [follows Robert Heath], a writer of Poems of about the same standing and the same

Rank in fame with the last mention'd, though not particularly influ-
enc'd, by any Nymph or Goddess, except his Maid Pru. That which is
chiefly pleasant in these Poems, is now and then a pretty Floury and
Pastoral gale of Fancy, a vernal prospect of some Hill, Cave, Rock, or
Fountain; which but for the interruption of other trivial passages might
have made up none of the worst Poetic Landskips'.

20. It is placed among 'Poems Probably by Cleveland' in the modern
     edition by Morris and Wittington (1967).

21. Early in the eighteenth century Dennis defends 'joining Poetry with
     true Religion' as a way of surpassing even the greatest ancient writers
     (*The Advancement and Reformation of Modern Poetry*, 1701), but
     Shaftesbury anticipates Johnson's concern about about whether
     Biblical material is 'too sacred to be submitted to the Poet's Fancy'
     (1710, 190).

22. After circulation in manuscript from 1667, this appeared, as 'Marvell's
     Further Instructions to a Painter' in *The Third Part of the Collections of
     Poems on Affairs of State* (1689).

23. See Osborne (1949) for a full annotated list. Waller's 'Instructions' and
     a series of the other 'Advice' poems are conveniently available in the
     first volume of *Poems on Affairs of State*.

24. For a brief account of eight other seventeenth-century poems, French
     or English, on premature ejaculation, including Etherege's 'The
     Imperfect Enjoyment' and Aphra Behn's 'The Disappointment', see
     Quaintance (1963).

25. How problematical modernising can be is exemplified here. While
     changing 'Meen' to 'Mien' or 'Alchimist' to 'Alchemist' seems practi-
     cal, how is the word 'lim'd' (l. 7) to be read: limbed or limned (drawn,
     painted, illuminated)?

3 Publike Calamities and Publike Sports

As is often the case, what everyone knows is not quite true. Asked about drama after 1642, the proverbial schoolboy would confidently reply that Puritans had put a stop to that. Certainly the Parliamentary resolution of 2 September 1642 rings with decisive phrases:

> whereas publike Sports doe not well agree with publike Calamities, nor publike Stage-playes with the Seasons of Humiliation, this being an Exercise of sad and pious solemnity, and the other being Spectacles of pleasure, too commonly expressing lacivious Mirth and Levitie: It is therefore thought fit, and Ordeined by the Lords and Commons in this Parliament Assembled, that while these sad Causes and set times of Humiliation doe continue, publike Stage-playes shall cease, and bee forborne. Instead of which, are recommended to the people of this Land, the profitable and seasonable Considerations of Repentance, Reconciliation, and peace with God, which probably may produce outward peace and prosperity, and bring againe Times of Joy and Gladnesse to these Nations. ('An Ordinance of both Houses, for the suppressing of Stage-Playes' 1642, facsimile in *Commonwealth Tracts 1625–1650*)

The 'Closing of the Theatres' was, however, not as conclusive as those words announce. The very existence of a series of further Parliamentary measures against the stage after the 1642 resolution indicates that there was something to put down, and that attempts to prevent public performances were, repeatedly, not successful for very long. Whatever the attractions of Repentance and Reconciliation, or the probability that they might lead toward Joy and Gladness, official ordinances did not fully wean the public from less edifying amusements.[1] Near the end of the decade, Parliament was continuing to take measures against drama. 'An Ordinance ... for the utter suppression and abolishing of all Stage-Playes and Interludes', passed on 9

February 1648, was sweeping in its attack. It called for sheriffs to 'pull down and demolish all Stage-Galleries, Seats and Boxes'. Actors were to be imprisoned and fined for a first offence, whipped for a second; a spectator 'at any such Stage-play, or Interlude, hereby prohibited, shall for every time he shall be so present, forfeit and pay the summe of five shillings to the use of the poor' (facsimile in *Commonwealth Tracts*). Nonetheless, although the interiors of three London play-houses were destroyed in 1649, some actors were rash enough, and some audiences eager enough, to keep at least occasional perfor-mance alive. On Tuesday 22 January 1650 the Red Bull Theatre in St John's Street was raided, the actors imprisoned, their costumes and properties confiscated, and the names of the spectators taken down. Lively accounts of the incident in royalist periodicals are sympathetic towards the actors – 'alas poor players they are acting their parts in prison' – and scathing in their descriptions of the parliamentary spoilsports: 'Me thinks the Supreme Poppet-players of State should have something else in their minds then suppressing Playes' (*Mercurius pragmaticus*, 22–29 January 1650; Hotson 1928; 1962, 46).

Continued vigilance was needed by those who opposed the stage. In February 1654 once again, 'instructions were given for suppressing of a wicked sort of people called Hectors, and Plays, and other wicked disorders' (Hotson 1928, 54). Intermittent performances nonetheless continued. As in other centuries, the pleasures or disorders of the prosperous classes attracted less interference than those of citizens further down the social scale. To entertain the Portuguese ambas-sador in 1653, James Shirley provided a masque entitled *Cupid and Death*. There are no reports of attempts to suppress private theatri-cals, such as those in which Dorothy Osborne participated (*Letters*, 10 July 1654). Professional actors performing commercially, however, needed to be discrete. James Wright reports in *Historia histrionica* that 'in *Oliver's* time they used to Act privately, three or four Miles, or more, out of Town, now here, now there, sometimes in Noblemens Houses, in particular *Holland-house* at *Kensington*, where the Nobility and Gentry who met (but in no great Numbers) used to make up a Sum for them' (1699, 9). More audaciously, a group at the Red Bull Theatre risked a series of raids (including one in December 1654 when they were playing Beaumont and Fletcher's *Wit without Money*, and other interruptions in May and September 1655), these interventions providing hard evidence about how resilient the actors and audiences were. A report in *The Weekly Intelligencer*, 11–18 September 1655 is self-consciously clever in its description of events:

> This Day proved Tragical to the *Players* at the *Red Bull*, their Acting being against an Act of Parlament, the Soldiers secured the persons of some of them who were upon the Stage, and in the Tyrin-house, they seized also upon their cloaths in which they acted, a great part whereof was very rich, it never fared worse with the spectators then at this present, for those who had monies payed their five shillings apeece, those who had none to satisfie their forfeits, did leave their Cloaks behind them, the Tragedy of the Actors, and the Spectators, was the Comedy of the soldiers. There was abundance of the Female Sex, who not able to pay 5s. did leave some gage or other behind them, insomuch that although the next day after the Fair, was expected to be a new *Faire* of Hoods, of Aprons, and of Scarfs, all which their poverty being made known, and after some check for their Trespasse, were civilly restored to the Owners. (Hotson 1928, 56–7)

This 'tragical' day turned to comedy at least for those whose poverty brought out the chivalry of the soldiers; an incident outside London two years earlier ended much less happily. When, at Witney in Oxfordshire, a group of amateurs from a neighbouring town staged the Elizabethan romance *Mucidorus* (published 1598, sometimes attributed to Shakespeare, Greene, Peele or Lodge) on the upper floor of the White Hart Inn, three or four hundred eager viewers flocked to see it, so many that halfway through the performance the floor collapsed, leaving six dead and dozens severely wounded. Under the title *Tragi-Comoedia* (1653), the Reverend John Rowe published an account of the disaster, complete with a sketch of the hall's construction and an analysis of which of the two beams supporting the floor broke. His emphasis, however, is not on material causes but on divine judgment: 'Do not quarrell with the Almighty for setting you up as the publik Theatre whereon he would manifest his holynesse, justice, & other Attributes to the world' (¶2^r). Particularly indignant about ridicule of 'all Godly persons under the name of Puritans' and about blasphemous language on stage, Rowe fervently denounces dramatic performances:

> Stage-playes are stuff'd with scurrilous, filthy, unbecomming speeches, passages, and gestures: they are the incentives, & occasions

of all lust; stage-playes are the very acting of wickednesse, they are a teaching of men to be vile, and wicked. What are all your Comedies, but onely bringing the wanton lusts of men upon the stage? as if so be the hearts of men were not corrupt enough by nature, but they must needs see lewednesse, and folly acted before their eyes, to provoke them to be wicked. (1653, 42)

The crowd at Witney for whom the play 'had a sad *Catastrophe*' (¶¶1ᵛ) and Rowe's diatribe are evidence of the enthusiasm drama provoked – in opposite directions.

   Restrictions on plays contributed to the development of a sub-genre, the 'droll'. Advertising that they had been acted in public and private, at fairs, in halls and taverns, the publisher Francis Kirkman collected some of these pieces, excerpts from work by Elizabethan and Jacobean dramatists. He printed two volumes of comic lollipops as *The Wits, or Sport upon Sport* (1662, 1673) with a preface briefly explaining their history:

> When the publique Theatres were shut up, and the Actors forbidden to present us with any of their Tragedies, because we had enough of that in earnest; and Comedies, because the Vices of the Age were too lively and smartly represented; then all that we could divert our selves with were these humours and pieces of Plays (1673, 1932, 267–8).

Although presented 'by stealth too, and under pretence of Rope-dancing, or the like' these short pieces became so popular that Kirkman claims he saw spectators turned away from the Red Bull playhouse for lack of room. In a table of contents to his first volume, he gives each 'droll' in *The Wits* a title of its own, and usually identifies the play from which it comes. He never bothers to name the play-wright; thus '*The Grave-makers*, out of *Hamlet P. of Denm.*' In '*The Imperick*, out of *the Alchymist*' the clockwork precision of Jonson's plotting is abandoned, but satire against the pious Ananias retained. All that remains of *A Midsummer Night's Dream* is 'Bottom the Weaver'. The effect is something like hearing only the livelier move-ments of a symphony, divorced from their context, an experience not uncommon in modern radio broadcasting.

   Surprisingly, despite the legal difficulties, there was enough opti-mism among theatrical entrepreneurs to encourage investment in buildings. Although soldiers had deliberately wrecked the interior of three theatres, the Fortune, the Cockpit and Salisbury Court in March 1649, before two years were up William Beeston was investing considerable sums in repairing and fitting the Cockpit, and taking 'Prentices, & Covenant Servants to instruct them in the quality of acting, & fitting them for the Stage, for which the said premises were so repaired & amended, to his great charge & damage'. A few years later, in 1656, Sir William Davenant persuaded four 'adventurers' to venture their capital on a project 'to build a structure for representations and shows' on land near the Charterhouse (Hotson, 43, 96, 139–40). Although the proposed theatre was not completed, the possibility of raising hundreds of pounds for such a scheme indicates that drama was far from dead.

Davenant (1608–68) is significant in a number of ways. As poet, playwright and theatre manager, he embodies continuity between Caroline (Charles I) and Carolean (Charles II) drama. Shakespeare was his godfather. Before the civil war, he wrote at least twelve plays, and he collaborated with Inigo Jones in staging *Salmacida Spolia* (1640), the last major masque at court. As a theatre manager, he governed the King's and Queen's company at the Cockpit in Drury Lane (June 1639 and following), and Charles I granted him permission to build a new playhouse, although that entrepreneurial project was not achieved until the Restoration. His life has details that could be called dashing, dramatic, indeed 'cavalier'.[2] Knighted by Charles I at the siege of Gloucester, he spent some time with Charles II in Paris. The alternative form of his name, D'Avenant, emphasises fashionable links with France. He was on his way to America as royal appointee for the governing of Maryland when captured by the Commonwealth navy, and then spent some time imprisoned in the Tower (1650–52), by report released through Milton's intervention. During the second half of the Protectorate period, Davenant tested the narrow path between official distrust of the theatres and a persistent popular appetite for staged entertainment. His first experiment, including scenes and music, but no action, was presented in a hall of his own London residence.

Cautiously entitled, 'The First Day's Entertainment at Rutland House' (1656) is only mildly theatrical. Here, as often with only a script rather than the bustle and buzz of an audience, the extravagance of lights and decorations, the swelling and the varied pace of music, a page offers very bare evidence of why the evening was a success. Conflict is reduced to single declamations; there is no dialogue and no action. Musical interludes and emblematic back-drops would to some extent relieve the austerity of the organisation: two sets of paired speeches. A figure representing the cynical philoso-pher Diogenes rails against drama, and the classical comic playwright Aristophanes (predictably, but not as wittily as readers of the *Symposium* might expect) speaks for the stage. The second pair of declamations offers more amusement. Setting against one another a visiting Frenchman complaining about London, and an Englishman describing Paris, Davenant provides a freshly detailed view both of the two capitals and of national stereotypes. Pepys and his French wife read the text aloud, to the merriment of both (*Diary*, 7 February 1664).

Considerably more adventurous, Davenant's second production in 1656, *The Siege of Rhodes*, is often mentioned along with Flecknoe's *Ariadne* (1654) as pioneering work in English opera. Performed first in the semi-private premises of Rutland House and later, more boldly, at the Cockpit in Drury Lane some time in 1658 or 1659, it was also Davenant's first production at Lincoln's Inn Fields after the Restoration. Since for the 1661 performances he changed recitative to speech, the completely sung version may have been devised to evade the regulations against stage-plays. In any case, there are enough innovations to make the play significant historically, even if it were not (as it is) entertaining in itself. Lavish scenery marks a link between court masques and Restoration theatres' showy productions, as does the appearance of female performers. The script, historical rather than mythological, set against a background of the Crusades, with an exotic setting, generous gestures by a non-Christian foe, and strong binary patterns of love and jealousy, makes a good starting point for the grandiose Restoration genre of 'heroic drama'; Dryden acknowl-edges its importance in his preface to *The Conquest of Granada* (1672). Four quarto editions (1656, 1659, 1663, 1670) demonstrate the impact and continuing popularity of *The Siege of Rhodes*.

The two earliest quartos include a prefatory letter To the Reader, apologising for the defects of the staging at Rutland House where, confined to a space eleven feet by fifteen feet, 'including the places of passage reserved for the Music', five changes of scenery represented 'the Fleet of Solyman the Magnificent, his Army, the Island of Rhodes, and the varieties attending the Siege of the City'. In this catalogue the disproportionately small space is less memorable than the splendours Davenant tried to squeeze into it. Riches in a little room characterise the whole project. The story is copious, but concentrated into a plot which can be presented with seven singers and a chorus. Music was composed by 'the most transcendent of England in that Art' (Henry Lawes, Matthew Locke, and Henry Cook); visual effects were provided by the designer John Webb, who had worked with Inigo Jones. Full of grand gestures and noble characters, the script also includes a jolly chorus of Soldiers whose final taunt to the Turks is that 'we drink good Wine, and you drink but Coffee'.

Restoration editions of the play include a dedication to the Earl of Clarendon, Lord High Chancellor of England. With a neatly turned reference to Lord Clarendon's judiciousness, Davenant presents his characters 'to be arraign'd at your Tribunal', but complains of those who persecute all dramatic poetry:

> And yet whilst those vertuous Enemies deny *heroique Plays* to the Gentry, they entertain the People with a Seditious *Farce* of their own counterfeit Gravity ... My Lord, it proceeds from the same mind not to be pleas'd with Princes on the Stage, and not to affect them in the Throne; for those are ever most inclin'd to break the Mirrour who are unwilling to see the Images of such as have just authority over their guilt. (1663, A2ᵛ–A3ʳ)

Along with the theatrical imagery, an interesting point about Davenant's dedication is his stress on the positive moral effects of drama. His final paragraph uses the old rhetorical device *occupatio*, drawing attention to topics in the process of claiming not to discuss them:

> If I should proceed, and tell your Lordship of what use Theatres have anciently been, and may be now, by heightening the Characters of Valour, Temperance, Natural Justice, and Complacency to Government, I should fall into the ill manners and indiscretion of ordinary Dedicators, who go about to instruct those from whose abilities they expect protection.

Curiously, given that 'Restoration drama' is often equated with bawdiness, the practitioners of the drama, particularly in the early years, emphasise its moral usefulness. Indeed, the introduction of actresses, many of whom became notorious as mistresses of noble, even royal, patrons, was originally presented as a reform, a device for eliminating the offensiveness of having male actors appear in women's clothing.[3]

As a theatrical entrepreneur, Davenant survived into the Restoration period. There was a flurry of activity in 1660–61, among builders and courtiers. When the royal palace at Whitehall was refurbished, one of the first projects was renovation of its theatre, the Cockpit at Court. On 19 November 1660, the king saw Jonson's *The Silent Woman* performed there; a payment to the Master Carpenter was made for the 'extraordinary pains' of making the theatre ready.[4] Despite the king's fondness for the stage, restrictions on theatrical activity were not simply swept away in 1660. Privilege and control, not freedom, were established. In principle, only Thomas Killigrew and William Davenant with the groups of actors they gathered under the sponsorship of Charles II and his brother James (thus called The King's Company and the Duke's Company) could legally produce plays in London. In practice, the situation was not quite as tidy as the king's exclusive patents to Davenant and Killigrew indicate. Early in the Restoration, several groups of actors were active in London. George Jolly, who led a company of travelling players on the continent during the Commonwealth period, brought them home. Intermittently the king granted special licences to foreign theatrical companies visiting London (Rosenfeld 1955). At 'nurseries' for the training of young actors plays were publically performed. And although London was the centre of theatrical activities there were amateur and professional performances elsewhere too. Dublin had a particularly notable permanent theatre in which Katherine Philips' *Pompey*, translated from Corneille, was produced.

From a distance of several centuries, squabbles over who should control the theatres may make amusing reading. How does an angry man accuse the king of unfairness? The petitions of Sir Henry Herbert, Master of the Revels under Charles I and in his own eyes still the rightful authority over the stage, show that it can be done with some forcefulness. Reading *The Dramatic Records of Sir Henry Herbert* is similar to reading a play; the script is augmented by imaginative projections of character and tone of voice. Some compromises were worked out. Herbert received twenty shillings from the acting companies for licensing an old play, and forty shillings for a new play. Until Queen Anne's death, the Master of the Revels continued to act as official censor, although his interventions usually amounted to no more than removal of blasphemous language.[5] Early in the Restoration period, the king's intervention in theatrical matters was apt to be positive rather than negative. He lent his coronation robes to the players for a production of Davenant's *Love and Honour*, and he sometimes suggested topics to courtier playwrights. In the preface to *The Adventures of Five Hours* (1663, printed 1671) Sir Samuel Tuke notes that his adaptation from a Spanish play was 'recommended to me by His Sacred Majesty, as an Excellent Design.' Frequent visits by the king to the public theatres, attested in the Lord Chamberlain's records, helped make them fashionable. In the later years of Charles II, however, when uneasiness about the succession of his Catholic brother was widespread, censorship was a more serious matter. Nathaniel Lee's *The Massacre of Paris* (written *c.* 1679–81) was banned; a play about the extermination of the Huguenots was provocative at the time when James was the nearest legitimate heir to the throne, and it was not acted until 1689 after the accession of William and Mary.

Fairs and trials

Competition for the two patent theatres came from a variety of quarters: puppet-shows, fairs, musical concerts (established by John Bannister in 1672), even church services. In James Wright's *The Humours and Conversations of the Town, Expos'd in Two Dialogues* (1693), the worldly Mrs Townley explains that 'our very Devotion too is not unpleasant, the Churches affording such a glorious sight of the Beau Monde' (126). There were permanent puppet-shows in London, which according to Colley Cibber were seen by Killigrew and Davenant as threatening their monopoly; 'a famous Puppet-shew, in Salisbury Change (then standing where Cecil-Street now is) so far distrest these two celebrated Companies, that they were reduc'd to petition the King for Relief against it' (1740; 1968, 57). Seasonally, the great fairs drew crowds to shows that ranged from tight-rope walking, dancing bears and freaks, to Biblical history presented by marionettes. In *Wit and Drollery* (1682) a poem entitled 'Bartholemew Fair' catalogues some of its attractions:

> Here's the Whore of *Babylon*, the Devil, and the Pope,
> The Girl is just a going on the Rope,
> Here's *Dives* and *Lazarus* and the Worlds Creation,

Here's the Tall *Dutch* Woman the like's not in the Nation;
Here is the Booth where the *High-Dutch* Maid is,
Here are the Bears that daunce like any Ladies ...

These lines indicate incongruous jostling of rival amusements, but in the patent theatres, too, the capacity of audiences to relish diverse kinds of entertainment was exercised by musical interludes and dancing introduced between the acts of tragic dramas. A letter from the Grub Street figure Thomas Brown emphasises the contrast between 'humble Stories' presented at puppet-booths in earlier times, when Ben Jonson used Bartholomew Fair as the setting of his comedy, and the entertainment now available at 'this noble Fair':

> it produces *Operas* of its own growth and is become a formidable Rival to both the Theatres. It beholds *Gods* descending from *Machines*, who express themselves in a Language suitable to their Dignity: It trafficks in *Heroes*, it raises *Ghosts* and *Apparitions*; it has represented the *Trojan Horse*, the workmanship of the divine *Epeus*: it has seen *St. George* encounter the *Dragon*, and overcome him. In short, for *Thunder* and *Lightning*, for *Songs* and *Dances*, for *sublime Fustian* and *magnificent Nonsense*, it comes not short of *Drury-Lane* or *Lincolns-inn-Fields*.' (28 August 1699, in Voiture 1705, 100–1)

Further evidence of how ambitious the puppet shows could be is provided in advertisements. A rare surviving playbill for Matthew Heatly's booth at Bartholomew Fair in 1701 lists fourteen scenes in his 'Little Opera, Call'd The Old *Creation of the World*, Newly Reviv'd' culminating in the spectacular presentation of 'Rich *Dives* in Hell, and *Lazarus* in *Abraham's* Bosom, seen in a most glorious Object, all in machines, descending in a Throne, Guarded with multitudes of Angels; with the Breaking of the Clouds, discovering the Palace of the sun, in double and treble Prospects, to the Admiration of all Spectators.' It is not entirely clear whether a marionette show called 'The State of Innocence, or Fall of Man' presented by Robert Powell in 1712 is a version of Dryden's rhymed adaptation of *Paradise Lost* or simply a renamed revival of Heatly's Biblical scenes (Stevenson and Seares 1998, 174–5). A Bartholomew Fair playbill advertising *The Tempest, or the Distressed Lovers*, roughly datable within Queen Anne's reign by the concluding words 'Vivat Regina', is an extreme example of Shakespearean adaptation (Figure 3.1). Even as a crowd-

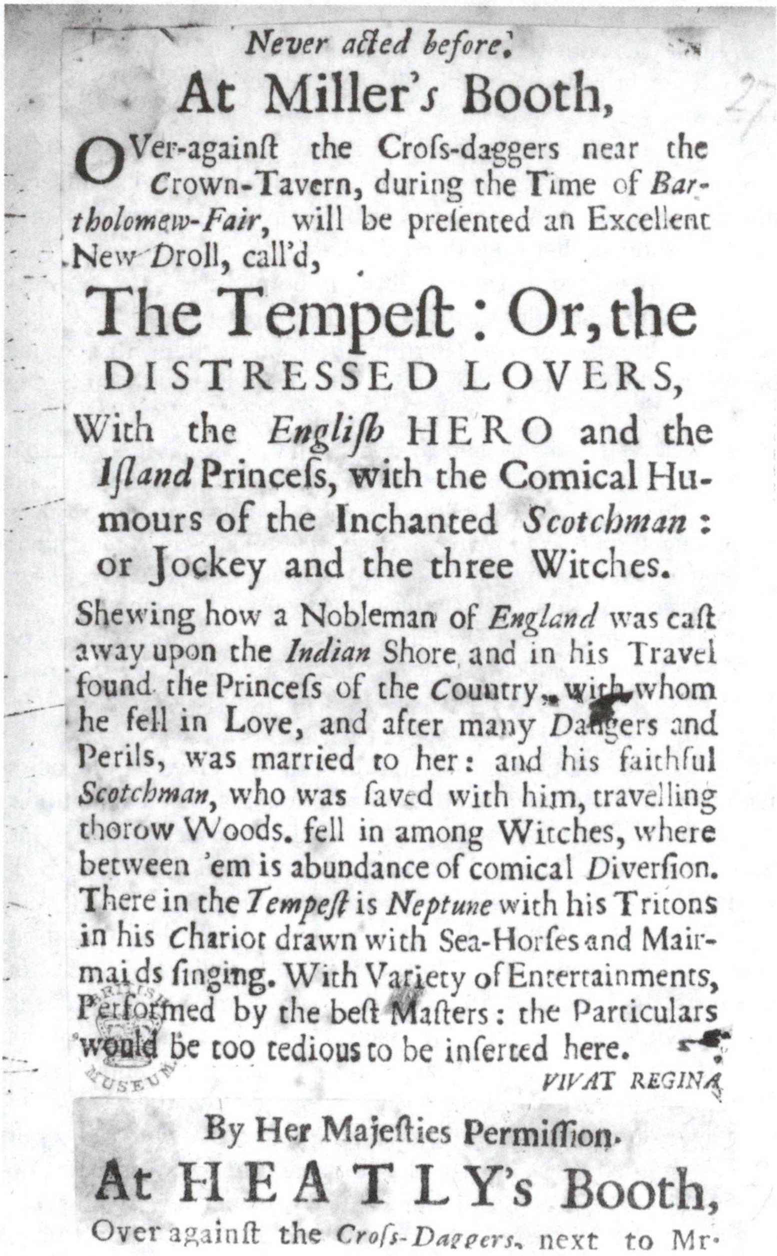

Never acted before.

At Miller's Booth,

OVer-againſt the Croſs-daggers near the Crown-Tavern, during the Time of *Bartholomew-Fair*, will be preſented an Excellent New Droll, call'd,

The Tempeſt : Or, the DISTRESSED LOVERS,

With the *Engliſh* HERO and the *Iſland* Princeſs, with the Comical Humours of the Inchanted *Scotchman* : or Jockey and the three Witches.

Shewing how a Nobleman of *England* was caſt away upon the *Indian* Shore, and in his Travel found the Princeſs of the Country, with whom he fell in Love, and after many *Dangers* and Perils, was married to her: and his faithful *Scotchman*, who was ſaved with him, travelling thorow Woods, fell in among Witches, where between 'em is abundance of comical *Diverſion*. There in the *Tempeſt* is *Neptune* with his Tritons in his *Chariot* drawn with Sea-Horſes and Mairmaids ſinging. With Variety of Entertainments, Performed by the beſt Maſters : the Particulars would be too tedious to be inſerted here.

VIVAT REGINA

By Her Majeſties Permiſſion.

At HEATLY's Booth,

Over againſt the *Croſs-Daggers,* next to Mr·

Figure 3.1   Advertisement for *The Tempest: Or, the Distressed Lovers* (early 18th century). Reproduced by permission of the British Library.

pleasing 'droll' it sounds like a crazy casserole of fragments from several plays: castaways from the The Tempest, witches from Macbeth, a faithful servant (Kent of King Lear transformed into a comic Scot?), with overtones of operatic splendours imitating spectacular productions in the patent theatres of The Tempest and of Fletcher's The Island Princess. 'There in the Tempest is Neptune with his Tritons in his Chariot drawn with Sea-Horses and Mairmaids singing.'

Trials, like fairs, drew spectators to alternative spectacles. As dialogue, trials are already rudimentary plays, with tense possibilities for suffering or happy outcomes. The quarto transcripts, published in profusion, are often about fifty pages long, approximately the same as a printed play. Occasionally they reward a reader with a hint of shapeliness as well as vivid moments, and they raise questions of genre, with tragedy, comedy, villainy or heroism in question until the final pages. The transcripts provide real-life courtroom dramas. On 18 July 1679 the diarist John Evelyn attended the trial of Sir George Wakeman, one of the queen's physicians, and three Benedictine monks accused of a plot to poison the king, subvert the government and introduce Popery. Evelyn notes that 'it was not my Custome or delight, to be often present at any Capital Trials, we having them commonly, so exactly published, by those who take them in short hand.' This trial drew a particularly large crowd; then as now many people regarded such procedures as entertainment. On this occasion, Evelyn reports, the courtroom was crowded with 'innumerable spectators.' He regards, with some scepticism,

> the chiefe Accusers Dr. Oates (as he called himselfe) and one Bedlow, a man of inferior note; but their testimony were not so pregnant, & I feare much of it from *heare-say*, but sworne positively to some particulars, which drew suspicion upon their truth; nor did Circumstances so agree, as to give either the bench or Jurie so intire satisfaction as was expected: After therefore a long & tedious tryal of 9 hours, the Jury brought them in not guilty to the extraordinary triumph of the *Papists*.

Always a careful observer, Evelyn makes an interesting witness both to the common practice of publishing precise shorthand accounts of trials, and of the uncertainties which promoted his attendance on this occasion: 'I was inclined to be at this signal one, that by the occular view of the carriages, & other Circumstances of the Manegers &

parties concerned, I might informe my selfe, and regulate my opinion of a Cause that had so alarm'd the whole Nation, & filled it with such expectations.'

Some of the trials end with horrifying explicitness. Ironically, an act passed in 1585 to protect Queen Elizabeth from plots associated with Mary, Queen of Scots was used to prosecute and execute a group of Catholic priests, simply for being priests, in the reign of Mary's grandson, Charles II, whose queen was Catholic. The chilling final speech of the trial is set in relief by the simple question of one of the defendants:

> *Marshall.*   May I ask one Question, Mr. *Recorder*, before you pronounce Sentence?
> Mr. *Recorder.*   No, Mr. *Marshall*, you can't speak now; but this is your Judgment, and the Court does award it, That you the several Prisoners now at the Bar, be conveyed from hence to the place from whence you came; and that you and every of you be conveyed from thence on Hurdles to the place of Execution, where every of you are to be severally Hang'd by the Neck; That you be severally cut down alive; That your Privy Members be cut off, your Bowels taken out and be burnt in your view; That your Heads be severed from your Bodies; That your Bodies be divided into four Quarters, which are to be disposed at the Kings pleasure. And the God of infinite Mercy, have mercy upon your Souls.
>
> Then the Prisoners were carried away, and the Court Adjourned the Sessions. (*The Tryals and Condemnation of Lionel Anderson* [et al.] 1680, 53)

At first sight, there seems little hope of happier reading in another legal transcript of early $16\frac{79}{80}$:

> *The Tryal of Sr Tho. Gascoyne Bar. for High-Treason, in Conspiring The Death of the King, the Subversion of the Government, and Alteration of Religion, On Wednesday the 11th of February 1679. At the Bar of the Kings Bench, before the Right Honourable Sir William Scroggs Lord Chief Justice, And the rest of the Judges of that Court.*

Despite the gravity of the charges, however, there are ludicrous notes from the first exchange in the arraignment on 24 January onwards:

> *Clerk of Crown.*   Sir *Thomas Gascoyne*, hold up thy hand.
>
> Sir *Tho. Gasc.*   I cannot hear.

Clerk.   He says he cannot hear.

L.C.J.   Then somebody must repeat it that stands by him.

Mr. Recorder.   Do you hear what I say to you?

Sir *Tho. Gasc.*   No, I cannot hear, I am very deaf.

There is some dickering about the date of the trial, with Sir Thomas, who declares himself 'above Fourscore and five years old', concerned about whether there will be time for his witnesses to arrive. Mrs Ravenscroft, his granddaughter, joins in to protest that since some witnesses are in Paris, a fortnight between the arraignment and the trial is not long enough; the Lord Chief Justice asserts that there is time to 'send to Paris a great many times between this and that' and another chimes in that as 'a man of an Estate' Sir Thomas can well afford the charge of a special messenger. It is hard, nonetheless, to silence a woman of Mrs Ravenscroft's social confidence once she begins to fret. She persists in raising difficulties about whether the witnesses can arrive in time: 'But if the wind should be contrarie, my Lord, and they cannot be brought over?' and again, 'What if the Letter miscarry, my Lord?' and a third time, 'But what if the winds be contrarie, must my Grandfather's life be lost?' (1680, 3–6)

As jury, judge and later readers sift through the evidence produced, a twofold movement appears. Against the damning testimony of Bolron and Mowbray that Sir Thomas plotted against the king is posed a counter-accusation of 'Conspiracy and Combination' (49). Did Bolron, heavily in debt, maliciously concoct his tale? At both ends of the trial, the complicated evidence includes a noticeable amount of evesdropping, with witnesses whose stories do not quite match. At summing-up time, the case against Sir Thomas seems dangerous enough. Mr Justice Pemberton clearly believes that given his association with Jesuits, Sir Thomas is capable of any wickedness, although he notes the implausibility of conspirators talking in public places when they could be overheard. The jury took half an hour to decide on a verdict of 'Not guilty'. There is one final, obscure question from the Clerk of the Crown, 'Did he fly for it?' to which the foreman of the jury replied 'Not that we know of.' Does the question hint at possible bribery? The whole, in any case, is a comedy both in dialogue, farcical action and happy ending.

Thinking of public, historical events in relation to the stage is common. Perhaps the best-known example is Andrew Marvell's description of Charles' execution, as the king acted his part on the scaffold high. How widespread such imagery was can be seen in more casual contexts than the *Horatian Ode*. When Lady Anne Clifford comments in her diary, on 30 January 1676, that twenty-seven years before the king had been beheaded, she recalls, with no particular signalling of metaphoric language, where she was on the day 'when this Tragedy was performed' (Clifford 1992, 244).

Audiences: spectators and readers

What was, and is, the audience for drama 1650–1720? From one point of view, the importance of 'Restoration drama' is highly inflated. The term, as a catchall for several hundred plays ranging from Davenant's entertainments in the late Commonwealth period to Georgian productions by Steele and by Gay, is itself problematical. At a time when a devotional work such as Andrew Jones' *The Dying Mans Last Sermon* reached a twelfth edition (1665) and Richard Baxter's *Call to the Unconverted* (1657) was read throughout the land, the two legitimate theatres in London had a limited seating capacity (variously estimated, but judging from the proportions of the buildings, between 400 and 1000 at most) and a new play with a run of more than three performances was considered a success. Robert D. Hume comments that 'The composition of the London audience, and changes in it, remain disputed matters, but we do know that it was tiny – a few thousand people in total, with a core of regular theatre-goers numbering only a few hundred' (Hume 1976, 16; see also Love 1980, Pedicord 1980).

When Davenant and Killigrew succeeded in gaining from Charles II exclusive patents for presenting plays, they both chose to use indoor spaces similar to the 'private' theatres like the Blackfriars before the civil war. The Red Bull Theatre, more like the Globe in its general construction, with an open-air pit for standing spectators as well as galleries, is important for its part in keeping performance alive in the most difficult years; it gained a reputation during the Commonwealth and Protectorate years for persistent flouting of the regulations, but in the selective freedom of the Restoration it was finally closed. For a short time it continued to be used, but when Pepys went there on 23 March 1661 he commented on the scanty audience, poor costumes

and rough performance. Fashionable London moved to the more intimate, more expensive theatres.

The organisation of space, and the social organisation of the audience, mark a shift from the earlier public theatres where the cheapest
places, standing space for 'groundlings', were close to the stage. Now
the least wealthy sat furthest from the stage, in the upper galleries.
Keenly aware of the social status of various spaces, Pepys records an
occasion when he 'was troubled to be seen by four of our office
Clerkes, which sat in the half-Crowne box and I in the 1s.6d' (19
January 1661). The benches of the pit were, at 2s.6d, a favoured position for ostentatious gallants and for the prostitutes who in an afternoon at the theatre, meeting potential clients, combined amusement
with business. The boxes, more expensive and more private, were
appropriate places for respectable women. In *The Country Wife*
(1675), the newly married Pinchwife is teased for his ill-advised and
unsuccessful attempt to conceal Margery from possibly lustful admiration by sitting 'in the eighteen-penny place with a pretty Country
wench'; she herself complains that 'we sat amongst ugly People. He
would not let me come near the Gentry, who sat under us, so that I
could not see 'em. He told me none but Naughty women sat there,
whom they toused and moused. But I would have ventured for all
that' (I.i. 430–1, II.i. 14–18). To be sure of a seat at a première, or a
performance when the king was expected to add lustre to the occasion, members of the audience might arrive hours in advance, or send
a servant to hold a place. Latecomers paid reduced prices, or escaped
without paying at all when they dropped in for only part of the performance. During the final act, the crowd who had paid one shilling for
places in the upper gallery was swollen by the servants required to
add dignity and perhaps some safety to their employers on the
journey homeward. In the opening scene of Southerne's *The Wives
Excuse* (acted December 1691, printed 1692), tired footmen waiting
for their masters to come out of a newly fashionable music-meeting
complain that at the theatres, at least, they have a less tedious time:
'There's no Fifth Act here, a free cost, as we have at the Play-Houses,
to make Gentlemen of us and keep us out of Harm's way' (I.i. 1–3).
What aesthetic sense latecomers could make out of a fraction of a play
is open to question. When, in search of one of his cousins, Pepys
tracked her down at the theatre and joined in watching the last act of
Beaumont and Fletcher's *Knight of the Burning Pestle* (1608), he noted
that it 'pleased me not at all' (*Diary*, 7 May 1662). A decision made in

1697 to allow footmen free admission to the Theatre Royal during the whole performance did not, however, have a positive effect, according to Colley Cibber, who complains about the 'Noise and Clamour of these savage Spectators' (1740; 1968, 129). He disdains 'playing to the gallery'. Estimating the number and composition of the theatre-going public is complicated by the fact that, like cinema-lovers today, habitués of the playhouses saw productions more than once. How frequently Pepys returns to performances of a given play is one of the mild surprises of his diary. The repeated visits sometimes strike even Pepys himself as excessive, notably on 25 October 1661: 'My wife and I to the Opera, and there saw again *Love and Honour*, a play so good that it has been acted but three times and I have seen them all, and all in this week; which is too much, and more than I will do again a great while.'

The relatively small audiences present in the theatre were extended by readers. Even when the theatres were officially closed, and surreptitious performances at risk of raids which criminalised both players and spectators, drama was easily available in print.[6] Along with cheap quarto editions of individual plays, booksellers found a profitable enough market to make worthwhile bringing out expensive collected works, in folio, of Beaumont and Fletcher (1647, 1679, 1711). Current playtexts made popular reading in the provinces as well as in London, as the country wife of Wycherley's play makes plain when she clamours to buy ballads or *Covent Garden Drollery* 'and a play or two' despite her husband's impatience (III.ii. 140–3). The appearance in print of almost all the new plays written after 1660 marks a major change from the Elizabethan-Jacobean theatre. In Shakespeare's time, the printing of playtexts was haphazard; the playwright had little to gain in terms of economics or reputation from publication. Jonson was exceptional in carefully seeing his plays printed, as *Works*, but the oxymoronic linking of plays and works was cause for mockery. In hopes of finding a more sympathetic reception in the closet than in the playhouse, even theatrical failures were published. A commendatory poem by Dryden printed with Southerne's *The Wives Excuse* attributes its lack of immediate success to want of taste among spectators in the pit, and the absence of the popular comic actor Robert Nokes from the cast; the older playwright generously assures the younger that 'The hearers may for want of Nokes repine; / But rest secure, the readers will be thine.'

The physical makeup of these printed volumes expands a sense of contemporary expectations. Facsimile reproductions offer particular insights, despite an immediate rebarbative impression. At first glance they are often less attractive to the eye than modernised editions, and because of the absence of annotations and line numbers, they may seem less immediately useful. Furthermore, being expensive and apparently arcane, they are not often found in local bookshops but only in academic libraries. Nonetheless, anyone who ventures beyond the most obvious plays produced between 1650 and 1720 is apt to handle facsimiles, whether from necessity or from scholarly curiosity about exactly what was originally presented. Less popular dramatists are often not available in inexpensive modern printings. Electronic editions, notably Chadwyck-Healey's Early Drama collection, often omit the informative 'preliminaries': dedicatory epistles, cast-lists, prefaces and additional commendatory poems.

Dedicatory epistles, at the beginning of early printings, may seem the most easily skipped of all pages; the effusive flattery characteristic of these letters is hardly to modern tastes. Reading one, and only one, is almost sure to produce distaste, but reading several becomes an exercise in discrimination. Hopes for a purely monetary reward from the dedicatee are seldom as wittily or openly announced as Lawrence Sterne was later to do in the first edition of *Tristram Shandy* (1760). At times, however, the dedicatory epistle is an announcement of political or moral alignment; Dryden's dedication of *The State of Innocence* to the Duchess of York declared his support for James at a time when the Catholic prince was far from popular. Flattery presents its own artistic challenges. Southerne offers an example of how to compliment without servile cringing, introducing a catalogue of praise for his dedicatee and potentially generous patron of *The Wives Excuse* with phrases whose apparent simplicity must be the result of considerable skill: 'Sir, I have the privilege of a dedication to say some fine things of my patron. But I will be as little impertinent as I can, and only beg leave to say some true ones.'

Wycherley, with splendid effrontery, plays off the conventions of dedications by addressing that of *The Plain-Dealer* (1676) 'To my Lady B – ' whose identity as no lady is plain indeed. Sixteen years before Wycherley's play, the reputation of Lady B – or Mother Bennet was already firmly established as 'a famous Strumpet' (Pepys, 22 September 1660). When Wycherley addresses her as 'the Great and Noble Patroness of rejected and bashful men' and asks her to take the book under her 'care and protection' so that 'by your recommendation and procurement' it may get into ladies' private rooms, a reader finds time spent reading duller dedications finally rewarded by recognition of routine phrases transformed into satire. With a self-conscious claim to originality, Otway disdains appealing to a wealthy aristocrat for patronage, and instead foregrounds the economic motives of introductory epistles by dedicating *The Souldiers Fortune* (1681) to his bookseller, who pays him honestly for the copy.

While dedications often include explanatory comment about the work, separate prefaces are also found in some early editions. Dryden's *Essay of Dramatick Poesie* (1668) and *Of Heroic Plays* (1672) are important enough as explorations of general principles and of a particular sub-genre that they are often printed divorced from the plays with which they first appeared. His preface to *Troilus and Cressida: or Truth Found Too Late* (1679) focuses more specifically on his procedures in adapting a Shakespearean play. He briskly lists his changes, in language and in design: 'I new modelled the Plot; threw out many unnecessary persons; improved those Characters which were begun and left unfinished.' Peter Motteux's preface to *Beauty in Distress* (1698), a mock apology for what is lacking in his play, provides an indictment of the late seventeenth-century audience's taste and a catalogue of popular stage-tricks. This play is

> divested of all the things that now recommend a Play most to the Liking of the Many. For it has no Singing, no Dancing, no mixture of Comedy, no Mirth, no change of Scene, no rich Dresses, no Show, no Rants, no Similes, no Battle, no Killing on the Stage, no Ghost, no Prodigy; and what's yet more, no *Smut*, no *Profaneness*, nor *Immorality*. Besides 'tis a single Plot.

Motteux's sense of what the audience preferred seems to have been entirely accurate. According to *A Comparison between the Two Stages* (1702) the play was 'Damned' (20).

Cast-lists, as a standard part of the printed playtext, were more or less an innovation in the later half of the seventeenth century. In the dialogue on actors, theatres and plays that makes up James Wright's *Historia histrionica: An Historical Account of the English-Stage* (1699), the older of the two speakers, Truman, can still remember who played 'the principal Women's Parts' or even particular roles in some of the theatrical companies before the Civil War. This gives his interlocuter, Lovewit, cause to comment, 'I wish they had Printed in the last Age (so I call the times before the Rebellion) the Actors Names over against the Parts they Acted, as they have done since the Restauration. And thus one might have guest at the Action of the Men, by the Parts which we now Read in the Old Plays'. With accuracy characterising Truman as an antiquary having some resemblance to Wright himself, the older speaker lists some eleven plays printed earlier 'that have the Names set against the Parts', but he acknowledges that 'It was not the Custome and Usage of those Days, as it hath been since' (3).

Prologues and epilogues, like dedicatory epistles, form a minor genre which is to some extent an acquired taste. Like cast-lists, they appear intermittently before 1642, but later become a regular part of the printed texts. When Marlowe chooses to have Machiavelli speak a prologue to *The Jew of Malta*, or when Shakespeare closes *The Tempest* with Prospero's epilogue 'Now my charms are all o'erthrown', these playwrights significantly affect interpretation of the major action. After 1660, prologues and epilogues are often less integrally a part of the plays with which they appear, but nonetheless of great interest in suggesting how intimate were the relationships of spectators, players and writers. Sometimes supplied by the playwright, sometimes by another poet, they were collected in drolleries and, in the highly political 1680s, were published as broadsides. Restoration audiences obviously delighted in them. One anonymous epilogue found in *Covent Garden Drollery* (1672), recycled for D'Urfey's adaptation of Shakespeare's *Cymbeline* as *The Injur'd Princess, or The Fatal Wager* (1682), promises:

> Our next new Play, if this Mode hold in vogue,
> Shall be half Prologue, and half Epilogue.
> The way to please you is easie if we knew't,
> A jigg, a Song, a Rhime or two will do't
> When you're i'th vein; and sometimes a good Play,
> Strangely miscarries and is thrown away.

Intimacy between audience and stage is defined and nourished in teasing description, rebuke or invitation. The framing verses often reflect the Restoration audience's interest in itself, and its familiarity with the popular actors who are identified as speaking the lines. The epilogue to Dryden's *Tyrannick Love, or The Royal Martyr* (1669), spoken by Nell Gwyn, depends on the reputation of the actress who 'though she lived a slattern, / Yet died a princess, acting in St.

Cathern'. Three major groups in the audience are identified in Wycherley's prologue to *The Plain-Dealer*: envious rival playwrights ('you who Scrible' only slightly differentiated from 'our Scribler', Wycherley himself), then 'the fine, loud Gentlemen, o' th' Pit' who borrow all their wit from the plays they ungratefully criticise, and finally those 'shrewd Judges' in the boxes who pay more attention to the ladies or to their own grooming and clothing than to the play that is going on. The rest of the prologue opens up questions about the playwright's theory and practice. Poets are compared to painters, specifically to the fashionable painter Lely who portrayed his clients in flattering and heroic poses. Wycherley, however, claims that he, 'the coarse Dauber of the coming Scenes', will not flatter, but 'follow Life, and Nature only'; his play will be realistic. (This is a half-truth in relation to unheroic characters, half-falsehood given a highly artificial plot including Fidelia's disguise.) Finally, Wycherley mocks the happy endings based on the principle which the critic Rymer was soon to term, and defend, as 'Poetical Justice' (*The Tragedies of the Last Age*, 1678, in Spingarn II. 188, 200). Sceptically, Wycherley asks, 'where else, but on Stages, do we see / Truth pleasing; or rewarded Honesty?'

Since the appearance of Pierre Danchin's multivolume collections of Restoration and eighteenth-century prologues and epilogues, it has become possible to read hundreds of these short pieces, in chronological order. They thus provide a miniature history of the drama, complete with traces of imitative rivalry. In January 1700, the character of Falstaff appears to speak a prologue to Betterton's version of *Henry IV*. In February, for Gildon's adaptation of *Measure for Measure*, the ghost of Shakespeare himself is introduced for an epilogue; indignantly he complains of being mangled by scribblers and murdered by lifeless actors (Danchin 6. 628–9, 632–3).

In early editions and their facsimiles, thrifty use for advertising of leaves which would otherwise be left blank is a final point of interest. At the end of Wright's *The Humours and Conversations of the Town*, the publisher advertises 'A Catalogue of some Plays Printed for R. Bentley'. The number of plays available in 1693 from a single publisher and bookseller is astonishing. First Bentley lists collected plays by Beaumont and Fletcher ('all 51 in large Fol.') and 'Mr. Shakespear's Plays In one large Fol. Volume, containing 43 Plays' (note that the canon is still at this point expanding beyond the thirty-six of the first folio published in 1623, and far beyond the thirty-seven or thirty-eight generally accepted today); next Nathaniel Lee, Otway,

Shadwell and Dryden. That buyers were more apt to recognise plays than playwrights is demonstrated by the list that follows: 112 titles (presumably quartos), alphabetical from *All mistaken, or the mad Couple*, to *Wit without Money*, and *Woman Bully*, without indication of authorship; apparently as late additions, twelve final titles are in miscellaneous order. On the opening flyleaf of Charles Gildon's *Measure for Measure, or Beauty the Best Advocate ... Written Originally by Mr. Shakespear: And now very much Alter'd; with Additions of several Entertainments of Musick* (1700) a larger proportion of the plays advertised are identified by author as well as by title. Also offered as books potentially attractive to readers of plays are Dennis's defence of the stage against Collier's attack, along with amusingly miscellaneous titles from *The Art of Swimming* (illustrated) to a medical text promising a 'compleat method of curing almost all Diseases, and description of their Symptoms'.

Secondary and primary materials

Drama 1650–1720 invites a variety of approaches: study of the companies, of their playhouses and audiences, of playwrights and critics, of plays. Whatever the major approach, the available evidence is bountiful (though not complete), almost dazzling in its plenitude. Even a single figure may offer a broad field for investigation. Dryden's career spans much of the period; his first play *The Wild Gallant* appeared in 1663, and his last dramatic work in 1700. He wrote for both acting companies, in a spectrum of genres: comedies, heroic dramas, semi-operas, adaptations of Shakespeare and Milton, critical essays. Over a hundred and fifty other playwrights active during some part of the period occupy a bafflingly large and cluttered field. Moreover, it is neither advisable nor possible to ignore the continuing presence of 'the giant race before the flood' as Dryden called the prewar dramatists ('To Congreve'). Some five hundred new plays and almost two hundred revivals or adaptations of earlier plays appeared on stage.[7] Within sixty years there was significant turnover in audiences, actors, playwrights, buildings, governments. The two outstanding comprehensive studies, Robert D. Hume's *The Development of English Drama in the Late Seventeenth Century* (1976) and Derek Hughes' *English Drama 1660–1700* (1996), divide their discussions chronologically into smaller sections, seldom longer than a decade. Informed and perceptive, Hume and Hughes offer stimulating guidance, complementary and perceptive overviews. Trying to reproduce their full surveys in condensed form would be absurd. Along with the invaluable volumes of *The London Stage 1660–1800* (Parts 1 and 2, 1965 and 1960) which digest information about the theatrical seasons year by year to present both summaries of developments and a calendar of performances, students are well-provided with secondary materials. Primary materials, too, exist in fascinating plenty.

Eyewitnesses: Pepys, Downes, Cibber

A remarkably full array of contemporary commentary is available. From different perspectives, the eyewitness accounts of a theatregoer, a theatrical bookkeeper, and an actor-playwright provide vivid, varied information. On the theatres as on almost every other aspect of London life, Pepys is a supreme observer; alas that failing eyesight prompted him to give up writing his *Diary* after 1669. Even his briefest accounts of an afternoon at one or another of the theatres are valuable. Many of the dates for première performances in the first decade after the Restoration rest on his entries, and studies of the social mix of the audience rely heavily on his observations. As a literary critic, he is often perfunctory. On *Love and Honour*, he notes 'a very good plot and well done' (21 October 1661); *A Midsummer Night's Dream* he finds 'the most insipid ridiculous play that ever I saw in my life' (29 September 1662). Occasionally he gives a useful glimpse of the grounds for his judgments, as when 'understanding the design better than I did' he enjoys a play more on a repeated visit to the theatre (26 December 1662). But it is not for literary criticism that he is read. More important are details that give a warm sense of the texture of play-going, not only in his recording of innovations such as 'the first time that ever I saw Women come upon the stage' (3 January 1661), or in comments on actors and acting, but through his observations of other members of the audience, how the women are dressed, who talks all during a performance. His own mixture of responses to the theatre and to his attendance there is sometimes marked. Finding himself 'lately too much given to seeing of plays, and expense and pleasure', he vows to amend his habits (31 August 1661), and, when irresistibly drawn back to them, he pays a self-imposed fine into a poorbox each time he breaks his resolution. What he fails to notice can be significant as an indication of how contemporaries thought of these theatrical productions. Although Pepys usually gives the titles of plays he sees, and often mentions particular actors, he rarely mentions a playwright's name.

The recollections of John Downes, who was prompter and book-keeper for Davenant's company, deal with the theatre from a businessman's point of view. In *Roscius Anglicanus, Or an Historical Review of the Stage* (1708), the plays he remembers as best are those which were 'most taking' in financial terms. (The title roughly translates as 'The English Actor'; the name of a great first-century actor who was of friend of Cicero had become conventional for an outstanding performer.) While Downes notes unusual splendour in costuming and scenery, he balances the costs of production against the profit. His post as prompter underlies praise for productions in which the actors spoke their parts 'exactly', but such praise is also related to a significant fact about the late seventeenth-century theatres, their rapidly changing repertories. The merest glance at calendars of performance raises admiration for the actors as quick studies. (Pepys complains on occasions such as 1 March 1662, when the players did not remember their lines.) On the balance between new plays and revivals of the 'old Stock Plays' from before the Civil War, Downes provides a perspective that is practical and economic rather than primarily aesthetic. The titlepage of Downes' book claims accuracy: *Non Audita narro, sed Comperta* (I relate not hearsay, but experience). His introductory epistle, however, although it spells out his qualifications for speaking authoritatively about one company from 1662 to 1702, sounds a note of cautious apology:

> He Writing out all the Parts in each Play; and Attending every Morning the Actors Rehearsals, and their Performances in Afternoons; Emboldens him to affirm, he is not very Erronious in his Relation. But as to the Actors of *Drury-Lane* Company, under Mr. *Thomas Killigrew*, he having the Account from Mr. *Charles Booth* sometimes Book-keeper there; If he a little Deviates, as to the Successive Order, and exact time of the Plays Performances, He begs Pardon of the Reader. (A2^{r-v})

Given not only possibilities of error, but also the enormous clutter of cast-lists and catalogues of plays, old and new, which are part of the book's value but not its most readable sections, a student is well-advised to consult *Roscius Anglicanus* in the generously annotated edition of Judith Milhous and Robert D. Hume (1987).[8] For those less than enthralled by studies of repertory, there are, mingled with all the lists of names and titles, vignettes of theatrical life: the actor Philip Cademan, maimed in a stage-duel during a performance of Davenant's last play, was supported by a pension for more than thirty-five years afterward (31). The stage career of the actress Mrs Johnson was cut short soon after 'Dancing a Jigg so Charmingly' in Shadwell's *Epsom Wells* (1672), for 'Loves power in a little time after Coerc'd her to Dance more Charming, else-where' (33).

A third collection of first-hand memories and observations makes up *An Apology for the Life of Mr Colley Cibber, Comedian, with an Historical View of the Stage during His Own Time, Written by Himself* (1740). Near the end of his long career, Cibber (1671–1757) provides the perspective of an actor, playwright and eventually manager, in years of important change, from 1690 onwards. When, after years of friction and frustration with management, Betterton led a secession from the United Company of the most experienced players, Cibber was left behind; he wryly acknowledges the inexpert performances and general muddle of the following seasons, but also indicates that new opportunities were opened for young actors and playwrights. Among the pleasures of the autobiography are Cibber's generous portraits of contemporary actors, including Betterton, Mrs Bracegirdle and Kynaston, one of the last male actors to excel in female roles (chapters 4–5). The practice and disadvantages of type-casting are illustrated in his account of Sandford, who so often appeared as a villain that, at a new play where he performed an honest part, the audience waited in vain for his 'well-dissembled Honesty' to be exposed, and when he remained honest to the end felt tricked by the playwright (77–8). A lament about alteration of Wren's design for the Theatre Royal in Drury Lane graphically conveys a sense of how the space worked for actors and audiences. In 1693, to fit more seating into the pit, the manager Christopher Rich shortened the forestage and added two stage-boxes at the sides, thus pushing the action back towards or into the inner stage. Cibber estimates that performers were at least ten feet further from the spectators (except those in the stage-boxes) than they had been before. His rhythmic catalogue of what was lost in impact and in subtlety conveys an artist's scorn for the mere financial advantage the manager gained by increasing the seating capacity.

But when the Actors were in Possession of that forwarder Space to advance upon, the Voice was then more in the Centre of the House, so that the most distant Ear had scarce the least Doubt, or Difficulty in hearing what fell from the weakest Utterance: All Objects were thus drawn nearer to the Sense; every painted Scene was stronger; every Grand Scene and Dance more extended; every rich or fine-coloured Habit had a more lively Lustre: Nor was the minutest Motion of a Feature (properly changing with the Passion, or Humour it suited) ever lost, as they frequently must be in the Obscurity of too great a Distance. (1740; 1968, 225)

Documents, dialogues, diatribes

Collections of documents quicken the imagination at some stages of learning about theatrical history, and anchor or test generalisations at another. Papers catalogued or edited by Milhous and Hume make it easy to venture beyond secondary texts. Dialogues which provide literary history in dramatic form offer genuine and more enticingly shapely contemporary views. Among James Wright's dialogues on London life, *Historia histrionica* (1699), the best-known, briefly and sympathetically surveys the history of the London theatre after the Restoration, placing both changes and continuities in perspective.[9] A subtitle defines Wright's scope: 'The ancient Use, Improvement, and Perfection, of Dramatick Representations, in this Nation. In a Dialogue, of Plays and Players'. In thirty-five small quarto pages, he avoids making 'a bustle' as he notes that Jeremy Collier and others had recently done, but instead presents an urbane overview of dramatic history. His use of dialogue eases transitions, so that the younger of two speakers can cut short a disquisition on theatres in Rome: 'That's a great way off, Truman. I had rather you would come nearer Home, and confine your discourse to Old *England*.' Dialogue also lightly veils, as in many didactic treatises, what might have been simply a lecture (although a clear and well-informed one, on parallels between the development of drama in Greece and Europe and on the history of mediaeval drama). For the last two-thirds of the text, Truman's account of mediaeval and Tudor Biblical plays and public pageants, complete with citations from books which he happens to have by him, is only occasionally interrupted by Lovewit, but these brief interruptions emphasise a serene perspective. To the comment that the pageants and Biblical plays described 'are far from that which we understand by the name of a Play', Truman replies, 'It may be so; but these were the Plays of those times' (1699, 14, 25).

Most pertinent in relation to seventeenth-century theatres, however, are the comparisons between the conditions in London before
and after the Civil War and Commonwealth. After Truman has
enumerated and described the theatres which flourished before the
war, Lovewit underlines the contrast in conditions by his surprise
'That the Town much less than at present, could then maintain Five
Companies, and yet now Two can hardly Subsist' (5). Truman's
answer defines the shrinking of the audience both economically and
morally:

> *Truman.* Do not wonder, but consider, That tho' the Town was
> then, perhaps, not much more than half so Populous as now, yet then
> the Prices were small (there being no Scenes) and better order kept
> among the Company that came; which made very good People think
> a Play an Innocent Diversion for an idle Hour or two, the Plays them-
> selves being then, for the most part, more Instructive and Moral.
> Whereas of late, the Play-houses are so extreamly pestered with
> Vizard-masks and their Trade (occasioning continual Quarrels and
> Abuses) that many of the more Civilized Part of the Town are uneasy
> in the Company, and shun the Theatre as they would a House of
> Scandal. (5–6)

The significance of scenery and showy productions, both economically and artistically, is something Wright emphasises, to the disparagement of the post-Restoration productions:

> It is an Argument of the worth of the Plays and Actors, of the last Age,
> and easily inferr'd, that they were much beyond ours in this, to
> consider that they cou'd support themselves meerly from their own
> Merit; the weight of the Matter, and goodness of the Action, without
> Scenes and Machines: Whereas the present Plays with all that shew,
> can hardly draw an Audience. (6)

Although the older of the two speakers has the lion's share of
dialogue, Lovewit can from his own memories supply a history of the
playing companies from 1660 onwards, neatly concentrated into a
single paragraph in which he calls attention to three innovations: the
use of scenery, the introduction of actresses, and the development of
playhouse music. With admirable succinctness he sums up the story
of rival playhouses: two decades during which there were competing
acting companies, their collapse into a united company, and their

subsequent division (10–12). Casually, having referred to 'severe' critics, he asks 'Have you seen Mr. Collier's Book?'

Jeremy Collier's *A Short View of the Immorality and Profaneness of the English Stage* (1698) is, aside from its own rhetorical vigour, interesting because of the replies it elicited, including John Dennis's *The Usefulness of the Stage* (1698). Facsimile editions of these two texts and many more are available in a convenient series from Garland, 'The English Stage: Attack and Defense, 1577–1730, A collection of 90 important works reprinted in photo-facsimile in 50 volumes', edited by Arthur Freeman. Among the more strident protests are two by Arthur Bedford, a clergyman whose knowledge of plays exceeds Mary Whitehouse's knowledge of pornography. Having in *The Evil and Danger of Stage-Plays* (1706) amassed 'almost Two Thousand Instances, taken from the Plays of the two last years' which demonstrate the relationship between drama and 'a General Corruption of Manners', he expands his study to 'almost Seven Thousand Instances, taken out of the Plays of the present Century' in *A Serious Remonstrance* (1719).

All that an enemy of the stage can say, however, may not be so damning as criticism by a lover of theatre. In 'Of the Modern Comedies', the first dialogue in Wright's *Country Conversations* (1694), one speaker takes a nostalgic backwards look confirming his sense that 'new' comedy, produced in the last decades of the seventeenth century, is inferior to that of the preceding age. He gives 'particular instances of the Defects and Blemishes of our late Comedies, and of the contrary Beauties of those before the Wars' (15–16). He praises the comic characters and dialogue of Jonson, Shakespeare, Beaumont and Fletcher, Massinger, Shirley and some at least of Dryden, describing them as being

> of a quite different Strain from those in the Modern Plays. Whose Conversation was truly Witty, but not Lewd, Brave and not Abusive; Ladies full of Spirit and yet Nicely Virtuous; with abundance of Passages discovering an admirable Invention, and quickness of thought, and yet decently facetious. On the contrary he gave infinite Examples out of Modern Comedies of another Stamp, mistaken Images of Bravery, Virtue despised, and the very Genius of Immodesty, not dropt here and there, but so diffused, that it seems the Soul of the Play. (16)

The mixture of comic scenes with tragic stories is also seen as better handled in the last age, when such scenes 'were always subservient to the main Design, and were used chiefly to Illustrate, Heighthen, and set off, the Moral of the Play' (17).

Concern with the ethical basis of comic drama, though less strident in recent decades, is not a completely dead issue. Clusters of words such as 'debauched', 'carnal', 'flagrantly indecent', 'depraved' appear along with informed historical scholarship in Allardyce Nicoll's *A History of Restoration Drama* (1940, 7, 22, 23, 24). On a single page he speaks of 'the unutterable coarseness which distinguished so much of Restoration workmanship', of 'incredibly indecent' songs in D'Urfey's *The Comical History of Don Quixote*, and the 'hideous pranks' of Rochester and Sedley (21). Studies of Restoration comedy often continue to focus on 'values' or 'morality' (Harwood 1982; Gill 1994). Although it would not be quite fair to call Christopher J. Wheatle a neo-Collierian, since he is concerned with defining moral presuppositions, not prescribing them, no reader of *Without God or Reason: The Plays of Thomas Shadwell and Secular Ethics in the Restoration* (1993) could complain that the title and subtitle did not give clear warning of its preoccupations. For those who find reading of comedy enhanced by demonstration that whereas Shadwell 'presupposes individual responsibility and recognition of one's role in society', in Steele's final play 'virtue is presented as deontological and not a social construction' (153, 170), this is the book.

Gildon's *A New Rehearsal* (1714), which examines Rowe's tragedies in unsympathetic fashion, alludes in its title to the full-fledged burlesque play *The Rehearsal* (1672), which mocked heroic plays. Its popularity can be gauged by the fact that Congreve expects his audience to recognise one of the characters, Volscius, in the epilogue he supplied for Southerne's *Oroonoko* (1695). The particular interest of this epilogue is not simply its evidence for continuing awareness of *The Rehearsal* but also its contribution to literary criticism of the term 'hip-hop' drama, used for double-plot plays involving 'a stitching together of apparently disparate story lines' (Hume 1976, 182):

> We weep, and laugh, joyn mirth and grief together,
> Like Rain and Sunshine mixt, in April Weather.
> Your different tastes divide our Poet's Cares;
> One foot the Sock, t'other the Buskins wears:
> Thus, while he strives to please, he's forc'd to do't,
> Like Volscius, hip-hop, in a single Boot.

At few other times in the history of the English theatre have there been so many major critics who were also practising playwrights. Dryden towers above the rest, but there are many others, including Farquhar, who published 'A Discourse upon Comedy' in 1702, and Addison and Steele, who included theatrical reviews in their periodical publications. The criticism of Gildon (five plays) and Dennis (six plays) is probably better-known now than their dramatic works. Certainly their criticism is nourished by their practical work in the theatres. This is a perspective lacking in Thomas Rymer's rational but unsympathetic *The Tragedies of the Last Age* (1678) and *A Short View of Tragedy* (1693). Dennis's extreme opposition to Italian opera reflects the threat posed to spoken drama as foreign performers and composers diverted audiences from the English acting companies. Some five years before the triumphal performance of Handel's *Rinaldo*, Dennis railed that Italian opera was 'a Diversion of more pernicious Consequence, than the most licentious Play that has ever appear'd upon the stage'; he contrasts tragedy, 'so reasonable and instructive an Entertainment' to opera which offers 'mere sensual Pleasure' (*Essay on the Operas after the Italian Manner*, 1706; 1939–43, I. 383, 388, 391).

Playhouses, playwrights, players
Keeping track of all the shifts as theatrical buildings were refurbished, devised from converted real-tennis courts, burned, newly-built or modified takes a clear head. Information about material and economic conditions, the physical dimension of buildings, bills paid to scene-painters or suppliers of candles can produce – when combined with imagination – insights about the shaping of texts. Historians concerned with the physical spaces in which plays were performed, and the implications of this space for acting styles, for interaction between players and audience, for a sense of what a playwright could plan in the way of spectacle, have contributed a good deal to understanding of theatrical experience in these decades.

There are two periods, 1660 to 1682 and from 1695 onwards, when rivalry between a pair of acting companies significantly affected the opportunities for new writers, and encouraged particular kinds of theatrical shows. At the Restoration, Killigrew initially seemed to have an advantage. In his group of actors were sturdy, experienced players who had been performing at the Red Bull. Secondly, Killigrew's company, under the protection of the king, claimed continuity with the prewar King's Men, and therefore rights to the plays which the earlier company had owned; this gave them the lion's share of popular scripts by Beaumont and Fletcher, Jonson, Shakespeare, and others. On the other hand, Davenant's enthusiasm for shows mingling music, scenery, dancing and words stood him in good stead. In the early years of Charles II, knights and peers of the realm outnumber those who write for money. Sir Samuel Tuke wrote only one play, but his Spanish intrigue was a great success. Sir Charles Sedley, one of the mob of gentlemen who wrote with ease, turned out plays along with lyrics. Roger Boyle, Earl of Orrery, followed Sir William Davenant in establishing the high heroic drama. When this line of heroic drama was lampooned by the Duke of Buckingham and fellow court wits, John Dryden, as Bayes, bore the brunt of ridicule. Dryden, under contract with the King's Company to provide three plays a year (a target he could not meet), was a lone professional for some years, but between 1668 and 1672 he was joined by Shadwell, Crown, Settle and Ravenscroft. John Oldham's 'A Satyr concerning Poetry' (1694) alludes to the fact that playwrights received the profits from the third day's performance at a theatre:

> *Sedley* indeed may be content with Fame,
> Nor care should an ill-judging Audience damn:
> But *Settle*, and the Rest, that write for Pence,
> Whose whole Estate's an ounce, or two of Brains,
> Should a thin House on the third day appear,
> Must starve, or live in Tatters all the year.

During the years when the Duke's Company and King's Company merged, 1682–95, the possibility of a young playwright's having work produced on stage was slight. After 1695, however, a scramble to provide audiences with new entertainment meant a flood of premières, although between the novice writers' inexperience and hasty rehearsals, few of these productions lasted to a third performance.

One general trend from 1660 onwards was towards theatres adapted for special effects and scenic splendour, towards public theatres which rivalled the prewar masques at court. Competition between the two acting companies contributed to the escalation of expensive sets. In Dryden's *Tyrannick Love* (1669), the temptation of Saint Catherine calls for elaborate stage-machinery; two figures descend on clouds, a bed arises, a scene of Paradise is revealed, and a guardian angel descends with a flaming sword. After the Bridges Street theatre used by the King's Company burned in January 1672, they were at a disadvantage. The bill for painting the *Tyrannick Love* sets, completely lost in the fire, had been over £350. Restaging the play in their temporary quarters at Lincoln's Inn Fields, the company had to omit all its spectacular effects. Dryden's plan for *The State of Innocence* (entered in the Stationers' Register 1674) calls for the most technologically advanced stage machinery. Act I is framed by the spectacle of 'rebellious Angels wheeling in the Air, and seeming transfix'd with Thunderbolts', and by acrobatic 'Flights and Dancing in Grotesque Figures'. Later, in Act III, Gabriel and Ithuriel 'descend, carried on bright Clouds; and flying cross each other, then light on the ground' and Uriel 'flies down from the Sun' (III.ii. 8 s.d.). In Act IV, a cloud machine sturdy enough to carry eighteen angels is required. When introducing a sea-battle into Adam's survey of future miseries, in Act V, Dryden evidently envisaged something even more ostentatious than 'a Tempestuous Sea in perpetual Agitation' seen in Shadwell's embellished *Tempest* (1674) which the Duke's Company produced in their elaborately equipped Dorset Garden building, opened in 1671.

Dryden may have planned *The State of Innocence* as the grand opening production at a newly-built theatre for the King's Company. The shareholders decided, however, to construct a plainer, less extravagant building, and never attempted to produce his rhymed, spectacular adaptation of Milton's epic. When the King's Men moved from makeshift accommodation to the Theatre Royal in Drury Lane in March 1674, Dryden's 'Prologue Spoken at the Opening of the New House' is an aggressively defensive apology for the defects of the building, attributed to the defects of the audience's taste:

> 'Twere folly now a stately pile to raise,
> To build a playhouse while you throw down plays;
> Whilst scenes, machines, and empty operas reign,
> And for the pencil you the pen disdain. (ll. 34–7)

The building, designed by Christopher Wren, was indeed better for spoken drama than the stately pile used by Davenant's troupe, and it remained in use until 1775. During the lean years of 1682–95 most plays were performed at Drury Lane; the larger Dorset Garden house was used mainly for operatic works.[10]

Dryden's attack on the masque-like spectacles echoes Jonson's belated criticism of 'Showes, mere Showes' with which he had been professionally implicated. Audiences, seldom improved by being harangued, continued to enjoy scenery, machinery and music. When Shadwell's *The Lancashire Witches* (1681) was revived in August 1711, Steele in the *Spectator* (no. 141) ridiculed athletic feats, 'gambols' or 'pranks' of flying, and hoped that when 'the People of Condition and Taste return to Town', a distinction between the 'Corporeal and Intellectual' attractions of the theatre would be appreciated. Steele does not mention that the acrobatics he deplores are directly in the line of Davenant's operatic *Macbeth*, with flying witches.

Although spectacle, associated with elaborate scenery as well as special effects, is one of the important characteristics of the post-Restoration theatres, so too is intimacy. On the apron stage three-quarters surrounded by the audience, players addressed their spectators directly in prologues and epilogues. Within the plays, a wealth of asides is a product of staging in which the distance between actors and audience is not sharply marked. Lighting as well as distance is significant here; the two groups were clearly visible to each other. Directors of some modern revivals show sensitivity to these matters. Early in the twentieth century, Sir Nigel Playfair recognised the importance of acting styles, and particularly of having actors address the audience directly, for the effects of these plays.

> When he began his work at the Lyric the whole technique of acting and production in England was based on a pretence of ignoring the audience and isolating the actors in their own world behind the foot-lights. Playfair's method was to accept the presence of the audience, to make them a partner in the play, and to establish a feeling of intimacy between the stage and auditorium. It was a method of production ideally suited to the Lyric with its small, friendly auditorium. (Marshall 1947, 41)

The rediscovery of appropriate acting styles and of suitable playing areas has contributed to the popularity of revivals, especially of comedies.

In Pepys' diary, Cibber's autobiography and other anecdotal material (including plays of the period, often full of allusions to playgoing), it is clear that observing the audience produced entertainment to rival what was presented on stage. On 23 February 1663, Pepys seems to have paid more attention to the king's responses to Dryden's *The Wild Gallant* than to the play, remaining confused at the end about which character had the title role. When by chance he sits next to Sir Charles Sedley at a performance of the Earl of Orrery's heroic play *The General*, Sedley's witty running commentary seems to have been the best part of the afternoon (4 October 1664). On 12 June 1663, he watches Cromwell's daughter Mary at a play with her husband, noting that 'when the House began to fill she put on her vizard, and so kept it on all the play; which of late is become a great fashion among the ladies, which hides their whole face. So to the Exchange, to buy things with my wife; among others a vizard for herself.' Given that the prostitutes regularly went masked at the theatre, this fashionable semi-disguise for respectable women too seems odd. It is tempting to speculate on the relationship between the plots of comedies such as Behn's *The Counterfeit Courtesans* and the behaviour of women in the audience, for whom masking is not simply a modest concealing of identity but a potentially dangerous assumption of a new role.[11]

Even at several centuries' remove the names of Betterton, Nell Gwyn and Anne Bracegirdle are as apt to be recognised as the names of playwrights Orrery, Sedley, Settle, Ravenscroft. Playwrights who worked under contract to one of the two companies could plan roles in relation to the particular qualities of available actors. Dryden's characterisation of Cleopatra in *All for Love* makes much more sense when it is compared to parts the ingénue Elizabeth Bowtell took in other plays. Tate defensively explains the failure of his farce *Cuckolds-Haven* as a problem in casting: 'The principal Part (on which the Diversion depended) was, by Accident, disappointed of Mr. *Nokes*'s Performance, for whom it was design'd, and only proper' (dedicatory epistle, 1685). Cibber put aside two acts of *The Careless Husband* because he could not imagine any actress in his company taking the role of Lady Betty Modish, Mrs Bracegirdle being with the rival company and Mrs Verbruggen too old or ill for the part; he resumed writing only after the talents of the young Mrs Oldfield became apparent, and he attributes a large share of the play's success to her (1740; 1968, 167). At a performance of Sir Robert Stapylton's *The Slighted Maid*, Pepys forgives inadequacies of the script in view of the personal charms of an actress, which he examined closely: 'the play hath little good in it – being most pleased to see the little girl dance in boy's apparel, she having very fine legs; only, bends in the hams as I perceive all women do' (*Diary*, 23 February 1663). As in Elizabethan comedies, a common turn of the plot in Restoration plays involves transvestite disguise; an appendix in Elizabeth Howe's *The First English Actresses* (1992) lists plays which include 'breeches roles'. Compendious information gathered by Highfill *et al.* in the volumes of *A Directory of Actors, Actresses, Musicians, Dancers, Managers and Other Stage Personnel in London 1660–1800* includes the locations of all known portraits of the performers.

Towards the end of the century, when the United Company split in 1695, the significance of buildings, rights to plays and the talents of personnel become particularly clear. Betterton and many of the other most experienced actors were so frustrated by Rich's management that they preferred independence in a cramped building, the once again refurbished playhouse at Lincoln's Inn Fields. The best actors were in the secession company; the greater composer of the day remained with the Theatre Royal group, which could mount spectacular effects. From the reopening of the theatre in April 1695 (after an obligatory three-month period of mourning for Queen Mary) to his death in November, Purcell contributed enormously to the drawing power of new productions, many of them revivals and adaptations designed to use the voice of the boy treble Jemmy Bowen. Richard Gould adapted Shirley's *The Maid's Revenge* into *The Rival Sisters: or, the Violence of Love* (1695) expanding opportunities for music. A revival of *The Indian Queen*, its original script substantially cut in order to allow time for Purcell's music, is only one of the many productions in 1695 to reflect a theatrical company's making the most of its assets.

Old plays and new

Dryden's first theatrical success, *The Indian Queen* (1664), written in collaboration with his brother-in-law Sir Robert Howard, suggests the advantages of coming to the theatre of the later seventeenth century by way of Shakespeare and his contemporaries, as most students do. Reading or seeing the plays easily turns into a game of spot-the-borrowing: how many strands from Elizabethan drama are here rewoven? The hero Montezuma, a warrior of obscure birth who overcomes almost every other figure in the play either through military might or force of character, takes his place in the line of Marlowe's *Tamberlaine*. As in Shakespeare's *Coriolanus*, a crucial turn in the plot is the decision of a highly successful general, reacting to insult and ingratitude, to go over to the enemy. When Montezuma is dishonoured by the Incan emperor he has served and is contemptuously refused the hand of the princess because of his low birth, he defects to the rival Mexican army. The witches of *Macbeth* are echoed in incantations by a sorcerer who is commanded by the usurping Mexican queen to reveal her future: 'By the croaking of the Toad ... By the crested Adders Pride, / That along the Cliffs do glide' (III.ii. 79, 83–4). In the final act, the unravelling of the plot, in which Montezuma is found worthy by blood as well as by deeds to wed the princess, calls for revelations like those of *Cymbeline*. Montezuma is the son of the rightful queen of Mexico, brought up in hiding by her faithful counsellor.

Made and moulded of things past, *The Indian Queen* is also very much a play of the 1660s. It belongs with a cluster, brilliantly discussed by Derek Hughes, of plays produced in this decade whose plots turn on the restoration of rightful rule. This group includes Davenant's four adaptations of Shakespeare, *The Law Against Lovers* (1662, an amalgamation of *Measure for Measure* and *Much Ado about Nothing*), *The Rivals* (1664, based on *Two Noble Kinsmen*), *Macbeth* (1664) and *The Tempest* (1667) which was rewritten in collaboration with Dryden (Hughes 1996, 30–7). Davenant's influence can also be seen more or less directly in *The Indian Queen*. Both *Love and Honour* and *The Siege of Rhodes* contribute to the shaping of the play, with strong binary patterns of opposition, triangles of love, and scrupulous explorations of honour. Although the theme of affinity between rivals owes something to *Coriolanus*, development of enormous admiration between men, which in this play binds together the rightful and wrongful princes of Mexico, Montezuma and Acacis, suggests indebtedness to Davenant as well. The sumptuousness of its staging by the King's Company exceeded anything Davenant had yet produced. That is the focus of praise given by John Evelyn in his diary: 'I saw acted the *Indian Queene* a Tragedie well written, but so beautified with rich Scenes as the like had never ben seene here as happly (except rarely any where else) on a mercenarie *Theater*' (5 February 1664). There were seven expensive sets, listed as a temple, a prison, Pleasant Indian Country, a Magicians Cave, the Chamber Royal, a pleasant grotto, the camp. Thriftily, sets and costumes could be reused in Dryden's sequel, *The Indian Emperour* (1665), as its prologue notes:

> The Scenes are old, the Habits are the same,
> We wore last year, before the Spaniards came.

Recycling has a long and respectable literary history, for as Bakhtin says, 'Something created is always created out of something given' (1986, 120). The status of 'originality' was much less high in the seventeenth century than it is now. Nonetheless, questions about plagiarising were sometimes raised, and while rewriting could be creative appropriation, Dryden in 1668 attacked the 'plunder' of older works:

> But this our Age such Authors does afford,
> As make whole Playes, and yet scarce Write one word.
> (Prologue to revival of Thomas Tomkis's *Albumazar*, 1668;
> *Miscellany Poems* 1684)

Productions and adaptations of Shakespeare have particular interest to modern students because of Shakespeare's present reputation, one which was being slowly established. It can be seen in Cibber's autobiography, full of praise for Shakespearean roles. In earlier references, however, it may come as a salutary shock that some of his contemporaries were more popular and more admired. Fletcher and Jonson are named as the 'Elder Brothers' of all who boast the estate of Wit in Dryden's preface to *The Wild Gallant* (1663). In *An Essay of Dramatick Poesie* (1668) he notes that the plays of Beaumont and Fletcher

> are now the most pleasant and frequent entertainments of the stage; two of theirs being acted through the year for one of Shakespeare's or Jonson's: the reason is because there is a certain gaiety in their comedies, and pathos in the serious plays, which suits generally with all men's humours, Shakespeare's language is likewise a little obsolete and Ben Jonson's wit comes short of theirs. (*Essays* 1962, I. 69)

Statistical evidence confirms Dryden's assertions, even when it is taken into account that their combined canon, at fifty plays (fifteen or so written together) is somewhat larger than Shakespeare's. Twenty of their plays were revived between 1660 and 1662 (Sorelius 1966, 46). Jonson's *Epicoene, or The Silent Woman* (the first play Charles II had performed in the Cockpit at Court) is Dryden's prime example of good English writing, in *Of Dramatick Poesie* (1668). Admiration for Jonson is one point on which Dryden and Shadwell concur. In the preface to *The Sullen Lovers* (1668), Shadwell attempts to define 'the practice of Ben Jonson, whom I think all Dramatic Poets ought to imitate, though none are like to come near; he being the only person that appears to me to have made perfect Representations of Human Life.' Distinguishing between comedy based on witty repartee and that based on character, Shadwell particularly praises Jonson's combination of realism and variety:

> most other Authors that I ever read, either have wilde Romantick *Tales* wherein they strein Love and Honour to that Ridiculous height, that it becomes Burlesque: or in their lower Comedies content themselves with one or two Humours at most, and those not near so perfect Characters as the admirable Jonson alwayes made.

Again, in the dedicatory epistle to *The Virtuoso* (1676), Shadwell gives Jonson the supreme place as 'incomparably the best Drammatick Poet that ever was, or, I believe, ever will be; and I had rather be Author of one Scene in his best Comedies, than of any Play this Age has produced.'

As models or raw materials, the new dramatists turned to work by Spanish and French as well as earlier English dramatists. What to make of this mass of rewritings is an open question. To look at the Restoration versions only in order to confirm a presupposition that the original was better would be, like all self-confirming prophecies, a tedious business of finding what one wanted to find. Sir Charles Sedley sets out a principle which would apply to Shakespeare (whose own sources and analogues are now fully documented) as well as to his successors:

> All that is now has been before tis true,
> And yet the Art, the Fashion may be new:
> Tho' old Materials the large Palace raise,
> The skilful Architect deserves his praise.
> (Prologue to Higden's *The Wary Widow*, 1693, reprinted in
> *The Gentlemen's Journal*, 1693, and Tonson's *Miscellany*, 1702;
> Sedley 1928, I. 50–1)

Playwrights working with old materials may choose to emphasise novelty or their links to the past. The prologue to Sir Samuel Tuke's *The Adventures of Five Hours* announces that 'The Dress, the Author, and the Scenes are new', but he obviously talked about his source as well as acknowledging it in the preface to the printed text (1663). Evelyn, who accompanied Tuke to a rehearsal of the play on 23

December 1662, notes in his diary entry that 'the plot was taken out of the famous Spanish Poet Calderon'. Shakespeare's name is not on the title page of *King Lear* 'Revis'd with Alterations. By N. Tate' (1681), but the dedicatory epistle acknowledges that Shakespeare provided the source, albeit in rough form: 'a Heap of Jewels, unstrung and unpolisht; yet so dazzling in their disorder, that I soon perceiv'd I had seiz'd a Treasure'. More deferential to Jonson, whose *Eastward Ho* he transformed into *Cuckolds-Haven* (1685), Tate refers to the earlier playwright in the prologue as 'that Master' and in the preface as 'great Ben'. Tate's decision to rewrite *King Lear* as a tragicomedy, with good characters preserved alive, might be seen as his participating in a seventeenth-century tradition of experimenting with endings. Edmund Waller provided a happy final act for Beaumont and Fletcher's *The Maid's Tragedy*, published in Waller's 1690 folio as 'The Maid's Tragedy Altered'. There is a particularly modernist touch in Sir Robert Howard's writing *The Vestal Virgin* (1664) in two versions, with a disastrous or happy conclusion. His brother James Howard revised *Romeo and Juliet* in the late 1660s or early 1670s, providing audiences with a choice of effects: 'when the Tragedy was Reviv'd again, 'twas Play'd Alternately, Tragical one Day, and Tragicomical another; for several Days together' (Downes 1708, 22).

Whether *The Forc'd Marriage* (1670), the first of Aphra Behn's plays to be performed, began as an adaptation of Ford's *The Broken Heart* (1633) is hard to tell. Certainly it is tantalising to look at them together. Ford's is in the list of plays which were allowed to the Duke's Company (20 August 1668, *London Stage*, I. 140); whether the company performed it is not recorded. The drama Behn provided for the Duke's Company uses France rather than Sparta as its setting, but recalls the name of Ford's character Orgilus in her character Orgilius. (Otway in *Caius Marius*, 1679, moves *Romeo and Juliet* from Verona to classical Rome.) Behn's play resembles Ford's in psychological intensity and strong dramatic patterns, as the plot piles up instances of blocked love matches and multiplies pairs of siblings. In Act II alone, which includes three brother–sister pairs sharing unhappiness about their love for someone unattainable, there are two duels and two scenes in which the princess Erminia invites men by whom she is loved to stab her. Scenes of quietly achieved dignity are even more memorable than those of violent action. A stylised masque-like scene in the final act separates more sensational moments by measured dancing. This transformation of Ford's materials, if it is transformation rather than coincidence, is satisfying on its own terms. The texture of Behn's play also includes some clearer borrowings from Shakespeare and from Dryden (Hughes 1996, 164–5). *The Indian Queen* provides the early episode in which a victorious general claims the hand of a princess. Stage-directions for her murder (IV.vii. 81) give alternative methods: strangling with a garter or smothering with a pillow; *Othello* lurks in the background. From *Much Ado about Nothing* or *The Winter's Tale* Behn takes her resolution of the central plot through the apparent resurrection of a virtuous woman whose husband suffers remorse. *Much Ado about Nothing* also contributes a pair of witty lovers reluctant to confess their feeling for each other.

Continuities in the practice of adaptation can be seen in Thomas Southerne's treatment of two narratives by Behn, within a few years of her death. His *The Fatal Marriage: or the Innocent Adultery* (1694), which rewrites Behn's *The History of the Nun, or the Fair Vow-Breaker* as a tragedy in blank verse, is chronologically slightly closer to its source than Shakespeare's *The Winter's Tale* is to Greene's prose romance *Pandosto, or The Triumph of Time* (1588). Like Shakespeare, Southerne freely modifies the ending of a recent popular romance, and for the same general purpose, to develop sympathy for a central character, despite transgression. At the end of Shakespeare's play, the violently jealous Leontes is rehabilitated, whereas in *Pandosto* the parallel character is killed. Although Southerne does not try to turn Behn's tale into a tragicomedy, rearrangement of the final events means that responses to its heroine Isabella are radically simplified. In both Behn's and Southerne's plots, Isabella is unwittingly guilty of bigamy. When after many years missing, presumed dead, her first husband reappears, Behn provides her with enough desperate clever-ness to dispose of both spouses. In Southerne's version, the first husband's younger brother is the murderer; Isabella goes mad and commits suicide. *The Fatal Marriage* joined Otway's *The Orphan* (1680) and *Venice Preserv'd* (1682) in a trio of outstandingly successful pathetic tragedies (Downes, 38). While Southerne was satisfying his audience's taste for pathos, he also nodded towards 'the present Humour of the Town' by introducing comic scenes, in prose. His dedicatory epistle betrays some uneasiness about the hybrids of comedy and tragedy popular at the time, but he manages to invent a comic plot in which a husband's apparent return from the dead can be seen as a neat enough variation on the serious plot, which at least in the final acts of the play emerges as the main plot. Less happily, he turned next to Behn's *Oroonoko* (1688), which suffered some violence when it became Southerne's *Oroonoko* (1695). Alongside the tragic story of the doomed African prince, he added a lively secondary plot complete with a breeches role and bed-trick, producing the curious hip-hop quality defined by Congreve's epilogue.[12] The play achieved, according to *A Comparison between the Two Stages*, an 'uncommon Success' even if 'the Comic Part is below that Author's usual Genius' (1702, 19).

Cibber considered adaptation a kind of busywork: 'And whenever I took upon me, to make some dormant Play of an old Author, to the best of my Judgment, fitter for the Stage, it was, honestly, not to be idle, that set me to work; as a good Housewife will mend old Linnen, when she has not better Employment' (1740; 1968, 146). Not all rewriting, however, is as routine as that. Nor can a playwright always be trusted in his comments on his work.

On the title-page of Dryden's *All for Love* (1677) are the words 'Written in Imitation of Shakespeare's Style.' How much should be made of this claim? To some extent, Dryden is emphasising an English tradition rather than a French or classical one. He asks in his preface 'to be tried by the laws of my own country; for it seems unjust to me that the French should prescribe here till they have conquered'. He moves, nonetheless, towards a much more obviously unified plot than Shakespeare's. Despite his claim that English tragedy 'requires to be built in a larger compass' than classical drama, and his opposition to the 'punctilios' of French poets, Dryden jettisons Shakespearean sweep in time and space. In design, there is very little resemblance to Shakespeare's play until the final act; Dryden begins after the battle of Actium, with the defeated Antony. By style, Dryden could mean not organisation but language, although he explains 'I have not copied my author servilely' since 'words and phrases must of necessity receive a change in succeeding ages'. What Shakespearean style involves for Dryden is, most obviously, the choice of blank verse rather than the rhyming couplets he used (and defended in prefaces) in his series of heroic plays and in his adaptation of Milton's epic as *The State of Innocence* (1677).

There are two contrasting trends in late seventeenth-century adaptations. Davenant's semi-operatic *Macbeth* and the Davenant–Dryden collaborations on *The Tempest* develop possibilities for the spectacular, astonishing, exotic, titillating. Other adaptations move toward simplification and sentimentality. Dryden's *All for Love: or, the World*

Well Lost and his *Troilus and Cressida: or, Truth Found Too Late* (1679) both announce a bland moral judgment in their subtitles. Oddly, Dryden presents a different view of Antony and Cleopatra in his preface, where he asserts 'the excellency of the moral, for the chief persons represented were famous patterns of unlawful love, and their end accordingly was unfortunate.' Nahum Tate's *King Lear*, later in the century, resembles these two adaptations in making an audience's responses to major characters and events easier, less challenging emotionally or morally. Something the adaptations have in common is a taste for symmetries: in *The Tempest*, Miranda and Caliban each acquire a sister, and the young women who have never seen a man are paralleled by a man who has never seen a woman. In Tate's *King Lear*, Lear's virtuous daughter Cordelia is finally paired with Gloucester's virtuous son Edgar. The staging of *All for Love* lacks the musical and visual embellishments which Davenant exploits in *Macbeth* and *The Tempest*, either through necessity, since the Drury Lane Theatre of the King's Company lacked the stage machinery, or aesthetic choice, Dryden pares down visual effects. Most of his scenes present very simple stage pictures, and the most dramatic moments of the play are tense dialogues between two characters.

Despite Dryden's invitation to think of *All for Love* in relation to Shakespeare's style, qualities of the play may be better illuminated by other approaches. One is placing it in the context of Dryden's development as a dramatist, his choice of materials and an evolving sense of genre. R. J. Kaufmann suggests that like his heroic plays, from *The Indian Emperour* onwards, it might be seen as 'terminal tragedy', centred on a character who is either literally or figuratively 'a dying emperor in the midst of a dying empire' (Kaufmann 1963, 89). Such an approach brings into focus Dryden's decision to frame the play by the Egyptian priest Serapion, with speeches on portents of disaster and on the imminent entry of Caesar after Cleopatra 'the last / Of her great race' has died. Alternatively, instead of reading *All for Love* as a successor to Dryden's heroic plays, it can be seen as a predecessor to the affective tragedies which dominate the stage at the turn of the century. Dryden's Antony invites sympathy rather than admiration. The play is full of tears. Cleopatra with her display of injured innocence, and unqueenly longings for quiet private life, belongs with Rowe's heroines of 'she-tragedy'. Nearer at hand, the proportion of the play devoted to the emotional, even self-indulgent, values rather than the public roles of the major characters aligns Dryden's work with that of Nathaniel Lee, his fellow in the service of the King's Company, in his treatment of major classical figures. In Lee's *Sophonisba, or Hannibal's Overthrow* (1675) the Carthaginian general is as concerned with his love for Rosalinda as with fighting against Rome. Similarly in *The Rival Queens* (1677), Lee achieved a popular success with a plot which, while it includes Alexander the Great, is focused on domestic matters.

Dryden's preface begins with a general compliment to his predecessors: 'The death of Antony and Cleopatra is a subject which has been treated by the greatest wits of our nation, after Shakespeare; and by all so variously, that their example has given me the confidence to try myself in this bow of Ulysses amongst the crowd of suitors.' The long series of plays on one or both characters (some, but by no means all, surveyed by Williamson, 1974) includes, shortly before and after Shakespeare's tragedy, two accounts which place emphasis on the female character: Samuel Daniel's *Cleopatra* (1594) and Thomas May's *The Tragedie of Cleopatra Queen of Aegypt* (acted 1626, printed 1639). The point of view of Antony's second wife is taken in Samuel Brandon's *The Tragicomedie of the Vertuous Octavia* (1598) and in a poem by Daniel in the tradition of Ovid's *Heroides*, 'A Letter from Octavia to Marcus Antonius' (1602). Fletcher's *The False One* was assigned to the King's Company in January 1669; whether it was performed is not recorded. A sympathetic portrayal of the young Cleopatra, before her meeting with Antony, appeared on Dublin and London stages in 1663 and 1664, in the translations of Corneille's *Pompée* prepared by Katherine Philips (Dublin 1663), and by a distinguished cluster of noblemen and poets, Waller, Sedley, Filmer, Godolphin, and Sackville, who took one act each (London 1664). Most interesting of all, for the sake of comparisons, is a play which precedes *All for Love* by only a few months.

In the theatrical season before *All for Love* was produced by the King's Company (December, 1677), the rival Duke's Company presented Sir Charles Sedley's *Antony and Cleopatra* (February 1677). Tart comments in Dryden's preface about rich men who 'not to be contented with what fortune has done for them', will not 'sit down quietly with their Estates' but expose themselves by writing without the excuse of poverty, could be directed against Sedley or his friend Rochester; the possibility that Sedley is a target is reinforced by Dryden's dry remark that 'there are many witty men, but few Poets; neither have all Poets a taste of Tragedy' (Novak 1984, 379).

In deference to Aristotle, as understood through French criticism and practice, both Sedley and Dryden contract their time-span to the period between Actium and Antony and Cleopatra's suicides. Note here the contrast between what Dryden says in his preface, which declares an English independence from rules of another country, and his practice. The unity towards which Dryden works also involves a restriction in his conception of characters, with emotion at the centre of attention. He focuses on Antony's initial lethargy and despair, on affection between him and the paternal Ventidius who replaces Shakespeare's bluff Enobarbus; both men weep easily in the course of the play. Antony's love for Cleopatra is never in doubt, although the passionate intensity with which he describes Dolabella provides an alternative homosexual bonding in mutual love. Dryden gives Antony a speech which plays with the inadequacy of metaphors to express their closeness:

> I was his Soul; he liv'd not but in me:
> We were so clos'd within each others brests,
> The rivets were not found that join'd us first.
> That does not reach us yet: we were so mixt,
> As meeting streams, both to our selves were lost;
> We were one mass; we could not give or take,
> But from the same; for he was I, I he. (III.i. 91–7)

Although when Dolabella enters, the embrace between the two men is compared to the joyful fondness of a bridegroom on his wedding night (III.i. 120–2), homoerotic possibilities are left largely undeveloped. There may here be little beyond a fashionable gesture towards classical ideas about love between men, a theme which appeared in Lee's *The Rival Queens* (March 1677). The major uses Dryden makes of the relationship are to intensify, as he had done in *The Indian Queen*, a triangular pattern in which two friends love the same woman, and to make more plausible Dolabella's responses to Cleopatra, in the fourth act, as a rekindling of an earlier attraction to her which had led to his parting from Antony. Dryden shapes a highly unified drama in which every major figure is motivated by passion. Even his characterisation of Octavia, initially introduced as a cold and formal contrast to Cleopatra, contributes to the plan. Antony is able to resist Octavia's magnanimity when, with no strings attached, she offers a formal reconciliation which will lead to her brother's withdrawing his troops, leaving Antony as ruler of the East. A neat passage of stichomythia is set up by his rejection of her dutifulness linked with reminders that he has injured her:

> Antony: Therefore you love me not.
> Octavia: Therefore, my Lord,
>   I should not love you.
> Antony: Therefore you wou'd leave me?
> Octavia: And therefore I should leave you – if I could. (III.i. 329–31)

His collapse in face of the compassion she thus invites is in keeping with the emotional focus of the play as a whole. Political discussion is minimal; the priests of Isis worry about the future of Egypt, but for Antony to spend his dying breath giving specific advice to Cleopatra about trusting none around Caesar except Proculeius, as he does in Shakespeare's play (IV.xv. 47–8), would be completely out of character.

Sedley's play is often condemned in comparison either with Shakespeare or with Dryden; in *The Development of English Drama in the Late Seventeenth Century*, it is briskly dismissed as 'awful' (Hume 1976, 314). In its own day, however, if the number of times it was printed is taken as evidence, it seems to have been at least as popular as Dryden's version; there were quartos in 1677, 1690, and 1696. It exemplifies the usefulness of reading 'minor' works for oneself. At the outset, Sedley's heroic couplets may present a difficulty. Over a decade before, Pepys complained that Dryden and Howard's *The Indian Queen* was 'spoiled with the Ryme, which breaks the sense' (*Diary*, 1 February 1664), and it is easy enough to pick out awkward couplets in any of the rhymed plays of the period. Although in his preface to *The Rival Ladies* (1664) Dryden defends the use of rhyme in serious plays, in the prologue to *Aureng-Zebe* (1675) he renounces it in preference for the natural: 'Passion's too fierce to be in Fetters bound.' Sedley chooses what in 1677 was already becoming old-fashioned; he writes heroic couplets at a time when Dryden was moving away from them, but at least sometimes the rhyme underlines the sense.

Like Dryden after him, Sedley simplifies the cast, using ten male characters and four actresses. Like Dryden, too, he gives Octavia an important role, and to preserve unity brings her from Rome to the Roman camp outside Alexandria. The play is, however, less narrowly focused than *All for Love*. Antony and Cleopatra are both active, political figures; it would be impossible to imagine Sedley's Cleopatra lamenting that 'Nature meant me / A Wife, a silly harmless household Dove; / Fond without art, and kind without deceit' (*All for Love*, IV.i. 91–3). This Cleopatra forestalls criticism of her conduct at Actium by announcing in her first scene that she has had the captain of her galleys executed for cowardice. Cant on wifely roles is neatly undercut in a scene between Octavius Caesar and his sister. Octavia primly expresses a standard line on obedience:

> Wives (like good Subjects, who to Tyrants bow)
> To Husbands though unjust, long patience owe:
> They were for Freedom made, Obedience We,
> Courage their vertue, ours is Chastity.
> Reason itself in us must not be bold,
> Nor decent Custom be by Wit controul'd.
> On our own heads we desperately stray,
> And are still happiest, the vulgar way.

Such a speech is set up only to be demolished by Octavius's impatient reply:

> Whoever did such Moral Nonsense hear?
> My Sister sure is turn'd Philosopher.
> But we Antonius' Pride will soon pull down. (1677, 35)

Views of love are explored which are less sentimental than swooning compassion and willing surrender of all the world; at the beginning of Act III, in dialogue among Caesar, Mecoenas and Agrippa, one rapturously defends passion through calling on divine precedents, the gods who forsook Olympus and took the shape of birds and beasts 'To pursue Mortals in an amorous way / And form their glorious Image in our clay'. A drier voice answers:

> The God that lov'd, what Nymph yet ever rul'd?
> He was again a God, his Lust once cool'd.

The satiric note (for which the chiming of heroic couplets is apt) expands and darkens to contemplation of love in relation to money and power, with personal sympathy and commitment left only to the socially insignificant.

Th'unable sure, the ugly, or the old,
First in affairs of Love, made use of gold.
Then Princes to out-bid 'em threw in pow'r,
Now heart for heart's the Traffick of the Poor. (1677, 21; Act III)

Thematically, Sedley's play is much richer than Dryden's. Three subplots are introduced, all centred on ambition. His title might have been *Octavius and Antony*, rather than *Antony and Cleopatra*, although the double orientation of interest can be assessed as fragmentation rather than enrichment. Sedley has almost too many ideas to keep under control. Expectations raised by the two strong opening acts are not fully satisfied in the final three acts. Late in life, Sedley adapted his own play into a more tightly organised version, called *Beauty the Conquerer*, now unfortunately difficult to find, since it appears only in the 1702 edition of his *Miscellaneous Works*. The revision suggests that he was capable of learning from Dryden about how to achieve dramatic focus.

Politics appears more subtly in Dryden's *All for Love* than in Sedley's play. By 1677, the restored Stuart monarchy had long outlived its honeymoon period. It was not only puritans who criticised the excesses of court life and Charles II's public flirtations with his French mistress, the Duchess of Portsmouth. Parallels between his self-indulgence and that of Antony, lover of another beautiful, foreign woman, are easily drawn. As Novak points out, Dryden 'shows how sensual passion on the level of a monarch and his mistress might be viewed as an heroic emotion. At a time when the country was enraged by the exalted position of a courtesan in the court, and a French and Catholic courtesan at that, Dryden surrounds such love with some magical virtues' (Novak 1984, 375–6).

Comparison between Dryden's play and Sedley's brings to the forefront a sense of Dryden's technical skill. Each of his acts is organised as a dramatic reversal, as Antony in particular changes his mind and mood. Approaching interpretation from a producer's viewpoint, Milhous and Hume provide a diagram for stage design. Towards the back of the stage, as they set it up, an exit to the left would indicate that the character is going towards the city of Alexandria, but to the right towards the Roman camp. Looking closely at the text, with a performance in the mind's eye, they illuminate Dryden's sharp patterns of shifting emotions and decisions, visually signalled in their arrangement of the stage by entrances and exits: 'Only after a major

change does a principal character go off some way other than he or
she came in' (1985, 128).

Both playwrights were writing for actors whose capacities they
knew. At first glance, the choice of Elizabeth Bowtell for the role of
Cleopatra in *All for Love* seems odd. Though attractive and popular,
she was far from regal; usually she played young innocent ladies. In
her mouth, however, the 'harmless household dove' speech must
have been more convincing than in any production since 1677. If the
object was to maximise sympathy for Cleopatra, the choice of
Katherine Corey for the role of Octavia is less surprising; taller and
almost twenty years older than Mrs Bowtell, Mrs Corey appeared
most often in shrewish roles. Even accompanied by two children,
therefore, it is difficult to imagine her setting up a strong rivalry with
the Egyptian queen. In his preface Dryden frets about whether
Octavia will draw too much of the audience's sympathy. The challenge for Mrs Corey might have been the reconciliation scene of Act II,
with her confession of irresistible love which briefly wins Antony over
to her. The production was only a modest success; Sedley's play, with
Betterton as Antony, Mary Lee as Cleopatra and Mrs Betterton as
Octavia, seems to have attracted larger audiences. There was a longer
run of *All for Love* in 1704, when Cleopatra was played by the seduc-
tive Elizabeth Barry and Octavia by Anne Bracegirdle, renowned on
stage and off stage for dignified purity.

Although Restoration comedies are often revived in modern times,
tragedies written in the decades after 1660 are less often produced.
The success of the Almeida Theatre's *All for Love* with Diana Rigg as
Cleopatra (1991) is a notable exception. Among two later tragedies
which have won applause in modern productions are Thomas
Otway's *Venice Preserv'd: or, A Plot Discover'd* (1682) and Nicholas
Rowe's *The Fair Penitent* (1703), both popular in their own time.
Perhaps it is fair to say that my immediate personal response to
Venice Preserv'd is dismay. Considering it may, however, produce
some bracing effects. Brought up on Shakespeare, a literary student
tends to be impatiently dismissive of critics (from Sir Philip Sidney
onwards) who condemn plays which mix tragic and comic scenes.
Confronted with Otway's concoction of sentimentality, politics, satire,
titillation and violence, one may suddenly discover a taste for chaste
simplicity after all. In the central act, a scene in which an elderly
Venetian senator's eloquence consists of baby-talk ('Nicky Nacky ...
hurry durry' III.i. 71) and his administrative policy consists of bribing

his indifferent mistress to treat him like a dog ('kick harder – harder yet, bough waugh, waugh' III.i. 110–11) sits oddly juxtaposed to the scene in which the heroine Belvidera bewails her fate as a modern Lucretia. It is part of Otway's manipulation of an audience's responses that he withholds for some hundred lines the information that although rape was threatened, it did not take place. If this shift in perspective seems to promise an easy resolution of difficult situations, the audience is doubly shocked at the end of the play when the group of conspirators (who have been seen more or less sympathetically, although their enmity towards the Venetian senate has seemed to rest on shaky or personal grudges) are first offered pardon, then cruelly executed with racks and torments. Was there real evil to combat after all? Was the sado-masochistic scene between Aquilina and Antonio in Act III introduced as a casual crowd-pleaser, or is it meant to be seen in relation to the scaffold scene in Act V, where Jaffeir's stabbing his friend Pierre is an expression of love?

Psychological approaches to *Venice Preserv'd* have some appeal. Here, as with the question of unmixed genres against mingling of comedy and tragedy, I find myself jolted into an unaccustomed position. Usually out of sympathy with critics who triumphantly exclaim, 'Aha, he didn't know what he was doing!' I wonder how clearly the character Jaffeir, or his creator Otway, could be sorting animosity from affection. Even the simplest summary of the action suggests a degree of intellectual and emotional confusion. In the opening scene Otway establishes that Jaffeir is young, handsome, beloved by Belvidera and, because he once heroically rescued her from drowning, deserving of some gratitude from her father. Otway also points up the imprudent waste of a small fortune, which in three years has brought the young couple and their small boy to destitution. It is a curious expression of love to have displayed his extravagance, and to boast to the father-in-law who (as expected) is refusing to provide money:

> the World must bear me witness,
> I have treated *Belvidera* like your Daughter,
> The Daughter of a Senator of *Venice*;
> Distinction, Place, Attendance, and Observance,
> Due to her Birth, she always has commanded;
> Out of my little Fortune I have done this,
> Because (though hopeless e'er to win your Nature)

> The World might see I lov'd her for her self,
> Not as the Heiress of the great *Priuli*.

There is a similar but much more charged blindness and perversity in his spontaneously offering as a hostage to the conspirators, who are invited to kill her if he wavers, this woman he loves and wishes to protect. And why is a child given them – to maximise pathos or to emphasise irresponsibility and instability? An alternative approach is through politics. The 'distracted times' of the Popish Plot, to which the play's prologue and its subtitle 'A Plot Discovered' refer, provide a provocative context for Otway's story. Since his plotters are a mixed bunch of grudge-holders, malcontents and idealists, by selective attention a spectator could go away with prejudices of any kind intact or reinforced.[13]

Theatrically, the play gave Betterton as Jaffeir and Elizabeth Barry as Belvidera an opportunity for displaying their talents. In 1682, Betterton also spoke the epilogue calling for approbation in stirring moral terms:

> Though the Conspiracy's prevented here,
> Methinks I see another hatching there.
> And there's a certain Faction fain would sway,
> If they had strength enough, and damn this Play;
> But this the Author bade me boldly say,
> If any take his plainness in ill part,
> He's glad on't, from the bottome of his heart.
> Poets in honour of the Truth should write,
> With the same Spirit, brave Men for it Fight. (ll. 3–11)

Decades after the first performances, Cibber names Belvidera as one of the two supreme roles played by Mrs Barry, affirming that 'In the Art of exciting Pity, she had a Power beyond all the Actresses I have yet seen, or what your Imagination can conceive' (1740; 1968, 92). Through the first half of the eighteenth century, Belvidera was hardly second to Lady Macbeth as a part in which actresses might make their mark. On twentieth-century stages, productions in 1904, 1920, and 1933 provoked disapproving analysis, but faults of design were overlooked in a later revival with a star cast. There was almost unanimous critical acclaim for Peter Brooks' production at the Lyric Theatre, Hammersmith, in 1953 (Hogg 1975). With a brilliant director, and with John Gielgud and Paul Scofield in the leading male roles, success was not entirely dependent on Otway.

Written twenty-one years after *Venice Preserv'd*, Rowe's *The Fair Penitent* provides another notable showcase for sensitive, suffering actors and a beautiful, doomed actress. The prologue announces that this tragedy will take a new line, something vaguely anticipating *The Death of a Salesman*:

> Long has the fate of kings and empires been
> The common bus'ness of the tragic scene,
> As if misfortune made the throne her seat,
> And none could be unhappy but the great.
>   . . .
> Stories like these with wonder we may hear,
> But far remote, and in a higher sphere,
> We ne'er can pity what we ne'er can share. (1–4, 9–11)

Rowe promises 'A melancholy tale of private woes' (16), where the audience will 'meet with sorrows like your own' (18). What follows is not, however, quite what these high or low promises would suggest. The scene is set far away in romantic Genoa, at the 'Palace and Garden' of the noble Sciolto; for the eight characters Rowe descends to no one lower in birth than 'a young Lord' or his friend.

One perspective on the tragedy would be to see it as anticipation of the lyric Goldsmith inserted into *The Vicar of Wakefield* (lines known to many modern readers because of their transformation by Eliot in *The Waste Land*, lines 253–6):

> When lovely woman stoops to folly
> And finds too late that men betray,
> What charm can soothe her melancholy,
> What art can wash her guilt away?
>
> The only art her guilt to cover,
> To hide her shame from every eye,
> To give repentence to her lover,
> And wring his bosom – is to die.

Since in *The Fair Penitent* the seducer is fatally stabbed well before the heroine accepts guilt, remorse and death, Goldsmith's final line and a half are not quite apposite, but the bosoms of father, husband,

husband's best friend and sympathetic members of the audience are thoroughly wrung. Rowe constructs the final acts as a piling up of highly charged, almost disastrous encounters or confrontations – between friend and friend, husband and wife, wife and father, all designed to produce the maximum emotional response.

Rowe is described, in *A Comparison between the Two Stages* (1702), as 'the first Man in the List of our present Dramatists'. That Charles Gildon chooses to attack his plays in *A New Rehearsal* is another sign of his contemporary importance. A general sense that for great tragedy the early eighteenth century was not a great age was evident at the time. This awareness qualifies the *Comparison* compliment: 'considering the degeneracy of our present Poets, Mr. *Rowe* has the fairest Pretence to succeed *Dryden* in *Tragedy* of any of his Brethren, excepting none' (1702; 1942, 96, 101). However much Rowe might try in his prologue to claim originality, his exploitation of sentiment is characteristic of the final decades of the seventeenth century and early decades of the eighteenth century. Like the many rewritings of Shakespeare in the period, *The Fair Penitent* is illuminating partly in terms of shifts in taste. Rowe's major source was Philip Massinger and Nathan Field's *The Fatal Dowry* (first acted 1615–20 and printed as a play 'often Acted at the Private House in Blackfriars, by His Majesty's Servants' in 1632). In the earlier play, the seducer is foppish rather than dangerously charming. Scenes in which he appears anticipate Restoration satire on empty flattery and sartorial excess. To the extent that sympathy for the adulterous wife is developed, it is through her shift from infatuation with her seducer to respect for her husband's solid virtue. Throughout, Massinger and Field emphasise judgment, and not simply sensation and pity.

Generically, Rowe's play invites thinking about how the social or moral transgressions of a rakish figure are handled. As in *Venice Preserv'd*, the relationships of suffering and comedy are problematical, but in a very different way. The villain, 'gay Lothario', is the only character in the play whose name is now recognised outside a group of students and specialists. What can a playwright do with a handsome, intelligent and charming seducer? Even the moralistic Jeremy Collier might be satisfied by Rowe's arrangements for removing Lothario from opportunities for further adventures. In comedy, however, such a character easily becomes a hero. In Ravenscroft's *The London Cuckolds* (discussed in more detail later in this chapter), the aptly named Ramble is repeatedly discomfited, but never vanquished.

Aphra Behn's Willmore occupies the title role of *The Rover* (1677), where 'cavalier', as in the subtitle 'The Banish'd Cavaliers', can suggest admirable, dashing political allegiance or culpable indifference to emotional obligations. One of the closest parallels to Lothario in personality is Dorimant in Etherege's *The Man of Mode* (1676). In the comedy, however, the consequences of the rake-hero's actions are not, as they are in *The Fair Penitent*, the centre of the plot. Etherege leaves largely unexplored the choices faced by Dorimant's mistress Bellinda after she has willingly been seduced and, like Mrs Loveit, cast off. In the final act she takes a share of responsibility, and admits that she has learned, expensively, too late, but not completely disastrously, a lesson. 'I knew him false and helped to make him so. Was not her ruin enough to fright me from the danger? It should have been, but love can take no warning' (V.i. 340–3). Dorimant is let off lightly. In the final scene of the play, Bellinda promises that if he leaves her reputation (and peace of mind) relatively intact by taking no notice of her, she will not hate him. The playwright, even kinder to the seducer than his mistress is, holds out the prospect of an intelligent, beautiful and rich wife, Harriet, subject to the very moderate pains required of visiting her family in the country.

As in the Elizabethan period, comedies far outnumbered tragedies by a ratio of at least three to one in the first sixteen years after the Restoration (Rothstein 1967, 51). There is nonetheless a tendency, from the first decade of the Restoration period onwards, to announce that the comedies can be reduced to a simple formula. In the preface to *The Sullen Lovers* (1668), Thomas Shadwell praises Ben Jonson as the creator of characters, and then moves on to sum up the practice of his contemporaries in one reductive, damning template:

> the two chief persons are most commonly a Swearing, Drinking, Whoring, Ruffian for a Lover, and an impudent ill-bred *tomrig* for a Mistress, and these are the fine People of the Play; and there is that Latitude in this, that almost any thing is proper for them to say; but their chief Subject is bawdy, and profaneness. (11)

That some of Shadwell's own writing looks perilously like a kit for comedy does not escape notice from an early date. *The Virtuoso* (1676) is an amusing work, especially when its title figure (who would have been quite at home in Swift's Academy of Lagado) is discovered lying on a table, connected by a string to a frog, and thus learning to swim. Its major characters, however, fall into recognisable patterns: there are two lively, marriageable young women and two men about town, plus blocking figures. One of these is a caricature of foppishness (Sir Formal Trifle) and another a frustrated older woman, jealous of her two young nieces (Lady Gimcrack). Less predictably, Shadwell adds a parody of scientific experiment and theory (Sir Nicholas Gimcrack). Such a collection of characters is almost exactly what is described in James Wright's *Country Conversations* (1694) when three friends lament how repetitive the comedies of the time are. One asserts that this cluster is found 'over and over again, the Names only vary'd'. Another protests so mildly as to confirm the charge: 'there is hardly any New Comedy that appears on the Stage, but has some New Part different from what has been before' (4–7). The phrase 'hardly any' and cautious argument on 'some' novelty form a demur which damns with faint revision.

The impulse to formalise the characters and situations of comedy as a single formula can be seen, too, in twentieth-century criticism. V. de Sola Pinto, writing in 1927, set out an account in which mirroring of society is combined with stylised patterning: 'It was clear that the centre of the new kind of comedy must be the Man of Wit and Fashion as he was conceived by the courtiers of Charles II, the ideal personage who had been to some extent embodied in the persons of such men as Rochester, Etherege, Sedley and Buckhurst.' As foils for such a hero, he suggests, the dramatists set up two kinds of contrast, on the one hand pretenders to wit and on the other hand, older and more puritanical characters. For the central contrast of the plays, however, he argues that 'a conflict between equals' was needed, and the hero therefore is placed against an equal 'in wit and grace and style', a woman who can 'at once conquer him and yield to him'. As attempts to sum up a great many plays in one template go, this one is attractive, and if it seems to fit Congreve's *The Way of the World* (1700) even better than plays produced under Charles II's rule, the critic anticipates the objection: 'To disentagle these motifs from the old elements of Jonsonian humour and boisterous horseplay and from such new attractions as "heroic" poetry was the work of a whole generation' (1927, 259).

There are also recurrent attempts to sum up comic conclusions neatly. Norman N. Holland epigrammatically suggests that 'Restoration comedy questions, earlier English comedy affirms' (1959, 224). In Laura Brown's discussion of 'transitional comedy' in the late seventeenth and early eighteenth centuries, the words 'incoherence', 'inconsistency' and 'incompatibility' recur so frequently that a clash between satiric action and moral conclusions almost establishes itself as a regular pattern (1981, 102–35). Pat Gill moves from description of *She Wou'd If She Cou'd* to broad assertions: 'The comic resolution in Restoration comedies is brought about by the movement away from the way of the world, the way of worldly experience, carnal desire, and deceit' (Gill 1994, 26). This is an optimistic reading, taking into account the open possibilities left at the end of many plays.[14] In Gill's formulation, the comic ending

> points to but does not enact a utopic future. The rake-hero, after sampling or exposing what his sophisticated society has to offer, perceives a fresher prospect, a vision that offers the best of the world without any of the dross that results from and sustains it: a virgin heroine, intelligent but inexperienced, sensual but not sexual, witty but not bawdy, who proposes to reclaim a hero and restore a world. (26)

Such a conclusion is seen as harmonious partly in contrast to other relationships dramatised as foils: 'this union always posits its mutual fitness over and against the [other] marriages or liaisons depicted within the plays' (27). Yes, probably. That is to say, a play or narrative contains or defines within itself a range of possibilities and values. (Hamlet is judged both by what he says about himself and by comparison with Horatio, Laertes, Fortinbras, Rosencrantz and Guildenstern, even Osric.) But 'always' in a critical pronouncement is risky. Later in this chapter, two twentieth-century productions of a single play are discussed in relation to the effect of an ending.

A search for similarities in plots can be a reductive exercise or, more positively, a preparation for analysing and savouring variations on a theme. When Chaucer in the fourteenth century made the comic motif of a jealous old husband and fresh young wife the centre of three tales on the road to Canterbury, the basic plot was already familiar. Reading the Miller's Tale, the Reeve's Tale and the Merchant's Tale together enhances enjoyment of how the events, and tone, of the story can be managed. Similarly, one late seventeenth-century play exploring the willingness of wives to take lovers is less interesting than a cluster dealing with the theme in contrasting ways. The focus can be on the husband, the wife or the would-be lover, all inviting ridicule or sympathy. Attention to several texts, rather than a single play, increases appreciation of what initially might seem a thin and predictable dramatic situation, whether the possibility of an affair is enthusiastically welcomed as in Wycherley's *The Country Wife* (1674) and Ravenscroft's *The London Cuckolds* (1681) or resisted as in Southerne's *The Wives Excuse; or, Cuckolds Make Themselves* (1692) and Sir John Vanbrugh's *The Provok'd Wife* (1697).

Susanna Centlivre's *The Basset-Table* (1709), revived in 1998 by the company Wild Iris, invites appreciation of neat recycling of stock materials. A Jonsonian ancestry is proclaimed in the humours names – Lady Reveller, Courtly, Worthy, Plainman. Mrs Centlivre presents a spectrum of assorted female types. Along with an outsider by class, the foolish social climber Mrs Sago, there are three wealthy cousins who are distinguished by personality: a frivolous widow, a prude and a scholar (a feminine version of Gimcrack, whose name is mentioned, from Shadwell's *The Virtuoso*). An opening scene in which servants discuss their employers' faults, soon to be exemplified, is an imitation of Southerne's *The Wives Excuse*, 1691–92). A four-couple plot, juggled with dexterity, has a long ancestry established in the *Commedia dell'arte* and frequent in British drama from *Love's Labour's Lost* and *As You Like It* to Etherege's *She Wou'd if She Cou'd* (1668) and Behn's *The Rover* (1677–81).

Competent in her handling of plot and dialogue, Centlivre was productive and successful enough to attract mockery, as 'Phoebe Clinket', in the farce *Three Hours After Marriage* (1717) by Gay, Pope and Arbuthnot. When this character exclaims, after a bundle of her papers is thrown on to the fire, that she is 'undone', her busy churning out of work is mocked in the catalogue of what she has lost: 'A Pindarick ode! five similes! and half an epilogue!' along with bits of a new comedy, a prologue, and commendatory verses (II. 158–65). At points the satire on Phoebe Clinket is broad enough to apply to any woman venturing outside the domestic sphere – 'instead of Puddings, she makes Pastorals' – but an argument that Centlivre is the particular target has been convincingly assembled (Hammond 1997, 203–4).[15] As in the burlesque of Dryden's heroic drama in *The Rehearsal*, satiric attack is partly a tribute to popularity, a sign of knowledge shared by audiences and attackers. It would be unrealistic to expect Mrs Centlivre both to succeed on stage and to anticipate the political correctness of future centuries.

In *The Basset-Table* her portrayal of a young woman with intellectual preoccupations is hardly more sympathetic than Gay, Pope and Arbuthnot's presentation of Phoebe Clinket. Plays by female playwrights do not automatically lend themselves to feminist analysis. When David Roberts calls on Veblen's sociological analysis as a key to understanding the female characters and female audiences of Restoration drama, however, he suggests a way in which Centlivre's farce could be contemplated (1989, 5–12). Does the play reflect how little scope women of the period had for their energies? Are the three major women characters, who devote themselves to gambling at cards, or to learning, or to morality, 'victims of leisure'? Analysis might also take into account the fact that the three leisured male suitors are (like Adam at the beginning of Book IX of *Paradise Lost*) more concerned with human relationships than their female counterparts are. Does this difference between men and women reflect society, define a value, or express wish-fulfilment?

The benign manipulator who brings about comic resolution, in the shape of three marriages and one reconciliation between an abused husband and his wife, is named Sir James Courtly. His own match is with the prim, consciously righteous Lucy, although he has been the lover of Mrs Sago, the grocer's wife. The former adultery between them is only alluded to, as a tedious affair from which he is glad to be freed. His benevolence in arranging her reconciliation with her husband is therefore coolly motivated. This is an unchallenging play, morally and socially. In contrast to comedies in which women take the initiative and test their lovers or husbands, the four major female characters of this play are largely passive. Signs of the decade in which the play was produced are evident in its surface morality, celebrated in the movement towards four happy couples at the end. The two card-playing women have 'learned a lesson' and renounced gambling. Mrs Sago will no longer aspire to move outside her class. Anyone attending this play in expectation of bawdiness associated with a vaguely conceived 'Restoration comedy' would be disappointed.[16] When Lady Reveller is shocked into reformation and attention to her lovelorn suitor, by an apparent attempt at rape, the audience is completely in the secret that the violence is staged by Sir James Courtly so that Lord Worthy can rescue her.

Statistics on performance gathered some two decades ago indicate that between 1660 and 1747 the most popular comedies were by Farquhar, Robert Howard, Dryden, Congreve, Cibber, Betterton, Behn and Shadwell; in the twentieth century, Wycherley, Farquhar,

Congreve and Vanbrugh lead the list (Styan 1986, 258). In recent years, adventurous theatre companies have ventured beyond the most familiar names, usefully providing chances to see how stageworthy the writing of figures such as Centlivre are. In general, as the statistics show, opinions on reputations held by the contemporaries of those dramatists and by readers contemporary with this book are in general alignment, with a few interesting exceptions. In seventeenth and early eighteenth-century accounts of comedy, the names of Etherege and Wycherley are often used as benchmarks for style and wit, as in Dryden's commendatory poem for Southerne's *The Wives Excuse* (1692). Shadwell was valued in his own time and for some decades afterward. Pepys saw his first play, *The Sullen Lovers* (1668), five times; Rochester names him along with Wycherley as an author of true comedy ('An Allusion to Horace'). When *Epsom Wells* was revived in 1709, Steele wrote in *The Tatler* that 'The whole comedy is very just, and the low part of human life represented with much humour and wit' (no. 7, 26 April 1709). Since most students first encounter Shadwell's name in *MacFlecknoe*, the disadvantages of having Dryden as a rival and enemy are clear. Refurbishment of Shadwell's reputation is now in progress; an entire issue of the journal *Restoration: Studies in English Literary Culture, 1660–1700* was devoted to him in the autumn of 1996 (20.2, ed. Slagle).

The study of revivals, their styles and implications, is a fruitful field (Taney 1985; Styan 1986). Kaplan's examination of Restoration comedies on the early twentieth-century London stage suggests contrasting views of the Restoration, as decadent or high-spirited, as brittle or genial (1995, 37–61). The process of adaptation goes on. Few members of the audiences for revivals of Ravenscoft's *The London Cuckolds* (first acted October 1681) are ready to recognise changes made in the script, although for over half a century it was immensely popular and staged every year until 1751 on the Lord Mayor's Day. Steele, who disapproved of it, notes on 16 April 1709 from Will's Coffee-house that 'The play of The London Cuckolds was acted this evening before a suitable audience, who were extremely well diverted with that heap of vice and absurdity' (*Tatler*, no. 8).[17] The freedom with which the text has been treated is in the tradition of late seventeenth-century adaptations of Shakespeare. Ravenscroft himself was active in such transformations. In the preface to his *Titus Andronicus, or The Rape of Lavinia* (1687), he announces that 'none in all that Author's Works ever receiv'd greater Alterations or Additions'.

Subtraction rather than addition is the first major change made by John Byrne, for a London production in 1985.[18] Ravenscroft's design includes three prosperous London citizens who have recently taken a wife. Byrne's simplifies the plot by eliminating Alderman Wiseacres and his child bride from the cast; only a gesture towards their place in the plot is retained in the opening dialogue between Dashwell and Doodle about whether a foolish, witty or godly wife is more apt to make a husband a cuckold. That all ageing husbands are doomed to wear horns is obvious from the start. The fun is the ingenuity with which Ravenscroft complicates this foregone conclusion once he introduces the wives along with an appropriate number of bachelors and motivates the husbands' absences from home by giving them a financial interest in a ship which docks at Gravesend. Byrne's trimming implies distrust of an audience's ability to follow three lines at once, although it is easy to find seventeenth-century intrigues involving four couples. An intelligent addition by Byrne, tightening the strands of plotting, is the theme of rum-smuggling, which links the husbands' concerns with shipping to one bachelor's habitual love of the bottle, and to another's story that he recently arrived in England. The most striking changes are at the end of the play, when rum-smuggling by the ship's captain precipitates legal intervention. Byrne has all the men – husbands, gallants and their servants – arrested by the Watch and led off together, leaving the stage to the two wives and their maids. All the men are humiliated; women are left in charge, to speak a severely truncated version of the original epilogue. This feminist affirmation radically shifts the emphasis of Ravenscroft's farce.

In the National Theatre production of 1998, Terry Johnson's rewriting and direction produced more subtle changes in mood. Teasing out exactly what he added and subtracted from Ravenscroft's text needs painstaking work, since the Methuen volume includes no annotations. A short, incongruous addition in the final act is an appeal by Loveday, who was enamoured with Eugenia before her marriage, to elope with him to a life of requited love. Some of the memorable moments of the production are not indicated at all in the printed text. At the outset of the performance, before a word was spoken, the stage filled gradually with musicians, an elegant string trio joined by five homelier street players with hurdy-gurdy and other robust instruments. Then, in a country dance, the three actresses who played the three wives of the plot were paired first with the three young bachelors, next with their husbands. In this communal scene, complete with the kind of dancing that is at once energetic, intricate and orderly, the play's director suggested a familiar festive ending for comedy. At the end of Act V, in contrast, he avoided contriving the sort of crowd scene which blends easily into curtain calls; instead, the stage emptied slowly, as one by one characters departed alone. A muted, almost desolate, appraisal of love, money and marriage was the result. As a late twentieth-century theatrical experience, this was admirable. It was hardly closer to Ravenscroft's poise between satiric gaiety and social accommodation than the spirit of Tate's *King Lear* was to Shakespeare.

Notes

1. Leslie Hotson's study, *The Commonwealth and Restoration Stage* (1928) remains a standard source, assembling a wealth of documentary evidence to disprove the view that 1642–60 was for the English theatre 'a homogeneous blank' (vii). More recently, Randall's *Winter Fruit: English Drama 1642–1660* (1995) is crammed with information.
2. Davenant's career includes more mundane details. An episode of syphilis deformed his nose. His second period in prison was not for royalist allegiance but for debt.
3. See Charles II's patent to Killigrew, 25 April 1662, quoted in the 'Introduction' to *The London Stage, Part I: 1660–1700*, xxiv–xxv.
4. Eleanore Boswell's study of *The Restoration Court Stage (1660–1702)* (1932) includes account records from His Majesty's Office of Works which illuminate the construction of both the Cockpit and the Hall Theatre at Whitehall, along with payments in 1662 and 1666 for construction of a stage in the apartments of Catherine of Braganza, used both for the queen's music and for 'drollery' or puppets.
5. For a full discussion, see Calhoun Winton, 'Dramatic Censorship' in Hume (1980), 286–308.
6. On Humphrey Moseley's importance as a publisher of plays, see Kewes (1995).
7. Statistics are further inflated by unperformed plays, including the twenty-six published by Margaret Cavendish, Duchess of Newcastle, sometimes dismissed as 'incoherent and virtually unperformable' (Shattock 1993, 313), sometimes read much more sympathetically (Wiseman in Grundy and Wiseman 1992, 159–77; Straznicky 1995, 355–90). A dramatic framework may enliven literary criticism (as in Gildon's *A New Rehearsal*) or political propaganda. *The Excommuni-*

cated Prince: or, The False Relique. A Tragedy (1679), perhaps written by Walter Thomas, has a villain 'who by the instigation of the Pope, Conspires the Prince's Death' (dedicatory epistle); on the title-page is the unlikely claim that this was 'Acted by His Holiness's Servants'.

8. Milhous and Hume usefully indicate original pagination, which is used here.

9. *Historia histrionica* was included in Robert Dodsley's eighteenth-century edition of *Old Plays*; extracts are printed in Bentley's *Jacobean and Caroline Stage*. The complete text is available in facsimile.

10. Perhaps, Edward A. Langhans suggests, Dorset Garden was 'too cavernous' for spoken plays ('The Theatres' in Hume 1980, 42). Langhans provides statistical tables on the construction of Restoration and eighteenth-century playhouses, with conjectures on their capacity (61–5).

11. Derek Hughes provides stimulating and sophisticated discussion of Carolean drama in relation to 'problematic ways of signifying the self' (1996, 27).

12. For contrary opinions, defending Southerne's comic scenes as providing a foil for the heroic figures, a means toward moral distinctions, and a choric function, see Rothstein (1967), 146–7. Hughes comments that 'the two plots of *Oroonoko* juxtapose two characters confronting a new world in new roles, which expose them to new and hitherto unexperienced categories of judgement' (1996, 426).

13. Susan Owen discusses *Venice Preserv'd* within the context of fifty-four plays written during the Exclusion Crisis (1996, 229–38). She concludes 'The fact that the play remains comparatively popular when other tragedies of the period are forgotten is probably due to its potential for contradictory interpretations' (238).

14. In considering alternative interpretations, Gill surveys proponents of the view that 'the harmonious alliance that occurs at the end of Restoration comedies represents the triumph of natural, sexually enlightened principles' and those who see the endings as a 'resurgence of traditional moral values' (27, 171).

15. In a chapter on 'The Scriblerians and Their Enemies' Hammond also invites comparison between Centlivre's two plays centred on card-playing, *The Gamester* and *The Basset-Table*, and Pope's *Rape of the Lock*. Among the common motifs, along with carefully worked-out card games, are symbolic or simulated rape, a contrasting female pair of coquette and prude, and emphasis on 'commodification' or luxury culture (1997, 211–14).

16. Centlivre's work falls in the self-consciously moral period of the early 1700s, but in any case Hume emphasises the very short period in

which comedy earned this reputation: 'Genteel smut is a development of the seventies: *The Country-Wife* (1675) could not possibly have been staged a decade earlier than it was' (Hume 1976, 249). The bawdiest play performed in the early Restoration was Thomas Killigrew's 1640 comedy *The Parson's Wedding*, made more titillating by its presentation in 1664 by an all-woman cast. On the other hand, Evelyn's diary provides a general denunciation of foul and indecent public theatres (18 October 1666).

17. Cibber is similarly unhappy about the play's popularity at the turn of the century, commenting that 'the most rank Play that ever succeeded, was then in the highest Court-Favour' (1740; 1968, 147).

18. *The London Cuckolds* opened at the Leicester Haymarket Theatre on 16 May 1985 and later transferred to the Lyric Theatre, Hammersmith.

4 An Aggregate of Various Nations

In *The Spectator*, no. 403 (12 June 1712) Addison describes a ramble around London coffee-houses on the day 'when we had a Current [false] Report of the King of *France*'s Death'. In his tour, he finds this news discussed with animation from the point of view of politics, poetry, law and commerce. At St James the succession of the European royal lines is reviewed. At Will's Coffee-House the assembled wits muse on whether Boileau, Racine or Corneille, if still alive, would have written the best elegy. In Fish-street speculation centres on whether mackerel will be in greater supply, through a reduction in the activity of French privateers. Whether or not the survey will bear the weight of Addison's opening thesis that London is 'an Aggregate of various Nations distinguished from each other by their respective Customs, Manners, and Interests', it does serve to illustrate his conclusion, mildly amused and mildly moralising, that on a given report, 'every one is apt to consider it with a regard to his own particular Interest and Advantage.'

The essay is a neat journalistic turn. It is also a nice piece of literary recycling, for Addison is expanding an idea of his friend and fellow editor Richard Steele, who used, in date-lines for *The Tatler*, names of the coffee-houses associated respectively with men about town, wits and poets, members of the Royal Society, and politicians. The first issue of *The Tatler* (12 April 1709) announced that 'All Accounts of *Gallantry*, *Pleasure*, and *Entertainment*, shall be under the Article of *White's Chocolate-House*; *Poetry*, under that of *Will's Coffee-house*; *Learning*, under the Title of *Græcian*; *Foreign* and *Domestick News*, you will have from St. *James Coffee-house*.'[1]

Although they play on the image of neatly divided, self-contained groups, Steele and Addison expressly set out to promote a larger community of discourse. The reader they construct can move as easily as the editors among these coffee-houses. In *The Spectator*, no.

10 (12 March 1711), Addison covets a reputation for opening up civil conversation. 'It was said of *Socrates*, that he brought Philosophy down from Heaven, to inhabit among Men; and I shall be ambitious to have it said of me, that I have brought philosophy out of Closets and Libraries, Schools and Colleges, to dwell in Clubs and Assemblies, at Tea-Tables, and in Coffee-Houses.' Later in this issue tea-tables are expanded to 'the female World'. Polite limits of tone and social class are nonetheless clearly drawn. Beyond the borders of Addison's 'Aggregate of various Nations' is unvisited territory. The editors deliberately avoid and deplore partisan controversy (*Spectator*, no. 10 and no. 125), probably a commercially shrewd decision which kept them from alienating a sector of potential readers. Intense religious experience, of the sort pejoratively called 'enthusiasm', is ignored or minimised.[2]

In *The Present State of Wit* (1711), John Gay extravagantly praised Steele's achievement:

> 'Tis incredible to conceive the effect his Writings have had on the Town; How many Thousand follies they have either quite banish'd, or given a very great check to; how much Countenance they have added to Virtue and Religion; how many People they have render'd happy, by showing them it was their own fault if they were not so; and lastly, how entirely they have convinc'd our Fops, and Young Fellows, of the value and advantages of Learning. (13–14)

Swift, who had fallen out with his Whiggish friends by the time he published *Gulliver's Travels* (1726), parodies these hyperbolic claims in 'A Letter from Capt. Gulliver to His Cousin Sympson', cataloguing the effects his own writing should have produced within half a year. During the short run of *The Tatler* (April 1709–January 1711), however, he contributed two poems, 'A Description of a City Shower' and 'A Description of the Morning', and one full essay (no. 230, 28 September 1710) which is of special interest in relation to standards for prose. Inventing a letter to the editor on three 'Abuses among us of great Consequence, the Reformation of which is properly your Province', Swift attacks ignorance, want of taste, and the corruption of the English language. Against these abuses, he proposes contrasting values, 'Wit, Sense, Humour, and Learning' expressed in a simple style, 'that Simplicity which is the best and truest Ornament of most Things in Life'.

Writing in simple civilised prose about 'most things in life', the periodical essayists provide few challenges to modern tastes. Across
almost three hundred years, moderate informed tolerance remains an
approved public attitude. There are continuities, too, in genre. Steele
and Addison invent something like a free-standing Op-Ed page,
amusing or thought-provoking. In the terms of *The Spectator*, no. 10,
they make instruction agreeable, and diversion useful, enlivening
morality with wit and tempering wit with morality. When in the
coffee-house essay Addison writes, not about the death of a great
prince (or about the falsity of rumours) but about reception of the
news, he explores the intersection of the public and private. His
description of individuals in the coffee-houses lingers on personality
revealed through turns of speech. In focusing on personal responses
and the texture of everyday life, the essay chimes with one strand of
the incipient novel. There are links, too, with the introspection of
diaries and autobiographies. Addison poses the question, 'is it not
much better to be let into the knowledge of one's self, than to hear
what passes in Muscovy or Poland?' (no. 10) This is a prose described
in its own day, and often since, usually without irony, as resembling
the conversation of gentlemen, in both the moral and social sense.[3]
Outside the coffee-house and beyond the tea-table there are other
worlds, and cruder or more ornate or more intense prose.

Even a casual glance at the essays raises the question of 'the canon'.
Some selections from the periodical essayists regularly appear on
university reading lists, but there is no agreement about particular
texts. What in prose 1650–1720, before Defoe's narratives towards the
end of the second decade of the eighteenth century, is clearly canonical? With the exception of Bunyan's *Pilgrim's Progress*, and perhaps in
recent decades Behn's *Oroonoko*, there has been little consensus.
Beyond fictional narrative, which takes up a very small proportion of
the publishers' catalogues, there is a tremendous clutter of miscellaneous prose – essays, letters and lives, writing which is occasional,
scientific, practical, religious, political, controversial. The diversity
can be seen as an advantage and opportunity. Almost every university
department of English periodically gives lectures on 'What is
Literature?' For these decades, when a canon of prose narrative hardly
exists, it is almost impossible not to be lured past a few familiar
names. If 'Al that is writen is writen for oure doctrine'[4] here is an invitation to sample philosophy and pastoral romance, pamphlets and
periodicals, jestbooks and courtesy books, diaries and sermons. As

with Addison's piece of news, responses to these varied materials are apt to be coloured by the 'particular interest and advantage' of those who encounter them.

While *The Spectator* and other periodicals of the early eighteenth century are best-known, properly so because of the quality of their contributors, it would be a mistake to ignore their predecessors in the late seventeenth century which had catered to the tastes of a more popular audience. Beginning in the 1690s, John Dunton published *The Athenian Gazette* (soon to be renamed *The Athenian Mercury*) the purpose of which lay in 'Resolving Weekly all the most Nice and Curious Questions Propos'd by the Ingenious.' It first appeared on Tuesday, 17 March $16\frac{90}{91}$,[5] and then twice weekly, on Tuesday and Saturday. As the 'History of the Athenian Society' prefixed to a collection of these papers into bound volumes indicates, it filled a need or gap, both commercial and educational, providing learning made easy even for those without much time for reading or money to buy hefty volumes. In single folio sheets these difficulties are vanquished: 'One hour a week is all the time, that is required to peruse them, and Two pence weekly sufficient to purchase those Papers, in which, every one may find the Marrow of what great Authors have writ on any curious subject' (4). At its first appearance, the periodical advertised that

> All Persons whatever may be resolved *gratis* in any Question that their own satisfaction or Curiosity shall prompt 'em to, if they send their Questions by a Penny Post letter to Mr. *Smith* at his Coffee-house in *Stocks Market* in the *Poultry*, where orders are given for the Reception of such Letters, and care shall be taken for their Resolution by the next Weekly Paper after their sending. (no. 1, 17 March $16\frac{90}{91}$)

As the weeks went on, this notice appeared with modifications, for as queries piled up, the promise of so swift a response was deleted and readers sending letters were reminded 'But pray pay the Postage, or they will not be taken in' (no. 3, and frequently thereafter). Soon, the publisher introduced a lure to readers still much in use in today's periodicals, announcements of the most interesting materials to come in the following issue. One or two more now familiar marketing ploys for serial publications were gradually introduced, notably an alphabetical table or index at the end of each year (though not yet a self-service binder) 'that so those Gentlemen, or Coffee-Houses, that keep by them the several Volumes, Supplements, or single Papers that are publisht from time to time may then Bind them up all together, and by the help of the said *Alphabetical Table* presently find any Subject or Question they have a mind to Consult' (*The Supplement to the First Volume of the Athenian Gazette*, 1691 [A1ᵛ]). Those gentlemen or coffee-houses that had not carefully accumulated individual issues could buy a complete volume, at two shillings and sixpence. Summaries and reviews 'of the considerable Books Printed in all Languages' complete the design.

So successful was the project that imitators appeared. In his autobiography, Dunton indignantly describes an attempt by writers of the *Lacedemonian Mercury* to 'ape our design', and asserts the idea of intellectual copyright: ''twas both *ungenerous* and *unjust* to interlope upon a Man, where he has the sole Right and Property, for the *Children of the Brain* are as much ours, as those we beget in *lawful Wedlock*.' He noted his own clever business practice in competition with the Lacedemonian upstarts, when he advertised that *The Athenian Mercury* would print its own, superior replies to all questions in the rival publication. A satiric play, *The New Athenian Comedy* seems to have demonstrated a standard rule of advertising too. Dunton triumphally notes that although it was written to expose, it actually promoted their cause (*Life and Errors* 1705, 257).

How many of the ingenious questions were devised by the editors themselves, how many were genuine, is beyond verification – but if Dunton is to be believed, the penny post brought dozens of letters each week to Smith's Coffee house, and it was not only immature and timid readers who posed questions. He declares in his autobiography that 'Our *Athenian Project* did not only obtain among the *Populace*, but was well receiv'd by the *Politer* sort of Mankind'. He reports compliments from the Marquis of Halifax and claims that there were frequent letters and questions from Sir William Temple (1705, 261).

Certainly the sheets make amusing reading, partly because of the highly miscellaneous questions posed, and partly because of the skilful handling of difficult answers. In the very first issue, questions range from the theological (Quest. 1. Whether the torments of the damn'd are visible to the Saints in Heaven?) to the domestic (Quest. 6. Whether 'tis lawful for a Man to beat his Wife?) and the scientific (Quest. 7. How came the Spots in the Moon?). On the question of wife-beating, the Athenian wisdom, or prudence, in formulating an answer is a marvel of facility designed to please all readers. First, assuming acceptance of the legal position that the Wife is part of the

Husband, a medical analogy is proposed: a patient may submit to violent treatment, such as lancing or cauterising, for curative ends. Yet,

> as none but Doctors are proper Judges of seasonable Violences to nature; so there are but few Husbands that know how to correct a Wife. To do it in a passion, and pretend Justice, is ridiculous; because that passion incapacitates the Judgment from it's Office; and to do it when one is pleas'd, is a harder Task; so that we conclude, as the legality is unquestionable, so the time and measure are generally too critical for a *Calculation*; when a Wife goes astray, 'tis safe to use a Sympathetick Remedy, as the rebuke of a Kiss: the Antipathetick may prove worse than the Disease. (*Athenian Gazette*, no. 1, 17 March $16\frac{90}{91}$)

Small books

Along with coffee-houses, the chapman's pack is a useful metaphor for diversity. When in the nineteenth century John Ashton attempted to arrange a sampler of chapbooks from the British Museum, an attempt at taxonomy quickly broke down. He announces that texts appear 'under the following heads: – Religious, Diabolical, Supernatural, Superstitious, Romantic, Humorous, Legendary, Historical, Biographical, and Criminal, besides those which cannot fairly be put in any of the above categories' (Ashton 1882, x). Recently reprinted, Ashton's 486-page anthology offers ready access (often, however, in summaries rather than full texts) to the popular, anonymous works underlying more imposing literature.[6] These small books reached far beyond London literary circles to the provinces and the poor. Bunyan ruefully looks back on a time when he preferred them to the Bible: 'the Scriptures thought I, what are they? ... give me a Ballad, a Newsbook, *George* on horseback, or *Bevis of Southhampton*, give me some book that teaches curious arts, that tells of old fables; but for the holy Scriptures I cared not' (*A Few Sighs from Hell* 1658; 1980, I. 333). That *Pilgrim's Progress* is indebted to fabulous adventures is clear; for those whose early reading was more austere, the heroic adventures of Bevis, complete with giants and castles and perilous journeys, can be found in Ashton's compilation (156–62). At least among the young, these stories were read across class divides. Bevis of Southampton and St George turn up again in a *Tatler* essay, as Steele catalogues the reading and indulgently notes the opinions expressed by an eight-year-old godson who had 'turned his Studies, for about a Twelvemonth past, into the Lives and Adventures of Don *Bellianis* of *Greece*, *Guy* of *Warwick*, the *Seven Champions*, and other Historians of that Age' (no. 95, 17 November 1709).

How large the reading public of the second half of the seventeenth century and the beginning of the eighteenth century was has been shown by studies approaching the question from the point of view of education, printing records and distribution of cheap and cheerful, or cheap and frightening, books (Cressy 1980; Spufford 1981). For purely physical reasons, inexpensive popular literature is less likely to survive than more costly volumes. Sold unbound like most other books of the period, and hardly worth the cost of binding, chapbooks were subject to wear and tear, and the more successful, the more popular, the more apt they were to being so tattered that they would not be preserved as valued objects.[7] Fortunately, a few middle-class collectors amassed and bound these ephemeral publications as curiosities. Samuel Pepys, notably, built up collections he called 'Penny Merriments' and 'Penny Godly', now in the library of Magdalene College, Cambridge. Other collections have survived in more specialised areas: by the 1670s the Society of Friends was methodically preserving the many tracts the movement produced (Wright 1932, 80–1).

In the welter of material available for a penny or two there was something for all tastes, from accounts of monstrous births (as in Autolycus' pack, attested as very recent and very true), ghost stories and cautionary tales, through retellings of mediaeval romance to practical handbooks to sermons. With a shilling or two to spare, a young man who liked to think of himself as sophisticated was apt to choose books slightly larger, though still small in the sense of trivial or frivolous. A quarto pamphlet called 'The Character of a Town Gallant' (1675), describes what might form the library of a young spark of the period: 'The *Academy of Compliments, Venus Undress'd, Westminster Drollery*, a *half a dozen plays* and a Bundle of *Bawdy* Songs in Manuscript' (in Sedley 1928, I. xii–xiii).

A glance at any edition of *The Academy of Complements* (1640, 1650, and thereafter) suggests its attractions, along with teasing links to other literature of the period. The 1650 volume, a duodecimo of 344 pages, is a thick pocket-book with a generous array of instruction and

amusement, from an opening ninety-six pages of compliments potentially useful to any Mr Collins, through songs of love and mirth,
sample letters, to a 'Table of hard words, and of Mythology'. An
octavo edition published in 1713 has much the same mix of materials.
Its title-page defines and flatters the readership – people of quality
who will take for granted an easy French phrase – and woos it with a
variety of promised contents:

> *The New Academy of Complements, erected for Ladies, Gentlewomen,*
> *Courtiers, Gentlemen, Scholars, Soldiers, Citizens, Countrymen; and*
> *all persons of what Degree soever of Both Sexes. Stored with variety of*
> *Courtly and Civil Complements, Eloquent Letters of Love and*
> *Friendship, with an Exact Collection of the Newest and Choicest Songs*
> *Alamode, Both Amorous and Jovial.* Compiled by L.B. Sir C.S. Sir W.D.
> and Others the most Refined Wits of this Age. London: Printed for
> John Churchill, at the Black Swan in Pater-Noster-Row, 1713.

Initials coinciding with famous court wits such as Sir Charles Sedley
give an impression of deliberately false advertising. As in earlier
editions, the reader is offered paragraphs of short flattering speeches
for men – 'Sir, your Goodness is as boundless as my Desires to serve
you' – and for women. A potential suitor may choose between clearly
studied praise – 'Madame, The perfume of your sweet breath informs
me, your Mother fed on Roses, when she bred you' – or apparently
unstudied apology: 'Mistress, To be plain with you, I love you; but I
want utterance, and that is a good sign' (1, 20–1).

The model letters are novels and dramas in embryo. Ninety-three
situations in which eloquence might be required include offering
service to the king, rendering thanks for a book, borrowing money,
appealing to parents who would have a daughter marry one she
cannot love, and bidding farewell to an inconstant mistress. The
headings alone are eloquent. Letter 56 is a model of how to propose,
for the second time, to a woman of greater wealth: 'A Gentleman of
good Birth, but small Fortune, to a worthy Lady, after she had given
him a denial.' In a pair of letters, an even more difficult episode is
sketched: 'Letter 57, A Lover to his Mistress, who had lately entertain'd another Servant to her bosom, and her bed', is instructive on
how to express outrage. The lady's reply asserts that she is amazed by
'the frenzy of your cracked Brain' in believing slanderous rumour.
Tactfully, she leaves open avenues for reconciliation, acknowledging

that 'a Lover may be allowed to be a little jealous' and closing, '*Yours, though hugely wronged.*'

The large number of 'courtesy books' suggests a readership charac-terised by a degree of self-consciousness and insecurity, or perhaps by a degree of social mobility. For a shilling *The Art of Complaisance, or the Means to oblige in Conversation* (2nd edition, 1677) supplied 180 pages of advice. In the prefatory 'Advertisement' to *The Rules of Civility* (1678), a translation of a popular French treatise which went through numerous editions in Paris, Brussels and elsewhere, embar-rassment about needing such a book is deflected: 'This Treatise was never intended for the Press, but in Answer to a Gentleman of Provence, who being the Authors particular Friend, desired some few Precepts of Civility for his Son, at that time come newly from the Academy, and designed for the Court.' On the other hand, it is quickly 'judged useful, not only to such as had Children to bring up but to others also, who though advanced in years, might be defective notwithstanding, in the exactness and punctilio of Civility, so indis-pensably necessary in the Conversation of the World' (A3^{r-v}). Part of the interest of the advice is its combination of punctiliousness on details of civility (advice to walk on the left side of a superior, remov-ing one's hat or leaving it on, arranging a letter on the page with a large space between the greeting and text), and glimpses of presum-ably common coarseness in behaviour which is expressly forbidden, such as combing the hair in church or spitting there on the floor; spit-ting into a handkerchief is solemnly advised as the alternative.

Romance

> let me assure you that the more you read of them you will like them still better. (Dorothy Osborne to William Temple, 25 June 1653)

For those with leisure, money to spare and adequate attention spans there were works like the six-volume *Parthenissa* (1654–65) by Roger Boyle (later first Earl of Orrery). In the 1650s, the English reader or writer of romance is fed by several streams. Aside from the mediaeval stories circulating in 'small books', romance has three major sources: Sir Philip Sidney's *Arcadia* (1590), translations of early Greek romances, and contemporary French fiction. To see these examples of fictional narrative as if their major importance were as forerunners of the novel is to think teleologically, to distort them, and to heighten the dissatisfaction or impatience of a modern reader. In the second half of the eighteenth century, Sterne's *Tristram Shandy* challenges and stimulates a reader at every turn to grow aware of assumptions and expectations, of conventions which are hardly recognised as culturally constructed until infringed; to a lesser extent, this is what exposure to earlier narratives does. The stock in trade (with a long shelf life, for the patterns are found at least as far back as Heliodorus's *Aethiopica*, in the third century AD, and survive today in science-fiction sagas) includes heroes and heroines who are aristocratic, often royal, invariably handsome or beautiful. Plots are cluttered with shipwrecks, combats, disguises, trials; families and friends long-separated are finally and wonderfully reunited. A short-breathed modern reader is most apt to have met romance conventions in the comedies of Shakespeare (*Comedy of Errors, Twelfth Night, The Winter's Tale*), but the popularity and influence of the earlier romances makes it worthwhile to read more widely.

The seminal Greek romances were translated into French by Jacques Amyot in the mid-sixteenth century, and thence into English, but in 1657, working directly from the Greek, George Thornley produced a new translation of Longus' *Daphnis and Chloe* so attractive and accurate that it continues to be easily available. Lightly corrected and modernised, it serves as the facing-page version in the Loeb Classical Library edition (1912, and numerous reprints). The story focuses on two innocent foundlings whose idyllic serenity as goatherd and shepherdess is complicated by their discovery of love and by external events including pirates, war, forced separations and unwanted suitors, until the eventual happy ending brings both marriage and, through discovery of their true parentage, money. Although making an announcement is not necessarily equivalent to constructing an audience, Thornley's title page calls *Daphnis and Chloe* 'A Most Sweet and Pleasant Pastoral Romance for Young Ladies', while the narrator's proem describes it as 'an oblation to Love and to Pan and to the Nymphs, and a delightful possession even for all men. For this will cure him that is sick, and rouse him that is in the dumps; one that has loved, it will remember of it; one that has not, it will instruct.' To forestall disappointment, one should be warned that the most sexually instructive passages (in Book III, paragraphs 18–20) are rendered into Latin rather than into English.

Whether or not the readers of romance can be neatly defined by gender, class and political allegiance,[8] the most direct expression of enthusiasm for particular texts is found in the letters of Dorothy Osborne, who fits the stereotype of the romance reader: female, socially and economically comfortable, and royalist. But the young William Temple, on his way to becoming a distinguished statesman and notable prose stylist, found time both to read the many volumes she lent him and to prepare for publication a set of romances himself. How soon, in the original and in translations, French romances by La Calprenède (1614–63) and by Mme de Scudéry (1607–91) reached an English audience can be seen in their correspondence. In early 1653, Dorothy Osborne was recommending La Calprenède's *Cléopâtre* (1647–56) and offering to send 'six Tomes'.[9] Like La Calprenède's ten-volume *Cassandre* (translated by Sir Charles Cotterell, 1667), which is set in the Greece of Alexander the Great, *Cléopâtre* takes place at the border of history and unfettered invention. Here his heroine is the daughter of Antony and Cleopatra. The influence of this vein of historical fiction is clearly marked in heroic plays such as Lee's *The Rival Queens*.

Only a small number of full-fledged English romances were published, but three, of varying degrees of interest and complication, appeared in the first decade of our period. Anna Weamys in *A Continuation of Sir Philip Sidney's 'Arcadia'* (1651) appeals directly to those who know the earlier work; she provides a happy ending for stories Sidney left unresolved. For *The Princess Cloria* (1653–61) Sir Percy Herbert of Powys picks up the name of one of Sidney's characters, Evarchus ('eu-archos' or 'good ruler'), and uses it for a thinly veiled Charles I. Dorothy Osborne looked forward to seeing the work Roger Boyle was known to be writing (September 1653; 1928, 91), but when the first volume arrived she was disappointed. Boyle's attempt to imitate French romances was in some ways oversuccessful. Although she praises the 'handsome Language' of *Parthenissa*, Dorothy Osborne complains that 'all the Story's have too neer a resemblance with those of Other Romances' (11 February 16$\frac{53}{54}$; 1928, 143). In the early eighteenth century, Delarivière Manley developed a more sensational vein of the *roman à clef* in *The Secret History of Queen Zarah and the Zarazians* (1705) and with *Secret Memoirs and Manners of Several Persons of Quality, of both Sexes, From the New Atalantis, an Island in the Mediterranean* (1709).

Sir Percy Herbert's *The Princess Cloria*, published anonymously as 'written by a person of honour', is a case in point of how different approaches may illuminate different qualities of a text. In 1653, the first (of five) parts of the narrative was published under the title *Cloria and Narcissus*; in 1654, a second part was entered in the Stationers' Register; the full text appeared in 1661, with a second edition in 1665. The preface 'To the Reader' of the 1661 edition invites comparisons among the texts, for it calls attention to differences between this edition and what was published during the Commonwealth period. Studying what is omitted, or what is added, has its interests both in relation to literary shaping and to the express political interests of the author. In the full title-page and in the prefatory address to the reader, attention is demanded not simply for a story, but for historical parallels. The title-page introduces the royal romance 'In Five Parts. Embellished with diverse political notions and singular remarks of modern transactions. Concerning the story of most part of Europe for many years last past.' Although there seems to be an invitation to match fictional names and historical personages, as if working out a puzzle, the preface warns:

> do not look for an exact history in every particular circumstance, though perchance upon due consideration you will find a certain methodical coherency between the main story and the numerous transactions that passed, both at home and abroad, as may render people competently satisfied.

Like Sidney's *Arcadia*, the five books mingle poetry with prose. In the author's description of his methods of characterisation, where 'not seldom one name stands for one or diverse parties, according as their faculties and employments were made use of', or remarks in particular that 'the Princess Cloria is not only to be taken for the King's daughter, but also sometimes for his national honour', a student of literature will recognise an intertextual link with Spenser's *The Faerie Queene* as well, and even suspect that some contribution to the princess's name may have come by way of Gloriana. Moreover, the author calls attention to the fact that Cloria, as royal and national honour, 'with some decorum ends every part'; her placing in the narrative is as carefully designed as that of Prince Arthur in Spenser's epic.

The significance of romance as a genre is more diffuse and more interesting than any one of these specific texts. First, it raises ques-

tions about psychological and aesthetic responses, about identification, imagination and sympathy. Secondly, romance is used as a standard in relation to which (often against which) other works are
defined. The vogue in the second half of the century for adopting
romance names implies some degree of adopting, along with names,
ways of imagining oneself. The poet Katherine Philips called herself
Orinda, and gave her friends similar pseudonyms. About half of her
poems are addressed to Mrs Anne Owen as Lucasia; her correspondence during the years 1661 to 1664 with Sir Charles Cotterell was
published as *Letters from Orinda to Poliarchus* (1705). John Locke and
Lady Damaris Masham, too, invented pastoral names for themselves.
Further down the social spectrum, John Dunton used romance
vocabulary in intimate nicknames. Dunton and his wife Ann (who was
sister-in-law to the elder Samuel Wesley) called each other Philaret
and Iris; he called his second wife (Sarah Nicholas) Valeria.

The relationship between a literary genre and formation of identity
is seen even in the syntax of the young Robert Boyle (1627–91, distinguished in his later life in chemistry and physics, his name preserved
in 'Boyle's Law') when he wrote *An Account of Philaretus, during his
Minority*, an unfinished autobiography covering his first nineteen
years. In a narrative which takes him from birth through schooling at
Eton and part of a Grand Tour of Europe, Boyle has little scope for
marvellous and complicated adventures, although he includes a few
providential escapes from mishaps in his childhood (1744, 25–7).
Choosing a name which means lover of excellence, he imitates the
sententiousness and balanced phrases of Sidney's tradition:
'Philaretus was born in a condition, that neither was high enough to
prove a temptation to laziness, nor low enough to discourage him
from aspiring' (19). How significantly the choice of genre, and thus of
style, contributes to conception of character is neatly illustrated by
such a sentence, where evaluative terms are carefully weighed against
one another. Twice he explicitly discusses his own reading of
romances, first at Eton when during convalescence from an illness he
was given *Amadis de Gaule* 'and other fabulous and wandring stories'
to aid his recovery. As a prescription for health, these books were far
from successful: 'for meeting in him with a restless fancy, then made
more susceptible of any impressions by an unemployed pensiveness,
they accustomed his thoughts to such a habitude of roving, that he
has scarce ever been their quiet master since, but they would take all
occasions to steal away, and go a-gadding to objects then unseason-

able and impertinent.' As antidote, amusingly, 'the most effectual way he found to be the extraction of the square and cube roots and especially those more laborious operations of algebra, which both accustom and necessitate the mind to attention' (28). A later bout of romance-reading, in Geneva during his tour, is described more favourably as having contributed to his linguistic abilities in French (38).[10] Like his older brother, he also tried his hand at fictional romance; *The Martyrdom of Theodora and of Didymus*, published semi-anonymously in 1687 as 'By a Person of Quality', has an afterlife in the libretto for Handel's oratorio *Theodora* (1750).

The stimulation of the imagination by romance could be seen as troubling, as it was for young Boyle when he was ill. Disapproval of romances expressed in the period goes beyond the obvious charge that they take time and, in an economic or moral sense, divert energy which could be used more profitably. Fénelon's argument against them in *Traité de l'education des filles* (1687) is concerned with inward effects on the imagination as well as outward effects on behaviour. He assumes that girls have restless imaginations which should be restrained rather than encouraged; George Hickes' version of Fénelon's comment, in *Instructions for the Education of a Daughter*, is that after reading about 'those imaginary Princesses who are in the Romances, always Charming, always Adored, always above all kind of Want', a young girl would find it disgusting 'to descend from this Heroical State to the meanest parts of Housewifery' (1707, 13). In *Marinda, Poems and Translations upon Several Occasions* (1716) Mary Molesworth Monck's gently comic verses 'On a Romantic Lady' call a reader back to reality, after both self-assessment and expectations of her wooers have been distorted. The sense of proportion she recommends is focused in contrasts between the grandiose names Cyrus or Orontes and the domestic Betty, between the adjectives 'grand' and 'pretty' in the opening and final couplet, and between the emotional responses indicated by 'tire' and 'frantic'. No striking pose could survive the lilting double rhymes:

> This poring over your grand *Cyrus*
> Must ruin you, and will quite tire us:
> It makes you think, that an Affront 'tis,
> Unless your Lover's an *Orontes*,
> And courts you with a Passion frantic,
> In Manner and in Style Romantic.

> Now though I count myself no *Zero*,
> I don't pretend to be an *Hero*,
> Or a By-blow of him that thunders,
> Nor are you one of the sev'n Wonders,
> But a young Damsel very pretty,
> And your true Name is Mistress Betty.

Charges of frivolity or of falsity could be brought against any fiction. A review of female education in Mary Chudleigh's poem 'The Ladies Defense', includes the recommendation that women be encouraged to study solid subjects and 'Instead of Novels, Histories peruse' (l. 557).

On the other hand, the audience for the romances includes men and women of intelligence and sophistication who celebrate their affective qualities. As Dorothy Osborne and William Temple are sharing views of stories in Mme de Scudéry's *Le Grand Cyrus*, she asks him to tell her 'which you have most compassion for' (September 1653; 1928, 81). When Hobbes comments on reading which nourishes an illusionary sense of oneself, he sounds as disapproving as Fénelon:

> the *fiction*, which is also imagination, of actions done by ourselves, which never were done, is *glorying*; but because it begetteth no appetite nor endeavour to any further attempt, it is merely *vain* and unprofitable, as when a man imagineth himself to do the actions whereof he readeth in some *romance*, or to be like some man whose acts he admireth (*Human Nature* 1650 [manuscript circulation 1640], IX.1; *Works* IV.41).

What Hobbes says about pity, however, provides a way of seeing the romance reader's imagination in a positive light.

> Pity is *imagination* or *fiction* of *future* calamity to *ourselves*, proceeding from the sense of *another* man's calamity ... The contrary of pity is *hardness of heart*, proceeding either from *slowness* of imagination, or from extreme great *opinion* of their own *exemption* of the like calamity (*Human Nature* IX. 10; *Works* IV. 45–6).

In *Leviathan* (1651), he sets side by side the creative activity of a poet in combining simple memories, and the process by which a reader constructs a multiple personality or sense of self. Simple imagination, the memory of a man or a horse, say, is contrasted with compound imagination:

as when, from the sight of a man at one time, and of a horse at another, we conceive in our mind a Centaur. So when a man compoundeth the image of his own person with the image of the actions of another man, as when a man imagines himself a Hercules, or an Alexander, which happeneth often to them that are much taken with reading of romances, it is a compound imagination, and properly but a fiction of the mind. (*Leviathan*, I. ii; Works III. 6)

Is he here being critical of romance, or suggesting a continuum between a poet's yoking unlike things together and a reader's identification with characters?

What Dorothy Osborne looked for, and did not find, in *Parthenissa* was novelty, and novel becomes a more fashionable term for fiction before the seventeenth century is out. This is not yet, however, the novel as recognised in the eighteenth and nineteenth centuries. In later decades of the seventeenth century, exactly what 'novel' means remains uncertain. In the often reprinted preface to *Incognita: or, Love and Duty Reconciled* (1692) Congreve defines novel and romance in contrast to each other, providing what at first glance seems a useful distinction:

> Romances are generally composed of the constant loves and invincible courages of heroes, heroines, kings and queens, mortals of the first rank, and so forth; where lofty language, miraculous contingencies and impossible performances elevate and surprise the reader into a giddy delight, which leaves him flat upon the ground whenever he gives off, and vexes him to think how he has suffered himself to be pleased and transported, concerned and afflicted, at the several passages which he has read, viz., these knights' success to their damsels' misfortunes and such like, when he is forced to be very well convinced that 'tis all a lie.
>
> Novels are of a more familiar nature; come near us, and represent to us intrigues in practice; delight us with accidents and odd events, but not such as are wholly unusual or unprecedented – such which, not being so distant from our belief, bring also the pleasure nearer us. Romances give more of wonder, novels more delight. (1692; Salzman 1991, 474)

This is very fine. But turning from the preface to the full text of *Incognita* involves a readjustment of expectations. The two rich young men who are its major characters are not, to be sure, knights, but at

short notice they provide themselves with silver or gold and enam-
elled suits of light armour in order to participate in a tournament,
where in the presence of the ladies they love they acquit themselves
with surpassing skill. The very first word of the narrative, 'Aurelian',
announcing the name of one of the two heroes, is enough to alert the
audience that its characters are not of a commonplace kind.

Judged as a realistic novel, or as a preparation for the realistic novel,
Incognita would produce only giggles. Both Aurelian, returning to
Florence after some years of study in Siena, and his similarly independent, handsome Spanish friend Hippolito fall in love at first sight, at a
masked ball. Congreve emphasises the extravagance and improbability of this development in his description of Aurelian's response to an
unidentified lady:

> For his part, he was strangely and insensibly fallen in love with her
> shape, wit and air, which, together with a white hand he had seen
> (perhaps not accidentally), were enough to have subdued a more
> stubborn heart than ever he was master of. And for her face, which he
> had not seen, he bestowed upon her the best his imagination could
> furnish him with. I should, by right, now describe her dress, which
> was extremely agreeable and rich, but 'tis possible I might err in some
> material pin or other, in the sticking of which, maybe, the whole
> grace of the drapery depended. (483)

After underlining the fact that Aurelian has not yet really seen her, the
narrator's calling attention to artifice and deliberate judgment in the
final bathetic sentence of this passage increases ironic distance from
the situation. The narrator piles up further absurdities. After the lady
teasingly gives Aurelian a choice between seeing her face or knowing
her name, he, in order to extend his period of freedom before
announcing to his father that he has arrived in Florence, impulsively
takes on the identity of Hippolito. Meanwhile the real Hippolito has
been accosted by Leonora, who because of the clothes he has hired
mistakes him for her cousin Don Lorenzo. Both she and her friend
Juliana, when they see him imprudently appearing 'in a habit which
so many must needs remember you to have worn upon the like occasion not long ago', fear that he will be ambushed by Juliana's brother,
who has hated him since a duel when he 'had the fortune to kill his
kinsman'. A reader who at this point turns back to the preface to
reread its comments on events 'not ... wholly unusual or unprece-

dented' is in danger of missing Leonora's information that, in some way that will mysteriously heal feuds between houses, a marriage is being arranged between Juliana, the Marquis's daughter, and Aurelian, son of Don Fabio. Other sensational and more or less unusual events accumulate. If a young lady chooses to meet her beloved at midnight at a convent gate, and if her letter specifying which convent she means is partially destroyed, it is all too likely that a villain will take advantage of her exposed position, although a kindly author may ensure that the wandering lover comes by at the crucial moment. If a second lover lurks in the garden of his beloved's house, it is not unprecedented that he should hear the lady sing, to the accompaniment of a lute, a poem confessing her love, and follow that with a soliloquy making her emotions even clearer. In an interpretative community formed by reading Sidney's *Arcadia*, that development is surprising only in the way that a second or third corpse is surprising to readers of detective novels.

Congreve's own prefatory comments about genre remain provocative and puzzling. In comparing romances and novels he writes: 'with reverence be it spoken, and the parallel kept at due distance, there is something of equality in the proportion which they bear in reference to one another with that between comedy and tragedy' (474). Both the two opening phrases and 'somehow' hedge the assertion, and what he does not mean is clearer than what he does. Unlike Dante he is not using 'comedy' primarily to indicate the movement of a plot towards a happy conclusion. In relation to *Incognita* he can hardly be thinking of the distinction, as old at least as Aristotle, that comedy deals with characters inferior to the audience, and tragedy with those greater. Only in youth and impetuosity are the heroes of *Incognita* inferior, and impetuous injudicious decisions are often the centre of tragedy. Another version of the Aristotelian division of genres is closer to being apt. A commonplace restated in Sir William Temple's essay 'Of Poetry' is that comedy provides 'the Images of common Life, and Tragedy those of the greater and more extraordinary Passions and Actions among Men' (1690; Spingarn, III. 90). That notion is congruent with Congreve's emphasis on courtship rather than affairs of state, at least until the suspicion arises that in reconciling feuding Italian families, *Incognita* is a happier version of *Romeo and Juliet*. The political implications of Congreve's story are much more lightly sketched than those of Sidney's *Arcadia*, which has a similar skeletal plot, as young lovers unknowingly choose exactly the match intended by their parents.

Congreve was by no means the first or only seventeenth-century author to invite judgment of his work by claiming a generic distinction which may or may not hold up under examination. That romance was almost synonymous with improbability can be seen in John Dunton's claim that 'Were all the Passages of my *Life* publish'd, it would be taken for more than a *Romance*. It is so full of Adventures which surpass the stories of *Gyants, Monsters, Enchanted Castles*, and the whole System of *Knight Errantry*. Such strange and unexpected Escapes as I have made from the very Jaws of *Death*, exceed the Fables of *Poets*'. He thus promises readers of his autobiography all the novelty and excitement of romance, and truth as well. Further, he suggests that his work is full of moral and religious instruction: 'had I no other Reason but the Remembrance of my own *Perils* and *Deliverances*, it were more than enough to convince me of an unerring Eye that watches over *Mankind*. This makes me chearful and easie in all humane Circumstances, and reconciles me to the *Stoicks*' (*Religio bibliopolae*, 1691, 17).

As the century wore on, 'history' was a more common word on title pages than 'romance', even when the events related had a very tenuous link to fact. Congreve's fellow-dramatist Aphra Behn develops, in *The History of the Nun: or, The Fair Vow-Breaker* (1689), a strand of exotic titillation. *Les lettres portugaises* (1669), purporting to be 'real' letters from a passionate nun deserted by her lover, were translated into English by Sir Roger L'Estrange in 1678, and reached a tenth edition by 1740. The situation of the amorous nun seems to have fascinated readers, and invited a number of spinoffs.[11] The artistic possibilities of a letter based on tension between absolute religious vows and passionate feeling is most memorably developed in Pope's *Eloisa to Abelard* (1717). Behn's *The History of the Nun*, far from historical, may owe something to the mediaeval *demands d'amour* which considered such hypothetical questions as how much guilt attaches itself to someone who takes a second spouse while mistakenly believing that the first is dead.

John J. Richetti, who in his full-length study of *Popular Fiction Before Richardson* (1969) approaches narratives published between 1700 and 1739 as 'fantasy machines', might be expected to consider Behn's romance in the same way. Instead, as co-editor of an anthology which usefully makes available modern-spelling texts of some *Popular Fiction by Women 1660–1730*, he introduces it as a political manifesto, thereby offering a startling demonstration of the victory of preconceptions over perception:

Behn's story is an implicit critique of the distorting effects of the monastic life, but it is also a shrewd presentation of the powerful satisfactions such a life could offer and the selfish and powerful ego it could produce. It is also a dramatisation of the traps and dead ends patriarchal society offers to beautiful and virtuous women, and Isabella is a sympathetic figure even when she murders two husbands. (Backscheider and Richetti 1996, 2)

Possibly Richetti is reading back into the story the generalisations he asserts in his overly neat summary of Behn's reputation – 'she has become an exemplar of the woman writer for feminist critics.' It is difficult, however, to find a fit between Behn's story of the fair vow-breaker Isabella and this commentary. So far as 'patriarchal society' goes, Isabella's father carefully stipulates that she is to have a choice between the convent and the world. The authority figure of her child-hood is an aunt, the abbess of a convent, who understandably hopes Isabella and her fortune will remain there, but who nonetheless 'to discharge her conscience to her brother', dresses the young heiress richly and organises outings for her with ladies of quality. The charac-ter most clearly trapped by patriarchal authority is Isabella's first husband Henault, whose 'cruel father' disapproves of his living idly, 'giving up his youth and glory to lazy love'; financial support and parental approval depend on the young man's joining a Venetian military campaign against the Turks (28–9). At every point in the story Isabella wins approval from all who see her. Although there are occa-sional references to 'austerities', convent life as she leads it resembles a fashionable salon; anyone of quality who passes through the town comes to speak with 'the lovely Isabella' at her grate. This is a fantasy machine indeed, a dream of unreserved praise. Even at the end of the tale when she appears on the scaffold after the double murder of her husbands, she looks so beautiful and speaks so eloquently that she 'set all hearts a flaming', and she is 'generally lamented and honor-ably buried' (42). Psychologically, the tale is strikingly self-indulgent; formally it is neat. Behn's handling of plot is, as in her other works, clear and competent; she provides a symmetrical structure in the wooing of Isabella by Villenoys, by Henault, and again by Villenoys when Henault is missing, presumed dead.

Jane Barker, whose rewriting of *The History of the Nun* suggests dry criticism of Behn's work,[12] gives conflicting generic signals on the title page of her prose publication, *Love Intrigues*:

> *Love Intrigues: Or, The History of the Amours of Bosvil and Galesia, As Related to Lucasia, in St. Germans Garden. A Novel. Written by a Young Lady. Omne tulit punctum qui miscuit utile dulci.* (1713)

The words 'History' and 'Novel' are both set in larger caps than 'Love Intrigues' and 'Amours'. While the names are characteristic of romance, the St Germain Gardens are not geographically remote. The transmission of the story is specific. The Latin quotation, from Horace (*Ars poetica*, l. 343) means 'He who mixes the useful and agreeable will win full praise'. Although some tensions of that page may be due to the publisher rather than the author, her dedicatory epistle to the Countess of Exeter also pulls in two directions, for the fictional quality of the story is suggested in its reference to 'this little Novel', while autobiographical facts are implied as the author wishes that the countess's young daughter 'may never entangle her Noble Person in those Levities and Misfortunes the ensuing Treatise describes me unhappily to have struggled with'.

Some modern readers find Barker 'strenuously moral' (Pearson 1993, 241), but the prose of *Love Intrigues* is teasingly ironic in its handling of sententious phrases. Note the brisk *'et cetera'*, implying some distance from standard accounts of dangers to be encountered in society, as the first-person narrator Galesia recounts being sent to London to finish her education in the care of her aunt 'under whose prudent Conduct, I might learn a little of the Town Politeness; its Civilities without its Vanities; its Diversions without its Vices, &c.' (1997, 9). She repeats this gesture when describing the first occasion on which she pretends not to believe young Bosvil's expressions of love: 'Thus Crimes and Folly mix themselves with our Vertues, Pride with Honour, Dissimulation with Modesty, &c.' (11). In an inversion of conduct books, this narrative demonstrates the damage of taking too seriously the common social advice to maidens not to expose their feelings openly. Like Jane Bennet in *Pride and Prejudice*, Galesia achieves cool social poise which might easily dismay an uncertain suitor.

Although apparently at a far remove from the elegant settings and psychological intricacies of romance literature, criminal biography plays on readers' familiarity with its conventions. *Don Tomazo* (1680), recounting 'the Juvenile Rambles' of Thomas Dangerfield, Mrs Cellier's 'matchless rogue', has multiple sources. Behind the rough and sometimes cruel adventures lies Nashe's *The Unfortunate*

Traveller (1594), as well as famous Spanish picaresque works, *Lazarillo de Tormes* (1554) and *Guzman de Alfarache* (1599). But when the adolescent thief arrives not at the castle his fellow-runaway has led him to expect but at a poor hovel, he describes it as 'very meanly thatched with oaten reeds, not such as the Arcadian shepherds piped withal, but plain, downright illiterate straw' (1991, 356). Tomazo's unsavoury progress through Scotland, England, Spain, Egypt, the Netherlands, France and Ireland is told in a prose which, though shorter-breathed, occasionally mimics Sidney's sonorous balance: 'The greatest historians have taken as much pains to recount the lives of bad men as of the most deserving subjects of their pens. Mirrors that do not show the deformities as well as beauties of a face are of little use' (351). After a brief period of prosperity, Tomazo and a companion rapidly run through his fortune, for 'as the sea itself would dry up without the continual supply of swelling rivers, so it was impossible for Tomazo's unreplenished bag, had it been as deep as Virgil's passage to Hell, to answer the expectations of a brace of scattergoods that thought it would never be evening' (382). As the elaborate simile with which the sentence begins winds its way past classical allusion to colloquialism, stylistic range and deliberate incongruity are emphasised. There is no moral lesson in *Don Tomazo*. The protagonist is resilient, clever, optimistic; he is more or less successful at robbery, soldiering, counterfeiting and seducing rich women. When his fellow counterfeiters are boiled in oil, and he escapes, luck is on his side. In seventeenth century discussions of heroic drama, the word 'admiration' is used for a kind of amazed wonder, not necessarily approval. This unheroic world of criminal biography may be similarly admired.[13]

In his younger days, well before he became one of the most respected diplomats of Europe, William Temple carefully prepared for the press a set of stories he called *A True Romance, or The Disastrous Chances of Love and Fortune*. Absent from his imposing two-volume *Works* (1720), edited by Jonathan Swift, the romances were not printed until 1930. Temple's prefatory letter, with its pretence of unwilling publication after copies had been taken from his 'scribbled papers', emphasises how conventional such claims were. His dedication to Dorothy Osborne describes the project as a solace during the time he was separated from her. In this group of stories translated and transformed from a French source, a combination of delight in the genre and relaxed willingness to mock it can be seen. The easy coexistence of the two should not surprise a modern reader, hardly the first generation capable of irony and multiple perspectives. When Temple inserts, between narratives whose characters have names such as Alidor and Amaryllis, the tale of John and his wife Jane, his juxtaposition of high romance and ironic parody is comparable to Chaucer's arrangement of the *Canterbury Tales*. The title of the collection celebrates piquant oxymoron, 'True Romance'.

In the most recent full-length study of Sir William Temple, these early stories are flattened into dull plot-summary, accompanied by an unhappy catalogue of apparent faults: loose episodic plotting, stock devices ('the secret entrance, the pining lovers, the brooding revenger, murder, suicide, illicit love'), sententious comments by the narrator, elaborate vocabulary and ornate comparisons. The concluding judgment is a mild apology: 'But most of these weaknesses are as characteristic of the seventeenth-[century] romance as they are of Temple's stories' (Steensma 1970, 30). Quite. But are these qualities necessarily weaknesses? Is the fault in the narratives or in expectations of another century's reader? Instead of condemning the plotting as 'loose', one might enjoy its unexpectedness, its open-endedness, its unpredictable variety and fecundity. It is possible to savour what Patricia Parker describes as characteristic 'detours, postponements, and suspensions' (1979, 220–1). When John in 'The Force of Custom' is separated from his wife, recognised on a faraway quayside by his son, and returned home, Temple's title and certainly his handling of plot suggest sophisticated pleasure in variation of stock episodes. Interplay between fictional events and a narrator's *sententiae* is still noticeable in modern fiction. Although the proportion of 'wise' comment is smaller than in the seventeenth century, passages of incidental insight can be found underlined in library copies of modern novels, and are not unknown amidst the fascinating improbabilities of series based on private investigators.

A title such as Dale Spender's *Mothers of the Novel: 100 Good Women Writers Before Jane Austen* (1986) seems misguided; thinking of earlier writers simply as ancestors of novelists means setting up inappropriate expectations. J. Paul Hunter's *Before Novels: The Cultural Contexts of Eighteenth-Century Fiction* (1990) invites relishing the different qualities of a wide variety of prose which contributes to later fiction. The texture of everyday life, often one of the joys of modern fiction, is not to be found in the romances which Dorothy Osborne read and William Temple wrote, but in her letters during their seven-year courtship. An account of their chance meeting in 1648, on the Isle of Wight, where Charles I was then prisoner, is recorded within the biography of Temple written by his sister, Lady Giffard. On the day of departure, Dorothy's brother used a diamond to inscribe on the window of the inn a verse from the book of Esther, a transparent warning of vengeance for the king's imprisonment. This cavalier gesture was soon noted; the party was overtaken and brought back before the governor of the castle, and the young man 'only escaped by his sister taking it upon herself' (Giffard 1690; 1930, 5). Such gestures are the stuff of 'true romance'.

The interest of Lady Giffard's biography goes well beyond such dramatic moments. It opens with a paragraph acknowledging aware-ness of conventions which here are not respected:

> I know it is not usual to write the life of any person till the last scene of it be ended, But since such a misfortune would make it impossible to me, I thought I could not chuse a better time than the retirement I am now in, to recollect some perticulars of a life which tis not unlikely his writeings & publick imployments for twenty years may give some the curiosity to know, & which haveing lived with him (except some small intervals) from the age of twelve years old till two and fifety, I am sure no body can give a more exact & faithfull account off. (Giffard 1930, 3)

At first glance, this opening suggests the beginning of a nineteenth-century novel, mingling promise of significant deeds with an assur-ance of truth. Interplay between the narrator's voice and the narrative recounted is apt to be one of the pleasures provided. Given that the subject of these memoirs is a man who refused the office of Secretary of State at least three times, historical and political material is promi-nent, but when the succession of William and Mary is mentioned it is drily described as 'the surprising revolution so well known to every-body'. In eighteenth-century editions (1727, with several reprints in the collected works of Temple), the standard honorific adjective 'glorious' is supplied as a replacement for 'surprising'. The eigh-teenth-century editors omit almost all the passages in which Lady Giffard's individual voice can be heard. Until her manuscript of the *Life* was published in 1930, printed versions lacked both the opening paragraph quoted above and a closing passage:

Hee has now past the age of sixty, which he used to say there was nothing worth liveing for after, that a man had nothing left to hope for more, & could only expect to be weary of himselfe and tire his friends, the last I am sure can never happen to him, & I hope the first never will. God Almighty give him & them patience for what ever is reserv'd for us. (31)

The eighteenth-century editor who deleted these paragraphs makes other significant changes, reducing to a parenthetical half-sentence the death by smallpox of Temple's beloved daughter Diana, at the age of fourteen. On the suicide of Temple's only son, soon after accepting from William III the post of Secretary for War, by drowning himself in the Thames, the early printed editions are completely silent. Lady Giffard refers to the incident with sad obliqueness: 'With this deplorable accident ended all the good fortunes soe long taken notice of in our Famely, & but too well confirm'd the rule that no man ought to think his life happy till the end of it' (Temple 1930, 25). Romance modulates towards Greek tragedy.

Diaries, autobiography, biography

> I began ... to have a sense of myself. (Roger North, *Notes of Mee*)

When in 1923 Arthur Ponsonby, MP, published his engaging *English Diaries: A Review of English Diaries from the Sixteenth to the Twentieth Century with an Introduction on Diary Writing*, he identified only twenty written 1650–1720. Of these twenty, only one, the *Diary and Letters of Elias Ashmole* (1717), was printed before 1720. Many were published by county historical societies in the nineteenth century, but a large number still survive only in manuscript. Growing attention to such material can be seen in William Matthews' *British Diaries: An Annotated Bibliography of British Diaries Written Between 1442 and 1942* (1950) which lists more than three hundred diaries written between 1650 and 1720, and further discoveries continue.[14] Arguing for a clear distinction between diaries and autobiographies, Matthews asserts:

> Autobiographers tend to read biographies and other people's autobiographies before writing their own; and it is under this tutelage that

they present their patterns of living – judicial pictures which share the lineaments and conventions of the most similar lives the writers knew. ... Any true diary includes a multitude of details about daily thoughts, emotions, and actions which would be pruned out in the careful topiary of a biography or autobiography. The diarist can see only the pattern of a day, not the pattern of a lifetime. (ix–x)

Matthews' essentialist notion of the true diary is, however, suspect, especially when it goes beyond the question of whether accounts are written each day, *chaque jour*, as the terms diary and journal imply, to questions about perceiving patterns. Although the contrast between retrospective views and immediate jottings is initially attractive, there is apt to be some blurring of these distinctions. Here diaries, autobiographies and biographies will be considered together, partly because of practical difficulties in sorting. As with other genres, the discussion here is necessarily only a sampling. Paul Delany's *British Autobiography in the Seventeenth Century* (1969) surveys some two hundred texts, with by far the greater proportion in the second half of the century. *The Journal of George Fox* (1694) is more autobiography than diary, but even when a journal is laid out day by day, it is not easy to tell whether the writing was done regularly, or retrospectively. The privacy, too, of journal-keepers is variable; Pepys used shorthand mixed with occasional longhand words, while in her later years Lady Anne Clifford dictated her diary to secretaries. Whether generic classification is fruitful seems dubious, but there are many more promising critical approaches. All the life stories, diaries, autobiographies or biographies, involve intersections between social and cultural conditions and individual perceptions of identity. Part of the interest, as in fictional narrative, is that of stories developing, difficulties overcome, characters defined by accretion of detail and by verbal rhythms. The accounts by Alice Thornton ($16\frac{26}{27}$–1707) of a declining fortune, along with the will and postmortem inventory of her possessions appended to her published *Life*, invite economic analysis. Attention to the writer's struggle to fit experience into a familiar form is particularly rewarding in the case of her never quite successfully shaped story. A large group of religious journals, which at first glance seem similar, repay attention to varying choices of imagery. Grateful as any reader must be for modern editions of writings which for many years survived unprinted, it is well to stay alert about how editorial decisions emphasise or obscure qualities in the texts.

Among diaries, the pair justly established as the big two are very big indeed. In the Oxford Standard Authors edition, John Evelyn's diary, spanning five decades, occupies 1126 pages before a transcription of his epitaph, and some eighty pages of index; this text omits his reports on sermons he heard 1660–1705, which can be found in the unabridged six-volume version. Samuel Pepys's diary, in full, is even more extensive, although it covers only the years 1660 to 1669; the standard edition runs to nine volumes of text, with two additional volumes for notes and index. These two detailed accounts of the Restoration decade occasionally intersect; the men became friends despite social and temperamental differences. One important temperamental similarity is their omnivorous curiosity. As a pair, they make stimulating, complementary reading; comparing their descriptions of major events, such as the Fire of London, is a common but still profitable enterprise. Within the diarists' mass of information, invaluable to social historians, there are justly famous bits, including Pepys on the execution of Major-general Harrison, 'he looking as cheerfully as any man could do in that condition' (13 October 1660), and Evelyn on the death of Charles II, who in his last hours asked his brother to make sure that Nelly (the actress Nell Gwyn, one of his many mistresses) might not starve (4 February 1685). Extensive reading of the diaries is, as with *Hamlet*, an experience of finding them oddly full of quotations, recognising phrases whose origin was only vaguely known.

Here both the usefulness and limitations of anthology selections become clear. There is hardly any introduction to the period more lively than reading these first-hand records of events, private and public, and of immediate responses. The bulk, however, is daunting to a newcomer to the second half of the seventeenth century, and the price of the standard editions prohibitive to those planning an undergraduate syllabus. On the other hand, passages change in meaning when they are isolated from their context. An anthology selection, or quotations in a book such as this one, should send a reader to look for the full text. As a case in point, my own experience of first reading, in a volume of selections for classroom use (1957), Evelyn's entry for 27 January 1658 recording the death of his dear son Dick and then encountering it within the Oxford Standard Authors edition (1959) was instructive. In any printing, the long account of young Dick's quartain ague, the accidents of a frozen river and broken coach which frustrated attempts to summon physicians from London, the catalogue of accomplishments of 'the prettiest, and dearest Child, that ever parents had, being but 5 yeares & 3 days old in years but even at that tender age, a prodigie for Witt, & understanding' and the quotation of his prayers are moving indications of the father's grief. In the final lines of the day's entry, Evelyn modulates from musing to prayer:

> thus God having dressed up a Saint fit for himselfe, would not permit him longer with us, unworthy of the future fruites of this incomparable hopefull blossome: such a Child I never saw; for such a child I blesse God, in whose boosome he is: May I & mine become as this little child, which now follows the Child Jesus, that Lamb of God, in a white robe whithersoever he gos. Even so Lord Jesus, *fiat Voluntas tua*, Thou gavest him to us, thou hast taken him from us, blessed be the name of the Lord, That I had anything acceptable to thee, was from thy Grace alone, since from me he had nothing but sinn; But that thou hast pardon'd, blessed be my God for ever Amen. (27 January 1658)

In the next entry, not included in the volume of 'selections', Evelyn describes an autopsy performed to determine the cause of the child's death, precisely observing the discovery of 'a membranous substance growing to the cavous part of the liver, somewhat neere the edge of it for the compasse of 3 Inches.' The juxtaposition of pious contemplation and scientific curiosity is not a contradiction but an expansion of Eveyln's character.

Whether the account of her life kept by Lady Anne Clifford (1590–1676) would fit Matthews' notion of a 'true diary', even in periods when it was written day by day, is doubtful. In her later diaries she often recalls what happened on the same date many years before. Thus, on 19 January 1676 she gives a circumstantial account of the Sunday afternoon, fifty-nine years ago, when 'in the withdrawing Chamber of Queene Anne the Dane in the Court of Whitehall' the queen advised her to persist in claims to her inheritance – an instance of female solidarity which involved not trusting the matter to King James (Clifford 1992, 239–40). At other points she takes a medium-range view of the recent past. Having at sixty moved north to the great estates which she finally inherited, after half a century of legal hassle, she reviews with zest and energy her activities in the twelve months between February 1650 and 1651; 'I enjoyed myself', she reports, in building and repairs of her many houses, and having the boundaries ridden; she records the settlement of some lawsuits with tenants and the continuation – 'God knows how long' – of others (106–7). Looking for what Matthews calls the pattern of a day, or of a lifetime, means attending to multiple patterns: the layering of memories, the networks of family and friends evoked by frequent entries about births or deaths, the persistence of legal disputes. One of the significant rhythms is a habit of mind which connects the writing of the greatest landowner of northern England with journals and autobiographies written by more humble men and women.

Repeatedly she cites Biblical passages with which her own experience resonates. A year after returning as a widow to the castle where she was born, she comments on finding there by experience 'that saying to be true: Eccles. 7.13, Pss. 104.13, 24, 16.6' (106). The last of these Biblical verses reads, 'The lines are fallen unto me in pleasant places; yea, I have a goodly inheritance.' Tantalisingly, her editor comments that in her last diary 'almost every entry is followed by copious quotations from the Old Testament, particularly the Psalms, Ecclesiastes, and Job, though, in the interest of brevity, most of these have been omitted' (1992, 230). To have only a bare citation, rather than copious quotation, dramatically shifts the pace. Determined to turn to advantage that editorial decision on brevity, a reader who looks up every Bible reference takes an active role in recovering the resonance of words Lady Anne knew by heart. The texture of the later diaries includes repetitions of Psalm 23 ('The Lord is my shepherd') and Psalm 121 ('I will lift up mine eyes unto the hills'). Other passages recalled over and over again are meditations on time (Ecclesiastes 3) and a haunting question from Proverbs 20:24, 'Man's goings are of the Lord; how can a man then understand his own way?'

The very large number of diaries and autobiographies written during the seventeenth century prompts speculation about causes. Did the turmoil of the times contribute to the activity of seeking patterns, searching for stability or for explanations of experiences? The influence of Locke is often mentioned in studies of eighteenth-century diaries and autobiographies. Certainly, in *An Essay Concerning Human Understanding* (1689) Locke encourages self-reflection as he analyses the source of all our knowledge:

> Our Observation employ'd either about *external, sensible Objects; or about the internal Operations of our Minds, perceived and reflected on by our selves, is that, which supplies our Understandings with all the materials of thinking.* (II. 1.2; 1975, 104)

Locke's epistemology, however, is too late to explain the proliferation of seventeenth-century introspective writing. Much of this is linked with a strand of Protestant theology, an increased emphasis on the individual's direct relationship with God which led to earnest, sometimes anxious, soul-searching. In the preface to *Grace Abounding to the Chief of Sinners* (1666), Bunyan lovingly urges his congregation:

> My dear children, call to mind the former days, the years of ancient times; remember also your songs in the night, and commune with your own heart (Psalm 77:5–12). Yea, look diligently, and leave no corner therein unsearched.

Intense attention to thoughts and feelings was encouraged by emphasis on what was called 'experimental' Christianity, a sense of salvation based on personal experience. In the absence of regular confessional practices, many Christians put their soul-searching on paper in a kind of spiritual bookkeeping. Rachel Wriothesley, Lady Russell (1636–1723), kept daily, weekly and monthly reviews of her faults (Reynolds 1920, 96–7).[15] The accounts kept by other Christians are less mechanical, more moving.

One approach to the religious autobiographies is a search for what is shared. Thus in introducing his Clarendon Press edition of Bunyan's *Grace Abounding*, Roger Sharrock neatly lays out typical patterns of pious biography and autobiography, developed by Puritans before the Civil War, and given increased vitality and fuller psychological exploration by members of the radical sects in the mid-century (1962, xxix). Such analysis clarifies generic expectations, explicitly for a reader, implicitly for those writers who found in others' spiritual narratives a framework into which individual experience could be fitted. For literary study, identification of the typical is most useful as a base for savouring differences, a project facilitated by compilations such as Stachniewski's edition of *Grace Abounding* alongside four contemporary nonconformist autobiographies (1998). While images of space and motion, fully developed later in *Pilgrim's Progress*, are rare in *Grace Abounding*, they are prominent in John Crook's account 'Concerning Some of his Spiritual Travels' (1706). Another early Quaker, Francis Howgill, sets up the metaphor of travel by the word 'return' when he entitles his life story *The Inheritance of Jacob Discovered after his Return out of Aegypt* (1656). Howgill's text is full of phrases indicating movement both literal and figurative, as he 'posted up and down after the most excellent sermons' or 'turned within' and 'walked mournfully in sorrow ... Thus I was tossed from mountain to hill' (Howgill 1828, 15, 16, 17). Finally he rejoices in a sense of arrival in the fold of God. Like George Fox, Crook and Howgill are apt to think of experience in terms of space, of 'Openings', a metaphor sometimes combined with that of inner light. In contrast, Bunyan's autobiography insistently emphasises words, which can burst upon him as invasive events: 'these words did with great power suddenly break in upon me' (1680, ¶ 206).[16] After overhearing the poor women of Bedford who 'spake as if joy did make them speak' (¶ 38), words assume an almost personified form as companions; 'their talk and discourse went with me' (¶ 40).

Bunyan's vocation as a preacher and author is manifest when his understanding of Scripture is immediately transformed into an urge to communicate it to others. Walking homeward after hearing a sermon on the Song of Songs, he finds the words 'Thou art my love' beginning to 'kindle' within him:

> I remember, I could not tell how to contain till I got home; I thought I could have spoken of his Love and have told of his mercy to me, even to the very Crows that sat upon the plowed lands before me, had they been capable to have understood me. (¶ 92)

How to interpret the Scriptures is a major theme throughout Bunyan's autobiography; for the greater part of *Grace Abounding*, he is troubled by conflicting passages of comfort and of warning. The dynamics of the narrative are found in his persistent effort to confirm a precarious sense of peace by finding 'a concurrence and agreement in the Scriptures' (¶ 195). Another important part the Bible has in *Grace Abounding*, and in other life stories of the time, is to provide structures for the imagination: models, parallels or metaphors for an individual's experience. Paul, who provides Bunyan's title (1 Timothy 1.15), is important in multiple ways, for his review of his own life in Acts 22 provides a precedent for public conversion narratives, and his continuing to practice his trade as a tentmaker (Acts 18.3) lends authority to an English tinker or tailor, a Bunyan or Evans, presuming to proclaim God's message in defiance of priestly condescension to artisans. Moreover, Paul's notorious opposition to Christianity before his conversion, and his wrestling with conflicts between the letter and spirit of the law, provide both model and comfort for those keenly aware of their transgressions and troubled about how to interpret Scripture. What other figures in the Bible various seventeenth-century Christians choose as models is a neat indication of how they define themselves. Whereas Bunyan often chooses to focus on sinners (Esau who sold his birthright, Peter who denied Christ, and many others), Arise Evans identifies with figures who bolster his authority, aligning himself with Old Testament prophets, Samuel and Jeremiah, or with John the Baptist.

Important as the Bible is as a source of identity, the range of autobiographical accounts is a reminder that models were also found closer to home. One thread which binds together the diaries and autobiographies of Lady Anne Clifford, Margaret Cavendish and Alice Thornton is that all linger on descriptions of their strong mothers. The hack journalist John Dunton tries to claim a great literary father when, in imitation of Sir Thomas Browne, he entitles two works about himself *Religio bibliopolae* (religion of a bookseller, 1691) and *The Life and Errors of John Dunton* (1705), thus inviting comparison with Browne's *Religio medici* (1642) and *Vulgar Errors* (*Pseudodoxia epidemica*, 1646). A scribbler of limited talent, whose copious output earned him places both in Swift's *Battle of the Books* and in Pope's *Dunciad*, Dunton may have been trying in the *Athenian Mercury* (1691–97), too, to follow Browne, transforming his curious enquiries about science and philosophy into a popular guise. At the outset of *Religio bibliopolae*, Dunton echoes Browne's carefully balanced, cadenced prose:

> Though Trades (as well as Nations) have Scandals fastn'd upon them in the Lump, yet there are some in all Professions to whom the abusive Character is not due. Booksellers in the Gross are taken for no better than a Pack of *Knaves* and *Atheists*; (tho' thanks to our few Kindred among the Stars, 'tis only by prejudic'd men) yet among them there is a Retail of men who are no Strangers to *Religion* and *Honesty*. I, that am one of the Calling, am bold to challenge the Title of a *Christian*, neither am I asham'd to expose my *Morals*. (1691, 1)

He aspires as well to Browne's open, tolerant tone and aphoristic turn of phrase, commenting on the futile irrationality of religious persecution: 'We find few edified by a Dungeon, or instructed by the spoiling of their goods' (4).

When Alice Thornton died in 1707, aged ninety, she left *A Book of Remembrances of all the remarkable deliverances of myself, husband*

*and children with their births, and other remarks as concerning myself
and family, beginning from the year 1626.* In three additional manuscript volumes she reworked her memories, sometimes explicitly
calling attention to the process of noting 'accidents and passages
forgotten to be entred' or of repeating something 'more at large
related by me in my First Booke of my own Life' (Thornton 1875, 3,
200). The fullest printed version, published in 1875 by a
Northumbrian historical society, partly obscures, deliberately, the
process of recurrent retrospection and evaluation which these
volumes contain. The editor, noting 'the very numerous repetitions',
tries to simplify the narrative, finding it 'necessary not only to make
omissions, but to transpose passages here and there, to preserve to a
certain extent the chronological sequence of events' (Preface, xv). He
thus semi-conceals what may be more important than sequential
history, Alice Thornton's repetitive attempts to shape and reshape her
memories.

Like Robert Frost, she seeks a momentary stay against disorder. She
makes multiple attempts to sort out memories of economic and
emotional disaster, searching for coherent patterns. Counting
provides a rudimentary order. She sees her life as passing through
three stages: 'virgin estate', marriage and widowhood (234). A longer
and sadder series places such events as 'The birth of my sonne
Christopher Thornton, my ninth childe, Nov. 11, 1667, and of his
death Dec. 1, 1667' (164). The editorial problems presented by her
four manuscript volumes are not unrelated to the difficulties she
herself found in making sense of a trail of misfortune and decline
from a prosperous childhood when her father was Lord Deputy of
Ireland, through 'sad and dismall times of distraction in church and
state' (204), to an impoverished widowhood.

Chaotic as her papers are, they open multiple paths for exploration.
Students with an eye for social and economic history will attend not
only to her accounts of turbulent decades but also to the final inventory which puts a price on everything she owns, furniture, linens,
haystacks. Feminist analysis of her experiences and of her own sense
of her experiences is interestingly complicated. It is easy to see her as
a victim, and she presents herself as one from time to time. At the
point of her marriage, she prefers to see herself as a willing sacrifice
for the family fortunes. Often she seems to be a Calamity Jane, but she
lives to ripe old age, outliving her husband and most of her nine children. Unshapely, repetitive, aesthetically unsatisfying though they

are, her books are nonetheless fascinating from the point of view of literary form; as product and as process, they record a desperate search for order.

Remarkable deliverances, emphasised in her long title, accumulate; there are escapes from fire, falls, flooded rivers, the Irish uprisings, smallpox, and a plotted rape. One characteristic narrative rhythm is description of an incident followed by pious ejaculation. But as deliverances mount up, so do disasters. The narrative is full of deathbeds, with at least a dozen significant ones: father, young Irish orphan, only sister after the birth of a sixteenth child, oldest and most dependable brother, mother, six out of nine children, husband. Try as she will to celebrate 'temporall comforts' and 'spirituall mercys' (144) in well-balanced binary patterns, it is not easy for her to come to terms with loss. Twice she needs reminding of what even a fool or child can grasp. When she lapses into depression after a son, William, dies at the age of two weeks, her four-year-old daughter Alice plays Feste to her Olivia, asking why she mourns. Doesn't she believe William to be in heaven? Would she want him to be sick and suffering here? The story is repeated, with further circumstantial details, soon after her husband's death; on a day when 'passion and a flood of teares over-came my reason and religion' (262–3), her only surviving son, six years old, plays the role of questioner.

One of Alice Thornton's difficulties in making sense of misfortune is her unwillingness to place blame on anyone to whom she owes love and obedience. Detailed financial accounts appear again and again, but long, circumstantial, legal troubles full of 'great burdens, and debts, and losses' are carefully phrased to avoid attributing to her husband anything worse than having had bad advisers (269). Although loyalty to the king and the established church cost her family dearly, lack of reward after the Reformation goes unquestioned. Finally, given her firm belief in providential history, a sentence which begins in complaint twists and turns its way past the attribution to God of all fortune good or bad towards a prayer for patience:

> it was a very pinching consideration to me that I was forced to enter the first conserne of my widdowed condition with bonds, debts, and ingagements for others, whereas I brought soe considerable a fortune, and never knew what debt was, to others, but what I had bin servicable to many in necessity to lend for charity; but it was the good

pleasure of my God to bring me into this dispensation, therefore I do
humbly beg His mercy and grace to indure it with patience. (261)

She knows that the Lord giveth and the Lord taketh away, and that the
right thing to say is blessed be the name of the Lord – and usually she
says it. But this formula from the Book of Job tends, through its parallel phrasing of loss and preservation, to emphasise the severe mysteries of divine providence:

> I ... am now left the most desolate and forlorne widow in the world by
> this seperation of soe dear a husand. *But, who may say to the Lord,
> What doest Thou? since the Lord giveth and the Lord taketh, blessed be
> the name of the Lord.* He pleased to lend me his life, tho' mixed
> comforts with many tribulations of this temporall evils falling uppon
> our own persons, posterity, and estate, which made injoyments to
> bitter to us. Yett while we injoyed each other's love (and, indeed,
> candid love) so intirely to each other, with the benifitt of Christian
> pietie and religion, it did sweeten our temporall troubles to us, and
> made us valew this world but as a troublesome passag into a better.
> And God there by these His dispensations, so wisely framed and
> molded us in the furnace of afflictions, drew our hearts to Him, and
> there fixed our anchor of hope, that affter this miserable life ended,
> we shall injoy each other in a glorious etternity. (234)

In citing the Biblical passage, she conflates the submissive verse ('the
Lord gave, and the Lord hath taken away; blessed be the name of the
Lord', Job 1:21) with a question from the anguished middle chapters
of Job: 'Behold, he taketh away, who can hinder him: who will say
unto him, What doest thou?' (Job 9:12). Her vocabulary rocks back
and forth: 'tribulations of this temporal evil' and 'benefitt of Christian
pietie', 'miserable life' and 'blessed etternity'.[17]

The pattern she consciously tries to find is a simple one, familiar to
readers of Puritan diaries from either side of the Atlantic. John Beadle,
in *The Journal or Diary of a Thankful Christian* (1656) explicitly
recommends 'a survey of all the good things God hath bestowed on
us, and continued to us' as an exercise which 'will much provoke us to
thankfulnesse.' That this is not a pattern exclusive to Puritan writing is
abundantly clear. Every reference to ecclesiastical matters places
Alice Thornton as a mainstream member of the Church of England,
bewildered by those who wanted change of any kind in prayerbook or
ritual. Throughout her books she valiantly strives to make her experi-

ence fit into an established devotional and literary pattern. She never, however, achieves the lucidity found in the autobiography of the New England minister Thomas Shepard, who sadly notes 'I have ever found it a difficult thing to profit even but a little by the sorest and sharpest afflictions' (Shepard [1646] 1972, 71).

Less concerned to fit into an established mould than to celebrate her originality, Margaret Cavendish, Duchess of Newcastle, published *A True Relation of my Birth Breeding and Life* along with her collection of stories *Nature's Pictures* (1656); it was reprinted with her biography of her husband (1667). Finding early modern women who pair autobiography and admiring accounts of their husbands' lives is somewhat easier than finding men who write about their wives.[18] A notable exception is Richard Baxter. He wrote the biographies of four female friends and relatives who died in 1680–81, his wife, his stepmother, his mother-in-law and his housekeeper. Unfortunately, friends persuaded him not to publish three of the four little biographies, and to shorten his account of his wife's life, on the grounds that 'public things are fittest for public notice'. Even with the cuts which his friends advised or editors have made, *A Breviate of Margaret Baxter* (1681) is full of interest, especially when read alongside Baxter's posthumous autobiography *Reliquiae Baxterianae* (1696). Baxter suggests that an account of his wife's life should be morally useful to readers in twenty-one specified ways, and a great deal of the narrative presents her history as an exemplary spiritual biography. There are also, however, personal glimpses; Baxter celebrates the mutual help and mutual love of a marriage which began with inequality of fortune, age and temperament. Twenty-one years younger than he, with a dowry of £2000, she first heard him preach in Kidderminster between 1656 and 1660; when he left for London, she and her mother followed. In the funeral sermon preached by John Howe (who had once been a chaplain to Cromwell), she is praised as a 'Godly Pattern for all Women', and especially praised for greatness of spirit, seen in the timing of her marriage to a nonconformist minister, doomed to silence or legal penalties by the Act of Uniformity in 1662. Practical and energetic in locating rooms where he could sometimes preach (at risk of £40 fine each time, since he would be violating the Conventical Act, forbidding religious gatherings of more than four or five persons, not members of the same household), she was, Baxter reports in his autobiography, 'never so cheerful a companion to me as in prison' where 'she had brought so many Necessaries, that we kept House as contentedly and comfortably as at home' (*Reliquiae Baxterianae*; 1925, 206). Details on differences of opinion give texture to the sense of a happy marriage:

> Her household affairs she ordered with so great skill and decency, as that others much praised that which I was no fit judg of: I had been bred among plain, mean people, and I thought that so much washing of Stairs and Rooms, to keep them as clean as their Trenchers and Dishes, and so much ado about cleanliness and trifles, was a sinful curiosity, and expence of servants time, who might that while have been reading some good book. But she that was otherwise bred, had somewhat other thoughts. (Baxter, *Breviate* 1681, 80)

He reports another contrast of judgment in relation to his voluminous literary output; she 'thought I had done better to have written fewer Books, and to have done those few better' (73). Despite her advice, he published 135 books between 1649 and 1691, and contributed prefaces to at least forty others. Readers of his own day did not, if publishers' sales are a reliable guide, join Margaret Baxter in wishing that he wrote less.

Sermons: a considerable branch of literature

> Why, Sir, you are to consider that sermons make a considerable branch of English literature; so that a library must be very imperfect if it has not a numerous collection of sermons. (Samuel Johnson, in Boswell's *Life*, IV. 105)

In sheer bulk, religious publications are a very considerable branch of literature indeed throughout the years 1650–1720, as they had been since the development of printing. For all incomes, godly books were best-sellers. While peddlers sold ballads and merry tales as well, roughly a third of the chapbooks published were pious (Keeble 1987, 134–5; Spufford 1981, 130). Theological treatises, devotional handbooks, personal experiences, sermons and controversial tracts were produced by and for all ranks of believers or inquirers, with divisions in the religious community unequally represented in the various categories. A very small proportion of the 2678 Quaker texts published between 1650 and 1725 are sermons. In Quaker meetings for worship, both prayer and preaching were supposed to express an outpouring of the spirit rather than formal preparation, About sixty Quaker sermons were nonetheless printed, after having been taken down in shorthand by 'an unknown admirer in another sect' (Wright 1932, xiii–xiv, 141–6). If it is easy enough to imagine that an early seventeenth-century printer might pay actors to reconstruct *Hamlet* from memory, the idea of pirated sermons seems more bizarre. A slight shock is produced by contemplating the activities of publishers rushing into print with surreptitious shorthand notes taken in Quaker meetings, or in 1695 competing to bring out collections of Tillotson's work.

Controversial writing reveals differences in temperament as well as in opinions. Bunyan, in *Grace Abounding*, emphasises the positive effect of his confrontation with Quaker errors (leading to his first book, *Some Gospel-truths Opened*, 1656), 'for as the Quakers did oppose his Truth, so God did the more confirm me in it, by leading me into the Scriptures that did wonderfully maintain it' (1680, 123).[19] Milton, in *Of True Religion, Hæresie, Schism, Toleration, and what best means may be us'd against the growth of Popery* (1673) asserts that 'There is no Learned man but will confess he hath much profited by reading Controversies, his Senses awakt, his Judgement sharpn'd, and the truth which he holds more firmly establish't' (*Prose Works* VIII. 437–8). But although Milton, like the warhorse of Job 39: 25, might feel invigorated by the scent of battle, others unsuccessfully sought concord. In a review of the great sins of the time, John Beadle considers first 'bitter contentions, and that amongst Brethren' (1656; 1996, 43). Gilbert Burnet suspected that intensifying a sense of divisions among the protestant groups was a plot of the papists.[20] A sad personal testimony by John Crook records that debates on minor points of faith and practice 'gendered unto much uncertainty and instability' within an independent congregation 'so that at last we did not meet at all, but grew by degrees into Estrangedness one from another' (Crook 1706; 1998, 166). While many of the debates are no longer of burning interest, the vocabulary in which they were conducted contributes to a stretching of assumptions about earlier centuries' proprieties. The learned Bishop of Chester responds to the 'distempered fancy' of published 'Aspersions and Calumnies' against his polyglot edition of the Bible by writing that his opponent 'like a wanton whelp runs round after his own stern' (Walton 1659, 15). Slanging-matches today are mealy-mouthed in comparison to 'The

Perils of False Brethren', a famous inflammatory sermon of 1709, in which Dr Henry Sacherverell characterises fellow-Christians of a different persuasion from his own as 'bloodsuckers' and 'a brood of vipers'.[21]

If it takes an exercise of the imagination to consider sermon-reading as recreational, that is partly a matter of considering 'which sermon?' In a study of 'The Puritan Death-bed, *c.* 1560–1660' Ralph Houlbrooke comments that 'the formulaic character of funeral sermons must not be exaggerated. One cannot read large numbers of these sermons without enjoying the skill with which the most varied individual character traits and idiosyncrasies were accommodated within the flexible framework of the basic models' (1966, 126–7). Given a choice among, say, recent theoretical essays, seventeenth-century sermons and popular romance, one could find material far more tedious than many a printed sermon. They are not, by any means, all alike. The variety of flavour is striking even within a restricted selection (such as those of the Anglican bishops edited by Simon), and the feast of diverse doctrines, even at the more respectable tables, ranges widely. In a letter of September 1653, Dorothy Osborne reports, with some asperity, having gone to hear the notable Stephen Marshall, 'soe famed that I Expected rare things from him.' (As a member of the Smectymnuus group, Marshall is still mildly famed, at least among readers of Milton's religious pamphlets.) He defended the compulsory payment of tithes to support an estab-lished church, a matter which roused strong feelings and civil disobe-dience, especially from Quakers, during the century, but the rest of his sermon was far from conservative. Dorothy Osborne objects both to Marshall's repetitiousness and to his levelling political theme: 'what doe you think hee told us? why that if there were noe kings no Queens, noe Lords no Ladies, noe Gentlemen nor Gentlewomen, in the world, 'twould bee noe losse at all to God Almighty. this wee had some forty times which made mee remember it whether I would or not.' She adds with a mixture of seriousness and wit: 'he does not preach soe always sure; if he does I cannot beleeve his Sermons will doe much towards the bringing any body to heaven, more than by Exercising their Patience' (1928, 85).

There is not much in common between such a sermon and those delivered by the last but one of the seventeenth-century Archbishops of Canterbury, John Tillotson, who can be found asserting (despite the whole century's demonstration of the opposite) that 'Religion tends to the public welfare of mankind; to the support of Government, and to the peace and happiness of human Societies' (Sisson 1976, II. 193).

Peace and respectability are far from the uniform qualities of religious activity and publication. Pejorative nicknames acquired by religious sects, from Levellers and Ranters to Quakers, call attention to affronts they offered to decorum, socioeconomic stability or complacency. But between 1650 and the end of the century, it would be hard to find any religious position which was not at some point outside the law. Even the most mainstream and unimaginative members of the established church found themselves for some years defined, and disadvantaged, as offenders. With a mixture of grief and bewilderment, Alice Thornton's autobiography reports a bonfire made by parliamentary soldiers 'under pretence of beeing popery in theire service-books' (1875, 37), and the outrage of a congregation whose minister (imposed on them by the government) refuses to allow use of the Lord's Prayer. Unable to think that a minister not episcopally ordained could properly administer the sacraments, she feels sadly 'wanting that benefitt of my salvation' (215). Quakers were imprisoned in great numbers, for owning or printing 'seditious books' among other offenses (Wright 1932, 94–6). Closer to the mainstream are the scrupulous ministers who chose nonconformity in the early years of the Restoration. In different circumstances, Richard Baxter might not have funnelled so much of his considerable energy into books. Persecution, it is well known, stimulates a sense of community; after the Declaration of Indulgence under James II (1687) and the Toleration Act passed under William and Mary (1689), attendance at unauthorised worship services lost something in daring and zeal.

Even in the parish church, the reception of a sermon could be something well beyond respectful and respectable passivity. George Fox was by no means the only listener to challenge a minister's discourse. A contemptuous account in Alice Thornton's autobiography of a Commonwealth clergyman who 'came to the church to prate, for preach he could not, beeing nothing of a scoller', suggests a degree of attention that a present-day minister might either envy or find daunting. Her comment as first phrased implies evaluation of the minister's rhetoric; she continues in a way which emphasises vigorous expression, across social classes, about doctrine. Heckling evidently interrupted the preacher in full flight:

the poore people in the church was soe greived, they came all out of it, and left him; nor did they ever goe againe to him, who, they said, spoke and railed against the Lord's Prayer in Yorke Minster, saing that they were all damned that used it, for it was popish invention. When he had uttered those railings against the Lord's Prayer, and blasphemous speeches against this most holy prayer, which was spoken and taught by our deare Saviour Himselfe, when He was on the earth, there was a poore old woman in the church att the time, when she heard him, rose of her seate in the ally and shooke it in her hand, ready to throw it att him, cryed out, 'They weare noe more damned then himselfe, old hackle backe', and made him come down with shame. (Thornton [1669] 1875, 210)

Not every congregation, of course, was so attentive. There is an anecdote, perhaps apocryphal, about Robert South, Publick Orator to the University of Oxford and Chaplain to the Lord High Chancellor of England (1634–1716):

Preaching before Charles II and his equally profligate courtiers, he perceived in the middle of his sermon that sleep had taken possession of his hearers. Stopping and changing the tone of his voice, he called thrice to Lord Lauderdale, who awakened, stood up: 'My Lord' says South very composedly 'I am sorry to interrupt your repose, but I must beg that you will not snore quite so loud, lest you should awaken his majesty', and then as calmly continued his discourse. (Simon 1976, I. 255–6, n. 3)

A sample of South's preaching, briefly discusssed below, is neither so sophorific nor so witty.

At one end of the best-selling range were little pamphlets like those published by Elizabeth Andrews, who in her widowhood continued the bookseller's trade of her husband. In 1665 she brought out 'the twelfth Edition with Additions' of Andrew Jones' *The Dying Mans Last Sermon. Or, The Fathers last Blessing. Left, and bequeathed as a Legacy unto his Children, immediately before his death. Being comfortable Meditations and Preparations for the day of death* (1665). Elizabeth Andrews used the twelfth, final leaf of the booklet to advertise other wares:

Courteous Reader.

There is lately published an excellent and profitable Sermon, called,

The Christians Blessed Choice. Likewise Christs first sermon, also
Christs last Sermon. And the Christians best Garment. Also Heavens
Glory, and Hells Horror. And the School of Grace. Also, a warning
piece for the Sloathful, Idle, Careless, Drunken, and Secure Ones of
these last and worst of times. Very godly Books, and are but three
pence price.

Likewise,

1. Englands Faithful Physician.
2. The dreadful character of a drunkard.
3. Dooms-day at hand.
4. The Fathers last Blessing to his children.
5. The sin of Pride arraigned and condemned.
6. The Black Book of Conscience.
7. Peters Sermon of Repentance.
8. The Plain Mans Plain Path-way to Heaven.
9. Death Triumphant.
10. The Charitable Christian.

All very necessary for these licentious times, and each of them
being but of two pence price. They are to be sold by Elizabeth
Andrews, at the White Lion near Pye-Corner. (B4^r)

Several of these titles are by the now obscure Andrew Jones. The
popularity of *Dying Mans Last Sermon* pales beside that of his *Black
Book of Conscience*, the sixth item on this numbered list, which was
in its forty-second printing when Pepys added it to his collection of
'Penny Godliness'. The appeal of such works may seem at first
remote or even distasteful, if meditation on hell means the satisfactions of seeing those outside one's own elect group condemned. But
it is worth sampling the prose at first hand. Jones writes in the pithy,
epigrammatic tradition of Bacon. His cadences owe a great deal to
the rhythms of the Bible; his images draw either on Herbert's poetry
or on the same stock of simple images Herbert used in *The Temple*. 'I
can go as willingly to my grave, as to a bed of down, or roses' (A7^r),
says the dying father, confident of God's comfort. Like Bunyan's
writing, these sermons are full of Biblical references. In the 1665
printing, shifts between black-letter type for the sermon proper and
Roman type for Biblical quotations make graphically clear the pleasures of reaching a passage both familiar and neatly joined to argument.

Jones' rhetoric is adapted to his subjects. As one would expect, the father's last blessing begins with sober meditations:

> The life of a Christian is, or rather should be, a continued daily meditation on, or a preparation for the day of his death. The first man living was called Adam (Gen. 2) which in the original signifies a clod of red earth: and he was arrayed and clothed by God with the skins of dead beasts, and adjudged to the Earth to dig and delve in it. God would have his very Name, his Apparel, his Employments, to be continual remembrances of his mortality. (A3^{r-v})

Jones speeds up as he considers the ubiquity and levelling force of death.

> The Daughters of Jersulem, as the Prophet Isaiah saith in the third Chapter and fifteenth Verse, which walk with stretched forth necks, and wanton enticing eyes, mincing as they go, and making a tinkling with their feet, must at last drop into the grave. And they that glory in their Birth and Blood, must make their Beds in the Dust, and acknowledge Corruption as their Father, and the Worms for their Mother. ... There is nothing more certain than Death, and yet nothing more uncertain: most certain it is that we must all dye, but when, where, or how we must dye, that is altogether uncertain. (A4^{r})

Where, except in a politician's oratory, is one apt to hear such control of repetition these days? A taste for sententiousness may not be strong in our times – except in political contexts – but it can be sensed here. It is not for originality one might enjoy Jones, but for sonorous expression of commonplaces.

For a modern reader attracted by the question of what were bestsellers in another age, it is an advantage to study near an older library with a substantial rare book collection. Few of even the most famous sermons are now in print. When the Archbishop of Canterbury John Tillotson (1630–94) died, there was a flurry of competition among booksellers. Readers soon had a choice between three folio volumes containing 254 sermons and a fourteen-volume octavo set. According to *The Tatler*, no. 101 (1 December 1709), Tillotson's widow was paid the enormous sum of £2500 pounds for 'his immortal Writings'.[22] The publishers' *Term Catalogue* for Michaelmas 1695 warns against surreptitious editions of sermons 'imperfectly taken from him in shorthand' (Simon 1976, II. 353). How is a student today to understand why Addison should celebrate him, or Burnet record in *The History of My Own Times* that 'He had the brightest thoughts, and the most correct style of all our divines; and was esteemed the best preacher of the age' (1724, I. 189)?

There were only occasional attempts in the last century to provide basic materials for judgment. James Moffatt's *The Golden Book of Tillotson* (1926, reprinted 1971) is a maddening collection of snippets, with no information about their context.[23] Selections arranged alphabetically by topic from 'Against Evil-Speaking' and 'Atheism' ('against' understood) to 'Zeal not according to Knowledge' amount to no more than a Reader's Digest introduction to opinions, with a concluding selection of 'Sayings and Sentences', shrewd little page-fillers. Although *The English Sermon Volume II: 1650–1750*, an anthology edited by C. L. Sisson, looks at first more promising, Sisson chooses a single sermon of Tillotson's, preached on Psalm 19: 11 about God's laws, 'And in the keeping of them there is great reward.' It serves to confirm his dismissive, damning view, diametrically opposed to that of Addison and Burnet, that 'Tillotson was one of those ordinary able men, common enough in the world of affairs, who owe their eminence to the utter suitability of their opinions to the political requirements of the times' (Sisson 1976, II. 190). Here the famous preacher appears as a major transitional figure in a sadly lessened religious tradition:

> The sermon in the new style was on the whole shorter than the old; it made three good points and sent people home to their dinner. Above all it said nothing that would strike sensible people as out of the way; and one might say that the respectable people at this time were becoming dangerously sensible, to the point of imagining that what decent people think must be right. (192)

The archbishop is, indeed, shockingly prudential in the sermon chosen by Sisson, which without exploration of paradox concludes that 'when all is done there is no man can serve his own interest better than by serving God' (II. 204). To make an independent judgment, perhaps somewhere between contemporary praise of Tillotson and Sisson's assertion, 'His mind was without originality and his expositions of doctrine are notably shallow' (II. 190–1), it is necessary to search either for early editions or for the admirable doctoral thesis by Irène Simon, *Three Restoration Divines* (1976), which presents nine of Tillotson's sermons in modernised spelling and punctuation, accompanied by a clear introduction and useful brief notes.

For an extreme contrast to Tillotson, we might go back slightly before mid-century to pick up a famous sermon which celebrates pure spirituality. *A Sermon Preached before the Honourable House of Commons, at Westminster, March 31, 1647* by Ralph Cudworth is an illuminating introduction to what Puritan could really mean, not the sadly rigidified legalism or prudery often now indicated by the term.[24] The spirit, rather than the letter, of the law is what Cudworth vigorously preaches:

> I do not ... mean, by *Holinesse*, the mere performance of outward Duties of Religion, coldly acted over as a task, not our habituall Prayings, Hearings, Fastings, multiplied one upon another (though these be all good, as subservient to an higher end) but I mean an inward *Soul* and *Principle* of *Divine Life*, that spiriteth all these; that enliveneth and quickeneth, the dead carkasse, of all our outward Performances whatsoever. (Cudworth 1647, 73)

At the peroration of the sermon, Cudworth's Platonism is an inversion of the ladder Socrates describes towards the end of the *Symposium*; beginning with love for God, the truly free Christian descends downward to love all that God creates:

> There is a Straitnesse, Slavery, and Narrownesse in all Sinne: Sinne crowds and crumples up our souls, which if they were freely spread abroad, would be as wide, and as large as the whole Universe. No man is truly free, but he that hath his *will* enlarged to the extent of Gods own will, by loving whatsoever God loves, and nothing else. Such a one, doth not fondly hug this and that particular created good thing, and envassal himself unto it, but he loveth every thing that is lovely, beginning at God, and descending down to all his Creatures, according to the severall degrees of perfection in them. He injoyes a boundlesse Liberty, and a boundlesse Sweetnesse, according to his boundlesse Love. He inclaspeth the whole World within his outstretched arms, his Soul is as wide as the whole Universe, as big as *yesterday, to day, and forever*. Whosoever is once acquainted with this Disposition of Spirit, he never desires any thing else: and he loves the *Life of God* in himself, dearer then his own Life. To conclude this therefore; If we love Christ, and *keep his commandments, his commandments will not be grievous to us: His yoke will be easie, and*

his burden light: it will not put us into a State of Bondage, but of perfect Liberty. For it is most true of Evangelicall Obedience, what the wise man speaketh of Wisdome; *Her wayes, are wayes of pleasantnesse, and all her paths are peace; She is a tree of Life to those that lay hold upon her, and happy are all they that retain her.* (Cudworth 1647, 78–9)

Learned though Cudworth is, his vocabulary incorporates homely words – 'Sin crowds and crumples up our souls'. He moves easily from concrete images to rapturous celebration in triple cadences of boundless liberty and sweetness and love. From 'love' there is an easy transition to an image of hugging the world in outstetched arms. From this enlargement, the soul which is as wide as the universe follows neatly on, the phrase 'as big as yesterday, today, and forever' placing the immediate and infinite very close together.

A Sermon Preached before the Court at Christ-Church Chappel in Oxford (1665) by Robert South takes as its text the verse about wisdom which Cudworth quotes at the end of his sermon: 'Her Wayes are Wayes of Pleasantness' (Proverbs 3: 17). When this urbane oration was reprinted in the eighteenth century, it was praised in *The Tatler*, no. 205 (1 August 1710), as an 'admirable Discourse' containing 'whatever Wit and Wisdom can put together'. There is little that is unworldly here. It seems a sad transition from Cudworth's pure holiness. South proceeds rationally to argue against the prejudice that religion is 'an Enemy to mens pleasures, that it bereaves them of all the sweets of Converse, dooms them to an absurd and perpetual Melancholy, designing to make the world nothing else but a great Monastery'; he claims that religion 'interferes not with any rational pleasure; that it bids no body quit the enjoyment of any one thing that his Reason can prove to him, ought to be enjoyed' (South 1665, 3–4). To be sure, he makes a distinction between sensuality and the more refined pleasures of the mind. Like Aristotle, whom he cites, he considers learning the liveliest pleasure, and he celebrates the pleasures both of a good conscience and of theological contemplation as more lasting than those of the table, 'For surely no man was ever weary of *thinking*' (28–9). Occasionally, a pithy comparison emphasises the contrast between appetite and the 'refined delights of a Soul Clarifyed by Grace and Vertue. The pleasures of an Angel can never be the pleasures of a Hogg' (9). Once, he gestures towards political-religious controversy in an attack on 'those affected, uncommanded, absurd Austerities, so much prized and exercised by some of the *Romish* Profession' (36). How much should the contrasts with Cudworth be attributed to individual or theological differences, how much to loss of fervour within the national church, how much to a particular occasion? This is a university sermon. One might wonder whether its relative brevity is an oblique commentary on the taste of Charles II's court. It is certainly clear, and well adapted to a hedonist audience in asserting that 'to exhort men to be Religious, is only in other words to exhort them to take their Pleasure' even if the pleasure is 'High, Rational, and Angelical' (38).

Greater stress on conversion, and spiritual transformation, is found in astonishingly popular writing by nonconformist ministers. In addition to those who risked fines for attending their sermons, a large audience was reached by men such as Richard Baxter and Joseph Alleine through their books. However unpromising *A Call to the Unconverted* (1657; in Baxter, *The Practical Works*, II. 481–520) may seem as the title of a best-seller, over 30 000 copies of this work of Baxter's were printed, and Alleine's *An Alarm to Unconverted Sinners* (1672) had a similar circulation. Uncompromisingly rational, Baxter sets up crisp alternatives. Under the stark heading 'Doctrine 1' he directly challenges his readers: 'If you will believe God, believe this: there is but one of these two ways for every wicked man, either conversion or damnation. I know the wicked will hardly be persuaded either of the truth or equity of this. No wonder if the guilty quarrel with the law.' There are echoes of Job, and anticipations of Pope's ironic half-line 'Be the God of God' (*Essay on Man*, I. 122) as he sets up questions for those who doubt the alternatives laid out in his opening text, Ezekiel 33: 11.

> When you find it in the Word of God that *so it is*, and *so it will be*, do you think your selves fit to contradict this Word? Will you call your Maker to the Bar, and examine his Word upon the Accusation of Falshood? Will you sit upon him and judge him by the law of your Conceits? (II. 489)

He can be almost peremptory in his urgent questions and commands, as he is near the beginning of the fifth section of his clearly marked exposition, but this is not his only tone:

> What now will you do Sirs? What is your Resolution? Will you turn or

will you not? Halt not any longer between two Opinions: If the Lord
be God follow him: If your flesh be God, then serve it still. If Heaven
be better than Earth and Fleshly Pleasures, come away and seek a
better Country, and lay up your Treasure where Rust and Moths do
not Corrupt, and Thieves cannot break thro' and Steal, and be awakened at last with all your might, to seek the Kingdom that cannot be
moved. (II. 499)

Note how the cadences shift in length, from the short questions,
through the imperatives with their alternatives, to the alluring invitation to come away to another country. A few pages later, enumerating
the calls to turn and live, there is a surge of eloquence in the description of the principal caller, God himself:

He commandeth all the Planets, and Orbs of Heaven, and they obey:
He commandeth the Sea to ebb and flow, and the whole Creation to
keep its course, and all they obey him: The Angels of Heaven obey his
Will, when he sends them to minister to such silly Worms as we on
Earth. (II. 500)

These cadences invite a participation in power and harmony. Picking
up the image of silly worms, Baxter shifts to satire as he describes a
fool's response to God: 'And yet if he command but a sinner to Turn,
he will not obey him; He only thinks himself wiser than God, and He
cavels and pleads the cause of sin, and will not Obey' (II. 500).

   As with other genres, religious literature published from 1650
onwards pulls a reader back to earlier works which continue to exercise an influence on new writing. A student of Baxter or of Bunyan is
drawn to read Arthur Dent's *The Plaine Mans Path-Way to Heaven*
(1601). While Bunyan never gives the name of his first wife, he does
record titles of the two books she brought to the marriage; 'this
Woman and I, though we came together as poor as poor might be,
(not having so much as a Dish or Spoon betwixt us both) yet this she
had for her part, *The Plaine Mans Path-way to Heaven*, and *The
Practice of Piety* [by Lewis Bayly, 1612], which her father had left her
when he died' (*Grace Abounding* 1680, ¶ 15). Dent's book is 'set forth
dialogue-wise, for the better understanding of the simple', with a
rudimentary fictional background, characterisation and plot as a
scoffer, a Christian and an ignorant man converse during a single day.
The conversational format, which enlivens theological doctrine and

encourages the creation of characters both lively and representative, contributes both to *Pilgrim's Progress* and to *The Life and Death of Mr Badman*. In *The Poor Man's Family Book* (1674) Richard Baxter is consciously following Dent's pathway, attempting 'to do somewhat like it to the same Ends' (Keeble 1982, 89). Dent's one-day conversation among typical characters becomes a nine-day conference between a minister named Paul and an ignorant man named Saul, further variety of tone being added when they are joined by Saul's rich landlord. Here lines of opposition are drawn both between the saved and the unsaved, and between rich and poor – as in Jones' *Dying Man* or Bunyan's early sermon on Dives and Lazarus, *A Few Sighs from Hell*.

Two final examples of religious writing, from within the established church, are much more concerned with this world and with political stability. *A Sermon Preached before the House of Peers in the Abbey of Westminster, on the 5th of November 1689, being Gun-Powder Treason-Day, As Likewise The Day of his Majesties Landing in England* by Gilbert Burnet, Bishop of Salisbury, expresses a phobia about France and the Catholic church which was as strong as right-wing American distrust of Russia and communism during the cold war. Twice, the bishop argues, the fifth of November has been a day revealing divinely ordered preservation of the country: 'who can reflect on these Two *Fifths of November*, without adoring the riches of God's Mercy and Goodness to us in them both?' he asks, and he celebrates the arrival of William of Orange even more than the events of 1605:

> it may be affirmed, That as the Danger which we lately run was greater, so by Consequence, the Deliverance which had its beginning this day, is not only the fresher Blessing, and so the more sensible to us; but is likewise the more Important in it self of the two.

Had James II retained the crown, Burnet argues, 'one half of that Authority that belongs to it, was to have been surrendred up to *Rome*, and the other half must have become tributary to *France*'. He goes on to a lurid account of dangers lurking across the Channel: 'when I have named *France*, I have said all that is necessary to give you a Compleat Idea of the Blackest Tyranny over Mens Consciences, Persons, and Estates' (1689, 26, 27, 28, 29). This oration is hardly an isolated example of cooperation between the government of William and Mary and the established church. In sermon after sermon preached after the arrival from the Netherlands of William and Mary, the date on which William landed is seen as significant, and much is made of the deliverance of the country from those who would threaten both the Protestant church and English independence from papist domination. In a study of royal propaganda 1689–1702, Tony Claydon shows how the court encouraged a view of courtly reformation, of contrast between their reign and that of Charles II and James II, to cope with political difficulties (1996).

A sermon *On Brotherly Love* (1717) displays how closely intertwined politics and religion continue to be (as closely as politics and economic theory are today). A familiar name but a not overly-familiar text can be found in Sisson's anthology of *English Sermons 1650–1750*: Jonathan Swift preaching on Hebrews 13: 1, 'Let Brotherly love continue'. First he examines the causes for the 'great want of brotherly love among us', defining enemies:

> This nation of ours hath, for an hundred years past, been infested by two enemies, the papists and fanatics, who, each in their turns, filled it with blood and slaughter, and, for a time, destroyed both the church and government. The memory of these events hath put all true protestants equally upon their guard against both these adversaries, who, by consequence, do equally hate us. The fanatics revile us, as too nearly approaching to popery; and the papists condemn us, as bordering too much on fanaticism. (Sisson 1976, II. 289–90)

Swift's summary of the middle ground occupied by the established church, and dissatisfaction on both sides, is apt. In addition, his suggestion that the extremes on both sides were viewed with equal suspicion, as an infestation of enemies, both given to blood and slaughter, summarises much of the trouble of the preceding century and the reason why what at first glance seems an entirely benign solution to strife, the attempt by James II to grant toleration at both ends of the religious spectrum, was viewed with great suspicion. Moderation within the Anglican church, in Swift's view, consists of 'due Christian charity to all who dissent from it out of a principle of conscience; the freedom of which ... ought to be fully allowed, as long as it is not abused, *but never trusted with power*' (II. 294, italics added).

Swift is clear-sighted enough about the effects of persecution, which dominates the history of the most fervent of seventeenth-century religious biographies, as a (positively deepening) force. With

insights which twentieth-century sociologists of religion have rediscovered, Swift identifies at the outset of his sermon *On Brotherly Love*
the situation of primitive Christianity, which (although he does not
say so) is parallel to that of English dissenters during much of this
period:

> In the early times of the gospel, the Christians were very much distin-
> guished from all other bodies of men, by the great and constant love
> they bore to each other; which, although it was done in obedience to
> the frequent injunctions of our Saviour and his apostles, yet, I
> confess, there seemeth to have been likewise a natural reason, that
> very much promoted it. For the Christians then were few and scat-
> tered, living under persecution by the heathens round about them, in
> whose hands was all the civil and military power; and there is nothing
> so apt to unite the minds and hearts of men, or to beget love and
> tenderness, as a general distress. (II. 289)

Some of the most lasting and moving prose of the late seventeenth
century was written by those who had been – or were at the time – in
prison for their consciences' sake. Alleine, Baxter, Bunyan come
quickly to mind. Continuing down the alphabet, Calamy reviewed
ejected ministers of the Church of England, and Whiting listed suffering Quakers. Sometimes comfortable in the seventeenth-century
sense, comforting, their writing was seldom comfortable in the pejorative sense proper for South or Tillotson. Indeed, these nonconformists are in a line which leads on towards the fervour of
Methodism and eventually to civil rights demonstrations organised
from within southern American churches.

Notes

1. The first number of *The Tatler* includes foreign news, reporting 'Letters
    from the *Hague* of the 16th' and 'Letters of the 17th from *Ghent*'. After
    the first six months, political news drops away; Steele and Addison
    abandon competition with the newspapers and concentrate on the
    precursors of modern centre-fold commentary.
2. When Addison includes two nonconformists in his coffee-house tour
    of *Spectator* no. 403, he makes their conversation earnest but entirely
    classical rather than spiritual; they are debating whether the king of
    France was more like Augustus Caesar or Nero.

3. See *Tatler*, no. 204; Samuel Johnson, *Lives* II. 149; Sutherland (1957) (quoted below, in Chapter 5). For Addison's self-congratulation on the success of the *Spectator*, and a compliment to the readers 'who give a much greater Attention to Discourses of Virtue and Morality, than ever I expected, or indeed could hope', see no. 262 (31 December 1711).

4. Chaucer, in the Retraction of the *Canterbury Tales*, paraphrases 2 Timothy 3:16.

5. There is some confusion in the use of old and new-style dating. The first two issues are, properly, o.s. 17 March and 24 March 1690, which would place no. 3 in 1691 whether o.s. or n.s. dating was used; the third issue is, however, dated 1690; no. 4 is Saturday, 4 April 1691.

6. It must be used with caution; transitions between reproduction of the original texts and Ashton's paraphrases are not clearly signalled, and his introductory discussion of dating is simply wrong, but an affordable paperback giving samples of title-pages, woodcuts, and at least outline summaries of over a hundred chapbooks is much better than mere second-hand comments. Thompson (1977) provides a small selection of the 'Penny Merriments' collected by Pepys.

7. The statistics on sales of popular works are sometimes remarkable: the Stationers' Company almanacs sold as many as 400000 copies a year in the 1660s. Although almanacs lie on the margins of literary studies, the 'simple chronological histories' they contain could, John Walter suggests, be linked to a changing conception of time, as the 'chronicles rendered the past as a story of sequential change' (Walter 1996, 216).

8. Although largely convincing, the patterns may be overstressed. See Patterson (1984), 159–202; Potter (1989); Smith (1994), 233–49.

9. In commenting 'there are some Stories in't you will like I beleeve' and in adding an afterthought, 'but what an Asse am I to think you can bee idle enough at London to reade Romances. noe i'le keep them till you come hither' (26 February 16$\frac{52}{53}$; 1928, 21), she emphasises the episodic quality of the work and the leisure it required. At the time she wrote, an English translation (by Robert Loveday, published 1652–59) was underway but far from complete.

10. The combination of the romance framework and mundane or scientific experiences during Boyle's Grand Tour of Europe with his brother, including a stop at Florence where he read Galileo, may invite further exploration. Of 'romance' in the modern sense of sexual attractions there is little sign; in Italy the embryonic scientist claims to visit 'the famousest Bordellos ... out of bare curiosity' (45), and he found his prejudice against the Catholic church confirmed when he was propositioned by two monks.

11. 'Five Love-Letters from a Nun to a Cavalier' (1678) and other works

including a seduced, forsaken nun can be found in the anthology of epistolary fiction edited by Würzbach (1969).

12. Retelling *The History of the Nun*, as 'Philinda's Story out of the Book' in *The Lining of the Patch Work Screen* (1727), Jane Barker reduces it to an illustration of the proverbial 'Marry in haste, and Repent at leisure' (1997, 214–16). Her account is a much cooler than Southerne's dramatic version *The Fatal Marriage*, briefly discussed in Chapter 3. For an overview of 'The History of *The History of the Nun*' which is sympathetic to Behn, see Pearson (1993).

13. For further criminal narratives, see Smith (1719), Peterson (1961), Todd and Spearing (1994).

14. An annotated list of female Stuart diarists, with asterisks marking those not included by Matthews, is provided by Mendelson, in Prior (1985), 181–210.

15. Compare with Pepys' regular reviews; see Sherman (1996) for a subtle and incisive analysis of changes in the perception of time, and comments on chronology, narrative, and self-construction in Pepys' diary.

16. References to *Grace Abounding* use the paragraph numbers related to the fifth edition (1680), found in Sharrock (1962) and in Stachniewski (1998). Carlton, having counted over ninety instances in which words drop into Bunyan's consciousness, offers a psychoanalytical explanation in which these 'disclaiming locutions' become signs of 'sublime self-deception' (1984, 22–3). Bunyan himself anticipates such criticism; in the opening pages of *Pilgrim's Progress* a neighbour of the major character labels Christian as one of 'a company of these Craz'd-headed Coxcombs'.

17. Compare with Evelyn's response to the death of his 'deare Child Dick', quoted above. His Biblical quotations and doctrine are generally similar to those of Alice Thornton, but her desperate rush to insist that she has a fixed 'anchor of hope' seems less convincing, less resolved, than his meditation.

18. Among the women who wrote both about their husbands and their own lives are Lucy Hutchinson and Lady Ann Fanshawe; see Hobby (1988), 76–84. Among several husbands who celebrated pious wives, the dissenting minister Samuel Bury abridged and published the *Diary* left by his learned and charitable wife Elizabeth Bury (Ballard 1752; 1985, 368). John Evelyn left in manuscript a *Life of Mrs. Godolphin*, an account of his virtuous and charming friend Margaret Blagg (1652–78), maid of honour, diarist and letter-writer.

19. Later after shared prison experiences with Quakers, Bunyan's opinions about their teaching became modified. Throughout, he attempted like

his mentor John Gifford to avoid controversy about non-essential religious details 'because I saw they engendered strife' (*Grace Abounding,* ¶ 284).

20. The title of Edward Stillingfleet's *Irenicon* (1659) is taken hopefully from *irene*, peace. A bishop himself, Stillingfleet suggests that episcopacy is a suitable but not essential structure, but the question of church government continued to vex and divide the Christian communities.

21. Sacheverell's sermon, which sold 100 000 copies, led to his trial for sedition and subversion, and to riots in which mobs destroyed dissenting meeting-houses. For a brief vivid description see Kishlansky (1996), 314–15, and for a full account Holmes (1973). On the issue of proper language for Christian controversies, see the discussion of Marvell in Patterson (1978), 178–89.

22. Compare with the £20 Milton received in 1667 from Samuel Simons for *Paradise Lost* (his widow was paid an additional £18 in 1680; Geduld 1969, 113–15). Dryden earned £1400 for *The Works of Virgil* (1697).

23. There is no identification of particular sermons and their dates. The claim that the copy-text is 'the folio edition in three volumes' (Moffatt, 39) might simply send a scholar off on a paper-chase. See Simon (1976), 354, notes 2–3, on three-volume 'sets' made up more or less randomly from different editions by one printer of *Fifty Four Sermons* and by another printer of *Two Hundred Sermons*.

24. Notoriously unstable as a term, 'Puritan' was often a used as criticism of scrupulous Christians. Cudworth is usually labelled a Cambridge Platonist.

5   Periods

> I undertook a history of the nation from its remotest origin; intending
> to bring it down, if I could, in one unbroken thread to our own times.
> I had already finished four books, when lo! (Charles's kingdom being
> reduced to a commonwealth) the council of state, as it is called, now
> first constituted by authority of parliament, invited me to lend them
> my services. (Milton, *Second Defence*, 1654)

As he explains why he left unfinished a *History of Britain*, Milton testi-
fies to breaking and tangling of threads, historical and literary. For my
own part, having emphasised for four chapters the complications of
tracing simple patterns between 1650 and 1720, I do not propose in
this final chapter to pull everything together in a tidy knot. What
follows, designed like the rest of the volume to open rather than to
close discussion, is in three sections: first, comments on how writers
of the time described or defined their age; second, a brief survey of
how it is cut into periods by our own contemporaries; and finally, a
return to a particular text, an ode presented to Queen Anne.

Viewpoints: Dryden and his contemporaries

How did writers during the years 1650 to 1720 think of period? First is
a small difference in vocabulary. They were more inclined to speak of
ages than of period: the Elizabethan age, the Augustan age. 'Age' was
already established, as 'period' was not, in classical terms such as 'age
of gold'. 'Age' – *aetas* – is closely linked to human experience while
'period', cooler, more rational, is related to rhetorical conclusions.
While commentators in the seventeenth century might well have
spoken of 'the age of Spenser', they would never have referred to 'the
period of Spenser.' On ages or period, as on everything else, they
spoke, however, in many different voices. One major contrast
between our own time and that is the scale by which historical events

are measured. We are, in comparison with our ancestors, short-sighted (as well as materialistic). To explain a disaster, we look to proximate causes. Marvell, to take as an example one of the most intelligent and discriminating of Restoration writers, takes a much longer view. He sees 'intermitting seasons of Discord, War, and publick Disturbance' in a huge time scale, running from the Fall through events of his own lifetime towards the millenium in a very serious sense (1673; 1971, 232). In Dennis's *The Grounds of Criticism in Poetry* (1704), this long view takes on particular significance in relation to literature, as Dennis asserts that 'The Great Design of Arts is to restore the Decays that happened to human Nature by the Fall, by restoring Order.'

Broad as well as long views characterise the many polymaths of the period. Lack of specialisation, especially clear in the wide curiosity exercised by members of the Royal Society, can be regarded as amateur, or alternatively as a rebuke to later, narrower endeavours. However eccentric or wish-fulfilling her publications, Margaret Cavendish, Duchess of Newcastle, regularly conveys a confident sweep of mind. When another titled but undereducated woman reviews favourite books, a 636-line poem is the result; in 'The Resolution' Mary, Lady Chudleigh, catalogues interests ranging from the writings of Archbishop Tillotson to Lucretius, from Homer to Congreve. Figures whose names come easily to mind as 'authors' were busy in other major roles: courtiers of Charles II, physicians, diplomats, architects. Never before or since in English history have so many peers of the realm also been poets and playwrights. At the same time, books by a multitude of commoners appeared, by gentlemen and tinkers, by women with titles and leisure, or with skills as midwives, or with zeal for religion or education. Within a single work, the range of allusion is sometimes startling; John Evelyn's *Sylva* (1664) combines speculation on the wood used for the Cross with more technical accounts of forestry. Sir William Temple, in 'Upon the Gardens of Epicurus' (1685), moves easily between practical gardening advice and meditations that in time go back to the golden age of Athens, where Epicurus was one of the first to have a garden in the city, and in space as far as to China. Although his own garden was designed symmetrically, like those in Holland where he spent much of his diplomatic career, Temple is open to ideas of a very different aesthetic, describing the asymmetrical ideal of Chinese 'sharawadgi'. In a letter expressing pleasure in English gardens, Pope seems to have both Sir Thomas Browne and Sir William Temple in mind when he mentions 'the hanging Gardens of Babylon, or the Paradise of Cyrus, and the Sharawaggis of China' (*Correspondence*, II. 314). Addison's *Spectator* papers 'On the Pleasures of the Imagination' (nos. 411–21, June–July 1712) freely intermingle theology, quotations from classical poets, and citations from Locke.

In contrast to such fluidity, binary thinking was encouraged by events. The Civil Wars polarised royalists and parliamentarians. In the religious settlement made after the Restoration, the nation's wide spectrum of belief and practice was simplified into conformist and nonconformist, the second term submerging into common hardship the differences among those who did not accept the Anglican prayer-book. By the end of the century, Whigs and Tories were allied into two opposing groups. In literature, divisions into 'them' and 'us' are sometimes prominent, sometimes implicit. Dryden's *Essay of Dramatick Poesie* (1668) focuses on three major literary polarities: French and English, Ancients and Moderns, the 'last' age and the present. Patriotic defensiveness about English poetry was spurred by the prestige of French culture at the court of Charles II, and given additional edge towards the end of the century when France became a literal, military rival. Conceding the literary achievements of France, Dryden and others sometimes make a conscious virtue out of English freedom from rules. Having in *An Essay on Translated Verse* paid tribute to French learning, the Earl of Roscommon moves on to ask:

> But who did ever in French Authors see
> The comprehensive English Energy?
> The weighty Bullion of One Sterling Line,
> Drawn to French Wire, would thro' whole Pages shine.
> (1684, ll. 27–30)

Towards the end of the century, comparisons between the Ancients and Moderns erupted into partisan evaluations of the classical and of contemporary learning, the 'Battle of the Books' treated most wittily by Swift and, in our day, most comprehensively in a lively study by Joseph M. Levine (1991).

In poetry, couplets foreground the binary divisions of debate. Antithetical pairings invite attention to the tensions between Art and Nature, Reason and Passion, Wit and Judgment. Pope deftly praises oxymoronic complications, an 'artful wildness', and mocks the

tedious regularity of poets or landscape artists who balance everything into predictable conclusions and symmetries ('Epistle to
Burlington,' ll. 115–18). Admiration for energy and for order coexists,
although some critics speak more in praise of sublimity, some in
defence of regularity. Reading the work of two outstanding critics of
drama in the later half of the seventeenth century shows that even on
common ground, temperamental differences are as interesting as
agreements. Although Dryden's *Essay of Dramatick Poesie* is set
against the background of a naval battle, and organised as a series of
debates, what is more striking is flexibility and generosity as Dryden
explores what can be said on opposite sides of the questions. It ends,
appropriately, with the four friends parting without having persuaded
one another, but with the sound of cannon replaced by the music of
dancers among whom they move as they come ashore. More polemi-
cally single-minded, Rymer in *The Tragedies of the Last Age Consider'd
and Examin'd by the Practice of the Ancients and by the Common
Sense of All Ages* (1678) rigorously lays down the law, and admits no
shred of pleasure in his prime example, Beaumont and Fletcher's
popular play *The Maid's Tragedy*.

Accumulating divergent or conflicting comments about 'this
present age' from 1650 to 1720 may be a tempting enterprise, more
amusing than persuasive. A spread of seventy years, two full generations, is only one of the reasons why such an exercise is easy, and
easily misleading. Description of one's time is seldom disinterested;
writers have axes to grind. When Edward Phillips asserts that
'nothing, it seems relishes so well as what is written in the smooth
style of our present language, taken to be of late so much refined'
(1675, 26), he is setting forth on a book largely devoted to 'Eminent
Poets among the Moderns'. When, on the other hand, the Earl of
Shaftesbury describes British writing as raw and immature, he is
clearing the way for his own aesthetic philosophy:

> The British Muses, in the Din of Arms, may well lie abject and
> obscure; especially being as yet in their mere Infant-State. They have
> hitherto scarce arrived to any thing of Shapeliness or Person. They
> lisp as in their Cradles: and their stammering Tongues, which
> nothing but their Youth and Rawness can excuse, have hitherto
> spoken in wretched Pun and Quibble. Our Dramatic Shakespeare,
> our Fletcher, Jonson, and our Epic Milton preserve this Style. And
> even a latter Race, scarce free of this Infirmity, and aiming at a false

Sublime, with crowded Simile, and mixed Metaphor (the Hobby-
Horse, and Rattle of the Muses) entertain our raw Fancy and unprac-
tised Ear; which has not as yet had leisure to form itself and become
truly musical. (1710, 64)

Most obvious of all is the interest behind the assertions of John
Vanbrugh (Sir John after 1714), the playwright and architect who
designed Blenheim Palace, when in 1709 he sweepingly claims:

> There is perhaps no one thing, which the most Polite part of Mankind
> have more universally agreed in; than the Value they have ever set
> upon the Remains of distant Times. ('Reasons for Preserving Part of
> the Old Manor, 11th June, 1709')

In the grounds of Blenheim he hoped to preserve the old Woodstock
Manor, where Henry II had kept his mistress Rosamond the Fair.
Tensions in his statement are clear: the absoluteness of '*universally*
agreed in' and of 'the Value they have *ever* set' (my italics) is tempered
by restriction of the group said to agree: only 'the most Polite part of
Mankind.' He exemplifies the habit of universalising opinions held by
oneself, or a small group. Vanbrugh failed, in the event, to convince
the Duchess of Marlborough, and the Old Manor was pulled down.

While Vanbrugh overstates universal agreement on the value of the
past, antiquarianism flourished. Sir Thomas Browne and other collectors blur what now seem sharper boundaries between literary, historical and scientific investigation. From the late sixteenth century, when
Camden wrote *Britannia* (1586), through into the eighteenth century
when the Elizabethan Society of Antiquaries was refounded, continuities can be traced. Delight in Britain's past attracted both sympathis-
ers and ridiculers. The comic lead in *Three Hours After Marriage*
(1717), a farce by Gay, Pope and Arbuthnot, is a character called
Fossile, based on Dr John Woodward (1665–1728), a noted naturalist
and fellow of the Royal Society. Its success was followed by the revival
of Shackerley Marmion's *The Antiquary* (1718, first presented in
1641). The interest in British antiquities, emotional as well as rational,
indicates a self-consciousness about changing times; as Graham Parry
has suggested, awareness that much has been lost or is in danger of
being lost intensified attempts to preserve traces of the past (1989,
173).

Occasionally, there is a confident assertion that change is only superficial. Denham, in a preface to his translation of Book II of the *Aeneid* (1656) comments on style in terms of clothing; his is a metaphor which implies not that people change, but that fashions do:

> Speech is the apparel of our thoughts, so are there certain Garbs and Modes of speaking which vary with the Times; the fashion of our Clothes being not more subject to alteration than that of our Speech ... and therefore if Virgil must needs speak English, it were fit he should speak not only as a Man of this Nation, but as a Man of this Age.

The young Pope, in the preface to his 1717 poems, calmly affirms:

> whatever is very good sense must have been common sense in all times; and what we call Learning, is but the knowledge of the sense of our predecessors. Therefore they who say our thoughts are not our own because they resemble the Ancients, may as well say our faces are not our own, because they are like our Fathers.

It is equally easy, however, to find quotations emphasising flux.

Given the welter of references to time and change, it is useful to distinguish between those musings on mutability which pose the temporal world against steadfast eternity (as in Milton's 'On Time' in his first volume of poems) and comments which divide cultural history into successive ages, whether declining from an Age of Gold or moving towards a Final Judgment. One of the most fascinating scholarly books in recent years, Stuart Sherman's *Telling Time: Clocks, Diaries, and English Diurnal Form, 1660–1785* (1996) focuses on neither of these, but on the interplay between technological innovation and psychological experience; with the development of reliable watches, mechanically measured time plays against biological rhythms or the communal, liturgically marked hours of churchbells. An admirable, clear analysis of contemporary views is provided by Achsah Guibbory who, in *The Map of Time: Seventeenth-Century English Literature and Ideas of Pattern in History*, discusses assessment of change in three major ways, as decay, cycle or progress (1986).

Translation poses in acute form the questions of whether, or how much, real change takes place from one time to another. Which classical authors attracted English translators is itself significant (See

Gillespie 1992 for a checklist). The epic poets chime with the struggle in later seventeenth-century literature to work out a satisfying image of heroism, whether in vernacular 'heroic drama' or in Milton's poetry. The Roman satirists present models for those writing in turbulent times, which Dryden in the bitter later years of his life called 'an Age, indeed, which is only fit for Satire' (Dedicatory epistle to the Duke of Ormond, *Plutarch's Lives*, 1693). Among the classical authors most attractive to English poets was Ovid, perhaps partly because his fictional letters from women to men, the *Heroides*, are in tune with the increasing taste for sentiment, developed especially in late seventeenth-century tragedy, and because *Metamorphoses*, directly concerned with flux and continuity, affirms – in Dryden's translation 'Of the Pythagorean Philosophy, from Ovid's Metamorphoses, Book XV' – that 'all things are but altr'd, nothing dies' (l. 239). Or, in an eloquent expansion of the point:

> Nature knows
> No steadfast station, but or ebbs or flows:
> Ever in motion: she destroys her old,
> And casts new figures in another mold.
>
> . . .
>
> Thus are their Figures never at a stand,
> But changed by Nature's innovating Hand;
> All Things are altered, nothing is destroyed,
> The shifted Scene, for some new Show employed. (262–5, 386–91)

Translation sharpened awareness of affinities and contrasts between different times. In the Preface to his translation of *The Iliad* (1715), Pope expresses a more discriminating view than Vanbrugh about the value of the past, and a less partisan position than those involved in the Battle of the Books. He challenges the sentimentalising of an earlier age by the French translator Mme Dacier who had asserted in the preface to her Homer (1711) 'that those Times and Manners are so much the more excellent, as they are more contrary to ours'. With a resounding rhetorical question he undermines such cant: 'Who can be so prejudiced in their Favour as to magnify the Felicity of those Ages, when a Spirit of Revenge and Cruelty, join'd with the practice of Rapine and Robbery, reign'd thro' the World, when no Mercy was shown but for the sake of Lucre, when the greatest Princes were put to the Sword, and their Wives and Daughters made Slaves and Concubines?' Immediately afterwards he equally criticises those 'shock'd at the *servile Offices* and *mean Employments* in which we sometimes see the Heroes of Homer engaged'. Without sentimentality or scorn, without denying either the otherness of the past or the possibility of growing acquainted with it, he celebrates the experience of contact with the ancient world:

> When we read *Homer*, we ought to reflect that we are reading the most ancient Author in the Heathen World; and those who consider him in this Light, will double their Pleasure in the Perusal of him. Let them think they are growing acquainted with Nations and People that are now no more; that they are stepping almost three thousand Years back into the remotest Antiquity, and entertaining themselves with a clear and surprising Vision of Things no where else to be found, the only true mirror of that ancient World. (*Poems* VII. 14)

Words emphasising distance (ancient, now no more, remotest Antiquity) are balanced by those that affirm closeness and understanding (growing acquainted, stepping, clear *and* surprising Vision, true Mirror). Pope's account of looking back three thousand years is a counterpart of our looking back three hundred, an amalgam of familiarity and strangeness, admiration and censure.

Looking back, whether to times before the Civil War or to the earliest records of Britain or to classical times, was one way of defining the present. Another, looking forward, was intensely charged. Especially, but not exclusively, the turbulent middle years of the seventeenth century encouraged millenarist thinking:

> Contemporary history was insistently interpreted in the light of biblical revelation, and of all the books in the Bible it was the Book of Revelation that was most eagerly read by Englishmen in this period, in order to elucidate the signs of the times and make them conform to the premonitions of the Apocalypse that were so cryptically described in the Bible. There was a wide consensus from high Anglican to radical Puritan that the present generation was living 'in this setting part of time', in Sir Thomas Browne's phrase. (Parry 1985, 13)

A sense of emergency can provide a source of energy, desperate or exhilarated. Good, or mad and dangerous to know, millenarists might gird up their loins to face the final trials of the time, or throw off artificial constraints. Although flamboyant enthusiasm wanes in the second half of the century, awareness of a looming Final Judgment remains strong.

In contrast to apocalyptic urgency, Addison in the *Spectator*, no. 253 (20 December 1711) expresses a curious sense of belatedness, of polishing as all there is left to do:

> It is impossible, for us who live in the later Ages of the World, to make Observations in Criticism, Morality, or in any Art or Science, which have not been touched upon by others. We have little else left us, but to represent the common Sense of Mankind in more strong, more beautiful, or more uncommon Lights.

There is a valedictory note even within the praise Waller's editor, Bishop Atterbury, bestows on the poet as a great refiner of the language, but perhaps the last:

> for I question whether in Charles the Second's Reign, English did not come to its full perfection; and whether it has not had its Augustean Age, as well as the Latin. It seems to be already mix'd with foreign Languages, as far as its purity will bear. (Preface to The Second Part of Mr. Waller's Poems 1690, A4ʳ)

Given modern scholarly use of the phrase, Atterbury's dating of an Augustan Age seems oddly early. Waller himself had used it even earlier. The time to which the label is attached floats freely, as a pair of poems by Waller shows. In about 1654 he wrote for Cromwell; in 1666 for Charles. In both cases, he celebrates peace after war, a period of prosperity and stability (and, in the case of Cromwell, international respect).

In 'A Panegyric to My Lord Protector, Of the Present Greatness, and Joint Interest, of His Highness, and this Nation' (*c.* 1654), Waller casts about for appropriate Biblical and Roman parallels. David, reared obscurely, destined to succeed the anointed king Saul, provides one deft compliment (stanza 34); Octavius another:

> As the vex'd world, to find repose, at last
> Itself into Augustus' arms did cast;
> So England now does, with like toil oppress'd,
> Her weary head upon your bosom rest. (stanza 43)

A dozen years later, in *Instructions to a Painter*, it is Charles II who, after the Battle of Lowestoft, can be portrayed like Octavius after Actium:

> Then draw the Parliament, the nobles met,
> And our great Monarch high above them set.
> Like young Augustus let his image be,
> Triumphing for that victory at sea,
> Where Egypt's Queen, and eastern kings o'erthrown,
> Made the possession of the world his own. (ll. 299–304)

Poetic 'invention' in Waller's time still carried its etymological weight of coming upon what to say, rather than making up something new. Despite a keen sense of change, Dryden could assert that the past offered ways of understanding the present, if one had wit enough to recognise it:

> For Mankind being the same in all Ages, agitated by the same Passions, and moved to action by the same interests, nothing can come to pass, but some Precedent of the like nature has already been produced; so that having the causes before our Eyes, we cannot easily be deceived in the effects, if we have Judgment enough but to draw the parallel. ('Life of Plutarch', 1693, 52)

Shaftesbury, too, praises the study of history, emphasising how limited understanding of the present is without awareness of the past:

> They who have no Help from Learning to observe the wider Periods or Revolutions of Human Kind, the Alterations which happen in Manners, and the Flux and Reflux of Politeness, Wit, and Art; are apt at every turn to make the present Age their Standard, and imagine nothing barbarous or savage, but what is contrary to the Manners of their own Time. (1710, 114)

Our contemporaries

In 1973, Martin Price could write, in the preface to a volume of the Oxford Anthology of English Literature with the title *The Restoration and the Eighteenth Century*, with a confident sense of period:

> Few moments seem so decisive a break in the continuity of English literature as the Restoration. While in exile in France, the court of Charles II had acquired a new tone of worldliness and self-conscious sophistication that was to affect literary as well as social forms. The fact that Milton's *Paradise Lost* or Bunyan's *Pilgrim's Progress* was published after the Restoration seems incongruous. (7)

Incongruous? In these assertions, the unspoken assumptions now seem clearly audible. If, and only if, the court is seen as the norm or as the centre, the religious poem and prose allegory are anomalies. Furthermore, Dryden's satire *Absalom and Achitophel* depends, as *Pilgrim's Progress* does, on the resonance of Biblical allusions; the poet laureate assumes a body of readers who know the Old Testament well enough to recognise and enjoy parallels between politicians and courtiers in the London of Charles II and the Jerusalem of David. Cowley's *Davideis* (1656), and extended verse 'Meditations on Genesis' probably by Anne Hutchinson frame *Paradise Lost* in time of publication.

The word Restoration in the title of the volume Price was editing is closely related to his focus on the culture of Charles II's court. One common way of dating periods is in relation to politics, with occasional claims for neat correlation between literature and government, so that, for example, the phrase 'Restoration drama' signals the enthusiasm of Charles II and his court for the stage. How blurred the period term becomes in general use is evident in Edward Bond's play *Restoration*, which owes more to Gay's *The Beggar's Opera* (1728), produced under a Hanoverian monarch, than to drama written during the decades of the Stuarts' return. After Charles II, direct and positive influence on literature by the later Stuarts is a rarity. James II reigned for only three years. In Samuel Johnson's ironic understatement, 'king William was not very studious of poetry' ('Life of Blackmore', *Lives* II. 239). Neither Mary nor her sister Anne provided compensating strength; a book on the reign of Anne is subtitled *The Decline of Court Culture* (Buckolz 1993). Nonetheless, within half a century the years of William and Anne were perceived as properly an English Augustan Age, characterised by a cluster of brilliant writers and by patrons ready to reward real worth; so Oliver Goldsmith portrays what for him is the glorious 'last age'.[1] In Joseph Warton's *Essay on the Genius and Writings of Pope* (1756), the rosiest of perspectives is proclaimed: 'If I was to name a time, when the arts and polite literature, were at their height in this nation, I should mention the latter end of King William, and the reign of Queen Anne' (161).

Whatever name is used for a 'period' has an immediate effect on ways of thinking about it. Consider for a moment the placing of 1650–1720 in relation to large and resonant period labels: Renaissance, Augustan, Enlightenment, Age of Reason, Neoclassical. Even apparently arbitrary or neutral references to dates are, in the case of the seventeenth and eighteenth centuries, fraught with demarcation disputes. Labels are attached to ideas and periods of varying stability and precision. Decades after the Restoration of 1660 are notably turbulent, with unsatisfactory religious settlements, foreign wars and, from 1688 onwards, Jacobite rebellions. In literature, the most direct impact of these troubled years is seen not only in the large number of politically engaged satires and dramas, but also in a steady stream of retirement poems. The popularity of Pomfret's 'The Choice' (1700), one such celebration of rural tranquillity, is noted by Samuel Johnson: 'Perhaps no composition in our language has been oftener perused' (*Lives* I. 302).

Evocative words and phrases can serve to present opposing views of the same decades. For household devotions, Sir William Temple composed a form of words which would avoid raising objections, but his sense of the need to do so is laid out in the heading he gave it:

> A Family prayer made in fanatic times when our servants were of so many different sects, and composed with the design that all might join in it, and so as to contain all what was necessary for any to know, or to do (Longe 1911, 187).

These 'fanatic times' are in other contexts claimed as part of the Age of Reason, or Enlightenment.[2]

Established labels carry with them the danger of established caricature. Restoration is sometimes a shorthand term for profligacy, merrymaking, and misbehaviour. Occasionally at least this image had graphic foundation. On 16 June 1663 young drinking companions of the king, Sir Charles Sedley (then about twenty-four years old) and Lord Buckhurst, stripped on the balcony of a Covent Garden inn, 'acted all the postures of lust and buggery that could be imagined' and preached a blasphemous mock sermon to the large crowd that gathered below. On this occasion, Sedley was reproved by the Lord Chief Justice, bound over for good behaviour, and fined five hundred pounds (Pepys, *Diary* 1 July 1663). Five years later, Pepys records the 'frolic and Debauchery' of Buckhurst and Sedley again. After running half-naked in the street and fighting the watch they were clapped in prison for the night. This time, however, the Lord Chief Justice reprimanded the constables for interfering with them. That Pepys' summary comment is 'a horrid shame' indicates, however, that contemporaries did not see either the court wits' behaviour or the judicial response as normative (*Diary* 23 October 1668).

In 1671 Dryden might celebrate the times as 'An Age more Gallant than the last' (Epilogue to *The Conquest of Granada, Part II*, and 'Defense of the Epilogue'). George Granville, Lord Lansdowne, looking back at the early restoration across some forty years, as we look at the 1960s, speaks of a 'frantick Age' ('Essay Upon Unnatural Flights in Poetry', 1701; Spingarn III. 294). The relatively staid years of William and Mary, however, are also perceived as too wild by some observers. Although the theatres were actually less deliberately shocking than in the 1670s, it is towards the end of the century that the Collier controversy erupts. In 1697, Mary Astell, in the second part of *A Serious Proposal to the Ladies*, concerned to dignify the role of single women, notes that 'Particular Obligations do not contract her mind, but her Beneficence moves in the largest sphere', so that 'perhaps the Glory of Reforming this Prophane and Profligate Age is reserved for you Ladies' (211). The official funeral sermon for Queen Mary, preached by Thomas Tenison, Archbishop of Canterbury, describes the times as materialistic and discontented, 'an Atheistical and Profane Age, the Seeds of which Impiety have been sowing for some years, and now seem to spring up in greater plenty than ever' and moreover 'a time of foreign War, and domestic Discontent reigning in those whose Resentments are stronger than their Reasons' (1695, 17–18).

Among especially stimulating studies of the significance and implications of nomenclature are Lawrence Lipking's 'Periods in the Arts: Sketches and Speculations' (1970) and Leah S. Marcus's article 'Renaissance/Early Modern Studies' (1992). Lipking draws attention to the way the word 'neoclassical' as used by art historians and literary historians 'refers to two periods which share little but a name' (181). Marcus surveys the different ways in which historians and literary scholars use the labels 'Renaissance' and 'early modern', neither of them precise, and the various connotations of the choice of terminology. Renaissance studies are apt to be orientated towards the past, 'concerned with questions of origin, influence, and filiation' while the phrase 'early modern' looks towards future developments. Renaissance is an 'upbeat' word, associated with a hierarchy and 'great' works; early modern is more prosaic, a term for greater cultural inclusiveness, 'lower and more egalitarian connotations' (42–4). Moreover, she suggests,

> We might suppose, since the Renaissance tends to push back into the past while the early modern period creeps up on the present, that study of the Renaissance would imply a sense of greater cultural distance than suggested by the more recent term. The reverse is usually the case. The idea of rebirth implies the perception of cultural disjunction, but also the possibility of renewed identity and therefore of essential similarity between two periods separated in time ... [In contrast,] more recent work of an early modern bent ... posits identity not as innate and unchanging but as culturally constructed and therefore unstable, never more than partly recoverable across time. (44–5)

Gathered in Lawrence Besserman's *The Challenge of Periodization* (1996) are a group of outstanding essays by various hands. J. Hillis Miller comments on placing individual works in the context of a period as both indispensable and problematical, not least because 'The singleness of the label implies the singleness of what is labelled' (197). Lee Patterson notes how 'remarkably unstable' the boundaries of the Renaissance are in different disciplines, and suggests that displacement of the term Renaissance by early modern can be seen as 'a shrewd tactical move in a postmodern cultural environment capable of sustained interest only in that which reflects itself' (51).

Occasionally, as in the Internet bibliography 'Iter: Gateway to the Middle Ages and the Renaissance', a project designed 'to increase access to all published materials pertaining to the Renaissance (1300-1700) and the Middle Ages (400–1299)'[3] there is a forthright claim that Renaissance extends to everything before the eighteenth century. It is rare, however, to find literary scholars who use the term Renaissance venturing beyond the first half of the seventeenth century, except for a habit of appropriating Milton, Marvell and Vaughan. An alternative term, Neoclassical, is common when Dryden and Pope are the centre of attention. Here again, the comparable implications of labels may be pondered. The metaphor of Renaissance is biological, spontaneous, warm, natural; Neoclassical is much more manufactured, artificial, cooler, separated from its parentage and deliberately trying to reinvent its ancestry. How much is this image destroyed by a closer look at the intimacy with the classical past assumed by Dryden, Pope and their contemporaries?

Less openly evaluative are labels which simply give the number of a century. Some arguments for 1700, the end of a century, as a convenient marking off of an era can be constructed. The death of Dryden in that year, like the death of Chaucer in 1400, falls neatly for students who associate a period with a major poet. Academic practice, however, complicates the matter. The scholarly journal entitled *The Eighteenth Century: Theory and Interpretation* is one of many which claim forty per cent of the seventeenth century as their own; an editorial announcement on the inside front cover spells out the range of interests: '*The Eighteenth Century: Theory and Interpretation*, published three times a year, welcomes essays concerned with the application of contemporary theory and methodology to all aspects of culture 1660–1800, including literature, history, fine arts, science, history of ideas, and popular culture.' The 'long eighteenth century' is so common a concept that while some journals such as *Restoration and Eighteenth Century Theatre Research* define their sense of continuity explicitly, others such as *Eighteenth Century Studies*, published by the American Eighteenth Century Society, take it for granted.[4]

Conversely, the Seventeenth Century is often but not explicitly a short century. As in the anthology edited by Dawson and Dupree (1994), 'seventeenth century English poetry' refers primarily to the earlier half; after Herrick, only Marvell, Vaughan, Traherne and Katherine Philips appear (and since anthologies favour shorter poems, Milton is represented primarily by work published in 1645, along with three later sonnets). When not short, the century is frequently broken, although there is no clear agreement on when it should be broken: 1642, 1649, 1660? Curiously, although 'Restoration' suggests return, a deliberate recovery or continuity with Charles I's reign, those who choose 1660 are least apt to connect the writing of the last fourth of the century with the first fourth.

Certainly in the awareness of those living in the later seventeenth century, the civil war and interregnum were a tremendous break in experience. If 'unimaginable' means so horrifying that it should not be imagined, the trial and execution of the king could be so described. A cataclysmic change had taken place. Dryden's brief reference to a 'race before the Flood' is a neat and apt phrase for the division made by the two central decades of the century. Yet the very importance of this cataclysm is an argument against making 1660 a starting point for the study of literature. One of the major themes of writing in the second half of the century is how to understand what had happened earlier. *Hudibras* is an obvious example. *The Tempest, The Indian Queen* and a host of other plays dramatise the restoration of rulers. Explicitly (in several of Dryden's prologues, and more extensively in the *Essay of Dramatick Poesie*) or implicitly, writers consider their relationship to predecessors before the war. Paradoxically, they are both defining a separation – 'this present age' as against 'the past age' – and, as they measure themselves against predecessors, revealing a sense of continuity.

Thinking in terms of a 'long seventeenth century' rather than the more common long eighteenth century has some advantages, for a university syllabus, say. By taking in a decade or so on either end of a hundred years, this long century could run from Spenser's *Shepherd's Calendar* (1579) and Sidney's *Arcadia* (1581) to Gay's *The Shepherd's Week* (1714). In versification it would invite considering the handling of heroic materials, original or translated, from Spenser's *The Faerie Queene* (1590 and 1596) and Fairfax's translation of Tasso (1600), through Dryden, to Pope. In drama, it sets Marlowe's *Tamburlaine* (c. 1587) in contrast to Rowe's *Tamerlane* (1701) and opens up study of the numerous rewritings of Shakespeare and his contemporaries. Roger Pooley's survey of prose between 1590 and 1700 (1992) demonstrates how useful the perspective of a longer seventeenth century can be.

Major shifts in perceptions of writing between 1650 and 1720 have occurred in recent decades. Roughly sketched, these are shifts which involve changes of emphasis within pairs of polarised terms: aristocratic–popular, secular–religious, gentlemen–radicals, male–female. A generation or so ago, the Age of Reason was an accepted term; it recurs throughout the 1957 Pelican Guide *From Dryden to Johnson*, along with the term Augustan, later more apt to be presented in sceptical quotation marks (Weinbrot 1978) or thoroughly explored as a complicated concept (Erskine-Hill 1983). In the mid-twentieth century, the late seventeenth century seemed to attract learned, urbane men who celebrated the learned, urbane men on whose work they concentrated. A case in point is James Sutherland, who in *On English Prose* presents interesting, but not always compatible, arguments about the attractiveness of prose style in the second half of the seventeenth century. Under the heading 'The Age of Prose', he praises fresh developments: 'A new prose was emerging in the seventeenth century, simpler, less ornate, more colloquial, more practical, and pitched at such a level that it could make sense, and immediate sense, to the average man.' (1957, 57–8) For this he gives several explanations: (1) a larger literate population; (2) 'the outburst of political and religious journalism (the two adjectives are often barely distinguishable at this period)' (58); (3) the Puritan distrust of decoration and ornament (62). What he emphasises, however, in a second half of his chapter, are not these strains but what he calls

> the fact that Restoration literature was dominated by the aristocracy, who set the tone for it and exercised an unquestioned control over the mode of expression. Restoration prose is, in the main, a slightly formalised variation of the conversation of gentlemen. The gentleman converses with ease, and with an absence of emphasis that may at times become a conscious and studied under-emphasis, but it is more often the natural expression of his poise and detachment. (67)

So gentlemanly is Sutherland's own prose, so apparently clear and poised, that the break in his argument between emphasis on a popular base (the points numbered above, one to three) and the assertion of aristocratic domination is easy to miss. He provides, at any rate, a sympathetic introduction to the seventeenth century as the age of attractive and direct prose, and ends the chapter with entertaining contrasts between the clarity he admires in Hobbes, Dryden and Addison and the pompous gentility of late eighteenth-century writing.

The gentleman is less prominent in studies published during the final decades of the twentieth century. Christopher Hill, in particular, has stimulated further research on radical writings. Enumerative bibliography, or regular review articles in *Studies in English Literature* and *The Yearbook of English Studies*, make clear the growing importance, in academic programmes and publishers' lists, of writing by women. John Sitter, for example, providing a subheading 'Gender Studies' in a survey of 'Recent Studies in the Restoration and Eighteenth Century' (1995), notes that 'If this category embraced all of the "Books Received" that have in some way been prompted by feminist criticism(s) – including monographs on women writers and editions unlikely to have been undertaken before the 1970s – it would cover more than one-third of all the titles published this past year' (609). Nowadays many university undergraduates read Aphra Behn before they read John Dryden.

On what was once seen as a smooth 'progress' from religious zeal at the time of the Commonwealth toward eighteenth-century secularisation and materialism, commonplaces have been challenged and eroded. Commenting in *William III and the Godly Revolution* on the 'ongoing reinterpretation of the late Stuart era', Tony Claydon argues that theology is as important as science and economics for the ideology of the 1690s. His study of Williamite propaganda analyses the language of 'Courtly reformation' and its basis in 'protestant and biblical idioms first developed during the Reformation of the middle of the sixteenth century' (1996, 4–5). He demonstrates the zeal with which societies for the reformation of manners were promoted in the final decade of the century, with existing laws against drunkenness, swearing or general 'debauchery' more actively enforced than since Cromwell's time, and a few new acts, including one on blasphemy, passed (110–21). In Anne's reign, too, as the riots following upon Sacheverell's sermon and trial indicate, trying to disentangle religious concerns from rhetoric and politics would be a perverse task.

Almost any modern label imposes a kind of stability which it was difficult for those living at the time to see. The 'Commonwealth' was precarious. 'Protectorate' implied (as Arise Evans happily pointed out) a temporary situation. Although 'Restoration' declares continuities, there were plenty of conspiracies and threats to Charles II's rule. A Protestant succession through the oldest of his illegitimate sons, the Duke of Monmouth, was much discussed, and somewhat more probable than what actually happened in 1688. Precisely because the right of William and Mary to the throne was constitutionally unsound, the Prince of Orange needed to set up arguments for it, beginning with his *Declaration of Reasons for Appearing in Arms in the Kingdom of England*, published a month before his landing at Torbay on 5 November 1688 – the date later exploited in celebrations of England's providential deliverance from papish plotters (Claydon 1996, especially 24–63). After James II fled the country, he and later his son James Edward made repeated attempts to return as rightful king.[5]

When after the death of Anne's son the Duke of Gloucester in 1700 an Act of Settlement was drawn up to prevent the succession of a Catholic ruler, specifying that the crown would pass to the Protestant heirs of Sophia of Hanover, Scotland did not ratify it. At the time of the War of Spanish Succession, Louis XIV recognised James III as King of England, and up to Anne's death canny politicians were in touch both with Sophia and her son George, in Hanover, and with James III in France. Jacobite pretensions (from Latin *Jacobus*, James, and *praetensus*, alleged or claimed) were a danger well into the eighteenth century, culminating in the 1745–46 Jacobite invasion led by Charles Edward Stuart (called in contrast to 'the old Pretender', his father James Edward, 'the Young Pretender' or, more romantically, Bonny Prince Charlie). Those events lie outside our period, but nevertheless serve as a reminder of persistent uneasiness about the line of succession to the throne. Only with the security of hindsight can one dismiss the seriousness of Jacobite uprisings in 1708, 1715 and 1718. A letter from Lady Giffard written on 23 July 1715 indicates how likely the success of a James III (whose claim to the throne might well appear stronger than those of George I) seemed at that time: 'we hear of the Pretender on one day in England and another in Scotland and talked of they say as familiarly at London as King William was before he came' (Longe 1911, 281).

Retrospection and simplification

In the collected *Poems on Several Occasions* by Mary, Lady Chudleigh (1703), the opening piece is an ode 'On the Death of his Highness the Duke of *Glocester*'. Like Dryden, the Duke died just at the end of the seventeenth century, in 1700. He was eleven years old, the only child of Anne's to survive infancy. How different English history might have been if he had lived on, ascending to the throne at the age of twenty-five following the death of his mother in 1714, is beyond conjecture. What is interesting for our purposes is the retrospective view of British history which Mary, Lady Chudleigh, provides in an elegy made and moulded of things past and also strikingly original.

'On the Death of his Highness the Duke of *Glocester*' invites comparison with other elegies and poems of consolation, remote or close in time. Like Chaucer's *Book of the Duchess* it approaches its subject, and the whole problem of tactful consolation of a social superior, indirectly. Chudleigh herself, in a Preface, called the elegy 'a very long' poem (although it is by no means the longest in the collection, far outstripped by the 636-line description of her reading, 'The

Resolution'). For over a fifth of its 378 lines, she describes her retirement from 'Business, Noise, and Care' (l. 1) to a 'little safe Retreat' of books and thoughts. Calm withdrawal to this 'dear Solitude' is not, however, sustainable. Midway through the fourth of the freely constructed stanzas, her reverie is interrupted:

> Behold! a wondrous Turn of Fate!
>   A hollow Melancholy Sound
>   Dispers'd an awful Horror round,
> And hideous Groans thro' all the Grove resound
>   Nature the dismal Noise did hear,
>   Nature her self did seem to fear:
> The bleating Flocks lay trembling on the Plains;
>   The Brooks ran murmuring by,
> And Echo to their Murmurs made reply:
> The lofty Trees their verdant Honours shake;
> The frighted Birds with hast their Boughs forsake,
> And for securer Seats to distant Groves repair. (ll. 80–91)

The grief and fright of Nature as a whole is the prelude to the appearance of the first of three personages used to define, in voices more authoritative than the poet's own, what the death of the young duke means. A resemblance to the series of figures who speak in Milton's *Lycidas* is notable, although, as with pathos expressed through nature, general conventions rather than specific borrowings can provide explanations. Laments for premature death are inevitable given the prince's eleven years. For four stanzas 'the British Genius' himself, solemn and venerable, describes with tears and sighs the loss which has occurred:

> He's Dead he cry'd! the young, the much belov'd!
> From us too soon, Ah! much too soon remov'd!
> Snatch'd hence in his first Dawn, his Infant Bloom!
> So fell *Marcellus* by a rigorous Doom.
> The Good, the Great, the Joy, the Pride of *Rome*! (ll. 114–18)

References to Augustus' heir, similarly cut off in his youth, and mourned in the sixth book of Virgil's *Aeneid*, common to this elegy and Dryden's poem 'On the Death of Mr Oldham', occur easily in literary works which set late seventeenth-century England against a classical background, and claim Augustan peace, prosperity and longed-for stability for postwar Britain as for postwar Rome. Within the same verse paragraph, Virgil is again cited in comparisons between the promise and grace represented by the young Duke of Gloucester and of Aeneas's son Ascanius, led from flaming Troy, or impersonated by Cupid at Dido's court (ll. 127–32).

The venerable, masculine figure of the British Genius is followed by Britannia, accompanied by river nymphs adding their pastoral voices of lament for a youth 'too soon, alas, too soon' dead, and then by St George, still patriotic in his contribution to the elegy since he appears as 'the fam'd Guardian of our Isle' (l. 259). The heaven which St George describes is like the honourable company of the Elysian Fields. He offers not Christian consolations, but the fellowship of the duke's forebears, the '*Caledonian* Chiefs' of the Stuart line and '*Danish* Heroes ... / Who long had ancient Kingdoms sway'd' (ll. 274, 279–80) of his father's side. These welcome him to 'th'Æthereal Court' (l. 327) of bliss, joy, glory, free from cares, pain, tempests. The most interesting version of seventeenth-century regal history is found in the thirteenth stanza of the ode, which presents a series of Stuart rulers in a symmetrical pattern: Mary, Charles, Charles, Mary. For those whose memories of monarchs make chants such as James, Charles, Charles, James a necessary mnemonic (and who then shift, at the point of the Bloodless Revolution, to William and Mary, with a stress on William), the variant is surprising; what is now provided is an enclosing feminine presence, from Mary, Queen of Scots to Anne's sister, 'the fair *Maria* ... / Who lately grac'd the *British* Throne' (ll. 304–5).

In the succession Mary, Charles, Charles, Mary, two martyrs are followed by their less unfortunate namesakes, and the hapless James II is simply ignored. Within the elegy, Lady Chudleigh manages to shape events into an orderly pattern, and one which may be personally comforting to the duke's royal mother and to the female poet. Shapeliness is produced, however, only by ignoring what will not fit into a consolingly simple formulation.

Notes

1. Goldsmith establishes this view in 'An Enquiry into the Present State of Polite Learning in Europe' (1759) and 'An Account of the Augustan Age in England' (1759).

2. In the introductory chapter of *The Enlightenment and Its Shadows*, Peter Hulme and Ludmilla Jordanova summarise alternative datings for the Enlightenment, a 'more exclusive' definition which focuses on France between 1715 and 1789, and a wider view in which earlier origins are emphasised (Hulme and Jordanova 1990, 2–3). Essays collected in *The Enlightenment and Its Shadows* often take for granted this wider definition, expressed in such parallel phrasings as 'the early decades of the seventeenth century, the beginnings of what we call the Enlightenment' (50).

3. http://iter.library.utoronoto.ca/iter/index.htm

4. In a sample issue of *Eighteenth Century Studies* (Winter 1995) two articles primarily concerned with material before 1701 occupy slightly more than half of the editorial space. See Lawrence Lipking, 'Inventing the Eighteenth Centuries: A Long View' on the institutional history and consequences of the very long and 'plural' period (in Damrosch 1992, 7–25).

5. For a brief vivid description of the first major attempt, and William's defeat of James II at the Battle of the Boyne, see Kishlansky (1996), 287–9.

Chronology

Births and deaths	Principal publications	Cultural and scientific events	Historical and political events
1650			
Jeremy Collier b. (d. 1726); René Descartes d. (b. 1596); Nell Gwyn b. (d. 1687); Edward Ravenscroft b. (*c.*) (d. *c.* 1700)	Baxter, *The Saints' Everlasting Rest*; Playford, *The English Dancing Master*; Henry Vaughan, *Silex scintillans*; Winstanley, *An Humble Request*	First coffee-house opened in Oxford; tea first imported into England	Edinburgh castle surrenders to Cromwell
1651			
	Davenant, *Gondibert*; Hobbes, *Leviathan*; Playford, *The English Dancing Master*		Charles II escapes to France
1652			
Inigo Jones d. (b. 1573); Thomas Otway b. (d. 1685); Nahum Tate b. (d. 1715)	Evans, *A Voice from Heaven to the Common-wealth of English*; Playford, *Musics Recreation*	Otto von Guericke invents the air pump at Magdeburg; opening of the first London coffee-house	Act of Pardon and Oblivion; first Dutch War begins
1653			
Thomas D'Urfey b. (d. 1723)	Margaret Cavendish, *Poems and Fancies*; Sir Percy Herbert, *The*		Cromwell made Lord Protector, expels the Long Parliament

Births and deaths	Principal publications	Cultural and scientific events	Historical and political events
	Princess Cloria pt 1; Shirley, *Cupid and Death*; Walton, *The Compleat Angler*		
1654 John Selden d. (b. 1584)	Boyle, *Parthenissa* (–1665); Comenius, *Orbis sensualium pictus*; Milton, *Second Defence*		First Protectorate parliament; coronation of Louis XIV
1655	Arise Evans, *The Voice of King Charles* and *The Voice of the Iron Rod*; *Musarum deliciae*		Parliament dissolved
1656 Jacob Tonson b. (d. 1737)	Margaret Cavendish, *A True Relation*; Cowley, *Poems*; Bishop Walton, *Biblia polyglotta*		Second Protectorate parliament
1657 John Dennis b. (d. 1734); Richard Lovelace d. (b. 1618); John Norris b. (d. 1711)			Cromwell offered title of king; powers of parliament enhanced
1658	Thomas Browne, *Urne- Burial* and *The Garden of Cyrus*; Comenius, *Orbis sensualium*		Oliver Cromwell d.; parliament dissolved

Births and deaths	Principal publications	Cultural and scientific events	Historical and political events
	pictus, trans. Hoole; Dryden, *Heroic Stanzas*		
1659 John Dunton b. (d. 1733); Henry Purcell b. (d. 1695); Richard Southerne b. (d. 1746)	Baxter, *Holy Commonwealth*; Evans, *A Rule from Heaven*; Hobbes, *De homine*; Lovelace, *Posthume Poems*; Molière, *Les précieuses ridicules*; Pepys begins diaries	Bunyan emprisoned	Long Parliament restored
1660 Daniel Defoe b. (d. 1731); Peter Antony Motteux b. (d. 1718); Diego Velázquez d. (b. 1599)	Charles II, *Declaration of Breda*; Clarkson, *The Lost Sheep Found*; Dryden, *Astraea redux*; George Mackenzie, *Arentina*		Restoration: Charles II re-enters London 29 May
1661	Boyle, *Some Considerations*; Brome, *Songs and Other Poems*; Davenant, *The Siege of Rhodes* pts 1 and 2; Sir Percy Herbert, *The Princess Cloria* (full text)		Coronation of Charles II; personal rule of Louis XIV (–1715)
1662 Richard Bentley b. (d. 1742); Henry	Butler, *Hudibras* pt 1; *Book of*	Royal Society founded;	Press Act (rigid censorship); Act of

Births and deaths	Principal publications	Cultural and scientific events	Historical and political events
Lawes d. (b 1595); Blaise Pascal d. (b. 1623)	Common Prayer, revised version; Molière, L'Ecole des femmes; Rump	Versailles palace begun	Uniformity (consent to revised Book of Common Prayer)
1663			
	Butler, Hudibras pt 2; Corneille/Phillips, Pompée; Dryden, The Wild Gallant	Theatre Royal opened	
1664			
Matthew Prior b. (d. 1721); Katherine Philips d. (b. 1631); John Vanbrugh b. (d. 1726)	Dryden, The Rival Ladies; Dryden/R. Howard, The Indian Queen; Etherege, Love in a Tub; Evelyn, Sylva; R.Howard, The Vestal Virgin; Molière, Le Tartuffe (3-act version); Racine, La Thébaide		Conventicle Act (against meetings of noncon-formists)
1665			
Nicholas Poussin d. (b. 1593/94)	Bunyan, The Holy City; Dryden, The Indian Emperor; Hooke, Micrographia; Lafontaine, Contes; London Gazette and Journal des savants begun; La Rochefoucauld, Réflexions et maximes		Plague in London; second Dutch war begins; Restrictions on non-Conformist ministers
1666			
Alexander Brome	Bunyan, Grace	Newton uses the	Fire of London 2-7

Births and deaths	Principal publications	Cultural and scientific events	Historical and political events
d. (b. 1520); Frans Hals d. (b. *c.* 1581); James Shirley d. (b. 1596)	*Abounding*; Dryden, *Annus mirabilis*; Molière, *Le misanthrope*	infinitesimal calculus	September
1667 Abraham Cowley d. (b. 1618); Jonathan Swift b. (d. 1745)	Dryden, *Annus mirabilis*; Margaret Fell, *Womens Speaking Justified*; Milton, *Paradise Lost* (10 book version); Playford, *Catch that Catch Can*; Racine, *Andromaque*; Sprat, *History of the Royal Society*		Peace of Breda between England and Holland
1668 William Davenant d. (b. 1606)	Dryden, *Essay of Dramatick Poesie*; Etherege, *She Wou'd if She Cou'd*; Lafontaine, *Fables*; Molière, *L'avare*; Racine, *Britannicus*; Shadwell, *The Sullen Lovers*	Dryden appointed Poet Laureate	
1669 Susannah Centlivre b. (d. 1723); John Denham d. (b. 1615) Rembrandt van Rijn d. (b. 1606)	Dryden, *Tyrannick Love; or, The Royal Martyr*	Pepys ends diary	
1670 William Congreve	Aphra Behn, *The*	Dryden appointed	

Births and deaths	Principal publications	Cultural and scientific events	Historical and political events
b. (d. 1729)	Forc'd Marriage; Dryden, The Conquest of Granada, pt. 1; Molière, Le bourgeois gentilhomme; Pascal, Pensées; Racine, Bérénice	Historiographer Royal	
1671 Colley Cibber b. (d. 1757)	Buckingham et al., The Rehearsal; Dryden, The Conquest of Granada, pt. 2; Milton, Paradise Regained and Samson Agonistes	Newton makes reflector telescope	
1672 Joseph Addison b. (d. 1719); Richard Steele b. (d. 1729)	Dryden, Marriage à la Mode; Molière, Les femmes savantes; Racine, Bajazet	First public concerts in London	Third Dutch War begins; Declaration of Indulgence toward nonconformists
1673 (c.) Anne Bracegirdle b. (d. 1748); Molière d. (b. 1622)	Aphra Behn, The Dutch Lover; Davenant, Collected Works; Milton, Of True Religion; Molière, Le malade imaginaire; Racine, Mithridate		Test Act excludes Roman Catholics from office under the Crown
1674 Robert Herrick d. (b. 1591); John Milton d. (b. 1608); Nicholas Rowe b.	Boileau, Art poétique; Milton, Paradise Lost (12 book version);		Third Dutch War ends

Births and deaths	Principal publications	Cultural and scientific events	Historical and political events
(d. 1718); Thomas Traherne d. (b. 1637)	Racine, *Iphigénie*; Shadwell *et al.*, *The Tempest*; Wycherley, *The Country Wife*		
1675 Barnaby Lintot (printer) b. (d. 1736); Jan Vermeer d. (b. 1632)	Dryden, *Aureng-Zebe*; Lee, *Sophonisba*; Rochester, *Satyr Against Mankind*	Royal Observatory, Greenwich	Wren begins St Paul's Cathedral
1676 John Phillips b. (d. 1709)	Etherege, *The Man of Mode*; Otway, *Don Carlos*; Shadwell, *The Virtuoso*; Wycherley, *The Plain Dealer*		
1677 (?) George Farquhar b. (d. 1707); Benedict de Spinoza d. (b. 1632)	Aphra Behn, *The Rover* pt 1; Dryden, *All for Love* and *The State of Innocence*; Lee, *The Rival Queens*; Racine, *Phèdre*; Sedley, *Antony and Cleopatra*		William of Orange marries Mary, daughter of James, Duke of York
1678 Andrew Marvell d. (b. 1621); Antonio Vivaldi b. (d. 1743)	Bunyan, *Pilgrim's Progress* pt 1; Butler, *Hudibras* pt. 3; Rymer, *The Tragedies of the Last Age Consider'd*; Madame de Lafayette, *La*		Popish plot

Births and deaths	Principal publications	Cultural and scientific events	Historical and political events
	princesse de Clèves		
1679 Roger Boyle d. (b. 1621); Thomas Hobbes d. (b. 1588)	Dryden, Troilus and Cressida	Newton's calculation of the lunar orbit	Duke of York banished; party names Whig and Tory come into use
1680 Samuel Butler d. (b. 1613); Rochester d. (b. 1647)	Bunyan, Life and Death of Mr Badman; Butler, Hudibras pt 3; Elizabeth Cellier, Malice Defeated; Otway, The Orphan	Comédie française established; Henry Purcell, Dido and Aeneas	Penny post instituted in London
1681	Behn, Aphra Behn, The Rover pt. 2; Dryden, Absalom and Achitophel and Religio laici pt 1; Marvell, Miscellaneous Poems; Ravenscroft, The London Cuckolds; Tate, King Lear		
1682 Sir Thomas Browne d. (b. 1605); Claude Lorrain d. (b. 1600)	Pierre Corneille, collected edition; Dryden, MacFlecknoe; Otway, Venice Preserv'd	Union of King's and Duke's companies	
1683 Elizabeth Elstob b. (d. 1756); Thomas			Monmouth exiled to Holland; Rye

Births and deaths	Principal publications	Cultural and scientific events	Historical and political events
Killigrew the Elder d. (b. 1612); Jean-Philippe Rameau b. (d. 1764); Izaak Walton d. (b. 1593)			House Plot
1684 Pierre Corneille d. (b. 1606)	Bunyan, *Pilgrim's Progress* pt 2; Dryden, *Religio Laici* pt 2		
1685 Johann Sebastian Bach b. (d. 1750); John Gay b. (d. 1732); Georg Friedrich Händel b. (d. 1759); Thomas Otway d. (b. 1652)	Dryden, *Albion and Albinus*; Tate, *The Cuckold-Haven*		Charles II d. 6 February; James II; Monmouth rebellion (beheaded 15 July)
1686	Aphra Behn, *The Lucky Chance*		
1687 George Villers, second Duke of Buckingham, d. (b. 1628); Charles Cotton d. (b 1630); Nell Gwyn d. (b. 1650); Edmund Waller d. (b. 1606)	Dryden, *The Hind and the Panther*, 'Song for Saint Cecilia's Day'; Fénelon, *De l'éducation des filles*	Newton, *Philosophiae naturalis principia mathematica*	James II receives the papal nuncio; parliament dissolved
1688 John Bunyan d. (b. 1628); Alexander Pope b. (d. 1744);	Aphra Behn, *Oroonoko*; Dryden, *Britannia Rediviva*; Shadwell, *The Squire of Alsatia*		William of Orange invited to England, lands 5 November (o.s.); James II abdicates, escapes to France on

Births and deaths	Principal publications	Cultural and scientific events	Historical and political events
			Christmas Day; the Glorious Revolution
1689 Aphra Behn d. (b. 1640); Samuel Richardson b. (d. 1761)	Aphra Behn, *The History of the Nun*; Lee, *The Massacre of Paris*; John Locke, *On Civil Government*	Thomas Shadwell (?1642–92) appointed Poet Laureate	James II arrives in Ireland
1690	John Locke, *Essay Concerning Human Understanding*	Huyghens proposes wave theory of light	William defeats James II at the Battle of the Boyne
1691 Richard Baxter d. (b. 1615); Robert Boyle d. (b. 1627); George Etherege d. (b. ?1634); George Fox d. (b. 1624)	Congreve, *Incognita*; John Dunton, *The Athenian Gazette/Mercury* (–1697) and *Religio bibliopolae*; Racine, *Athalie*; Rochester, *Poems*	Purcell, *King Arthur*	New East India Company formed; Protestant farmers settled in Ireland
1692 Nathaniel Lee d. (b. ?1649); Thomas Shadwell d. (b. ?1642)	Southerne, *The Wives Excuse*	Purcell, *Fairy Queen*; Nahum Tate (1652–1715) appointed Poet Laureate	Massacre of Glencoe; Lloyd's coffe-house becomes centre of maritime insur-ance
1693	Congreve, *The Old Bachelor*; Higden, *The Wary Widow*; John Locke, *Ideas on Education*;		National Debt established

Births and deaths	Principal publications	Cultural and scientific events	Historical and political events
	Rymer, *A Short View of Tragedy*; Wright, *The Humours and Conversations of the Town*		
1694 Voltaire b. (d. 1778)	Congreve, *The Double Dealer*; Dryden, *Love Triumphant*; Southerne, *The Fatal Marriage*; James Wright, *Country Conversations*	Purcell, *Te Deum* and *Jubilate*	Queen Mary II d.; Bank of England established
1695 Henry Purcell d. (b. 1659); Henry Vaughan d. (b. 1621)	Congreve, *Love for Love*; Leibniz, *Système nouveau de la nature*; Southerne, *Oroonoko*	Purcell, *The Indian Queen*	End of press censorship in England; window tax imposed
1696 Edward Phillips d. (?) (b. 1630); Giambattista Tiepolo b. (d. 1770)	John Aubrey, *Miscellanies*; Behn/Gildon, *The Younger Brother*; Vanbrugh, *The Relapse*	Rich shortens the stage of the Drury Lane Theatre	Licensing of plays by the Lord Chamberlain
1697	Dryden, *Alexander's Feast*; Vanbrugh, *The Provok'd Wife*		
1698 Robert Howard d. (b. 1626)	Collier, *A Short View of the*	Purcell, *Orpheus Britannicus*, pt 1	

Births and deaths	Principal publications	Cultural and scientific events	Historical and political events
	Immorality and Profaneness of the English Stage; Dennis, The Usefulness of the Stage; Fénelon, Télémaque		
1699 Jean Racine d. (b. 1639)	D'Urfey, Wit and Mirth; Farquhar, Love and a Bottle; Wright, Historia histrionica		
1700 Dryden d. (b. 1631); Edward Ravenscroft d. (c.) (b. c. 1650)	Congreve, The Way of the World; Dryden, Secular Masque; Gildon, Measure for Measure		German Protestants adopt the Gregorian calendar; Whigs create the Kit-Kat Club
1701 Charles Sedley d. (b. ?1639)	Dryden, Collected Plays; Rowe, Tamerlane		Act of Succession (Protestant succession of the house of Hanover); James II d.; Start of the war of the Spanish succession (–1714)
1702	Anon., A Comparison between the Two Stages; Bysshe, Art of English Poetry; Daily Courant, first English daily newspaper; Sedley, Beauty the	Purcell, Orpheus Britannicus, pt 2	William III d.; Queen Anne; Vanbrugh builds Castle Howard, Yorkshire (–1714)

Births and deaths	Principal publications	Cultural and scientific events	Historical and political events
	Conqueror (revision of his *Antony and Cleopatra*)		
1703 Samuel Pepys d. (b. 1633)	Mary, Lady Chudleigh, *Poems on Several Occasions*; Rowe, *The Fair Penitent*		
1704 John Locke d. (b. 1632)	Dennis, *The Grounds of Criticism in Poetry*; Swift, *Tale of a Tub* and *The Battle of the Books*	Newton, *Optics*; corpuscular theory of light	
1705	Centlivre, *The Basset-Table*; Dunton, *Life and Errors*	Opening of The Queen's Theatre, Haymarket; Halley calculates the cometary orbit	Vanbrugh builds Blenheim Palace
1706 John Evelyn d. (b. 1620); Charles Sackville, 6th Earl of Dorset d. (b. 1638)	Farquhar, *The Recruiting Officer*	Excavations begun at Pompei and Herculaneum	
1707 George Farquhar d. (b. ?1677); Henry Fielding b. (d. 1754)	Farquhar, *The Beaux' Stratagem*; Locke, *An Essay for the Understanding of St. Pauls Epistles*; Isaac Watts, *Hymns and Spiritual Songs*		Union of England and Scotland

Births and deaths	Principal publications	Cultural and scientific events	Historical and political events
1708	Downes, *Roscius Anglicanus*; Swift, *An Argument Against Abolishing Christianity*; John Whiting, *A Catalogue of Friends Books*	Handel, *Agrippina*	Unsuccessful expedition of Old Pretender to Scotland; East India and New East India Companies merge
1709	Berkeley, *An Essay Towards a New Theory of Vision*; Centlivre, *The Basset-Table*; Rowe's edition of Shakespeare; Steele, *The Tatler* (–1711)	First European porcelain at Meissen	First Copyright Act
1710 Thomas Betterton d. (b. 1635)	Berkeley, *Principles of Human Knowledge*; Swift, *Meditations Upon a Broomstick*	Handel, *Rinaldo*	Christopher Wren finishes St Paul's Cathedral
1711	Gay, *The Present State of Wit*; Pope, *Essay on Criticism*; Steele and Addison, *The Spectator* (–1712)		Handel comes to London; South Sea Company formed
1712	Pope, *The Rape of the Lock* (2 canto version)		Last execution for witchcraft in England

Births and deaths	Principal publications	Cultural and scientific events	Historical and political events
1713 Thomas Rymer d. (b. 1641)	Addison, *Cato*; Pope, *Windsor Forest*; Steele and Addison, *The Guardian*	Scriblerus Club formed	Swift becomes Dean of St Paul's
1714	Gay, *The Shepherd's Week*; Gildon, *A New Rehearsal*; Mandeville, *Fable of the Bees*; Pope, *Rape of the Lock* (5 canto version)	Fahrenheit makes mercury thermometer	Queen Anne d. George I (–1727)
1715 Nahum Tate d. (b. 1652); William Wycherley d. (b. 1641)	Elstob, *The Rudiments of Grammar for the English-Saxon Tongue*; Pope's translation of the *Iliad* begun (–1720); Le Sage, *Gil Blas*	Nicholas Rowe (1674–1718) appointed Poet Laureate	First Jacobite rebellion
1716 Gottfried Leibniz d. (b. 1646)			James (III) in Scotland
1717	Gay/Pope/Arbuthnot, *Three Hours After Marriage*; Pope, *Works*; Voltaire, *Édipe*	Society of Antiquaries refounded	
1718 Peter Antony Motteux d. (b.	Gildon, *Complete Art of Poetry*;	Lawrence Eusden (1688–1730)	

Births and deaths	Principal publications	Cultural and scientific events	Historical and political events
1660); Nicholas Rowe d. (b. 1674)	Marmion, *The Antiquary*	appointed Poet Laureate; Handel, *Acis and Galatea*; beginning of vaccination against smallpox; Halley discovers movement of fixed stars	
1719 Joseph Addison d. (b. 1672)	Defoe, *Robinson Crusoe*; D'Urfey, *Wit and Mirth* (–1720)		
1720	John Gay. *Collected Poems*	Handel, *Esther*	South Sea Bubble bursts

Annotated Bibliography

Ezell, Margaret J. M. *The Patriarch's Wife: Literary Evidence and the History of the Family*. Chapel Hill: The University of North Carolina Press, 1987.

This book provides a vigorous antidote to reductive assumptions about women's roles and their writings, and specifically about what 'patriarchy' meant in the seventeenth century. Chapter 1 succinctly reviews female education, mobility and matriarchal power. Chapter 2 discusses courtesy books and antifeminist satires. Chapter 3 emphasises the significance of manuscript circulation (an important topic which can be pursued in Love 1993) and epistolary networks. Chapter 4 deals with 'The Female Perspective' as expressed in ballads on good and bad husbands, and in writing proposing alternatives to marriage. Chapter 5 provides case studies of three contemporary essays on women which circulated in manuscript (these are printed as appendices). Portraits of Sir Robert Filmer and his competent wife Dame Alice complement the discussion of her character. See also Ezell (1993), an invigorating review of feminist literary history.

Griffin, Dustin. *Literary Patronage in England 1650–1800*. Cambridge: Cambridge University Press, 1996.

Griffin studies the 'cultural economics' of patronage, the rhetoric of dedications, and the mutually advantageous relationships of patrons and authors in a system which survived well after the Copyright Act. There are individual chapters on Dryden, Swift, and Pope and on some later eighteenth figures. Griffin is especially interesting on the rhetoric of dedications which sometimes, as *The True Briton* commented in 1723, 'do not give us the least Insight into the *Virtues* of the Person they are ascribed to, yet acquaint us with what are in *Vogue*' (quoted 17 n. 20). Students concerned with the economic and social context should read Griffin's study alongside Brean S. Hammond's *Professional Imaginative Writing in England, 1670–1740: 'Hackney for Bread'* (1997).

Hotson, Leslie. *The Commonwealth and Restoration Stage*. Cambridge, Mass.: Harvard University Press, 1928.

Hotson demonstrates how much theatrical activity survived the closing of the theatres in 1642. There are chapters on 'Players and Parliament' with a particularly useful section on 'Surreptitious Drama, 1642–1655', on five Playhouses, on Davenant's 'Opera' 1655–60, and on George Jolly and the Nursery (English actors on the continent, and training companies in London). The final four chapters are devoted to acting companies in the Restoration period. An appendix lists 119 'Chancery Bills and Answers: New Documents from the Public Record Office used for the History of Stage, 1640–1710' (315–26) and reprints some of the documents (327–407). Despite its age, this remains the best introduction to the subject.

Hughes, Derek. *English Drama, 1660–1700*. Oxford: Clarendon Press, 1996.

Complementing Hume's earlier history of dramatic development, Hughes' study offers stimulating, often brilliant, readings of individual plays within the context of 'the whole span of theatrical activity' (vi). The chronological and generic survey is divided into short spans, usually no longer than half a dozen years. Within this clear framework Hughes discusses significant recurrent themes, as 'competing and serpentine cross-currents, not parallel and linear advances towards the future' (15). Among his 'recurrent and interacting motifs' are dramatists' handling of hierarchy and of dislocation, of ways of signifying the self and portrayals of the stranger.

Hume, Robert D. *The Development of English Drama in the Late Seventeenth Century.* Oxford: Clarendon Press, 1976.

Concerned with 'what defines this period in dramatic history, and how the plays change over a span of nearly two generations' (vii), Hume traces the development of drama between 1660 and 1710. Analysis of formulas and variables provides a taxonomic basis for considering the great mass of comic and serious drama produced during these years. Challenging any homogeneous notion of period in relation to Restoration drama, he emphasises differences between drama of the 1670s and 1690s. In a chronological survey which achieves clarity without sacrificing complexity, the development of theatrical fashion is treated decade by decade, with attention to smaller periods of significant change.

Hume, Robert D., ed. *The London Theatre World, 1660–1800*. Carbondale: Southern Illinois University Press, 1980.

Gathered under Hume's editorship are twelve essays by other outstanding theatrical historians. Here are lucid introductions to company management, the theatres, scenery and technical design, the evidence from promptbooks, performers and performing, the making of the repertory, music as drama, the changing audience, political and social thought in the drama, dramatic censorship, the publication of plays, and the London theatre at the end of the eighteenth century. Although on each individual topic later work has been done, this convenient volume offers a good starting point.

Hunter, J. Paul. *Before Novels: The Cultural Contexts of Eighteenth Century English Fiction*. New York: W.W. Norton, 1990.

The most readable of recent, informed studies of the prehistory of the novel, this is devoted to 'other kinds of reading material that ministered to the same needs novels later came to address' (67): journalistic, didactic, private and personal, and historical writing. The first two sections offer thoughtful analysis of how the novel is defined and the contexts within which readers do their reading. The third section, making up about half the book, is of particular interest to students of prose 1650–1720: eight chapters on the publication of varied books and pamphlets, not seen condescendingly as 'background' or 'subliterary' (226) but as illumination of the narrative pleasures, whether in 'immediacy and minutiae' (193) or in finding links between astonishment and providential pattern.

Kishlansky, Mark. *A Monarchy Transformed: Britain 1603–1713*. The Penguin History of Britain. London: Allen Lane, The Penguin Press, 1996.

Kishlansky's zest for the seventeenth century enlivens this historical survey. Each chapter except the two introductory ones (on 'The Social World' and 'The Political World') opens with description of a particular dramatic moment related to political issues of the period. In the preface, Kishlansky plays with publishing conventions, as seventeenth-century writers often do, remarking after he has acknowleged the help of a great many scholars, students and friends, 'In this context, I shall refrain from taking sole responsibility for any errors that remain.' The volume includes a substantial section of annotated suggestions 'For further reading.'

The London Stage 1660–1800: A Calendar of Plays, Entertainments & Afterpieces Together with Casts, Box-Receipts and Contemporary Comment, compiled from the Playbills, Newspapers and Theatrical Diaries of the Period. Part I: 1660–1700, ed. William Van Lennep, with intro. by Emmet L. Avery and Arthur H. Scouten. *Part II: 1700–1729*, ed. and intro. by Emmet L. Avery. Carbondale: Southern Illinois University Press, 1965, 1960.

As the long title indicates, this is a rich, indeed an indispensable compendium of information about the theatre in London. Organised by theatrical season, it gives overviews of each year along with the detailed calendar of performances. For supplementary information, consult *A Register Of English Theatre Documents 1660–1737*, ed. Judith Milhous and Robert D. Hume (1991), and *Vice Chamberlain Coke's Theatrical Papers 1706–1715*, also edited by Milhous and Hume (1982). Pierre Danchin's collection of prologues and epilogues complements materials in *The London Stage* and sometimes corrects the dates of première performances.

Love, Harold. *Scribal Publication in Seventeenth-Century England*. Oxford: Clarendon Press, 1993.

Love both identifies and contributes to remedying a problem of period divisions: 'Literary scholars working on the early Stuart period define themselves as Renaissance specialists, inhabiting a different conceptual as well as historical world from those working on the later Stuart period who define themselves as Augustan specialists' (8). Thus connections are seldom made, as they are here, between the significance both for Donne and for Rochester of manuscript circulation. Love's bridge-building is also interdisciplinary, as he discusses the scribal publication of music, of scientific and legal materials, and of newsletters, as well as poetry. The study is divided into three parts: a clear exposition of 'Scribal Publication'; analysis of the relationship between 'Script and Society', which includes discussion of manuscript publication in relation both to censorship and to the establishment of communities; and finally, more briefly, 'Editing Scribally Published Texts'.

Mack, Maynard. *Alexander Pope: A Life*. New Haven: Yale University Press, 1985.

Modestly subtitled 'a life' rather than 'the life', this 900+ pp. account will comfortably fill a winter's reading, especially with pauses to read or reread each poem of Pope as it is discussed – as Mack's descriptions make one want to do. A generous appreciation of Pope's work, the biography was criticised by some reviewers for making Pope sound too much like Mack himself. (For an account of the controversial reception of the book, see Hammond 1997, 245–6.) There could be worse fates. Consider Mack someone like the wife who is remembered and longed for by John Le Carré's Smiley, because she could have helped him find a way to like a new acquaintance. For those who would like to be wooed into sympathy with a poet, and a kind of poetry, not to all tastes, this is a perfect companion.

Sherman, Stuart. *Telling Time: Clocks, Diaries, and English Diurnal Form, 1660–1785*. Chicago: The University of Chicago Press, 1996.

The intersection of technology, psychology and literature forms the base of this perceptive book. Like Lynn White Jr. on the stirrup, Sherman reveals how thoroughly a mechanical invention can affect a culture. He moves easily between the history of chronometers and theories of narrative. Detailed attention is given to how a changing sense of time affects varied prose genres: diaries, newspapers, periodical essays, travel writing, biography, the novel. In the first half of the book, his key texts are Pepys' *Diary* and *The Spectator* papers; later chapters discuss Defoe, Johnson and Boswell, and Burney.

Spufford, Margaret. *Small Books and Pleasant Histories: Popular Fiction and Its Readership in Seventeenth-Century England*. London: Methuen, 1981.

An economic historian illuminates questions about who could read and what they read. Spufford's fascinating review of evidence about literacy in the period includes the correlation of opportunities for schooling with geography, economic status and gender. More among the poorer classes could read than was once thought, for reading and writing were taught separately, so that inability to sign one's name did not necessarily mean illiteracy. Small books carried in the packs of some 2500 chapmen selling their goods in England and Wales provided a wide range of reading; Pepys' collection of chapbooks and the trade-lists of chapbook publishers contribute to the analysis of available publications.

Winn, James Anderson. *John Dryden and His World*. New Haven: Yale University Press, 1987.

Often the most efficient way to learn about many things is to try to learn about one. This biography of Dryden, like Mack's biography of Pope, combines the advantages of focus and of range. In tracing the life of an author who was the outstanding Restoration figure in drama, poetry and criticism, Winn adroitly mingles history, cultural studies and commentary on individual works. Among the special strengths of Winn's writing, here and elsewhere, is that he is knowledgeable about both literature and music.

Bibliography

Primary Texts

For works published before 1801 the place of publication is London unless otherwise stated.

Academy of Complements, The. 1650. Other eds 1640, 1685.

Addison, Joseph. *Works.* 1721.

Alleine, Joseph. *An Alarm to Unconverted Sinners.* 1672.

Art of Complaisance, or the Means to oblige in Conversation, The. (1673) 2nd edn 1677.

Ashton, John. *Chapbooks of the Eighteenth Century.* London: Chatto & Windus, 1882. Repr. Bronz, NY: Benjamin Blom, 1966; Welwyn Garden City: Seven Dials Press, 1969; London: Skoob, 1997.

Astell, Mary. *A Serious Proposal to the Ladies, for the Advancement of their True and Greatest Interest.* 2 pts 1697. A facs. of Part I only is included in *The Pioneers: Early Feminists,* ed. Marie Mulvey Roberts and Tamae Mizuta. London: Routledge/Thoemmes Press, 1993. This also includes the anonymous *An Essay in Defense of the Female Sex,* 1696.

Athenian Gazette, The. Renamed *The Athenian Mercury.* Ed. John Dunton. 1691–97.

Ault, Norman, ed. *Seventeenth Century Lyrics from the Original Texts.* London: Longmans, Green & Co. 1928. 2nd edn 1950.

Backscheider, Paula R. and John J. Richetti, eds. *Popular Fiction by Women 1660–1730: An Anthology.* Oxford: Clarendon Press, 1996.

Ballard, George. *Memoirs of Several Ladies of Great Britain who have been Celebrated for their Writings or Skill in the Learned Languages, Arts and Sciences.* (Oxford, 1752, 1775). Ed. Ruth Perry. Detroit: Wayne State University Press, 1985.

Barker, Jane. *The Galesia Trilogy and Selected Manuscript Poems.* Ed. Carol Shiner Wilson. Oxford: Oxford University Press, 1997. Contains *Love Intrigues* (1713), 1–47; *Love Intrigues* also in Backscheider and Richetti (1996), 81–111.

Baxter, Richard. *The Practical Works.* 4 vols 1707.

—— *The Saints Everlasting Rest.* 1650. 8th edn 1659, and 12th edn 1688. There is an abridged modern edn by John T. Wilkinson, 1962.

—— *A Call to the Unconverted to Turn and Live.* (1657) In *The Practical Works,* II. 481–520.

—— *A Breviate of the Life of Margaret ... Baxter.* 1681. Modern edition ed. John T. Wilkinson under the title *Richard Baxter and Margaret Charlton: A Puritan Love-Story.* London: George Allen & Unwin, 1928.

—— *Reliquiae Baxterianae.* (1696). Ed. and abridged J. M. Lloyd Thomas (under the title *The Autobiography of Richard Baxter*). London: J. M. Dent, 1925. There is a later Everyman edition, ed. Neil Keeble, 1974.

Beadle, John. *The Journall or Diary of a Thankfull Christian.* (1656). Ed. Germaine Fry Murray. New York: Garland, 1996.

Bedford, Arthur. *The Evil and Danger of Stage-Plays, Shewing their Natural Tendency to Destroy Religion, and Introduce a General Corruption of Manners.* 1706. Facs. New York: Garland, 1974.

—— *A Serious Remonstrance in Behalf of the Christian Religion.* 1719. Facs. New York: Garland, 1974.

Behn, Aphra. *The Works.* Ed. Janet Todd. 7 vols. London: William Pickering, 1992–96.

B[ehn], A[phra]. *Covent Garden Drollery.* 1672.

—— *The Unfortunate Happy Lady* (1698). In Salzman (1991), 527–53.

Beveridge, William. *Of the Happiness of the Saints in Heaven: a Sermon Preach'd before the Queen at White-Hall, October the 12th 1690.* 1690.

Bold, Henry. *Poems Lyrique, Macaronique, Heroique, &c.* 1664.

—— *Latine Songs, with their English; and Poems.* 1685.

Boswell, James. *Life of Johnson.* (1791) Ed. G. B. Hill. 6 vols. Oxford: Clarendon Press, 1934–50.

Boyle, Robert. *Some Considerations Touching the Style of the H. Scriptures.* 1661. 4th edn 1675.

—— *The Martyrdom of Theodora and of Didymus.* 1687. Published semi-anonymously as 'By a Person of Quality'.

—— *An Account of Philaretus, during his Minority.* In Thomas Birch, *The Life of the Honourable Robert Boyle.* 1744, 18–48.

Brome, Alexander. *Songs and Other Poems.* 1661.

—— *Poems.* Ed. Roman R. Dubinski. 2 vols. Buffalo: University of Toronto Press, 1982.

Brown, Thomas. *The Fourth and Last Volume of The Works ... Serious and Comical, in Prose and Verse.* 1715.

—— 'Original Letters'. In Voiture (1705), 65–140.

Browne, Sir Thomas. *The Works.* Ed. Geoffrey Keynes. 6 vols. London: Faber & Faber, 1928–31. New edn, 4 vols, 1964.

Bunyan, John. *Grace Abounding with Other Spiritual Autobiographies.* (1666). Eds John Stachniewski and Anita Pacheco. Oxford: Oxford University Press (World's Classics), 1998. Contains Lawrence Clarkson, *The Lost Sheep Found*, 1660; John Crook, *A Short History of the Life*, 1706, and others.

—— *Grace Abounding to the Chief of Sinners.* (1666). Ed. Roger Sharrock. Oxford: Clarendon Press, 1962.

—— *The Life and Death of Mr Badman.* 1680. Extract in Salzman (1991), 447–70.

—— *The Miscellaneous Works.* Ed. Roger Sharrock *et al.* 13 vols. Oxford: Clarendon Press, 1962–94.

—— *The Pilgrim's Progress.* 1678, 1684.

—— *A Relation of the Imprisonment of Mr. John Bunyan.* (1765) In Bunyan, ed. Stachniewski and Pacheco (1998), 95–122.

Burnet, Gilbert. *A Sermon Preached before the House of Peers in the Abbey of Westminster, on the 5th of November 1689, being Gun-Powder Treason-Day, As*

Likewise The Day of his Majesties Landing in England by the Right Reverend Father in God GILBERT Lord Bishop of SARUM. 1689.

—— *The History of My Own Times.* 2 vols. 1724, 1734.

Bysshe, Edward. *The Art of English Poetry.* 1702. Facs. Menston: Scolar Press, 1968.

Calamy, Edmund. See Matthews.

Cavendish, Margaret, Duchess of Newcastle. *Playes Written by the Thrice Noble, Illustrious and Excellent Princess, The Lady Marchioness of Newcastle.* 1662.

—— *The Blazing World.* (1666) In Salzman (1991), 249–348.

—— *The Life of William Cavendish Duke of Newcastle to which is added the True Relation of my Birth Breeding and Life.* (1667). Ed. C.H. Firth, 1906. The *True Relation* had been previously included in her *Natures Pictures Drawn by Fancies Pencil to the Life,* 1656.

—— *Plays, Never before Printed.* 1668.

—— *The Sociable Companions; or, The Female Wits: A Comedy.* (1668). Ed. and int. Amanda Holton. Oxford: Seventeenth Century Press, 1996.

Cellier, Elizabeth. *Malice Defeated* and *The Matchless Rogue.* 1680. Facs. ed. Anne Barbeau Gardiner. Los Angeles: William Andrews Clark Memorial Library, 1988.

—— 'A Scheme for the Foundation of a Royal Hospital and...for the Maintenance of a Corporation of skilful Midwives, of such Foundlings, or Exposed Children, as shall be admitted therein. As it was proposed and addressed to his Majesty King James II.' (1687). In *The Harleian Miscellany: or, A Collection of Scarce, Curious, and Entertaining Pamphlets and Tracts, as well in Manuscript as in Print, found in the Earl of Oxford's Library.* 1745. IV. 136–40. A headnote reads: 'Now first published from her own MS. found among the said King's Papers. folio, containing nine pages.'

Cellier. 'To the praise of Mrs. Cellier, the Popish Midwife'. 1680. Broadside ballad.

Charles II, King of England. 'His Majesties Declaration from Breda to all His loving Subjects'. In *A Collection of His Majesties Gracious Letters, Speeches, Messages and Declarations Since April $\frac{4}{14}$ 1660'.* 1660. Thomason Tracts E.191.

Chudleigh, Lady Mary. *The Poems and Prose of Mary, Lady Chudleigh.* Ed. Margaret J.M. Ezell. New York: Oxford University Press, 1993.

Cibber, Colley. *An Apology for the Life of Colley Cibber, with An Historical View of the Stage during His Own Time, Written by Himself.* (1740). Ed. and int. B. R. S. Fone. Ann Arbor: The University of Michigan Press, 1968.

Clarkson, Lawrence. *The Lost Sheep Found.* (1660) In Bunyan, ed. Stachniewski and Pacheco (1998), 173–90.

Cleveland, John. *Poems.* 1653. Facs. Menston: Scolar Press, 1971.

—— *The Poems.* Ed. Brian Morris and Eleanor Withington. Oxford: Clarendon Press, 1967.

Clifford, Lady Anne, Countess of Pembroke. *The Diaries of Lady Anne Clifford.* Ed. D. J. H. Clifford. Stroud: Alan Sutton, 1990. Reprint with corrections, 1992.

Collection of Poems, Written upon Several Occasions, by Several Persons. Never before in Print, A. 1672.

Collier, Jeremy. *A Short View of the Immorality and Profaneness of the English Stage.* 1698.

Comenius, Johann Amos. *Orbis sensualium pictus.* 1664. English trans. by Charles Hoole. 1659. Facs. int. by John E. Sadler. London: Oxford University Press, 1968.

Other facs.: (1) English Linguistics 1500–1800, No. 222. Menston: Scolar Press, 1970. Reproduces the Dr Williams' Library copy, Wing C5523; (2) Third London ed. 1672, int. James Bowen. Sydney: Sydney University Press, 1967.

Commonwealth Tracts 1625–1650. Facs., with preface by Arthur Freeman. New York: Garland, 1974.

Comparison between the Two Stages, A. (1702). Ed. and intro. Staring B. Wells. Princeton: Princeton University Press, 1942.

Congreve, William. Incognita: Or, Love and Duty Reconciled. (1692) In Salzman (1991), 471–525. Facs. Menston: Scolar Press, 1971.

—— The Judgment of Paris: A Masque. 1701.

—— A Pindaric Ode Humbly Offer'd to the Queen ... To which is prefix'd A Discourse on the Pindarique Ode. 1706.

—— The Comedies. Ed. Anthony G. Henderson. Cambridge: Cambridge University Press, 1982.

Cotton, Charles. Works, 1663–1665. Ed. A. I. Dust. New York: Garland, 1992.

Cowley, Abraham. Poems, viz.: I. Miscellanies, II. The Mistress, or Love Verses, III. Pindarique Odes, and IV. Davideis. 1656.

—— The Third Part of the Works of Mr Abraham Cowley, being His Six Books of Plants, Never before Printed in English: viz. The First and Second of Herbs. The Third and Fourth of Flowers. The Fifth and Sixth of Trees. Now made English by several Hands. 1689. Book VI trans. by Aphra Behn.

Cromwell, Oliver, Lord Protector. Letters and Speeches. 3 vols (1845). Ed. Thomas Carlyle. London: Chapman & Hall, 1857.

Crook, John. A Short History of the Life of John Crook. (1706) In Bunyan, ed. Stachniewski and Pacheco (1998), 157–69.

Cudworth, Ralph. A Discourse Concerning the True Notion of the Lords Supper (1642) to which is added two Sermons (1 Jn.2: 3–4, 1 Cor. 15: 57). 1670 and 1676.

—— A Sermon Preached before the Honourable House of Commons, at Westminster, March 31, 1647. Cambridge, 1647.

Danchin, Pierre, ed. The Prologues and Epilogues of the Eighteenth Century: The First Part 1701–1720. Nancy: Presses Universitaires de Nancy, 1990.

—— The Prologues and Epilogues of the Restoration, 1660–1700. 4 parts in 7 vols. Nancy: Publications Université Nancy II, 1981–88.

Dangerfield, Thomas. Don Tomazo, Or the Juvenile Rambles of Thomas Dangerfield. (1680) In Salzman (1991), 349–445.

Davenant, Sir William. Love and Honour [1649] and The Siege of Rhodes [1656]. Ed. James W. Tupper. Boston: D.C. Heath, 1909.

—— The Siege of Rhodes. Made a Representation by the Art of Perspective in Scenes, And the Story sung in Recitative Musick. At the back part of Rutland-House in the upper end of Aldersgate-Street, 1656.

—— The Siege of Rhodes....The first part being lately Englarg'd. 1663.

—— Works. 1672/3. Facs. New York: Benjamin Blom, 1968.

Dawson, Terence and Robert Scott Dupree. Seventeenth-century English Poetry: The Annotated Anthology. New York: Harvester Wheatsheaf, 1994.

Defoe, Daniel. 'An Academy for Women'. In An Essay upon Projects. 1697. Facs. Menston: Scholar Press, 1969.

DeMaria, Robert, Jr. *British Literature 1640–1789: an Anthology.* Oxford: Blackwell, 1996.

Denham, Sir John. *Poetical Works.* Ed. T. Banks. New Haven: Yale University Press, 1928.

Dennis, John. *The Critical Works.* Ed. Edward Niles Hooker. 2 vols. Baltimore: The Johns Hopkins University Press, 1939–43.

—— *The Plays.* Ed. and int. J. W. Johnson. New York, Garland, 1980.

Downes, John. *Roscius anglicanus.* (1708). Ed. Judith Milhous and Robert D. Hume. London: The Society for Theatre Research, 1987.

Dryden, John. *Works.* Ed. H.T. Swedenberg, Jr. *et al.* 15 vols. Berkeley: University of California Press, 1956–94.

—— 'Dryden's Miscellanies'. See Miscellanies.

—— *Of Dramatic Poesy, and Other Critical Essays.* Ed. and intro. George Watson. 2 vols. London: Dent (Everyman's Library), 1962.

—— 'Life of Plutarch'. In *Plutarch's Lives* 1693, I. 1–79.

Dunton, John. *Religio bibliopolae. In Imitation of Dr. Browns Religio Medici. with a Supplement to it.* 1691.

—— *Life and Errors.* 1705.

—— See also *Athenian Gazette.*

D'Urfey, Thomas, ed. *Wit and Mirth: or Pills to Purge Melancholy.* (1719–20). Int. Cyrus L. Day. 6 vols. New York: Folklore Library Publishers, 1959.

Elledge, Scott, ed. *Eighteenth-Century Critical Essays.* Ithaca: Cornell University Press, 1961.

Elstob, Elizabeth. *The Rudiments of Grammar for the English-Saxon Tongue, First Given in English: with An Apology for the Study of Northern Antiquities. Being very useful towards the understanding our ancient English Poets, and other Writers.* 1715. Facs. Menston: Scolar Press, 1968.

—— translator. [Aelfric.] *An English-Saxon Homily on the Birth-day of St. Gregory.* 1709.

Essay in Defence of the Female Sex. In which are inserted the Characters of A Pedant, A Squire, A Beau, A Vertuoso, Poetaster, A City-Critick, &c. In a Letter to a Lady, An. Written by a Lady. 1696. 2nd edn 1696, 4th edn 1721.

Etherege, Sir George. *The Plays.* Ed. Michael Cordner. Cambridge: Cambridge University Press, 1982.

Euing Collection of English Broadside Ballads in the Library of the University of Glasgow, The. Int. John Holloway. Glasgow: University of Glasgow Publications, 1971.

Evans, Arise. *An Eccho to the Voice from Heaven, or A Narration of the Life, and manner of the special Calling, and Visions of Arise Evans.* 1652.

—— *A Voice from Heaven to the Common-wealth of English.* 1652.

—— *The Voice of the Iron Rod, To His Highness The Lord Protector: Being A seasonable Admonition presented to him and to all Judicious men.* 1655.

—— *The Voice of King Charls the Father, to Charls the Son.* 1655.

Evelyn, John. *The Diary.* Ed. E. S. de Beer. 6 vols. Oxford: Clarendon Press, 1935.

—— *Selections from the Diaries of John Evelyn and Samuel Pepys.* Ed. James Gibson. London: Chatto & Windus, 1957. Repr. 1975.

—— *The Diary.* Ed. E. S. de Beer. London: Oxford University Press, 1959.

—— *Fumifugium, or The Inconvenience of the Aer and Smoak of London Dissipated.* 1661.

—— *Sylva, or A Discourse of Forest Trees.* 1664.

Fanshawe, Ann, Lady. *See* Halkett.

Farquhar, George. *The Recruiting Officer and Other Plays.* Ed. William Myers. Oxford: Clarendon Press, 1995.

Fell, Margaret. *Womens Speaking Justified, Proved and Allowed of by the Scriptures.* (1667). Intro. David J. Latt. Los Angeles: William Andrews Clark Memorial Library, 1979.

Female Wits, The. (performed 1696, printed 1704). Facs. with intro. Lucyle Hook. Los Angeles: William Andrews Clark Memorial Library, 1967. This satiric play is also included in Morgan (1981), 390–433.

Fowler, Alastair, ed. *The New Oxford Book of Seventeenth Century Verse.* Oxford: Oxford University Press, 1991.

Fox, George. *The Journal.* (1694). Ed. John L. Nickalls. Cambridge: Cambridge University Press, 1952.

—— John Stubs and Benjamin Furly. *A Battle-Door for Teachers & Professors to Learn Singular & Plural* 1660. Facs. Menston: Scolar Press, 1968.

Fuller, Thomas. *The History of the Worthies of England.* 1662.

Garman, Mary *et al.*, eds. *Hidden in Plain Sight: Quaker Women's Writings 1650–1700.* Wallingford: Pendle Hill Publications, 1996.

Gay, John. *Poetry and Prose.* Ed. Vinton A. Dearing with Charles E. Beckwith. 2 vols. Oxford, Clarendon Press, 1974.

—— *The Present State of Wit.* 1711.

Giffard, Martha Lady. *The Life and Character of Sir William Temple, Baronet.* 1728. Her 1690 text is in Temple (1930), 1-31.

Gilbert, Sandra M. and Susan Gubar, eds. *The Norton Anthology of Literature by Women.* New York: Norton, 1985. 2nd edn 1996.

Gildon, Charles. *Measure for Measure, or Beauty the Best Advocate ... Written Originally by Mr. Shakespear: And now very much Alter'd; with Additions of several Entertainments of Musick.* 1700.

—— *The Complete Art of Poetry.* 2 vols. 1718.

—— *Remarks on Mr. Rowe's Tragedy of the Lady Jane Gray, and All His Other Plays.* 1715. Reprints *A New Rehearsal, or Bays the Younger,* 1714, paginated 1–88, with additional prefatory material. Facs. New York: Garland, 1974.

—— *Plays.* Ed. and int. Paula R. Backscheider. New York: Garland, 1979.

Goldsmith, Oliver. *Collected Works.* Ed. Arthur Friedman. 5 vols. Oxford: Clarendon Press, 1966.

Graham, Elspeth, *et al.*, eds. *Her Own Life: Autobiographical Writings by Seventeenth-Century Englishwomen.* London: Routledge, 1989. Repr. 1996.

Greer, Germaine *et al.*, eds. *Kissing the Rod: An Anthology of Seventeenth-Century Women's Verse.* London: Virago, 1988.

Grierson, H.J.C. and G. Bullough. *The Oxford Book of Seventeenth Century Verse.* Oxford: Clarendon Press, 1934.

Halifax, George Savile, marquess of. *A Lady's New Year's Gift, or Advice to a Daughter.* 1688.

Halkett, Anne, Lady; Fanshawe, Ann, Lady. *The Memoirs of Anne, Lady Halkett and Ann, Lady Fanshawe*. Ed. John Loftis. Oxford: Clarendon Press, 1979.

Haller, William and Godfrey Davies, eds. *The Leveller Tracts 1647–1653*. (1944). Gloucester, Mass.: Peter Smith, 1964.

Harrington, James. *The Commonwealth of Oceana*. (1656). In *The Political Works of James Harrington*, ed. J. G. A. Pocock. Cambridge: Cambridge University Press, 1977.

Herbert, Sir Percy. *The Princess Cloria, or The Royal Romance*. 1653/1661. Extract in Salzman (1991), 209–47.

Hickes, George, trans. and reviser. *Instructions for the Education of a Daughter, by the Author of Telemachus* [Fénelon]. *To which is Added a Small Tract of Instructions for the Conduct of Young Ladies of the Highest Rank. With Suitable Devotions Annexed*. 1707.

Hobbes, Thomas. *The Collected Works*. Ed. Sir William Molesworth. 12 vols. London, 1839–45. Repr. London: Routledge/Thoemmes Press, 1992.

Horace. *Satires, Epistles and Ars Poetica*. With an English translation by H. Rushton Fairclough. Cambridge: Harvard University Press, 1961. Loeb Classical Library.

Howard, Edward. *Spencer redivivus, Containing the first book of the Fairy Queen, his Essential Design Preserv'd, but his Obsolete Language and Manner of Verse Totally Laid Aside. Deliver'd in Heroick Numbers*. 1687. Published as by A Person of Quality.

Hutchinson, Lucy. *The Life of Mrs. Lucy Hutchinson, written by herself*. In *Memoirs of the Life of Colonel Hutchinson*, ed. Julius Hutchinson. 2 vols. London: John C. Nimmo, 1885. I. 1–26.

—— *Translation of Lucretius: 'De rerum natura'*. Ed. Hugh de Quehen. London: Duckworth, 1996.

Johnson, Samuel. *Lives of the English Poets*. (1779–81). Ed. George Birkbeck Hill. 3 vols. Oxford: Clarendon Press, 1905.

Jones, Andrew. *The Black Book of Conscience, or God's High Court of Justice in the Soul*. 6th edn 1658, 22nd edn 1663.

—— *The Dying Mans Last Sermon. Or, The Fathers last Blessing. Left, and bequeathed as a Legacy unto his Children, immediately before his death. Being comfortable Meditations for the day of death* ... 3rd edn 1659, 12th edn with Additions, 1665.

—— *The Dreadfull Character of a Drunkard*. (10th edn 1663) 1681.

Kenner, Hugh, ed. *Seventeenth Century Poetry: The Schools of Donne and Jonson*. New York: Holt, Rinehart & Winston, 1964.

Langbaine, Gerard. *An Account of the English Dramatic Poets*. Oxford, 1691. Facs. Menston: Scolar Press, 1971.

Locke, John. *An Essay Concerning Human Understanding*. (1690). Ed. Peter H. Nidditch. Oxford: Clarendon Press, 1975.

—— *An Essay for the Understanding of St. Paul's Epistles, By Consulting St. Paul himself*. 1707.

Longus, *Daphnis and Chloe*. [3rd century AD?]. Trans. George Thornley [1657] Revised J.M. Edmonds. London: Heinemann, 1912. Repr. 1962. Loeb Classical Library.

Lonsdale, Roger, ed. *Eighteenth Century Women Poets: An Oxford Anthology*. Oxford: Oxford University Press, 1989.

Lord, George deForest, *et al. Poems on Affairs of State: Augustan Satirical Verse, 1660–1714*. 7 vols. New Haven: Yale University Press, 1963–75.

Lyons, Paddy and Fidelis Morgan, eds. *Female Playwrights of the Restoration: Five Comedies*. London: J.M. Dent, 1991. Anthology: Aphra Behn, *The Feigned Courtesans* (1679); 'Ariadne', *She Ventures and He Wins* (1695); Mary Pix, *The Beau Defeated* (1700); Susannah Centlivre, *The Basset Table* (1705) and *The Busybody* (1709).

McHenry, Robert W. Jr., ed. *Contexts 3: Absalom and Achitophel*. Hamden: Archon Books, 1986.

Makin, Bathsua. *An Essay to Revive the Antient Education of Gentlewomen, in Religion, Art and Tongues*. 1673. Facs. with int. by Paula L. Barbour. Los Angeles: William Andrews Clark Memorial Library, 1980.

Marvell, Andrew. *The Complete Poems*. Ed. Elizabeth Story Donno. Harmondsworth: Penguin, 1972.

—— *The Rehearsal Transpros'd* (1672) and *The Rehearsal Transpros'd, the Second Part* (1673). Ed. D. I. B. Smith. Oxford, Clarendon Press, 1971.

Massinger, Philip. *The Fatal Dowry*. (Written and first produced 1617–19?, published 1632) In *The Plays and Poems of Philip Massinger*, ed. Philip Edwards and Colin Gibson. Oxford: Clarendon Press, 1976. I. 1–103.

Matthews, A. G. *Calamy Revised, being a Revision of Edmund Calamy's Account of the Ministers and Others Ejected and Silenced, 1660–2*. Oxford: Clarendon Press, 1934, repr. 1988.

Mennis, Sir John and James Smith. *Musarum deliciae: or, The Muses Recreation, Conteining severall select Pieces of sportive Wit*. 1655. Other eds. 1656, 1661. Facs. of *Musarum deliciae* (1655) and *Wit Restor'd* (1658), intro. Tim Raylor. Delmar: Scholars' Facsimiles & Reprints, 1985.

Milhous, Judith and Robert D. Hume, eds. *A Register of English Theatrical Documents 1660–1737*. 2 vols. Carbondale: Southern Illinois University Press, 1991.

—— *Vice Chamberlain Coke's Theatrical Papers 1706–1715*. Carbondale: Southern Illinois University Press, 1982.

Milton, John. *Complete Prose Works*. Ed. Don M. Wolfe *et al.* 8 vols. New Haven: Yale University Press, 1953–82.

—— *Paradise Lost* (1667). Ed. Alastair Fowler. (1968, 1971) Sixth impression, with corrections. London: Longman, 1981.

Miscellanies of poetry by various hands, in chronological order:

Miscellany Poems, Containing a New Translation of Virgills Eclogues, Ovids Love Elegies, Odes of Horace, and Other Authors, with Several Original Poems; by the most Eminent Hands. 1684. The first of the six volumes called 'Dryden's Miscellanies' or 'Tonson's Miscellanies'; others appear in 1685, 1693, 1694, 1704, 1709. Tonson published a six-volume collection, not identical to the previous six volumes, in 1716.

Miscellany, Being a Collection of Poems by several Hands. 1685. Dedicatory epistle signed A. Behn.

Miscellany Poems and Translations. By Oxford Hands. 1685.

Sylvae, or the Second Part of Miscellany Poems. 1685. (The second 'Dryden's Miscellany' or 'Tonson's Miscellany'.)

Miscellany Poems upon Several Occasions. 1692. Compiled by Charles Gildon.

A New Miscelllany of Original Poems: on Several Occasions. 1701. Dedication signed Charles Gildon.

Miscellaneous Poems and Translations. 1712, 1714, 1720, 1722. (Bernard Lintot's miscellany, including Gay's poem about how to assemble such a collection.)

Mish, Charles C. *Restoration Prose Fiction.* Lincoln: University of Nebraska Press, 1970. Anthology.

Molière. *Plays from Molière by English Dramatists.* Int. by Henry Morley. London: Routledge, 1883. Contains Dryden, *Sir Martin Marr-all*; Vanbrugh, *The Mistake*, and Wycherley, *The Plain Dealer*, together with two plays by Fielding and one by Cibber.

Monck, Mary Molesworth. *Marinda, Poems and Translations upon Several Occasions.* 1716.

Morgan, Fidelis. *The Female Wits: Women Playwrights on the London Stage 1660–1720.* London: Virago, 1981. Part II is an anthology: Aphra Behn, *The Lucky Chance* (1686); Catherine Trotter, *The Fatal Friendship* (1698); Mary Delarivier Manley, *The Royal Mischief* (1696); Mary Pix, *The Innocent Mistress* (1697); Susannah Centlivre, *The Wonder: a Woman Keeps a Secret* (1714), and as an appendix, the anon. satiric *The Female Wits* (see above).

Motteux, Peter. *Beauty in Distress: A Tragedy.* 1698.

New Academy of Complements. Compiled by L.B. Sir C.S. Sir W.D. and Others the most Refined Wits of this Age. 1713.

Norris, John, Vicar of Bemerton. *A Collection of Miscellanies: Consisting of Poems, Essays, Discourses, and Letters.* Oxford, 1687.

North, John. *A Sermon Preached before the King at Newmarket October 8, 1671.* Cambridge, 1671.

Norton Anthology of English Literature, The. Ed. M.H. Abrams *et al.* 6th edn. New York: Norton, 1993.

Oates, Titus. *The Popes Ware-house, or the Merchandise of the Whore of Rome. Published for Common Good.* 1679.

—— *The Witch of Endor; or the Witchcrafts of the Roman Jesebel: In which you have an Account of the Exorcisms or Conjurations of the Papists.* 1679.

Ogilby, John. *The Entertainment of His Most Excellent Majestie Charles II in His Passage through the City of London to His Coronation.* 1662. Facs. Binghamton: Medieval and Renassance Studies, 1987.

Oldham, John. *The Works...together with his Remains.* 1684.

—— *Selected Poems.* Ed. and int. Ken Robinson. Newcastle upon Tyne: Bloodaxe Books, 1980.

Osborne, Dorothy. *Letters of Dorothy Osborne to Sir William Temple.* Ed. G. C. Moore Smith. Oxford: Clarendon Press, 1928.

—— *Letters to Sir William Temple.* Ed. and intro. Kenneth Parker. London: Penguin, 1987.

Otway, Thomas. *Works: Plays, Poems, and Love-Letters.* Ed. J.C. Ghosh. 2 vols. Oxford: Clarendon Press, 1932. Repr. 1968.

Ovid. *Ovid's Epistles. Translated by Several Hands.* 1680.

Pepys, Samuel. *The Diary of Samuel Pepys.* Ed. Robert Latham and William Matthews. 11 vols. London: Bell & Hyman, 1970–83.

Pepys Ballads, ed. W. G. Day. Facs. 5 vols. Cambridge: D. S. Brewer, 1987.

Peterson, Spiro, ed. *The Counterfeit Lady Unveiled and Other Criminal Fiction of Seventeenth Century England: A Selection.* New York: Doubleday Anchor, 1961.

Philips, Katherine. *Poems.* 1667.

—— *The Collected Works.* Ed. Patrick Thomas *et al.* 3 vols. Stump Cross: Stump Cross Books, 1990–93.

Phillips, Edward. *Theatrum poetarum, or A Compleat Collection of the Poets, Especially of The most Eminent of all Ages. The Ancients distinguish'd from the Moderns in their several Alphabets. With some Observations and Reflections upon many of them, particularly those of our own Nation. Together with a Prefatory Discourse of the Poets and Poetry in Generall.* 1675.

Phillips, John. *The Mysteries of Love and Eloquence Or, the Arts of Wooing and Complementing.* 1658. Facs. Menston: Scolar Press, 1972.

Playford, John. *The English Dancing Master.* 1651. Facs. with int., bibliography, and notes by Margaret Dean-Smith. London: Schott & Co., 1957.

—— *Choyce Ayres, Songs, and Dialogues ... 1673–1679.* Int. by Ian Spink. London: Stainer & Bell, 1989.

Pope, Alexander. *The Correspondence.* Ed. George Sherburn. 5 vols. Oxford: Clarendon Press, 1956.

—— *The Twickenham Edition of the Poems.* General ed. John Butt. 10 vols. New Haven: Yale University Press, 1950–69.

Price, Martin, ed. *The Restoration and the Eighteenth Century.* New York: Oxford University Press, 1973.

Purcell, Henry and Nahum Tate. *Dido and Aeneas: an Opera.* (1689) Ed. Curtis A. Price. New York: Norton, 1986.

Ravenscroft, Edward. *The London Cuckolds.* (1682) In *Restoration Comedies*, ed. Montague Summers. London: Jonathan Cape, 1921.

—— *The London Cuckolds: A Play.* (1682) Adapted by John Byrne. London: Samuel French, 1986.

—— *The London Cuckolds.* (1682) In a version by Terry Johnson. London: Methuen, 1998.

—— *Titus Andronicus, or The Rape of Lavinia...A Tragedy, Alter'd from Mr Shakespears Works.* 1687.

Rochester, John Wilmot, 3rd Earl of. *The Complete Poems of John Wilmot, Earl of Rochester.* Ed. David M. Vieth. New Haven: Yale University Press, 1968.

—— *The Complete Works.* Ed. Frank H. Ellis. London: Penguin, 1994.

Rollins, Hyder Edwards, ed. *The Pack of Autolycus; or, strange and terrible news of ghosts, apparitions, monstrous births, showers of wheat, judgments of God, and other prodigious and fearful happenings as told in broadside ballads of the years 1624–1693.* Cambridge, Mass.: Harvard University Press, 1927. Repr. 1969.

Rowe, John. *Tragi-Comoedia.* (Oxford, 1653) Facs. prefaced by Arthur Freeman. New York: Garland, 1973.

Rowe, Nicholas. *Tamerlane.* (1702) Ed. Landon C. Burns, Jr. Philadelphia: Pennsylvania University Press, 1966.

—— *The Fair Penitent* (1703). Ed. Malcom Goldstein. Lincoln: University of Nebraska Press, 1969.

Rules of Civility; or, Certain Ways of Deportment observed amongst all persons of Quality upon several Occasions, The. Newly revised and much Enlarged. 1678. Trans. of a popular French treatise (by Antoine de Courtin) which went through numerous eds in Paris, Brussels and elsewhere.

Rump: or An Exact Collection of the Choycest Poems and Songs Relating to the Late Times. By the most Eminent Wits, from Anno 1639 to Anno 1661. 1662.

Rymer, Thomas. *The Tragedies of the Last Age.* 1678.

—— *A Short View of Tragedy; Its Original, Excellency, and Corruption. With Some Reflections on Shakespear, and other Practitioners for the Stage.* 1693.

Salzman, Paul, ed. *An Anthology of Seventeenth Century Fiction.* Oxford: Oxford University Press, 1991. Includes selections from Percy Herbert's *The Princess Cloria* and from Bunyan's *Mr Badman*, along with all of Margaret Cavendish's *The Blazing World*, Thomas Dangerfield's *Don Tomazo*, William Congreve's *Incognita*, and Aphra Behn's *The Unfortunate Happy Lady.*

Sedley, Sir Charles. *The Poetical and Dramatic Works.* Ed. V. de Sola Pinto. 2 vols. London: Constable, 1928. Does not include *Beauty the Conquerour.*

—— *Beauty the Conquerer, or the Death of Marc Antony. A Tragedy in imitation of the Roman way of Writing.* 1702. Separately paginated, but bound in *The Miscellaneous Works of the Honourable Sir Charles Sedley,* with a preface by W. Ayloffe. 1702.

Selden, John. *Table-Talk, being the Discourses of John Selden, Esq. or his Sence of Various Matters of Weight and High Consequence Relating especially to Religion and State.* Ed. R. Milward. (1689) Ed. Sir Frederick Pollock, London: Selden Society, 1927.

Shadwell, Thomas. *The Complete Works.* Ed. Montague Summers. 5 vols. London: The Fortune Press, 1927.

Shaftesbury, Anthony Ashley Cooper, 3rd Earl. *Soliloquy: or, Advice to an Author.* 1710. Also included in his *Characteristicks of Men, Manners, Opinions, Times* 1727, I. 176.

Shepard, Thomas. *God's Plot: The Paradoxes of Puritan Piety, Being the Autobiography and Journal of Thomas Shepard.* Ed. Michael McGiffert. Amherst: The University of Massachusetts Press, 1972.

Simon, Irène, ed. *Three Restoration Divines: Barrow, South, Tillotson: Selected Sermons.* 3 vols in 2. Paris: Société d'Edition 'Les Belles Lettres', 1967.

Sisson, C. H., ed. *The English Sermon, Vol II: 1650–1750: An Anthology.* Cheadle: Carcanet Press, 1976.

Smith, Alexander. *A Complete History ... of the Most Notorious Highwaymen.* (5th edn 1719). Ed. Arthur L. Hayward, London: Routledge, 1926.

South, Robert. *A Sermon Preached before the Court at Christ-Church Chappel in Oxford.* Oxford, 1665.

Southerne, Thomas. *The Works,* ed. Robert Jordan and Harold Love. 2 vols. Oxford: Clarendon Press, 1988.

Spectator, The. Ed. Donald F. Bond. 5 vols. Oxford: Clarendon Press, 1965.

Spingarn, Joel Elias, ed. *Critical Essays of the Seventeenth Century.* 3 vols. Oxford: Oxford University Press, 1908, 1909. Repr. 1957.

Sprat, Thomas. *History of the Royal Society.* (1667). Facs., ed. with critical apparatus Jackson I. Cope and Harold Whitmore Jones. London: Routledge, 1959.

Steiner, T.R. *English Translation Theory 1650–1800*. Assen: Van Gorcum, 1975.

Suckling, Sir John. *The Non-Dramatic Works*. Ed. and intro. Thomas Clayton. Oxford: Clarendon Press, 1971.

—— *Aglaura*, 1638. Facs. Menston: Scolar Press, 1970.

Tate, Nahum. *The History of King Lear*. 1681.

—— *Cuckolds-Haven: or, An Alderman No Conjurer*. A Farce. Acted at the Queen's Theatre in Dorset Garden. 1685.

Tatler, The. Ed. and int. Donald F. Bond. 3 vols. Oxford: Clarendon Press, 1987.

Temple, Sir William, Baronet. *The Works*. 2 vols. 1720. New eds 1731, 1740, 1750.

—— *The Early Essays and Romances of Sir William Temple Bt. with the Life and Character of Sir William Temple by his sister Lady Giffard*. Ed. G. C. Moore Smith. Oxford: Clarendon Press, 1930.

Tenison, Thomas, Archbishop of Canterbury. *A sermon concerning the coelestial body of a Christian, after the resurrection: preached before the King and Queen at Whitehall, April 8, 1694, being Easter day*. 1694. 2nd edn 1695.

—— *A Sermon Preached at the Funeral of Queen Mary ... March 5, 1694/5*. 1695.

Thompson, Roger, ed. *Samuel Pepys' Penny Merriments, Being a Collection of Chapbooks, full of Histories, Jests, Magic, Amorous Tales of Courtship, Marriages and Infidelity, Accounts of Rogues and Fools, together with Comments on the Times*. London: Constable, 1976 and New York: Columbia University Press, 1977.

Tillotson, John, Archbishop of Canterbury. *The Golden Book of Tillotson: Selections*. Ed. James Moffatt. London: Hodder and Stoughton, 1926. Repr. Westport, Conn., 1971.

Tonson, Jacob. See Miscellanies.

Todd, Janet and Elizabeth Spearing, eds. *Counterfeit Ladies: The Life and Death of Mal Cutpurse* [by Mary Frith, 1662]; *The Case of Mary Carleton, lately stiled The German Princess* [by Mary Carleton, 1663]. London: William Pickering, 1994.

Triall of Henry Carr, Gent ... Also the Tryal of Elizabeth Cellier at the King's-Bench-Bar, July the 11th, 1680, where she was cleared, and Mr. Thomas Dangerfield, the chief Witness against her, for some defect in his Pardon, committed to the Kings-Bench Prison, The. 1681. In this volume the second trial has a separate title-page: *The Triall of Elizabeth Cellier, at the Kings-bench-Barr, on Friday July the 11th, 1680*. 1680.

Tryal and Conviction of John Tasborough and Ann Price, The. February 1679/80.

Tryal and Sentence of Elizabeth Cellier; for Writing Printing, and Publishing, A Scandalous Libel, called Malice Defeated, at the Sessions in the Old-Bailey, held Saturday the 11th and Monday the 13th of Sept. 1680, The. 1680.

Tryal of Sr Tho. Gascoyne Bar. for High-Treason, The. 1680.

Tryals and Condemnation of Lionel Anderson [*et al.*] ... *for High Treason, as Romish Priests, Upon the* Statute *of 27. Eliz. Cap. 2, Together with the Tryal of Alexander Lumsden a Scotchman, and the Arraignment of David Joseph Kemish for the same Offence. At the Sessions of Oyer and Terminer in the Old-Baily, on Saturday January 17th, 1679, The*. 1680.

Voiture, Vincent. *The works of Monsieur Voiture ... containing his Familiar Letters to Gentlemen and Ladies ... with three collections of Letters on Friendship and several other Occasions*. 1705.

Wain, John, ed. *The Oxford Anthology of English Poetry. Volume 1: Spenser to Crabbe.* (1986) Oxford: Oxford University Press, 1990.

Waller, Edmond [*sic*]. *Poems, &c. Written upon Several Occasions and to Several Persons.* (1664) 5th edn with several Additions Never before Printed, 1686.

—— *The Second Part of Mr. Waller's Poems. Containing His Alteration of the Maids Tragedy, and whatever of his is yet unprinted.* 1690.

Walter, Thomas. *The Excommunicated Prince: or, The False Relique. A Tragedy. As it was Acted by His Holiness's Servants. Being the Popish Plot in a Play.* by Capt. William Bedloe. 1679. The Selden copy in the Cambridge University Library, in a bound collection of works related to the Popish Plot has, written on the title page in an old hand, 'This play was writ all, or the most part of it by Thomas Walter of Jes:Col:Oxon: son of Jn. Walter of Percefield in Monmouthshire'. A note on the flyleaf indicates that this attribution of authorship to Thomas Walter 'is taken from Wood, Fasti Oxonienses' (= in the 1820 edn, pt. 2, col. 373).

Walton, Brian. *The Considerator Considered: or, A Brief view of certain Considerations upon the Biblia Polyglotta, the Prolegomena and Appendix thereof.* 1659.

Walton, Izaak. *The Compleat Angler.* 1653.

Warton, Joseph. *An Essay on the Genius and Writings of Pope.* 1756.

Weamys, Anna. *A Continuation of Sir Philip Sidney's 'Arcadia'.* (1651) Ed. Patrick Colborn Cullen. New York: Oxford University Press, 1994.

Whiting, John. *A Catalogue of Friends Books; Written by many of the People, called Quakers, from the Beginning or First Appearance of the said People.* 1708.

—— *Persecution Exposed in Some Memoirs.* 1715.

Winstanley, Gerrard. *The Works.* Ed. George H. Sabine. Ithaca: Cornell University Press, 1941.

Wit and Drollery. Jovial Poems. Corrected and Amended, with New Additions. 1682.

Wits, or, Sport upon Sport, The. (1662, 1673). Ed. John James Elson. Ithaca: Cornell University Press, 1932. A modern edn of Francis Kirkman's 1662 and 1673 collections of 'drolls'.

Woolley, Hannah (?). *The Gentlewoman's Companion; or a Guide to the Female Sex.* 1675.

Wright, James. *Country Conversations.* 1694.

——(?) *The Humours and Conversations of the Town, Expos'd in Two Dialogues.* 1693. Facs. with int. by Brice Harris. Gainesvile, Florida: Scholars' Facsimiles & Reprints, 1961.

—— *Historia histrionica: An Historical Account of the English-Stage.* 1699. Facs. New York: Garland, 1974.

Würzbach, Natascha, ed. *The Novel in Letters: Epistolary Fiction in the Early English Novel 1678–1740.* London: Routledge & Kegan Paul, 1969.

Wycherley, William. *The Plays of William Wycherley,* ed. Arthur Friedman, Oxford: Clarendon Press, 1979.

Secondary Works Cited

Allison, Alexander Ward. *Toward an Augustan Poetic: Edmund Waller's 'Reform' of English Poetry.* Lexington: University of Kentucky Press, 1962.

Bakhtin, M. M. 'The Problem of the Text', *Speech Genres and Other Late Essays.* Trans. Vern W. McGee, ed. Caryl Emerson and Michael Holquist. Austin: University of Texas Press, 1986. 103–31.

Bell, Maureen, George Parfitt and Simon Shepherd. *A Biographical Dictionary of English Women Writers 1580–1720.* New York and London: Harvester Wheatsheaf, 1990.

Benedict, Barbara M. *Making the Modern Reader: Cultural Mediation in Early Modern Literary Anthologies.* Princeton: Princeton University Press, 1996.

Besserman, Lawrence, ed. *The Challenge of Periodization: Old Paradigms and New Perspectives.* New York: Garland, 1996.

Bond, Edward. *Restoration: A Pastoral* (1981), in *Plays,* IV. London: Methuen, 1992.

Boswell Eleanore. *The Restoration Court Stage (1660–1702).* London: Allen & Unwin, 1932.

Bradner, Leicester. *Musae Anglicanae: A History of Anglo-Latin Poetry 1500–1925.* New York: Modern Language Association, 1940.

Brooks, H. F. 'Rump Songs: An Index with Notes,' *Proceedings and Papers of the Oxford Bibliographical Society* 5 (1936–39), 281–304.

Brown, Laura. *English Dramatic Form 1660–1760.* New Haven: Yale University Press, 1981.

Buckolz, R. O. *The Augustan Court: Queen Anne and the Decline of Court Culture.* Stanford: Stanford University Press, 1993.

Burns, Landon C. *Pity and Tears: The Tragedies of Nicholas Rowe.* Salzburg: Institut für Englische Sprache und Literatur, 1974.

Cambridge History of the Bible: The West from the Reformation to the Present Day, The. Ed. S.L. Greenslade. Cambridge: Cambridge University Press, 1963.

Capp, B. S. *The Fifth Monarchy Men: A Study in Seventeenth-century English Millenarianism.* London: Faber & Faber, 1972.

Cappelli, A. *Cronologia, Cronografia e Calendario Perpetuo.* 6th edn. Milan: Ulrico Hoepli, 1988.

Carlton, Peter J. 'Bunyan: Language, Convention, Authority', *English Literary History,* 51 (1984), 17–32.

Case, Arthur E. *A Bibliography of English Poetical Miscellanies 1521–1750.* Oxford: The Bibliographical Society, 1935.

Chernaik, Warren L. *The Poetry of Limitation: A Study of Edmund Waller.* New Haven: Yale University Press, 1968.

Claydon, Tony. *William III and the Godly Revolution.* Cambridge: Cambridge University Press, 1996.

Crawford, Patricia. 'Women's Published Writings 1600–1700'. In Prior (1985), 211–82.

Cressy, David. *Literacy and the Social Order: Reading and Writing in Tudor and Stuart England.* Cambridge: Cambridge University Press, 1980.

Culler, A. Dwight. 'Edward Bysshe and the Poet's Handbook', *Proceedings of the Modern Language Association of America* 63 (1948), 858–85.

Damrosch, Leo. *The Profession of Eighteenth-Century Literature: Reflections on an Institution.* Madison: The University of Wisconsin Press, 1992.

Day, Cyrus Lawrence and Eleanore Boswell Murrie. *English Song-Books 1651–1702: A Bibliography with a First-line Index of Songs.* London: The Bibliographical Society, 1940.

Delany, Paul. *British Autobiography in the Seventeenth Century.* London: Routledge & Kegan Paul, 1969.

DeLuna, D. N., ed. 'The Yale Poems on Affairs of State Thirty-Five Years Later,' *1650–1850: Ideas, Aesthetics, and Inquiries in the Early Modern Era* 4 (1998): 305–82.

de Sola Pinto, V. *Sir Charles Sedley 1639–1701: A Study in the Life and Literature of the Restoration.* London: Constable, 1927.

Erskine-Hill, Howard. *The Augustan Idea in English Literature.* London: Edward Arnold, 1983.

Everett, Barbara. 'The Sense of Nothing' in *Spirit of Wit: Reconsiderations of Rochester.* Ed. Jeremy Treglown. Oxford: Basil Blackwell, 1982, 1–41.

Ezell, Margaret J. M. *Writing Women's Literary History.* Baltimore: The Johns Hopkins University Press, 1993.

Fiske, Roger. *English Theatre Music in the Eighteenth Century.* 2nd edn. Oxford: Oxford University Press, 1986.

Ford, Boris, ed. *From Dryden to Johnson.* Harmondsworth: Penguin, 1957.

Fortescue, G. K. *Catalogue of the Pamphlets, Books, Newspapers, and Manuscripts Relating to the Civil War, the Commonwealth, and Restoration, Collected by George Thomason, 1640–1661.* 2 vols. London: British Museum, 1908.

Gaskell, Philip. *A New Introduction to Bibliography.* New York: Oxford University Press, 1971.

Geduld, Harry M. *Prince of Publishers: A Study of the Work and Career of Jacob Tonson.* Bloomington: Indiana University Press, 1969.

Gill, Pat. *Interpreting Ladies: Women, Wit, and Morality in the Restoration Comedy of Manners.* Athens: The University of Georgia Press, 1994.

Gillespie, Stuart. 'A Checklist of Restoration English Translations and Adaptations of Classical Greek and Latin Poetry, 1660–1700', *Translation and Literature* 1 (1992), 52–67.

Graham, Elspeth et al., eds. *Her Own Life: Autobiographical Writings by Seventeenth-century Englishwomen.* London: Routledge, 1989.

Griffin, Dustin. *Regaining Paradise: Milton and the Eighteenth Century.* Cambridge: Cambridge University Press, 1986.

Grundy, Isobel and Susan Wiseman, eds. *Women, Writing, History 1640–1740.* London: B.T. Batsford, 1992.

Guibbory, Achsah. *The Map of Time: Seventeenth-Century English Literature and Ideas of Pattern in History.* Urbana: University of Illinois Press, 1986.

Hale, John K. 'The Significance of the Early Translations of *Paradise Lost*', *Philological Quarterly* 63 (1984), 31–53.

Hammond, Brean S. *Professional Imaginative Writing in England, 1670–1740: 'Hackney for Bread'.* Oxford: Clarendon Press, 1997.

Harwood, John T. *Critics, Values, and Restoration Comedy.* Carbondale: Southern Illinois University Press, 1982.

Havens, Raymond D. 'Changing Taste in the Eighteenth Century: A Study of Dryden's and Dodsley's Miscellanies' *Proceedings of the Modern Language Association of America*, 44 (1929), 501–36.

Highfill, Philip H., Jr., Kalman A. Burnim and Edward A. Langhans. *A Biographical Dictionary of Actors, Actresses, Musicians, Dancers, and Other Stage Personnel in London, 1660–1800*. 16 vols. Carbondale: Southern Illinois University Press, 1973–93.

Hill, Christopher. *Change and Continuity in Seventeenth-Century England*. Revd edn. New Haven: Yale University Press, 1991.

Hobby, Elaine. *Virtue of Necessity: English Women's Writing 1646–1688*. London: Virago Press, 1988.

—— 'A Woman's Best Setting Out is Silence: the Writings of Hannah Wolley.' In MacLean (1995), 179–200.

Hogg, James. 'The 1953 Production of *Venice Preserv'd*'. In *Poetic Drama and Poetic Theory*, ed. James Hogg, *Salzburg Studies in English Literature*, 16 (1975), 2–11.

Holland, Norman N. *The First Modern Comedies: The Significance of Etherege, Wycherley, and Congreve*. Cambridge, Mass.: Harvard University Press, 1959.

Holmes, Geoffrey. *The Trial of Doctor Sacheverell*. London: Eyre Methuen, 1973.

Houlbrooke, Ralph. 'The Puritan Death-bed, *c.* 1560–1660'. In *The Culture of English Puritanism, 1560–1700*, ed. Christopher Durston and Jacqueline Eales. Houndmills: Macmillan Press, 1996, 122–44.

Howe, Elizabeth. *The First English Actresses: Women and Drama 1660–1700*. Cambridge: Cambridge University Press, 1992.

Hulme, Peter and Ludmilla Jordanova, eds. *The Enlightenment and Its Shadows*. London: Routledge, 1990.

Kaplan, Deborah, 'Representing the Nation: Restoration Comedies on the Early Twentieth-Century London Stage.' *Theatre Survey* 36.1 (1995), 37–61.

Kaufmann, R. J. 'On the Poetics of Terminal Tragedy: Dryden's *All for Love*' in *Dryden: Twentieth Century Views*, ed. Bernard N. Schilling. Eastwood Cliffs: Prentice-Hall, 1963, 86–94.

Keeble, N.H. *Richard Baxter: Puritan Man of Letters*. Oxford: Clarendon Press, 1982.

—— *The Literary Culture of Nonconformity in Later Seventeenth-Century England*. Leicester University Press, 1987.

Kenyon, John. *The Popish Plot*. London: Heinemann, 1972.

Kewes, Paulina. '"Give Me the Sociable Pocket-Books ...": Humphrey Moseley's Serial Publication of Octavo Play Collections.' *Publishing History* 38 (1995), 5–21.

Korshin, Paul J. *Typologies in England 1650–1820*. Princeton: Princeton University Press, 1982.

Levine, Joseph M. *The Battle of the Books: History and Literature in the Augustan Age*. Ithaca: Cornell University Press, 1991, repr. 1994.

Lewis, C.S. *A Preface to Paradise Lost*. London: Oxford University Press, 1942.

Lipking, Lawrence. 'Periods in the Arts: Sketches and Speculations,' *New Literary History* 1 (1970), 181–200.

Longe, Julia G. *Martha Lady Giffard: Her Life and Correspondence (1664–1722)*. London: George Allen & Sons, 1911.

Love, Harold. 'Who were the Restoration Audience?' *Yearbook of English Studies* 10 (1980), 21–44.

Lynch, Jack. 'Political Ideology in Translations of the *Iliad*, 1660–1715', *Translation and Literature* 7 (1998), 23–41.

McAleer, John J. 'The King's Pamphlets', *The Library Chronicle* 27.2 (Spring/Summer 1961), 163–75.

McKenzie, D. F. *Bibliography and the Sociology of Texts: The Panizzi Lectures 1985.* London: The British Library, 1986.

Mack, Phyllis. *Visionary Women: Ecstatic Prophecy in Seventeenth-Century England.* Berkeley: University of California Press, 1992.

MacLean, Gerald, ed. *Culture and Society in the Stuart Restoration: Literature, Drama, History.* Cambridge: Cambridge University Press, 1995.

Marcus, Leah S. 'Renaissance/Early Modern Studies' in *Redrawing the Boundaries: The Transformation of English and American Literary Studies.* New York: The Modern Language Association of America, 1992, 41–63.

Markley, Robert. *Fallen Languages: Crises of Representation in Newtonian England, 1660–1740.* Ithaca: Cornell University Press, 1993.

Marsden, Jean I. *The Re-Imagined Text: Shakespeare, Adaptation, & Eighteenth-Century Literary Theory.* Lexington: The University Press of Kentucky, 1995.

Marshall, Norman. *The Other Theatre.* London: John Lehmann, 1947.

Matthews, William. *British Diaries: An Annotated Bibliography of British Diaries Written Between 1442 and 1942.* Berkeley: University of California Press, 1950.

Medoff, Jeslyn. 'The Daughters of Behn and The Problem of Reputation'. In Grundy and Wiseman 1992, 33–54.

Mendelson, Sara Heller. 'Stuart Women's Diaries and Occasional Memoirs'. In Prior 1985, 181–210.

Milhous, Judith and Robert D. Hume. *Producible Interpretation: Eight English Plays 1675–1707.* Carbondale: Southern Illinois University Press, 1985.

Nicoll, Allardyce. *A History of Restoration Drama 1660–1700.* 3rd edn. Cambridge: Cambridge University Press, 1940.

Norbrook, David. 'A devine Originall: Lucy Hutchinson and the "woman's version"' *Times Literary Supplement* (19 March 1999), 13–15.

Novak, Maximillian. 'Commentary' on *All for Love*, in California Dryden, XIII. 357–440, 1984.

Nussbaum, Felicity. *The Brink of All We Hate: English Satires on Women, 1660–1750.* Lexington: The University Press of Kentucky, 1984.

Nyberg, Lennart. 'Restoration Comedy in the Modern British Theatre', *Restoration and Eighteenth-Century Theatre Research.* 2nd series 10.2 (Winter 1995), 1–16.

Osborne, Mary Tom. *Advice-to-a-Painter Poems 1633–1856: An Annotated Finding List.* Austin: The University of Texas Press, 1949.

Owen, Susan J. *Restoration Theatre and Crisis.* Oxford: Clarendon Press, 1996.

Parker, Patricia A. *Inescapable Romance: Studies in the Poetics of a Mode.* Princeton: Princeton University Press, 1979.

Parry, Graham. *Hollar's England: A Mid-seventeenth-century View.* Wilton: Michael Russell, 1980.

—— *Seventeenth-Century Poetry: The Social Context.* London: Hutchinson, 1985.

—— *The Seventeenth Century: the Intellectual and Cultural Context of English Literature 1603–1700.* London: Longman, 1989.

Patterson, Annabel. *Marvell and the Civic Crown*. Princeton: Princeton University Press, 1978.

—— *Censorship and Interpretation: The Conditions of Writing and Reading in Early Modern England*. Madison: The University of Wisconsin Press, 1984.

Pearson, Jacqueline. 'The History of *The History of the Nun*'. In *Rereading Aphra Behn: History, Theory, and Criticism*, ed. Heidi Hutner. Charlottesville: University Press of Virginia, 1993, 234–52.

Pedicord, Harry William. 'The Changing Audience' in Hume 1980, 236–52.

Ponsonby, Arthur. *English Diaries: A Review of English Diaries from the Sixteenth to the Twentieth Century with an Introduction on Diary Writing*. London: Methuen, 1923.

Pooley, Roger. *English Prose of the Seventeenth Century, 1590–1700*. London: Longman, 1992.

Potter, Lois. *Secret Rites and Secret Writing: Royalist Literature 1641–1660*. Cambridge: Cambridge University Press, 1989.

Prior, Mary, ed. *Women in English Society 1500–1700*. London: Methuen, 1985.

Quaintance, Richard E. 'French Sources of the Restoration "Imperfect Enjoyment" Poem', *Philological Quarterly*, 42 (1963), 190–9.

Randall, Dale B. J. *Winter Fruit: English Drama 1642–1660*. Lexington: University Press of Kentucky, 1995.

Reed, Joel. 'Restoration and Repression: the Language Projects of the Royal Society'. *Studies in Eighteenth Century Culture* 19 (1989), 399–412.

Reynolds, Myra. *The Learned Lady in England, 1650–1760*. Boston: Houghton Mifflin, 1920.

Richetti, John J. *Popular Fiction Before Richardson: Narrative Patterns 1700–1739*. Oxford: Oxford University Press, 1969.

—— 'The Portrayal of Women in Restoration and Eighteenth-century English Literature'. In *What Manner of Woman: Essays on English and American Life and Literature*, ed. Marlene Springer, Oxford: Basil Blackwell, 1977.

Roberts, David. *The Ladies: Female Patronage of Restoration Drama*. Oxford: Clarendon Press, 1989.

Rothstein, Eric. *Restoration Tragedy: Form and the Process of Change*. Madison: The University of Wisconsin Press, 1967.

Shattock, Joanne. *The Oxford Guide to British Women Writers*. Oxford: Oxford University Press, 1993.

Sherwood, Roy. *The Court of Oliver Cromwell*. London: Croom Helm, 1977.

—— *Oliver Cromwell: King in All but Name 1653–1658*. Thrupp: Sutton Publishing, 1997.

Simpson, Claude M. *The British Broadside Ballad and its Music*. New Brunswick, N.J.: Rutgers University Press, 1966.

Sitter, John. 'Recent Studies in the Restoration and Eighteenth Century' *Studies in English Literature 1500–1900*, 35 (1995), 599–639.

Slagle, Judith Bailey, ed. *Thomas Shadwell Reconsider'd: Essays in Criticism*. Special issue of *Restoration Studies in English Literary Culture 1660–1700*, 20.2 (Fall, 1996).

Smith, Nigel. *Literature and Revolution in England, 1640–1660*. New Haven: Yale University Press, 1994.

Sorelius, Gunnar. *'The Giant Race Before the Flood': Pre-Restoration Drama on the Stage and in the Criticism of the Restoration.* Uppsala: Almqvist & Wiksells, 1966.

Spender, Dale. *Mothers of the Novel: 100 Good Women Writers Before Jane Austen.* London: Pandora, 1986.

Steensma, Robert C. *Sir William Temple.* New York: Twayne Publishers, 1970.

Stephens, Frederick George. *Catalogue of Political and Personal Satires Preserved in the Department of Prints and Drawings in the British Museum.* Vol. I, 1320–1689 [1870]. London: British Museum Publications, 1978.

Stevenson, Kay Gilliland and Margaret Seares. *Paradise Lost in Short: Smith, Stillingfleet, and the Transformation of Epic.* Madison: Fairleigh Dickinson University Press, 1998.

Straznicky, Marta. 'Reading the Stage: Margaret Cavendish and Commonwealth Closet Drama', *Criticism* 37.3 (1995), 355–90.

Styan, J. L. *Restoration Comedy in Performance.* Cambridge: Cambridge University Press, 1986.

Sutherland, James. *On English Prose.* Toronto: University of Toronto Press, 1957.

Taney, Retta M. *Restoration Revivals on the British Stage (1944–1979).* Lanham, Maryland: University Press of America, 1985.

Thickstun, Margaret Olofson. '"This was a woman that taught": Feminist Scriptural Exegesis in the Seventeenth Century', *Studies in Eighteenth-Century Culture* 21 (1991), 149–58.

Todd, Janet. *Gender, Art, and Death.* Cambridge: Polity Press, 1993.

Walter, John. 'The Commons and their Mental Worlds'. In *The Oxford Illustrated History of Tudor & Stuart Britain*, ed. John Morrill, Oxford: Oxford University Press, 1996, 191–218.

Watts, Michael R. *The Dissenters from the Reformation to the French Revolution.* Oxford: Clarendon Press, 1978.

Wedgwood, C. V. *Poetry and Politics under the Stuarts.* Cambridge: Cambridge University Press, 1960.

Weinbrot, Howard D. *Augustus Caesar in 'Augustan' England.* Princeton University Press, 1978.

Wheatley, Christopher J. *Without God or Reason: The Plays of Thomas Shadwell and Secular Ethics in the Restoration.* London: Associated University Presses, 1993.

Williamson, Marilyn L. *Infinite Variety: Antony and Cleopatra in Renaissance Drama and Earlier Tradition* Mystic, CT: Lawrence Verry, 1974.

Wiseman, Susan. 'Gender and Status in Dramatic Discourse: Margaret Cavendsh, Duchess of Newcastle'. In Grundy and Wiseman (1992), 159–77.

Wright, Luella M. *The Literary Life of the Early Friends, 1650–1725.* New York: Columbia University Press, 1932.

Index